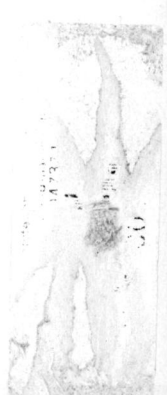

GRAZING IN TERRESTRIAL AND MARINE ENVIRONMENTS

THE BRITISH ECOLOGICAL SOCIETY
SYMPOSIUM NUMBER FOUR

GRAZING IN TERRESTRIAL AND MARINE ENVIRONMENTS

A Symposium of
THE BRITISH ECOLOGICAL SOCIETY
Bangor 11-14 April 1962

Edited by
D. J. CRISP
Ph.D.

Professor of Marine Biology
University College of North Wales

BLACKWELL
SCIENTIFIC PUBLICATIONS
OXFORD

Printed in Great Britain by
ADLARD AND SON LTD, BARTHOLOMEW PRESS, DORKING
and bound by
THE KEMP HALL BINDERY, OXFORD

CONTENTS

[1] Now at the Nature Conservancy, Monkswood Experimental Station, Abbots Ripton, Huntingdonshire, England.

v

PART III

GRAZING IN THE MARINE ENVIRONMENT

GRAZING BY PLANKTONIC ORGANISMS

GRAZING BY LITTORAL AND BENTHIC ORGANISMS

[1] Now at Department of Zoology, University of Bristol.

PREFACE

The fourth symposium arranged by the British Ecological Society took as its theme the subject of 'grazing'. The Programme Planning Committee decided that the subject should be interpreted in its broadest sense to include not only pasture and range grazing but also planktonic grazing and other grazing-like phenomena in marine and freshwater habitats.

The symposium members and contributors were drawn from a wide spectrum of biologists. Both botanists and zoologists were well represented and their interest ranged from agronomy to freshwater and marine biology. Members of the British Grasslands Society also took part in the meeting. Seven overseas contributors were able to attend and their presence greatly added to the value of the meeting.

The sessions were held at the University College of North Wales, Bangor, in the Department of Botany, at the invitation of the President of the Society, Professor P. W. Richards. The visitors were welcomed by the Principal of the College, Dr R. Charles Evans, and accommodation was provided in University Hall where the symposium dinner was held.

In addition to the formal papers which are included in the published account and the discussions that followed them, the participants enjoyed several excursions. Parties visited the Marine Science Laboratories at Menai Bridge, the University farm at Aber, the Nature Conservancy experimental areas in Snowdonia and Lord Aberconway's gardens at Bodnant in the Conway valley.

Thanks are due to all those who shared in the organization of the symposium; to the Programme Planning Committee and those who helped it in consultation, to the contributors and the sponsoring organisations who generously supported them, to the Warden of University Hall and other members of the College staff, to those whose hospitality made the excursions possible and finally to Dr G. R. Sagar and Mr J. Foster, who acted most willingly and efficiently as local secretaries.

D. J. Crisp

INTRODUCTION

Primitive man was able to hunt and fish as he required without impoverishing or modifying his environment. He imposed no undue pressures on the natural communities of which he formed a part. Civilized man, however, from the very outset effected changes disproportionate to his stature and immediate needs. He altered the vegetation by the use of fire and by other means so that he could maintain stocks of animals and plants capable of supporting his ever-increasing numbers. Human populations are now so large that it is only by the most efficient use of the resources of land and sea that they can be adequately supported.

One of the major problems so created is the increased need for animal food and products. The risk is already apparent that man's predatory activities, enlarged and intensified by technological advance, may destroy the stocks of animals and fish on which he depends. A basis for rational harvesting without endangering the stocks formed the subject of an earlier volume. This symposium is concerned with the same need for animal products but approaches the problem from a different standpoint. It deals with the production of animal tissue from plant food rather than with the utilization of existing populations of animals in the wild.

The most primitive and still the most effective means of changing plant into animal tissue is through the grazing animal. It is convenient to extend the term 'grazing' to include all transfers at the second trophic level. In this symposium it will therefore be used to describe the feeding activities of all kinds of herbivores, whether domestic or wild, and all types of environment: terrestrial, freshwater and marine.

Clearly the over-riding issue of practical importance is to develop means of increasing animal productivity by canalizing as much as possible of the organic matter formed by primary production to flow into profitable forms of animal tissue. The aim is the same whether domestic ruminants, range animals or fish are considered. Two areas of knowledge

are necessary to achieve this degree of control. The first is a broad understanding of what is now called 'energy flow' and by which is meant a fully
quantitative description of the food chains, beginning with the transformation of solar into chemical energy and finishing with the regeneration of
inorganic components. The second area of knowledge is a detailed familiar-
ity with the dynamics of the particular grazing animal and its pasture, the
animal's behaviour, its powers of selection and the long and short term
responses of the pasture to grazing. These two lines of approach re-
inforce each other in the same way that generalized thermo-dynamics
and detailed kinetics each play their part in man's mastery over the
physical world.

The study of energy flow in ecosystems where grazing plays a part must
begin with the primary production of organic matter from solar energy
by the plant. It has been increasingly recognized of late that it is not the
obvious quantities of plant material present as standing crop that determines primary productivity but the unseen turnover of energy and
organic matter. From comparisons of terrestrial ecosystems and those of
the open sea a fundamental difference emerges. Terrestrial ecosystems are
characterized by large amounts of standing crop in relation to energy flow
and by the high proportion of primary production passing, not directly to
herbivores, but into plant detritus which is slowly attacked by decomposers.
Ecosystems of the open sea have a relatively small standing crop of
phytoplankton and the bulk of primary production is consumed directly
by the herbivores. These differences are perhaps to be expected. Land
plants, rooted in the soil and exposed to desiccation, require materials like
cellulose and lignin to give them ridigity, and materials like cutin, suberin
and sporo-pollenin to resist water-logging and water loss. These polymeric
substances are, moreover, inert and not readily digestible by animals.
Consequently, in relation to its metabolic activity, the biomass of a land
plant is considerably increased by these structural elements, which in
turn tend to remain uneaten or to resist digestion and so to accumulate as
plant detritus. The primary producers of the open sea, on the other hand,
are floating microscopic plants which must multiply rapidly enough to
keep pace with intensive grazing by zooplankton if they are to survive.
The standing crop, especially in warmer seas, is therefore small in relation
to the flow of organic matter and energy. In cooler seas the standing
crop is sometimes relatively large, but this is a seasonal phenomenon probably resulting from temporary imbalance between phytoplankton and
herbivores. Though the detritus food chain in the open sea is considered

to be relatively small it must be recognized that the fate of uneaten or partially eaten plant material is not so easy to trace in this environment.

The freshwater environment was only briefly touched upon at the symposium but it may nevertheless be appropriate in this introduction to mention it. Of the various freshwater environments, the open waters of lakes most obviously resemble conditions in the open sea and may show somewhat similar cycles of plant and animal growth, though their productivity varies considerably with depth and with the composition of the lake bed. The other extreme type of freshwater environment is the turbulent stream or 'rhithron'. Here the standing crop of plant material is so small and unproductive that it cannot act as a primary source on which the animal life has to depend. Hynes has argued elsewhere (Hynes, H. J. N. *Proc. Int. Congr. Zool.* Washington 1963, **4**, 324–9) that the high productivity of such environments can be explained only in terms of the organic matter that enters the stream from the surrounding terrestrial environment. Allochthonous nutrients probably form an important additional source of energy, not only in streams and rivers, but also in other environments occupying the margins of land vegetation, such as estuaries, saltmarshes and mangrove swamps.

It is clearly essential for progress that valid comparisons of both primary and secondary productivity should be possible between different ecosystems and between ecosystems under different forms of management. For this purpose conformity is desirable in the units used and essential in the definitions of the quantities compared. Macfadyen, in stressing this point, illustrates some of the confusingly different meanings attached to the term 'ecological efficiency'. A framework such as that recommended by Macfadyen for a wide variety of ecosystems offers a rational basis for comparing and improving grazing practice.

The upper limit of potential herbivore production is clearly that determined by the kind of plants that function as primary producers. Yields from managed crops with added fertilizer are as great as or greater than, the most productive of natural systems. However, Ovington has demonstrated that grassland, such as natural prairie, is a relatively inefficient primary producer and uses the available space and energy far less economically than savannah or woodland. Furthermore, the primary productivity of grassland will itself depend on the grazing pressure, since the activities of the grazing animal will normally add fertilizer, reduce light interception by foliage, stimulate leaf regeneration, and reduce the growth of roots, as is discussed fully by Alcock. There is presumably an optimum grazing pressure that will extract the highest yield from any particular pasture.

Nutrient supply rather than solar energy appears to be the factor most generally limiting primary productivity in terrestrial ecosystems. Interference with the soil and with the plant communities naturally present can easily render it less productive. The consequences of man's activities and his deployment of grazing stock on the natural grassland of America is seen in the perspective of geological and historical time by Dix, and as an urgent contemporary issue by Costello. Changes affecting range lands of widely different character are described by Marr, Flook and Carr. Pitelka and Schultz suggest that the regular crash in the populations of Arctic microtines can be ascribed to extreme nutrient depletion which is made good by slow regeneration in the succeeding two years. If the nutrient cycle that they suggest is operative in controlling microtine populations is substantiated by further research it will provide an interesting parallel in the terrestrial environment to the annual nutrient cycle of the euphotic zone of temperate seas.

The alternative approach to the problem of grazing, namely the detailed study of inter-relationships between specific herbivores and their pasture, has been carried out most fully in the case of the sheep. The investigations described here show how the animal's behaviour greatly complicates the relationship between yield and population density on a given pasture type. Arnold describes how sheep partially compensate for shortage of suitable pasture by increasing the time that they spend in grazing. Sheep are highly selective, choosing certain plants and certain parts of the plant. The results of faecal analyses, carried out by Martin to investigate the diet of sheep under natural conditions, reveal a pattern of preferences recurring annually on a given pasture. However, it cannot be simply assumed that all the sheep present have an independent choice of the most favoured areas of pasture, since Hunter has clearly demonstrated that sheep roam in family groups each restricted to one of several overlapping home ranges, each differing in altitude, aspect and vegetation.

In the open sea a major difficulty is the problem of sampling. Copepods of cool temperate waters and the diatoms on which they feed are patchy in distribution and are constantly on the move. One may grasp the nettle, as Cushing has done, using scattered field data to derive statistical relationships and, where feasible, to select a large uniform patch of zooplankton predominantly composed of *Calanus* grazing on diatom cells in order to follow the changes occurring in the same patch over a long period of time. The alternative method is to observe the feeding of *Calanus* in the laboratory and to construct a nutritional balance sheet as

Marshall and Orr have done. The results of field and laboratory observations are not entirely in accord. In the laboratory *Calanus* utilizes algal cells efficiently but, according to Cushing's interpretation, in the sea *Calanus* feeds wastefully when diatoms are abundant. Walne's results, obtained by feeding lamellibranch larvae in the laboratory, also lead to discrepancies when related to conditions prevailing in the sea.

The remaining papers on grazing in the sea form a miscellany illustrating some of the great variety of food relationships in benthic and littoral environments. The minute organisms living in spaces between sand grains consume autotrophs from the illuminated superficial layers of sand, bacteria attached to sand grains, and detritus washed in from the surface of the sand. They in turn provide an important food source for the larger burrowers. The nudibranchs, a bizarre group of carnivorous browsers, not true grazers, justify their inclusion because they illustrate two contrasting patterns of exploitation. Some are prodigal feeders; they mature rapidly, eliminate their prey, and depend thereafter for survival on their disseminated progeny. Others browse more sparingly on highly specific prey which is always present in relative abundance; these forms breed only once a year.

Of all the examples of grazing described from the marine environment, only the grazing by limpets on algal sporelings resembles at all closely the stereotyped pattern of terrestrial grazing. Browsing by periwinkles and topshells on permanent beds of fucoids, though not among the topics discussed, represents an even closer analogy – for the limpets, unlike most terrestrial grazers, usually destroy their pasture completely. Limpets depend therefore on a continuous supply of algal spores which must be transferred to, and germinate within, each individual homing area. In their reliance on food derived from elsewhere, limpets show a similarity to wholly sessile feeders such as barnacles, filter-feeding molluscs and annelids. Such sedentary forms are dependent entirely on the turbulence of the surrounding water to bring their food within range, and the plant material that they consume is removed quite unselectively with other forms of suspended matter. Nevertheless, these animals are so numerous that they must be responsible for transforming a greater proportion of primary energy than the much more limited numbers of purely herbivorous gastropods.

The subject of grazing gives an opportunity to bridge two divisions among ecologists. It provides a meeting point for terrestrial and marine ecologists, though it seems that the characteristic processes of grazing on land and in the sea illuminate each other by their contrasts rather than by their similarities. It also provides an area of cooperation between animal and plant ecologists. The contributions that follow are presented in the hope of stimulating and encouraging this cooperation in a field of immediate practical importance to agronomists and of wide theoretical significance to biologists as a whole.

PART I

ENERGY FLOW

ENERGY FLOW IN ECOSYSTEMS AND ITS EXPLOITATION BY GRAZING

A. MACFADYEN

Department of Zoology, University College, Swansea

ABSTRACT

A brief discussion of the definition and measurement of energy flow in ecosystems is followed by an analysis of some known ecosystems. These are broken down into their trophic components. The relative magnitudes of respiration, yield to grazing, production of non-grazed organic matter by plants and of metabolic and growth efficiency by animals are compared over a range of contrasting systems including grassland and plankton. It is shown that the various routes of energy flow and the relationships between stock and productivity vary over several orders of magnitude depending on the biology of the organisms involved. This is reflected in the greatly different yields obtained by conventional grazing practices. The ecological framework within which it is possible to manipulate ecosystems for the purpose of increasing grazing yields is then defined and present performance is compared with the potential yields.

In this paper I shall attempt to deal with the factors which limit the productivity of ecological systems involving grazing. I must stress that my qualifications for tackling this task are meagre; my own research is hardly relevant to the ecology of grazing and I should be grateful if experts would correct any mis-statements I may make. It seemed useful at the outset, before treating the more specific aspects of the symposium, to look for the major factors which different grazing systems have in common, to compare the conclusions which have been reached in published work and to devise a scale by which estimates of grazing quantities for different systems can be compared. This is the more necessary because our topic is covered by many kinds of biologists who write in many different journals, and they do not all speak the same language. As a result, we find the situation, so familiar in ecology, in which a number of different terms are employed for the same concept whilst the same term is used by different authors to mean different things. A more elusive variant of the latter difficulty is the way in which concepts effectively change their meaning — or at least their significance — when transposed from one field to another on account of differences in the magnitude of the quantities involved. I propose to try to use a consistent set of words, but if in doing so I misinterpret their implications

3

in a particular field I hope — and expect — that this will be clarified in discussion.

In outline, I propose to begin by considering in theory what happens to the solar energy which flows through a closed ecological system. Then I shall dismantle this theoretical system and, by means of figures from a range of published examples, I shall attempt to fit typical magnitudes to some of the component parts, and then reassemble the complete system and examine the effects of the idiosyncrasies of the parts on the structure of the whole.

Finally, I want to consider the boundaries which ecological theory would seem to impose on the returns which are to be obtained by manipu- lating ecological systems for human gain. I hope that you will not misun- derstand me here; I realize that farming and other methods of food pro- duction are dominated by what is economically possible, but on this occasion I suggest that we concern ourselves with the wider range of what is ecologically possible because we are, after all, ecologists and therefore interested in generalizations about the structure of living systems. In a world which is getting hungrier today's impractical ideas have a way of becoming tomorrow's technical realities.

The first figure is a grossly oversimplified illustration of the pathways of energy through an ecosystem. In this I have made the following assump- tions. First, that one can validly think of energy as flowing between orga- nisms when in fact it takes the form of separate individual creatures and separate meals; secondly, that the system is isolated from all other systems; and thirdly, that organisms can clearly be separated into 'trophic levels' as plants, herbivores, carnivores and decomposers. The main points I want to illustrate are the differences between the schemes in relation to energy flow, to organic matter containing energy and to inorganic matter from which energy has been removed. If the system is assumed to be in a steady state, the quantity of solar energy taken up by photosynthesis is equal to the sum of energy losses derived from respiration of all the organisms, plant and animal, present. The metabolism of the plants is limited either by solar energy or by nutrients; if the non-photosynthetic components of the system were to break down the plants would be denied fresh supplies of nutrients and would eventually be unable to maintain active photo- synthesis. From this point of view, given unlimited light, the more rapidly that organic foods are oxidized and their energy and nutrients are liberated the more rapid will be the rate of plant metabolism; any bottlenecks in the cycle of breakdown will reduce plant productivity.

Let us now examine in more detail what happens at the plant level. In Fig. 2, the area of the central rectangle represents the stock of organic material in the living plants. The flow channels from six o'clock to ten o'clock represent the flow of energy into and out of the system. The channel at twelve o'clock represents the output of organic matter as green food to herbivores and the channel at two o'clock the output as dead plant matter to decomposers. The arm at three o'clock represents the interchange of inorganic nutrients and carbon dioxide mostly into but partly out of the

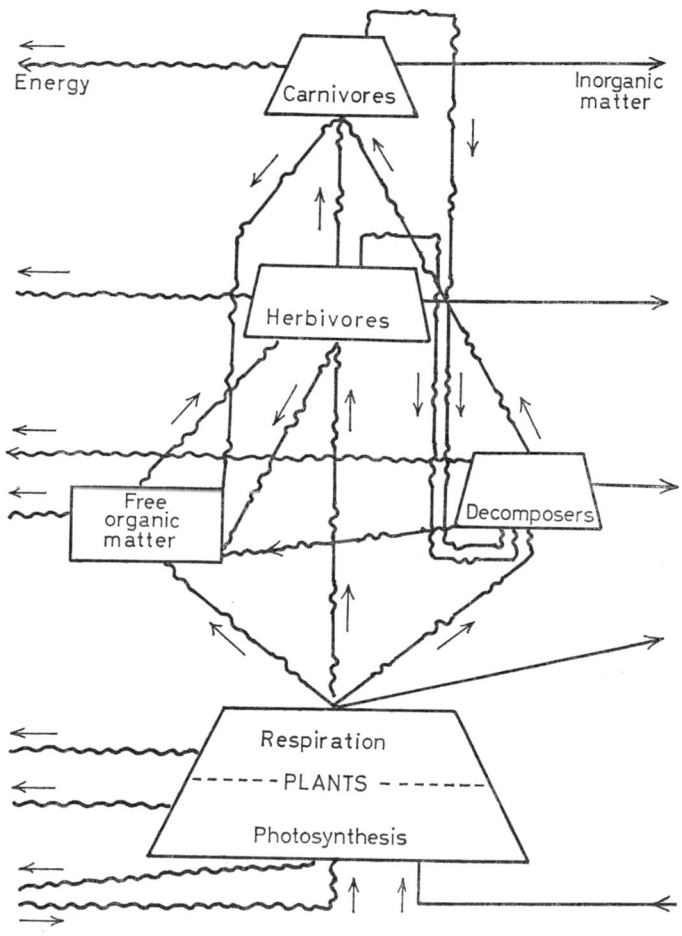

FIG. 1. Theoretical energy flow scheme in an isolated system. 〜〜〜 = paths of Energy; ━〜━〜 = paths of organic matter; ------ = paths of inorganic matter.
Solar energy enters only from the bottom. Details see text.

plant stock. Since this cannot usually be analysed under natural conditions we shall omit it from later diagrams. The conventional positions occupied by each form of energy flow will be adhered to in describing six examples of primary production systems from nature, which are shown in Fig. 3.

A. A managed forest of *Picea omorika* in Britain described by Ovington and Heitkamp (1960). This is assumed to be cut down once every 21 years and to be provided with fresh supplies of fertilizer; it represents about the most productive primary system in the open in our climate. The stock is taken to be the average throughout the period of growth.

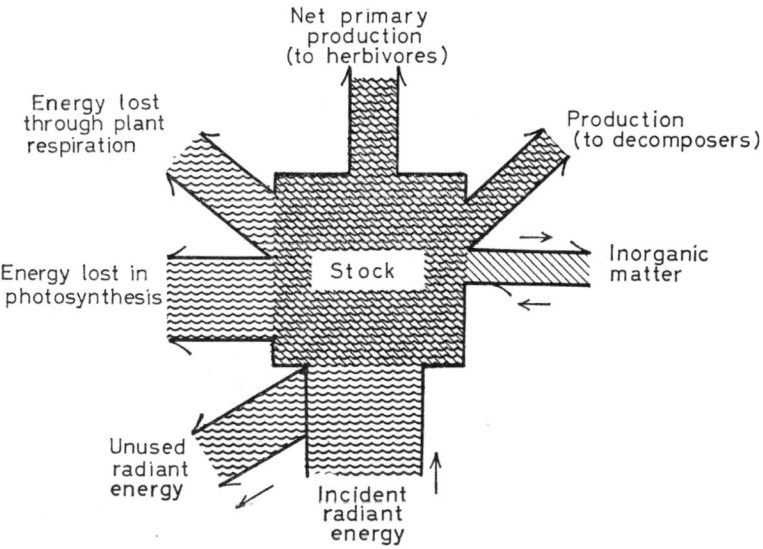

Fig. 2. Scheme for energy and matter flow through plant level. ≈≈≈ = energy paths; ▨▨▨ = paths of organic matter; \\\\\\\\\\ = paths of inorganic matter.

B. A normal reasonably fertile grass field exploited by grazing under British conditions (data modified from Golley (1960), Stamp (1958), Odum (1959), Albriton (1953)).

C and *D.* Two examples from an unexploited salt marsh at Sapelo island described by Odum and his colleagues (Odum, 1960; Pomeroy, 1959; Teal, 1959; Smalley, 1960). Firstly (*C*) the food chain based on the algae which live on the mud (Pomeroy, 1959) and secondly (*D*), that supported by *Spartina* (Smalley, 1960).

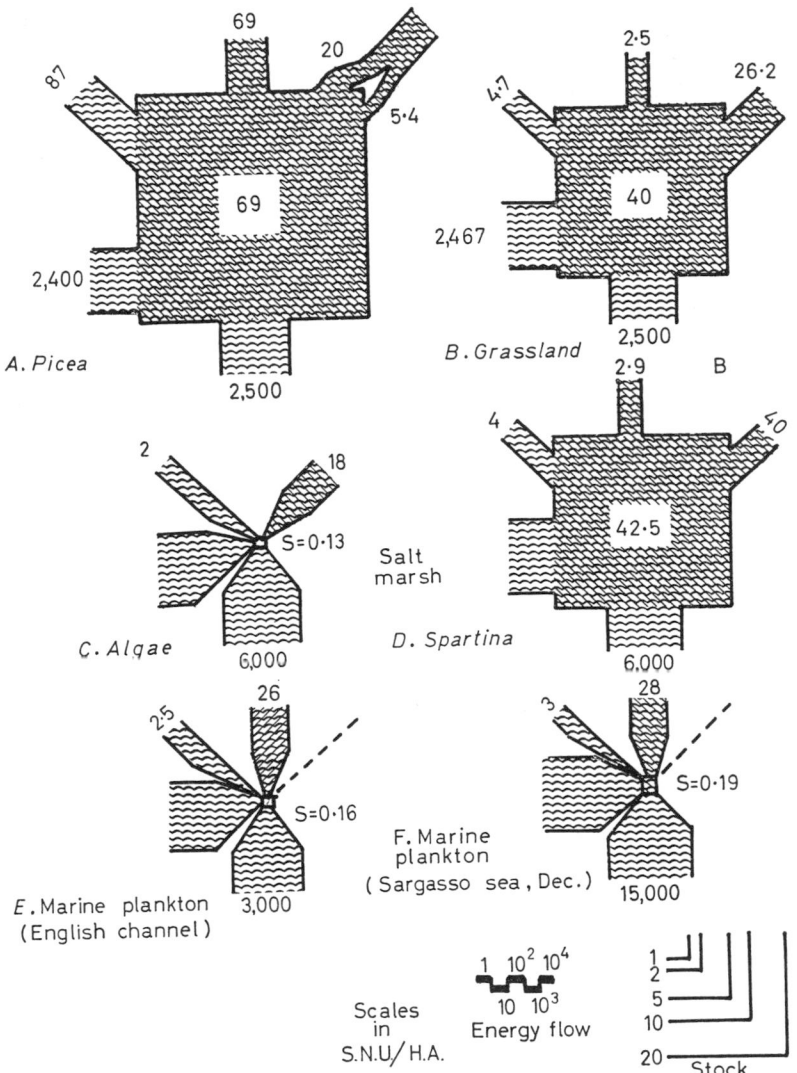

FIG. 3. Scaled flow paths for six actual plant systems. Mean stock is proportional to the area of the central square.

Flow channels are logarithmically proportional to mean annual energy flow. The units are S.N.U. (= 10^6 Calories) per hectare. Conventions as in Fig. 2.

E and *F*. Two examples of marine plankton communities discussed by Cushing (1955, 1959a, 1959b).

An appreciation of energy flow may be made difficult by unfamiliarity with the magnitude of the different units employed. I am therefore adopting the S.N.U. or Standard Nutritional Unit proposed by Stamp (1958) which has the advantages that it can usually be employed without using too many zeros or decimals and that it is the amount of energy which we ourselves consume in a year assuming a daily ration of 2,640 cal and a 10 per cent loss of calories in cooking. This unit is exactly a million large Calories. The unit of area is the Hectare (2·47 acres). If you are unfamiliar with hectares you can divide the figures given by 10 and think of them as applying to a quarter-acre vegetable garden. The time unit for flow is the year. Stock, of course, is not a rate of flow but a quantity of matter and the relation between the flow 'channels' and the stock 'boxes' is therefore arbitrary. Where possible I have used known calorific coefficients but where, as is usually the case, these are not known I have assumed that one gram dry-weight of organic matter has an energy content of four Calories; this is only one of the factors which make these calculations extremely rough. The flow scales in all these diagrams are logarithmic and the stock scales are proportionate in *area* to the logarithm of the caloric value of the stock.

The most interesting differences between these diagrams seem to me to be these. Firstly, the algae, as opposed to the higher plants, do comparable amounts of metabolic work with the aid of a very much smaller stock of material. This confirms expectations that metabolic rates per unit of mass increase with the surface-to-volume ratio (Zeuthen, 1947). Secondly, notice that by far the greater part of solar energy which is actually absorbed by the plant is lost through the relative inefficiency of photosynthesis. As a result there is little relation between yield to herbivores and incident solar radiation. This is something we cannot do very much about. Note, however, that losses are greater for grass and *Spartina* than for the *Picea* forest. Thirdly, of the energy which is incorporated in plant tissue a fairly constant amount is respired, again except in the case of the forest. Fourthly, from the plant's point of view as it were, what happens to the remainder of the energy going to herbivores and decomposers is not of great moment; but from the point of view of the whole system there is a very great difference between the 'productive' systems, such as the phytoplankton, of which nearly all is eaten by herbivores and a negligible quantity allowed to die 'naturally', and the grass of which by far the greater amount is never eaten during the growing season but goes to feed the decomposer industries. At this point, therefore, there is a major division in the energy flow scheme which decides whether a community shall contain a high or a low proportion of plant-derived dead organic matter on the one hand and a small or large herbivore industry on the other.

Presumably this reflects some special features of the biology of the higher land plants as compared with aquatic algae; perhaps their evolution of defence mechanisms such as silica spines on the edges of leaves ensures that they are not so readily eaten during life. At all events the result of this contrast is that most of the biomass of animals in most terrestrial habitats is to be found in decomposer organisms whilst there are very few of these in the plankton.

Notice too that the ratio of stock to herbivorous production varies enormously. In the case of the grasses, much plant material remains free from herbivore attack at the end of the season, whilst in the plankton the algae are grazed many times over. This means that turnover of nutrients is necessarily much slower in the former whilst in the latter the very growth of later generations of algae depends on their ancestors having been eaten and the nutrients released by zooplankton earlier in the year.

All this serves, of course, to underline the falsity of relying on stock figures as a guide to production rates. This point has been further clarified by Cushing (1959a, 1959b) in his comparison between temperate marine plankton and that in the Sargasso. The diagram shown here is for the peak season of activity in the winter and a similar diagram for summer would have shown a much smaller stock. In fact, there is remarkably little difference between the primary production picture for the Sargasso and for the English Channel, because in the Sargasso the much greater depth of planktonic activity and sunlight penetration compensates for a more dilute plankton.

Notice too, that the *Picea* forest is a managed system in which most of the production is removed as timber. Naturally, in an unexploited woodland, by far the greater part of the 69 S.N.U. yield would join the unexploited roots (20 S.N.U.) and the litter (5·4 S.N.U.) which at present go to the decomposer organisms.

In order to give scale to some typical man-managed systems I have given in Table 1 a few yield figures in S.N.U. Apart from the enormously greater yields obtainable under a tropical sun I think perhaps the most interesting points to observe here are firstly that intensive cultivation can produce comparable yields to natural systems depending on the trouble taken over the different methods of culture and secondly that the great increases due to fertilizer application indicate that nutrients and not solar energy are often the limiting factors in production.

TABLE I

Approximate net annual primary production from some man-managed
systems

Vegetation	S.N.U./ Hectare	Source
Old Field Grass	3·2	Minnesota. Bray *et al.*, 1959
Maize unfertilized	8·2	
,, fertilized	24·4	
Typha	31·2	
British Farming		Stamp, 1958
Grazing (improved)	1·0	
National average	7·0	
Best	13·6	
Europe. Wheat max.	8·3	
Sugar beet	60·5	4 months only. Best Gaastra, 1958
Sugar mean	65·5	Odum, 1959
max.	254	
Cassava	280	Kalle, 1948
Algal culture	300	Fogg, 1958

The next figure (Fig. 4) is intended to show what happens to the food which is obtained by herbivores from plants. Much of the energy available in the form of plant matter is not, of course, grazed by economically favoured species because it is used by rival herbivores or because it is simply not available in the right form at the right time. Of the calorific value in food ingested a considerable proportion, varying usually from about 40 per cent to more than 90 per cent is rejected as faeces, only a reduced amount being actually assimilated. A proportion of the assimilated food is stored in the tissues of the animal or is used in the formation of eggs or young and thus contributes to the growth of the stock of the population. The rest of the food is broken down to produce excreted matter of reduced energy content and, at the same time, energy is liberated in the form of heat or mechanical work. This exploitation of the potential energy is an irreversible process which can only occur once in the ecosystem and this explains the value to the ecologist of respiration measurements as an index of ecological importance. The stock in turn is exploited by predators which therefore stand to benefit from a high secondary net production rate.

The ratios of energy flows at different stages represent efficiencies and a great many such ratios have been recognized according to the viewpoint of the investigator (see Slobodkin (1960) Pattern (1959)). For instance, the ecologist interested in the community as a whole is concerned with losses in energy content between equivalent stages in succeeding trophic levels and concentrates on the *ecological efficiency* E4/E1. (See Fig. 4.) The pig

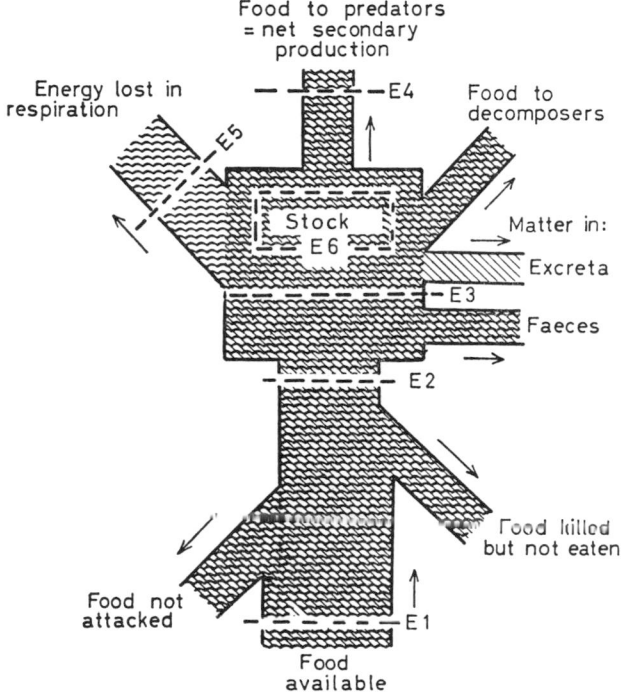

FIG. 4. Scheme for energy and matter flow through herbivore level. Conventions as in Fig. 2.

Ratios of the flows at points marked are efficiencies: $E4/E1 = $ ecological efficiency; $E6/E2 = $ growth efficiency when measured throughout development; $E5/E3 = $ Teal's efficiency; $E6/(E3-E5) = $ efficiency in the sense used by fisheries biologists.

farmer who wants to obtain as much pig meat per unit of feeding stuff as possible can eliminate losses to rival herbivores provided he can control the depredations of rats and grain weevils. He can also avoid losses through disease which would feed the decomposers, but he must take into account the metabolic cost to the sow of producing piglets as well as the feeding cost of raising weaners. He is therefore concerned with what Slobodkin

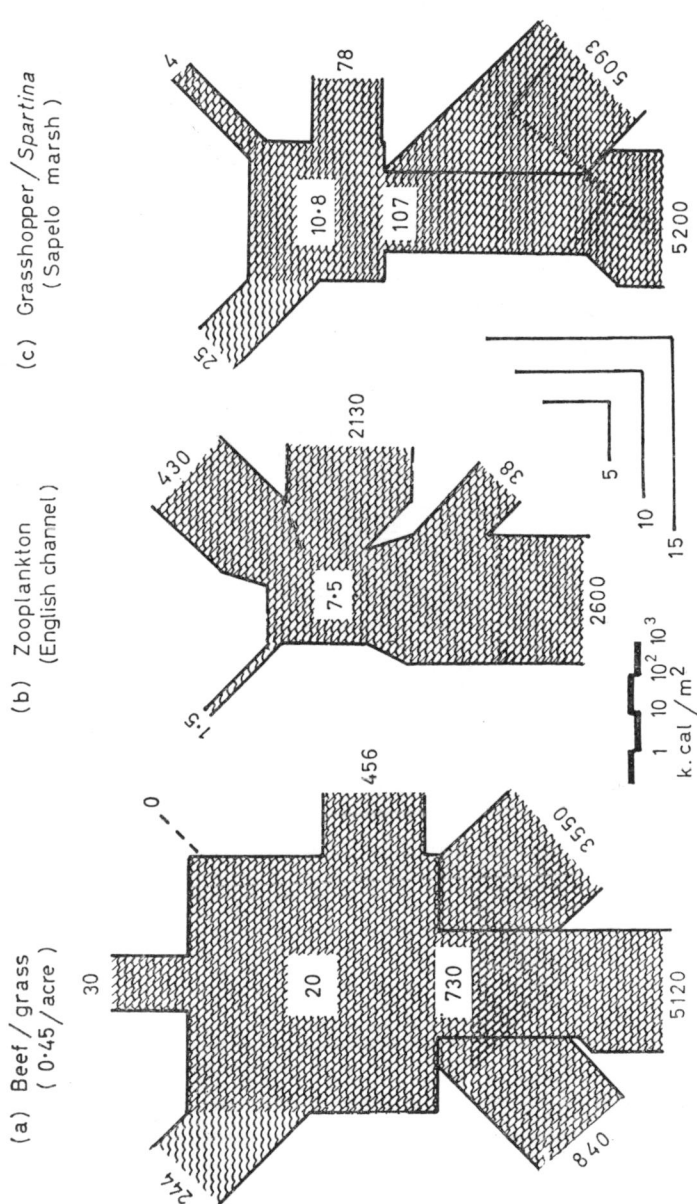

(a) Beef / grass
(0·45 / acre)

(b) Zooplankton
(English channel)

(c) Grasshopper / *Spartina*
(Sapelo marsh)

FIG. 5. Scaled flow paths for three herbivore systems. Conventions as in Fig. 4.

has defined as *growth efficiency*. Other measures of efficiency, each of which is perfectly logical and legitimate in its appropriate context, are indicated in the figure; I only want to stress at this stage that the undefined use of the term 'efficiency' by different groups of people has, in the past, lead to a good deal of confusion.

If we now examine some actual examples of energy flow through the herbivore levels of some of the communities we are studying (Fig. 5) we find that there are very great discrepancies even in the order of magnitude of the different flow paths. First, I should point out that the scales are about 100 times larger than those for primary production (Fig. 3) and that this is reflected by the use of a unit one hundredth of the S.N.U. per hectare, namely the Calorie per m². Secondly, it is important when considering grazing animals and their food to take account of the time factor. Most frequently the food organisms breed more rapidly than their consumers and this can result in apparently small stocks of food organisms supplying herbivores at a very rapid rate. This evidently happens in the case of the zooplankton as we shall see below, and is equally obvious in the case of carnivores grazing on herbivores. For instance Allen (1951) showed that the trout in the Horokiwi stream grazed the bottom living invertebrates to an extent of over forty times the maximum standing crop in the course of a year and Horton (1961) has since found a similar situation among trout in a Dartmoor stream. Thirdly, I have had to amalgamate the yields to herbivores and to decomposers in most cases because we do not know the proportions which go to each. As I said of the plant level, it is not of fundamental importance to the herbivores whether they succumb to predators or to disease; it is only the human predator who tries to maximize the first and minimize the latter and it is in this direction that man has a chance to switch the energy flow to his own advantage with least influence on the metabolism of the ecosystem as a whole. Thus the successful raiser of bullocks can hope for a maximum yield of 30 calories per square metre from an initial grass production of over 5,000. Notice (Fig. 5a) that the bullocks have selected only about one seventh of the available herbage in favour of other herbivores and decomposers, have rejected nearly two thirds of their food in faeces and have respired nearly 90 per cent of what they do assimilate. If he fails to keep his stock healthy much of the 30 calories of yield will go to feed the decomposers also.

The Sapelo marsh Grasshopper *Orchellimum fidicinium* (Fig. 5c) which was studied by Smalley (1960) seems fairly typical of most herbivorous insects in that feeding is very selective but the proportion of ingested food which is actually assimilated is fairly high — about 25 per cent. Also notice that a very high proportion of the assimilated food is respired again. This is a particularly characteristic feature of terrestrial arthropods and perhaps reflects the high metabolic demands of life on land. In the case of such an animal and for the purpose of comparing different species, the near equality between respiration and assimilation may make it permissible to measure whichever is more convenient, as Phillipson has done in his studies on the harvestman *Mitopus morio* (1960a, 1960b). In the case of fishes, on the other hand, which lay down as body flesh a higher proportion of their food, this is often not legitimate.

The third part of this diagram (Fig. 5b) represents the English Channel zooplankton. It is rather badly distorted by the fact that values are averaged over the year although in fact most of the activity is confined to three or four months in the summer. It will be remembered that they press so closely on the heels of the phytoplankton that very little of the latter remains un-eaten. However, as Cushing has shown (1959a, 1959b) the free organic matter in the sea is derived largely from a different source, namely the fact that copepods, when food is abundant, become fantastically inefficient feeders and defecate five and even ten times as much plant food as is required for metabolism. This has important consequences for the community as a whole, it accelerates the liberation of nutrients to plants and to some extent it provides a reserve of food for the long period between summer plankton blooms, but in the present context it results in the copepods liberating the energy from only a small proportion of the food available to them and thus contributing enormously to the free organic matter of the sea. The story of the marine zooplankton is far from unique. Slobodkin found the same overfeeding phenomenon in his culture experiments with *Daphnia* (1954), Gajevskaya (1959) found that marine Isopods fed wastefully on higher plants in the Black Sea and a number of authors have detected similar behaviour among land arthropods such as Diplopods (Dunger, 1960). In each case we have an important diversion of organic matter, usually readily accessible to microbial attack, from the herbivorous food chains.

Before material is attacked by the decomposers it is present in the form of undecomposed organic matter, a feature of most natural systems which we are inclined to overlook. However, according to Fogg (1959) the quantities of dissolved organic matter present in lake waters may be from six to four thousand times that in particulate form. Again, soils of the möder type are known which almost entirely consist of the faeces of arthropods (Kubiena, 1953). Fox (1955) has estimated a free organic content of the world's oceans about fifty times as great as the annual photosynthesis. This, of course, implies a very slow rate of turnover but the significant point in the present context is the existence of vast reserves of nutrients and energy locked up and only slowly being exploited.

Some of the organic material is known to be oxidized directly; this happens to copepod faeces in tropical seas (Cushing, 1959b) and also under high temperature conditions in desert soils (Bunt et al., 1954). Direct chemical oxidation is presumably a useful supplement to biological breakdown, provided it does not imply loss of nitrogen and soluble salts nor unfavourable physical changes in the medium, as happens when vegetation is burned. The relative importance of direct oxidation is not yet clear but it seems to be appreciable in some conditions in warm climates.

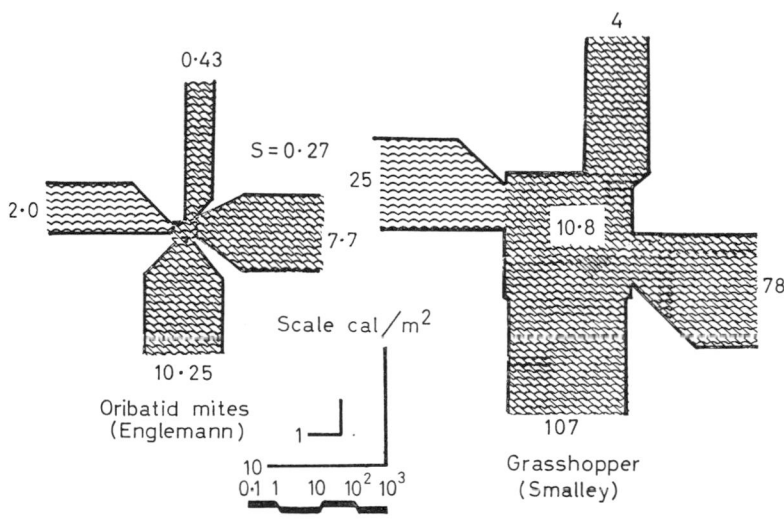

FIG. 6. Scaled flow paths comparing a decomposer with a herbivore system (Oribatid mite population after Englemann, 1961 and Grasshopper population after Smalley, 1960).

This leads to a brief consideration of the organisms which are responsible for the breakdown of most of the free organic matter in all its forms. A full treatment of this subject would be a lengthy matter, especially in the case of terrestrial environments, such as grassland, where by far the greater part of both species and biomass are involved in this decomposer industry. From the present point of view, however, I want first to point out that a great many organisms are involved and that organic matter is subjected to a whole succession of processes, such as concentration, comminution, mixing with mineral matter and changes in physical structure by animals as diverse as filter feeders, millipedes, earthworms and fiddler crabs.

I have one figure (Fig. 6) which allows us to compare the flow sheet for the grasshopper *Orchellimum* with Englemann's (1961) field results from a small arthropod decomposer population in a meadow. The main feature to notice is that the detritus feeding Oribatid mites, as we might expect, seem able to process proportionately more material and energy with much less biomass than the herbivore. It is my guess that this is a valid generalization and my conviction, based on knowledge of metabolic activity, that a similar comparison of Collembola with *Orchellimum* would show an even greater discrepancy. On the whole detritus feeders abstract rather little energy in proportion to the material they handle but the effects of their activities are important because the material is usually made more accessible to attack by bacteria and fungi especially when, as in the case of soil, it is both moistened and aerated. We have also recently become aware (Van der Drift, 1959 ; Witkamp, 1960; Macfadyen, 1961) that the effects of such detritus feeders are out of all proportion to their own metabolic activities because, by spreading of spores, by breaking down microbial antagonisms and in other ways, they greatly accelerate the activities of the microorganisms.

Next I should like to consider what happens when we re-synthesize something like a complete ecosystem from its components. Fig. 7 is the scaled version of my first diagram on the basis of some figures from grassland. Apart from the points I raised before about photosynthetic inefficiency and energy loss from beef as faeces, the outstanding feature must surely be the enormous accumulation of organic matter in the soil, mostly at the surface. The greater part of this comes from the grass but an appreciable quantity exists in the form of cow pats. The stock of decomposer organisms as a whole contains about the same quantity of energy as the grass but compared to the cattle and to other herbivores it is slow in processing the organic material which is its food. It seems clear from other analyses (Macfadyen, 1961) that the animals in soil and litter contribute barely 10 per cent to the total metabolism of the decomposers, the remainder being carried out by microorganisms. For the reasons mentioned above, however, this does not imply that removal of the animals would decrease the energy flow and nutrient liberation from the organic matter by only 10 per cent. Indeed, to judge from what happens in acid mor conditions or when animals are suppressed by toxic chemicals it is clear that when all decomposition is left to the microorganisms, organic matter usually accumulates from year to year. The decomposer industry is clearly a complex one

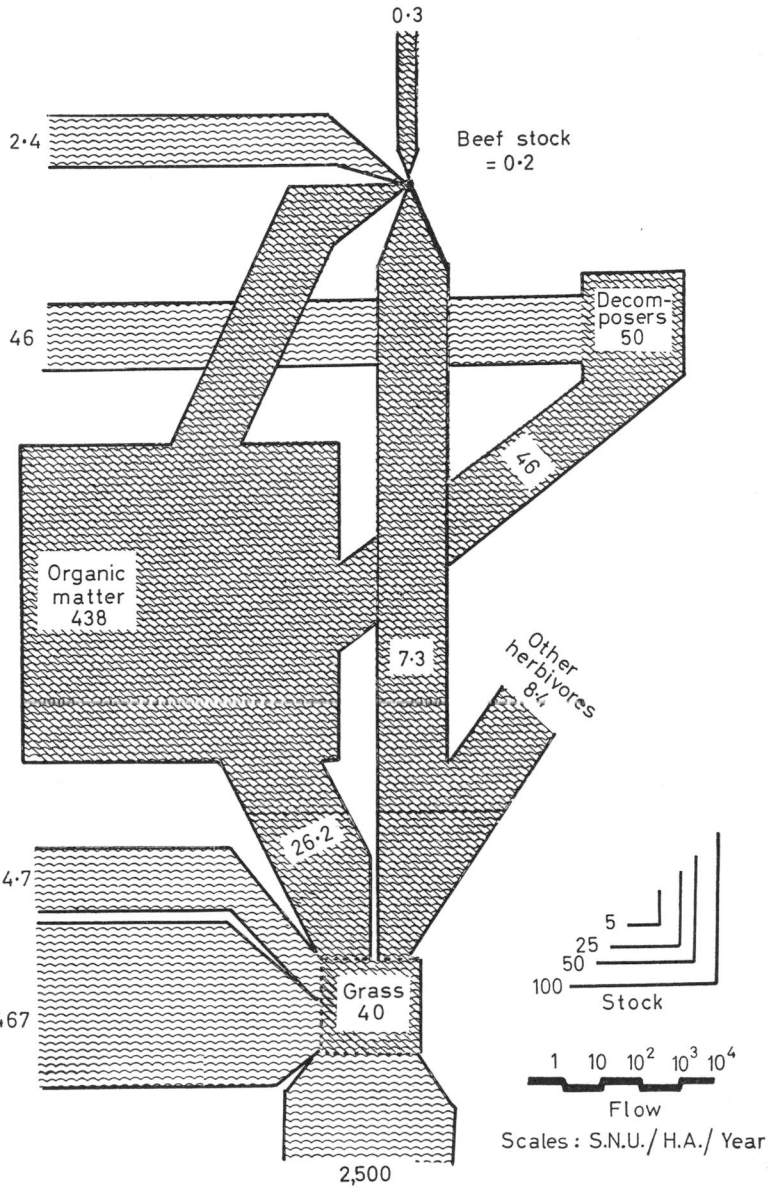

FIG. 7. Scaled version of Fig. 1 with values obtained from meadow subject to grazing by beef cattle.

3

involving many different stages and subject to dislocation in many
different ways. In the case of the permanent grassland shown in Fig. 7, it is
clearly the activity of the decomposers which limits the productivity of
the whole system, grazing included.

I have not the data to construct a similar scheme for the salt marsh and
the marine plankton, but in both these systems we have noticed that a high
proportion of the plant production appears in the form of accumulation of
organic matter and it seems most likely that here too the decomposer
organisms limit the overall turnover.

This survey of the ecological potentialities of a highly theoretical scheme
does not, of course, give the ecologist the right to tell practical people how
to conduct the detailed management of living systems. It does, though,
indicate some possible ways in which they might consider diverting
organic production for human use. We know, from experience with terrestrial systems that we can profitably supplement or substitute chemically
derived nutrients for those which a too slothful soil community is failing
to supply. There was a period when similar fertilization was advocated as
a stimulus to marine systems, but it now seems that a more profound
knowledge of the rather lengthy food chains is required. In principle there
are likely to be more losses in such a system between photosynthetic and
predatory fish production than between the farmer's pasture and arable
crops and agricultural food products. In the case of already fertile systems
such as salt marshes, Odum's (1960) suggestion that the exploitation of
detritus feeding molluscs and crustacea should take precedence over attempts to harness a not very prolific herbivore chain deserves careful consideration.

This raises the further point, which I have omitted hitherto for the sake
of simplicity, that calorific content is far from being the only criterion of
a satisfactory human diet. The crops which produce the highest calorific
yield for instance, are those which are most deficient in proteins. It is now
generally accepted that the human diet requires about 20 gm of protein
per 1,000 Calories. Clearly at the present time there is much to be said for
encouraging the production of animal food, especially where this can be
done by using detritus feeding animals and with relatively little expense.
The relative economic advantages of more ambitious schemes both for
cereal production and for protein production by unconventional methods,
such as Pirie (1958) has advocated, are matters of economics and human
need which must be weighed by others; the ecologist can only indicate
new fields which seem to have been overlooked and the rules within which
human endeavour must operate.

REFERENCES

ALBRITON E.C. (1953) Editor. *Standard values in Nutrition and Metabolism*. Committee on the Handbook of Biological Data American Institute of Biological Sciences. U.S. Air Force, Ohio

ALLEN K.RADWAY (1951) The Horokiwi stream. *New Zealand Marine Dept., Fish Bull.*, No. 10. 239 pp.

BRAY J.R., LAWRENCE D.B. & PEARSON L.C. (1959) Primary production in some Minnesota terrestrial communities for 1957. *Oikos* 10, 38–49

BUNT J.S & ROVIRA A.D. (1954) Oxygen uptake and carbon dioxide evolution in heat-sterilized soil. *Nature, Lond.*, 173, 1242

CUSHING D.H. (1955) Production and a pelagic fishery. *Min. of Ag. Fish and Food. Fisheries Investigations* (2) 18 (7), 104 pp. H.M.S.O.

CUSHING D.H. (1959a) On the nature of production in the sea. *Min. of Ag. Fish and Food. Fisheries Investigations* (2) 22 (6), 40 pp. H.M.S.O.

CUSHING D.H. (1959b) The seasonal variation in oceanic production as a problem in population dynamics. *J. Conseil internat. Exp. Mer.* 24, 455–464

DUNGER W. (1960) Zu einigen Fragen zu Leistung der Bodentiere bei der Umsetzung organischer Substanz. *Zentralbl. f. Bak, Paras., Infekt. u Hyg.* 2 (113), 245–255

ENGLEMANN M.D. (1961) The role of soil arthropods in the energetics of an old field community. *Ecol. Monogr.* 31, 221–238

FOGG G.E. (1958) Actual and potential yields in photosynthesis. *Adv. Sci.* 14, 395–400

FOGG G.E. (1959) Dissolved organic matter in oceans and lakes. *New Biology* 29, 31–48

FOX D.L. (1955) Organic detritus in the metabolism of the sea. *The scientific monthly* 80, 256–259

GAASTRA P. (1958) Light energy conversion in field crops in comparison with photosynthetic efficiency under laboratory conditions. *Medeleel. Landbouwhogeschool Wageningin* 58, 1–12

GAJEVSKAYA N.S. (1959) Sur l'étude quantitative de l'alimentation des animaux aquatiques. *Proc. XV. Int. Cong. Zool., London*, pp. 769–772

GOLLEY F.B. (1960) Energy dynamics of a food chain of an old-field community. *Ecol. Monogr.* 30, 187–206

HORTON P.A. (1961) The bionomics of brown trout in a dartmoor stream. *J. Anim., Ecol.* 30, 311–338

KALLE K. (1948) Zur Frage der Produktionlseistung des Meeres. *Dtsch. hydrogr. Zeits.* 1, 1–17

KUBIENA W.H. (1953) *The Soils of Europe*. London Murby

MACFADYEN A. (1961) Metabolism of soil invertebrates in relation to soil fertility. *Ann. appl. Biol.* 49, 216–19

ODUM E.P. & ODUM H.T. (1959) *Fundamentals of ecology*. Philadelphia & London. 546 pp.

ODUM E.P. (1960) The role of tidal marshes and streams in estuarine production. *19th Annual Meeting Atlantic States Marine Fisheries Commission, S. Carolina*. Sept. 1959

OVINGTON J.D. & HEITKAMP D. (1960) The accumulation of energy in forest plantations in Britain. *J. Ecol.* 48, 639–646

PATTERN B. C. (1959) An introduction to the cybernetics of the ecosystem: the trophic-dynamic aspect. *Ecology* **40**, 221-231

PHILLIPSON J. (1960a) A contribution to the feeding biology of *Mitopus morio* (F) (Phalangida). *J. Anim. Ecol.* **29**, 35-42

PHILLIPSON J. (1960b) The food consumption of different instars of *Mitopus morio* (F) (Phalangida) under natural conditions. *J. Anim. Ecol.* **29**, 299-307

PIRIE N. W. (1958) Unconventional production of foodstuffs. pp. 115-126 in YAPP W.B. & WATSON D.J. *The Biological Productivity of Britain.* Institute of Biology, Symposia No. 7, London

POMEROY L.R. (1959) Productivity of algae in salt marshes. *Proc. Salt Marsh Conf. Sapelo Island, Georgia* 1958. Marine Inst. Univ. Georgia, pp. 88-95

SLOBODKIN L.B. (1954) Population dynamics in *Daphnia obtusa* Kurz. *Ecol. Monogr.* **24**, 69-88

SLOBODKIN L.B. (1960) Ecological energy relationships at the population level. *The American Naturalist* **94**, 213-236

SMALLEY A.E. (1960) Energy flow of a salt marsh grasshopper population. *Ecology* **41**, 672-677

STAMP L.D. (1958) The land-use pattern of Britain. pp. 1-10 in YAPP W.B. & WATSON D.J. *The Biological Productivity of Britain.* Symposia of the Inst. of Biol. No. 7, London

TEAL J.M. (1959) Energy flow in the salt marsh ecosystem. *Proc. Salt. Marsh Conf. Sapelo Island, Georgia* 1958. Marine Inst. Univ. Georgia, pp. 101-107

VAN DER DRIFT J. & WITKAMP M. (1959) The significance of the breakdown of oak litter by *Enoicyla pusilla* Burm. *Arch. Néerl. de Zool.* **13**, 486-492

WITKAMP M. (1960) Seasonal fluctuations of the fungus flora in mull and mor of an oak forest. *I.T.B.O.N. Medeling* No. **46**, Arnhem

ZEUTHEN E. (1947) Body size and metabolic rate in the animal kingdom. *Compt-rend. Lab. Carlsberg Sér. Chim.* **26**, 17-165

PART II

GRAZING IN THE TERRESTRIAL ENVIRONMENT

NUTRIENT CIRCULATION IN VARIOUS ECOSYSTEMS

THE PHYSIOLOGICAL SIGNIFICANCE OF DEFOLIATION ON THE SUBSEQUENT REGROWTH OF GRASS-CLOVER MIXTURES AND CEREALS

M. B. ALCOCK

Department of Agriculture, University College of North Wales, Bangor

ABSTRACT

The importance of grassland as an agricultural crop and as a source of ruminant feed in the temperate regions of the world is emphasized. The problem of achieving maximum output of animal products from grassland is ultimately concerned with the close interrelationship between the plant community and the grazing animal. There is need for further fundamental knowledge of the underlying principles of plant and animal growth.

Grazing is controlled by Man through (1) The season and stage of growth at which grazing takes place, (2) The frequency of grazing, and (3) The severity or closeness of grazing. These three variables are discussed in relation to their known effect on the yield of grassland. The paper then outlines three basic theories for such responses: (1) The effect of grazing on root growth and its implication in respect of mineral and water uptake. (2) The effect of grazing on 'carbohydrate reserves' and their possible role in initiating regeneration after grazing. (3) The effect of grazing on leaf development and its implication to the interception of light and in rate of growth after defoliation. The basic theories behind this form of analysis are outlined.

Autumn sown cereals, because of their ability to grow at lower temperature than the majority of grasses are an attractive proposition for providing grazing in the early spring. Evidence obtained in Bangor on the growth and yield of spring grazed cereals and its implication to the general theory of grazing response in graminaceous plants is discussed.

1. INTRODUCTION

In the temperate regions of the world grassland predominates as an agricultural crop. It provides the most important single source of ruminant feed and is most usually, and also most economically utilized by grazing animals on it. The problem of increasing animal production from grassland is therefore mainly concerned with the complex interdependence of the plant community and the grazing animal. Logically in developmental research the experimental unit should be the animal and its pasture, both being studied as an entity. Where such an approach has been attempted in recent years it has become apparent that there is still insufficient knowledge

25

of the underlying principles of both plant and animal growth to satisfy completely the requirements for such complex experimentation.

In this paper are outlined some of the major contributions that crop physiologists are making to the basic problem of how and why plants react to various systems of grazing.

2. THE PROBLEM

Investigation into the effect of grazing on the grassland sward is essentially concerned with the various ways in which grazing can be controlled. Donald (1941) has outlined these as being:

1. The season of grazing, with particular reference to the stage of growth.
2. The frequency of grazing.
3. The severity of grazing.

In the past the effect of these variables has been widely studied. Details of these investigations are given in reviews by Singh (1958), Perks (1961), Kennedy (1950) and Brougham (1959). Much of this early work revealed that increasing the frequency and severity of grazing lowered annual production as measured in terms of dry matter yield. There was also found to be an inverse relationship between the frequency and severity of grazing; for example, the adverse effects of severe grazing could largely be mitigated by decreasing the frequency. Evidence of species and varietal differences in the response of the plant to grazing was often found, usually attributable to differences in morphology (Jones, 1933; Cooper and Saeed, 1949; and Cooper, 1960). For example, erect growing species suffered greater reduction in yield from close defoliation than did prostrate species, because in the latter a greater proportion of foliage escapes defoliation. The stage of growth was also found to be important in relation to grazing, there being greater adverse effects if this was carried out at an early stage of development (Jones, 1933). While these results have been found to occur over a wide range of circumstances there have been a number of conflicting observations. This has been particularly so with regard to the height of defoliation, there being several examples where close defoliation has given higher dry matter yields than has lax defoliation (Robinson et al., 1952; Reid, 1959; Wilson and McGuire, 1961; Appadurai, 1961; Burger et al., 1962).

3. THEORIES OFFERED IN EXPLANATION OF THE EFFECT OF DEFOLIATION OF GRASSLAND SPECIES

Various attempts have been made to explain the response to defoliation in terms of developmental physiology. The various theories suggested can be

considered most conveniently in three groups with respect to the effect of defoliation on:
1. The growth of roots and uptake of minerals and water.
2. The amount and re-utilization of reserve carbohydrates.
3. The development of leaf area and capacity to intercept light.
Although discussed separately complete independence is not suggested for any one theory. This aspect will be considered later.

4. THE SIGNIFICANCE OF ROOT GROWTH AND CAPACITY FOR WATER AND MINERAL UPTAKE IN DETERMINING THE RESPONSE TO DEFOLIATION

Grazing has often been found to reduce the size and growth of roots, the intensity of the response increasing with increasing frequency and severity of grazing. For a review of this subject Troughton (1957) should be consulted. The rate of recovery after grazing is usually slower in the roots than in the top growth and Troughton (1960) has suggested that this is in fact an adaptive mechanism, whereby a constant balance is maintained between the absorptive function of the root and the photosynthetic function of the shoot, since otherwise grazing would leave the plant with relatively more absorbing than photosynthetic tissue. On the other hand, existing roots may rapidly decompose after grazing in which case the efficiency of the new root system is of great importance. There is little evidence on this subject, but it does appear that reduced absorptive efficiency cannot simply be deduced from a reduction in root size and surface area, since these factors are not closely correlated with ability to absorb nutrient (Drake *et al.*, 1951; Williams, 1960; Williams and Waledge, 1961). Reduction in the concentration of soluble carbohydrates often occurs in the roots after defoliation and there is some evidence to suggest that this may result in lowered absorption of mineral ions (Alberda, 1948; Humphries, 1958).

Perhaps the most important effect of reduced root growth after grazing is a restriction of the plants' absorptive potential to the upper limits of the soil, this having particular significance under dry conditions. Oswalt *et al.* (1959), working in America, have demonstrated this point. They found that existing roots of orchard grass and bromegrass decomposed within 36 to 48 hours after defoliation of top growth. The phosphorus isotope (P^{32}) which had been placed 6 in. deep in the existing root zone was not detected in the shoots until new roots reached the activated zone, this occurring no earlier than 24 days after defoliation.

Poor growth after grazing has also been explained in terms of lowered ability of a defoliated plant to absorb water. Jäntti and Kramer (1956) have indicated that defoliation of pasture plants reduces the diffusion pressure deficit in the roots from values between ten and twenty atmospheres to levels as low as one or two atmospheres, depending on the severity of defoliation. In dry soils where water is held at a tension greater than two atmospheres, the defoliated plant would be unable to absorb water.

5. CARBOHYDRATE RESERVES AND THEIR SIGNIFICANCE IN THE REGENERATIVE CAPACITY OF HERBAGE PLANTS FOLLOWING DEFOLIATION

Grazing systems have often been based on the theory that an adequate supply of carbohydrate reserves is necessary to initiate and sustain regrowth after grazing. These reserves are considered to be mainly non-structural carbohydrates laid down as sugars, fructoses and starch in the roots, rhizomes and leaf bases of the plant. For recent reviews on this subject May (1960) and Weinman (1961) should be consulted. The concentration of these substances may vary between species and more particularly they are reduced by increasing the frequency and severity of defoliation.

Recently considerable doubt has arisen as to whether these carbohydrate reserves have in fact a causal role in initiating regrowth (Davidson and Donald, 1958). It appears that much of the evidence for such a role is circumstantial; for example, it is based on the apparent correlation of periods of active seasonal growth and growth after defoliation with lowered concentration of these carbohydrates. With respect to defoliation this is classically demonstrated by the work of Sullivan and Sprague (1943) illustrated in Fig. 1. In this experiment plants of a single perennial ryegrass clone were defoliated to a height of an inch and a half. The concentration of water soluble carbohydrates was followed in the stubble and roots following defoliation. There occurred a rapid decrease in these substances expressed as a percentage on a dry weight basis. It was assumed that since no increase in weight occurred in the stubble and roots over this period, the soluble carbohydrates were being translocated to the growing tops and utilized, partly as raw material for new growth, and partly as a source of energy for such growth to occur. After about 11 days recovery the photosynthetic area of new top growth had increased sufficiently to allow restorage of carbohydrates to occur, slowly at first and then at an increasing rate, reaching pre-defoliation levels in approximately 30–36 days.

Despite numerous experiments illustrating similar cyclic changes in soluble carbohydrates following defoliation there is no definite evidence as yet of a correlation between initial variation in carbohydrate level and subsequent extent of regrowth (May, 1960). While it is obvious that re-

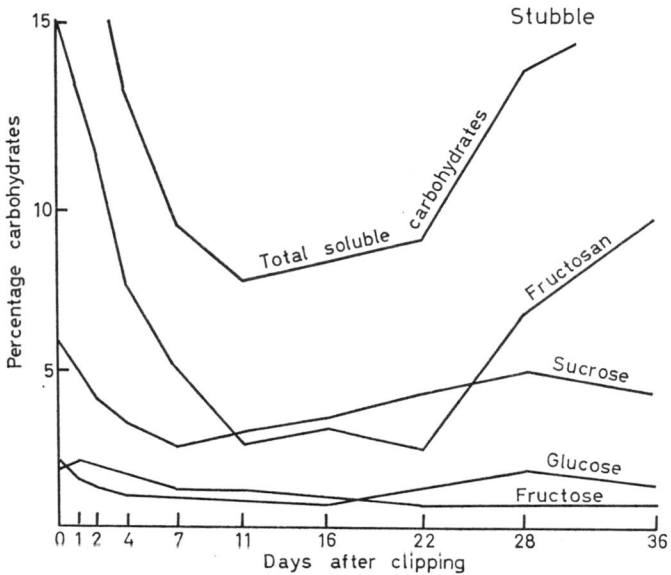

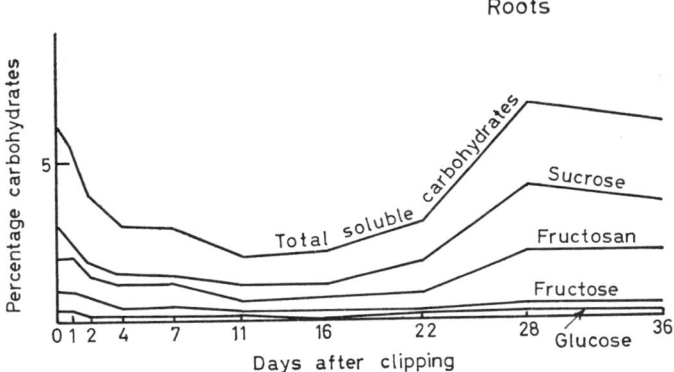

FIG. I. Water soluble carbohydrates in the stubble and roots of *Lolium perenne* plants growing in the greenhouse for 36 days after removal of the tops (redrawn from Sullivan & Sprague, 1943).

growth of a completely defoliated plant must depend initially upon a source of readily available energy already present in the plant, it is not so obvious how much importance can be attached to varying concentrations of carbohydrate reserves in the more usual circumstance where some green leaf is left after defoliation. Perhaps then the function of carbohydrate reserves is in promoting leaf expansion in the early stages of regrowth, bringing about the greatest recovery of total leaf area where there are a large number of leaf initials. There is, at present, at least some evidence of the former (Nottingham, 1961). Mitchell (1954a), studying the effect of partial defoliation on the growth of ryegrass, found no evidence of any utilization of carbohydrate reserves in re-growth. He suggests that a rapid rate of leaf growth after defoliation is more likely to be due to a re-direction of dry matter within the plant. When the supply of energy metabolite available to the plant is decreased, as after partial defoliation, the proportion of that metabolite used by the active meristematic centres lying closest to its point of origin in that plant increases.

Depletion of carbohydrate reserves may have an indirectly beneficial effect on the plant. May (1960) has suggested that in certain circumstances the rate of translocation of the products of assimilation is a limiting factor in photosynthesis. Lowered carbohydrate reserves would, in fact, represent a larger 'sink' which, in turn, would result in increased translocation away from the leaves. The view that translocation has an important role in determining photosynthetic activity is held by Thorne (1961) and is supported by evidence of an experiment (Alcock, 1963) where the artificial reduction of the soluble carbohydrate content of the leaf sheaths and roots of a winter wheat resulted ultimately in a greater rate of growth.

Clearly considerable more work is needed to evaluate the significance of carbohydrates accumulated in the various organs of the plant. The use of the C^{14} isotope as a tracer may well provide the means to this end.

6. THE THEORY OF LEAF GROWTH AND LIGHT INTERCEPTION

Mitchell (1954b) states that pasture growth is basically a process of transferring light energy into plant tissue. The response of a pasture plant to defoliation may, therefore, ultimately be described in terms of its capacity and efficiency for photosynthesis following defoliation. This can be described in terms of classical growth analysis (Watson, 1947; 1952; 1958.)

Thus at any one instant

$$\frac{dw}{dt} = \frac{1}{L} \cdot \frac{dw}{dt} \times L \tag{1}$$

where w = dry weight, L = leaf area;
or expressed in another way

$$C = \text{N.A.R.} \times \text{L.A.I.} \tag{2}$$

where C = the crop growth rate, N.A.R. = net assimilation rate, L.A.I. = leaf area index.

Donald (1961) has recently suggested in these terms how the rate of growth of a sward is dependent on the L.A.I. (Leaf area index). As illus-

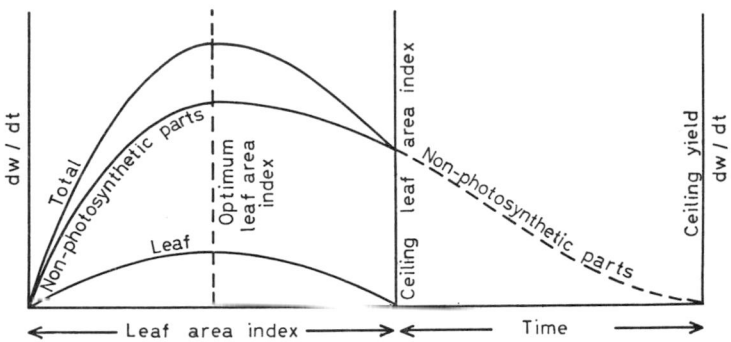

FIG. 2. Showing the relationship between crop growth rate (dw/dt) and leaf area index (redrawn from Donald, 1961).

trated in the left half of Fig. 2, with increase in L.A.I. the amount of light intercepted by the sward increases and growth proceeds at an increasingly rapid rate until a point is reached when, as a result of increasing mutual shading, the lowermost leaves in the canopy are assimilating dry matter only at the same rate as they are losing dry matter through respiration.

At this compensation point for the lower leaves in the canopy the N.A.R. (net assimilation rate) and C (crop growth rate) of the whole sward is at a maximum and leaf development is considered to be at a stage of optimum L.A.I. With further rise in L.A.I. an increasing proportion of the lower leaves fall below compensation point and as a result of their negative contribution in photosynthesis the N.A.R. and C of the sward begins to decline. Leaves below the compensation point 'respire themselves away' and are shed, their death rate and rate of shedding increasing with further rise in L.A.I. A final stage of leaf development is reached where the rate of death and production of new leaves is the same, L.A.I. then becomes static having reached a ceiling value. The canopy is still capable of positive photosynthesis and a further increase in non-photosynthetic parts occurs, although at a rapidly decreasing rate of growth as the ratio of respiration to photosynthesis approaches unity. When respiration losses equal photosynthetic gain in terms of carbon balance then ceiling yield has been reached.

If a pasture could be constantly maintained at optimum L.A.I. by merely grazing off excess growth as it accumulates, then theoretically maximum production, in terms of dry matter, would be achieved, as the pasture would be constantly growing at a maximum rate.

It is therefore possible to interpret the way in which different systems of grazing effect yield by considering the degree by which they approach this ideal. For example at one extreme, close and very frequent defoliation depresses annual dry matter production by limiting leaf growth thereby resulting in poor interception of light and low growth rates. Equally differences in species and varietal response to defoliation may be partly interpreted in terms of differences in optimum L.A.I. White clover for example produces its maximum rate of growth under closer grazing than grass because it has a lower optimum L.A.I. (3·5) than have most grasses such as perennial ryegrass with an optimum L.A.I. of 7·1 (Brougham, 1958). The value at which the L.A.I. is optimal will depend on the light intensity above the crop. It therefore varies between seasons. The critical value depends also on the optical properties of the leaves, involving the ability to transmit light, and on their spatial arrangement, particularly the inclination of the laminae, being higher when foliage is erect than when it lies horizontally (Monsi and Sacki, 1953; Kasanaga and Monsi, 1954; Davidson and Donald, 1958; Brougham, 1958; Mitchell and Calder, 1958; Saeki, 1960; 1961; Warren-Wilson, 1960; Donald, 1961; Stern and Donald, 1961). The response to defoliation of a sward of varied composition will be largely influenced by the response of the dominant species which in turn may vary throughout different seasons of the year (Brougham, 1958).

The experimental evidence which directly supports these theoretical considerations is as yet limited and has been mainly obtained by Brougham in New Zealand, Davidson and Donald in Australia and more recently Appadurai working at Wye College in Kent.

Brougham (1956) has shown how variation in height of defoliation may affect yield. This he demonstrated by defoliating a ryegrass–clover pasture association from a uniform height of 9 in. down to a height of 5 in., 3 in., and 1 in. Recorded over a period of 32 days' regrowth, were the dry weight increase, leaf area and the percentage of daylight intercepted at a level of 1 in. above the ground surface. The course of light intercepted in the various treatments indicated that in the 5 in. cut, 95 per cent of the light was intercepted within 4 days of defoliation, whereas it took 16 days for the 3 in. cut and 24 days for the 1 in. cut.

At this level of light interception the L.A.I. of the sward was 5, irrespective of the severity of defoliation. Also at this stage of development of L.A.I. the maximum crop growth rate was achieved. Theoretically if this represents the optimum L.A.I., then it would be expected that the crop growth rate would decline as L.A.I. increased further. In fact maximum growth rates were maintained up to a L.A.I. of 9. This was possibly due to an increase in light intensity as the season progressed but more probably due to a change in the profile of light intensity in the sward as it became grass dominant. As a result of this and because of the early attainment of maximum growth rate after the 5 in. cut, the dry matter yields at the end of 32 days of growth were 20 per cent in favour of the 5 in. cut when compared with the yields from the 1 in. cut. Yields of herbage from the 3 in. cut were intermediate.

Davidson and Donald (1958) working with monoculture swards of subterranean clover were able to demonstrate a clearly defined optimum L.A.I., with lower growth rates both below and above a L.A.I. value of 4·5. These experiments were primarily designed to study the effect of growing subterranean clover at different densities and subjected to different times of defoliation during the growing season.

These experiments demonstrated clearly the interelationship between the stage of growth at which defoliation occurs, the optimum L.A.I. and dry matter production. Defoliation was severe and consisted of removing 50 per cent of the fresh weight of tops which was equivalent to 80 per cent of the laminae.

The results indicated that the effect of initial L.A.I. on the rate of subsequent leaf production depended upon whether L.A.I. was above or below the optimum at the time of defoliation. If, for instance, L.A.I. was higher than 4·5 then any defoliation reducing L.A.I. towards the optimum increased the rate of leaf production. If L.A.I. was lower than 4·5 and was further decreased by defoliation then the subsequent rate of leaf production was drastically reduced.

Of even greater significance, this pattern of leaf development was repeated in the subsequent dry matter production.

4

Both these experiments confirm the theory that high pasture production could be obtained by maintaining L.A.I. as closely as possible to the optimum. This interpretation of the response to defoliation clearly explains a large body of evidence which indicates that increasing the severity of defoliation results in lowered annual yield whereas higher yields are obtained from more lax defoliation. It does not, however, at first sight explain those circumstances where close defoliation has in fact resulted in higher annual dry matter yield than has less severe defoliation. This is particularly so where such results have been obtained irrespective of the grazing frequency between close and lax defoliation treatments (Burger et al., 1962). The explanation offered is bound up with a consideration of the effect that the transition from vegetative to reproductive growth has on the pattern of development in grasses (Langer, 1957; 1958; 1959). Lax grazing often allows relatively uninterrupted development of the flowering shoot resulting in an ultimate check to increase of leaf area in the sward. This is because flowering is accompanied by a decline in leafy vegetative tillers and with limited leaf development on the flowering shoot. Close defoliation, on the other hand, inhibits the development of the flowering shoot and results in increased tillering and leaf development, the extent of which largely depends on the species or variety (Cooper and Saeed, 1949).

Appadurai (1961) working with perennial ryegrass-white clover swards found that such increased leaf production particularly in the early part of the season was a major factor in determining the higher yields obtained from close defoliation. A further factor involved was that the N.A.R. was also greater after close defoliation. This was similarly found by Brougham (1956) and is a result that needs further investigation.

7. THE EFFECT OF GRAZING ON THE DEVELOPMENT AND YIELD OF AUTUMN SOWN CEREALS

With a few exceptions autumn sown cereals are capable of growing at lower temperatures than the majority of grasses. This makes them an attractive proposition for providing grazing in very early spring. While in some countries autumn sown cereals are used solely to provide such grazing, in Great Britain it is considered economically necessary that they should also provide an adequate yield of grain. It is known that in the majority of circumstances grazing cereals in the spring will reduce grain and straw yield, the extent of the reduction depending on the stage of growth and frequency and severity of defoliation (Holliday, 1956; Alcock, 1963).

Alcock (1963) has investigated the effect of grazing autumn sown wheat, rye and oats in the spring. In these investigations a single grazing with dairy cattle was carried out on the 1st April. At this date the different cereals were approximately 10 in. high and yielded between 4–5 cwt of dry matter per acre. The growing apices showed the beginning of inflorescence initiation and were on average between 0·1 in. and 0·7 in. above soil sur-

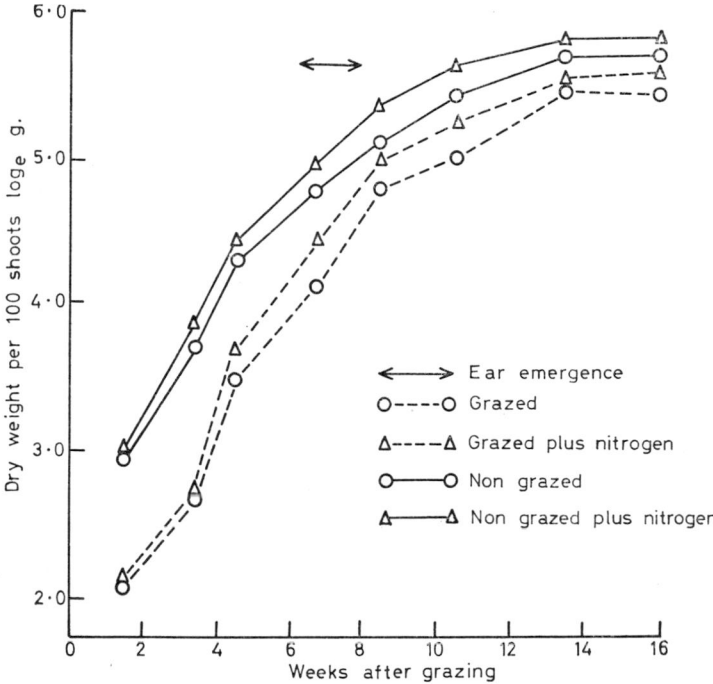

FIG. 3. The effect of grazing and nitrogen on the dry weight increase per 100 shoots — average effect on autumn sown wheat, rye and oats when grazed on 1 April.

face. Grazing was severe, all laminae being removed leaving a 2½ in. high stubble. Immediately after grazing a nitrogen treatment consisting of 1½ cwt of sulphate of ammonia per acre was applied. The results obtained showed that the three cereals did not differ in their response to grazing, and that grain yield was reduced by 38 per cent and straw yield by 46 per cent in the absence of nitrogen. Application of nitrogen brought about complete recovery in grain yield but a less complete recovery in straw yield. Reduction in the dry weight of individual shoots was a major factor in determining the reduction in yield.

In Fig. 3 the natural logarithm of the dry weight per shoot is plotted for the nitrogen and grazing treatment combinations after averaging the results for the three cereals. The slope of the lines $d \log_e w/dt$ is therefore proportional to the relative growth rate (R.G.R.) which at any instant is

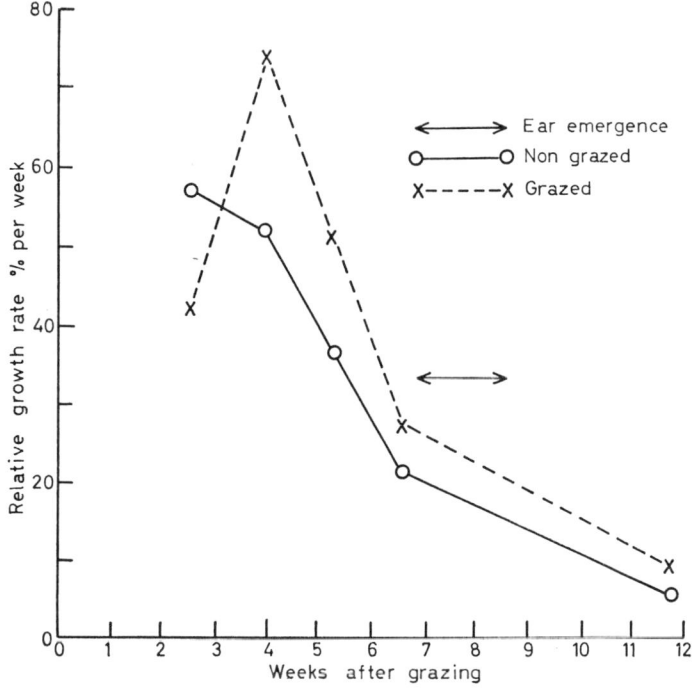

FIG. 4. The effect of grazing on the relative growth rate.

expressed as $1/w \cdot dw/dt$ (where w = dry weight). Grazing reduced the dry weight per shoot by 57 per cent at the first sampling after grazing and then this increased to a reduction of 65 per cent at the second sampling. At ear emergence the reduction had diminished to 27 per cent and at harvest to 22 per cent. Fig. 3 indicates that recovery was a result of a higher R.G.R. The average effect of grazing on the R.G.R. is shown in Fig. 4. Grazing depressed the R.G.R. over the first three weeks of regrowth and then increased the R.G.R. with a maximum increase of 27 per cent above the R.G.R. of the non-grazed treatment. The difference was significant at a probability level, $P = 0\cdot001$. The extent of this increase diminished with time but a higher rate was always maintained. Relative growth rate can be analysed in terms of N.A.R. and the leaf area ratio (L.A.R.) according to Equation 3 (Briggs et al., 1920; Gregory, 1926).

$$\frac{1}{w} \cdot \frac{dw}{dt} = \frac{1}{L} \cdot \frac{dw}{dt} \times \frac{L}{w} \qquad (3)$$

where w = dry weight, L = leaf area.

Grazing initially depressed N.A.R. and then showed either little effect or a slight increase at about the 6th and 7th week (Fig. 5). The effect of

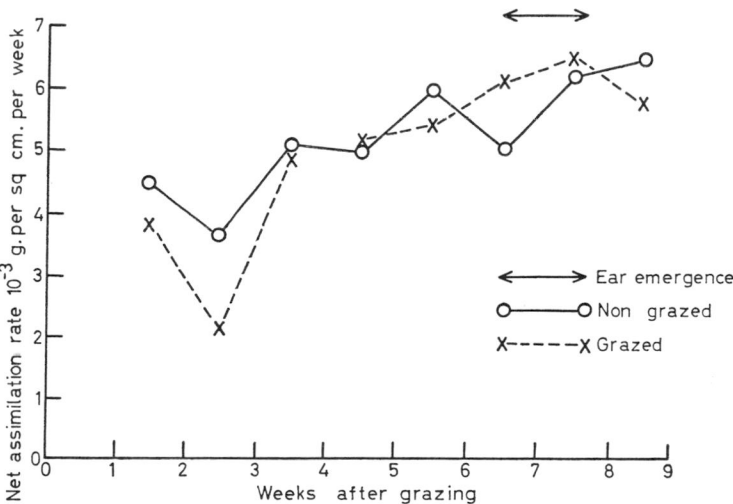

FIG. 5. The effect of grazing on the net assimilation rate.

grazing on L.A.R. is shown in Fig. 6. Grazing decreased L.A.R. during the first two weeks of re-growth and then increased L.A.R., the trend showing a close parallel to that of the R.G.R. It was evident that the higher R.G.R. that was attained after grazing was due almost entirely to a higher L.A.R. which in turn was a result of a rapid increase in leaf area. Thus the relative leaf growth rate over the first four weeks of regrowth was 52 per cent per week (± 6 per cent) for the grazed treatment and 26 per cent per week (± 6 per cent) for the non-grazed treatment. The effect of nitrogen in increasing recovery and yield was also entirely a result of an increase in L.A.R. Gardner and Wiggans (1960) and Holt (1962) both found rapid leaf growth following defoliation of spring sown oats and suggest that this was due to reutilization of carbohydrate reserves. In this present experiment the initial increase in leaf area was accompanied by a low dry weight increase and a low N.A.R. These results appear to support the above theory, at least in the early stages of regrowth after complete defoliation. They do not preclude, however, the possiblity of preferential utilization of energy metabolite by the expanded leaves as suggested by Mitchell (1954A).

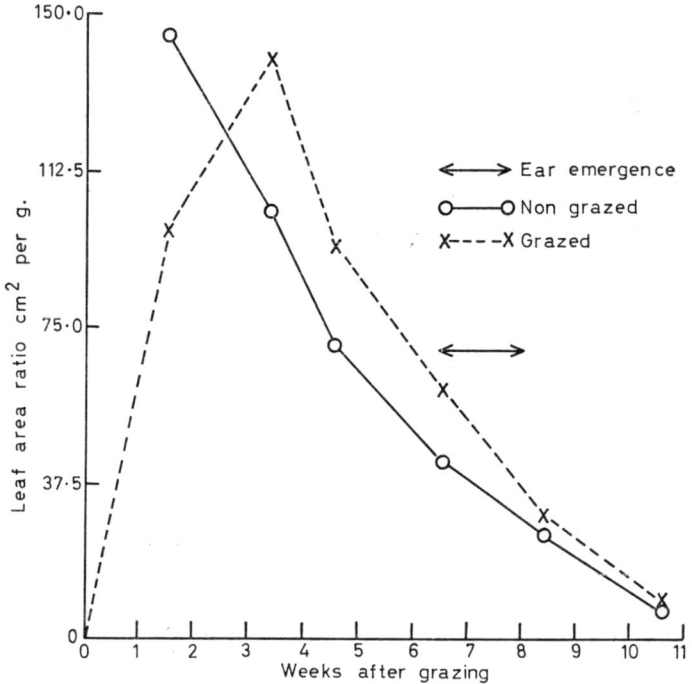

FIG. 6. The effect of grazing on the leaf area ratio.

8. CONCLUSION

The theories suggested to explain the response of grasses, clovers and cereals to defoliation have been outlined. The most precise interpretation is made in terms of classical growth analysis. Thus the regrowth and annual dry matter yield under various grazing systems will be dependent upon the extent of leaf growth and interception of solar energy and upon the efficiency of photosynthesis. In the majority of examples where growth analysis has been carried out, the effect of defoliation on leaf area has been the major factor influencing yield. This in turn may eventually be proved to show an interaction with the water and mineral status of the plant and possibly with re-utilization of carbohydrate reserves.

One of the most important questions arising from recent work on this subject is whether it is the residual leaf area left after defoliation or the concentration of carbohydrate reserves that is the more important in determining the rate and extent of regrowth. Experiments such as those carried out by Ward and Blaser (1961), while seemingly indicating an interplay of these two factors, with carbohydrate reserves being the more important in the initial stages of regrowth, have not, in fact, conclusively identified their role. More attention could be profitably paid in the future to assessing their relative significance. Meanwhile it is apparent that, while considerable knowledge has been obtained of the physiological effects of defoliation, the application of this in rationalizing grazing systems still remains a formidable task.

REFERENCES

ALBERDA TH. (1948) The influence of some external factors on growth and phosphate uptake of maize plants. *Rec. Trav. bot. neer* **41,** 542

ALCOCK M.B. (1963) The physiological effects and practical implications of grazing winter wheat, rye and oats in the spring. Unpublished Thesis. University of Wales

APPADURAI R.R. (1961) Studies in pasture growth. The influence of stage of growth and closeness of defoliation on the growth and productivity of a perennial ryegrass white clover sward under different moisture regimes. Unpublished Thesis. University of London

BRIGGS G.E., KIDD F. & WEST C. (1920) A quantitative analysis of plant growth. Parts I and II. *Ann. Appl. Biol.* **7,** 103–123, 203–223

BROUGHAM R.W. (1956) The effect of intensity of defoliation on regrowth of pasture. *Aust. J. Agric. Res.* **7,** 377–387

BROUGHAM R.W. (1958) Interception of light by the foliage of pure and mixed stands of pasture plants. *Aust. J. Agric. Res.* **9,** 39–52

BROUGHAM R.W. (1959) The effects of frequency and intensity of grazing on the productivity of a pasture of short-rotation ryegrass and red and white clover. *N.Z. J. Agric. Res.* **2,** 1232–1248

BURGER A.W., JACKOBS J.A. & HITTLE C.N. (1962) The effect of height and frequency of cutting on the yield and botanical composition of Smooth bromegrass and Orchard grass mixtures. *Agron. J.* **54,** 23–26

COOPER J.P. (1960) Selection for production characters in ryegrass. *Proc. 8th Int. Grassl. Congr.* 41–44

COOPER J.P. & SAEED S.W. (1949) Studies on growth and development in Lolium. I. Relation of the annual habit to head production under various systems of cutting. *J. of Ecol.* **37,** 233–259

DAVIDSON J.L. & DONALD C.M. (1958) The growth of swards of subterranean clover with particular reference to leaf area. *Aust. J. Agric. Res.* **9**, 53–72

DONALD C.M. (1941) *Pastures and pasture resarch.* Univ. Sydney 57–72

DONALD C.M. (1961) Competition for light in crops and pastures. *XVth Symp. Soc. Exp. Biol.* 282–313

DRAKE M., VENGRIS J. & COLBY W.G. (1951) Cation-exchange capacity of plant roots. *Soil Sci.* **72**, 139–147

GARDNER F.P. & WIGGANS S.C. (1960) Effect of clipping and nitrogen fertilization on forage yield of spring oats. *Agron. J.* **52**, 566–568

GREGORY F.G. (1926) The effect of climatic conditions on the growth of barley. *Ann. Bot.* **40**, 1–26

HOLLIDAY R. (1956) Fodder production from winter-sown cereals and its effect upon grain yield. *Field Crop Abstr.* **9**, No. 3 129–135; **9**, No. 4, 207–213

HOLMES W. (1962) Grazing management for dairy cattle. *J. Brit. Grassl. Soc.* **17**, 30–40

HOLT E.C. (1962) Growth behaviour and management of small grains for forage. *Agron. J.* **54**, 272–275

HUMPHRIES E.C. (1958) Entry of nutrients into the plant and their movement within it. *Proc. No. 48 Fertilizer Soc. London*

JÄNTTI A. & KRAMER P.J. (1956) Regrowth of pastures in relation to soil moisture and defoliation. *Proc. 7th Int. Grassl. Congr.* 33–42

JONES M.G. (1933) Grassland management and its influence on the sward. *Emp. J. Expt. Agric.* **1**, 43–57, 122–127, 223–234, 361–367

KASANAGA H. & MONSI M. (1954) On the light transmission of leaves and its meaning for the production of matter in plant communities. *Jap. J. Bot.* **14**, 304–324

KENNEDY W.K. (1950) Simulated grazing treatments. Effect on yield, botanical composition and chemical composition of a permanent pasture. *Memoir 295 Cornell Univ. Agric. Exp. Sta.*

LANGER R.H.M. (1957) The effect of time of cutting on ear production and seed yield in S48 Timothy. *J. Brit. Grassl. Soc.* **12**, 97–102

LANGER R.H.M. (1958) A study of growth in swards of Timothy and Meadow Fescue. I. Uninterrupted growth. *J. Agric. Sci.* **51**, 347–352

LANGER R.H.M. (1959) A study of growth in swards of Timothy and Meadow Fescue II. The effects of cutting treatments. *J. Agric. Sci.* **52**, 273–281

MAY L.H. (1960) The utilization of carbohydrate reserves in pasture plants after defoliation. *Herb. Abstr.* **30**, No. 4, 239–245

MITCHELL K.J. (1954a) Influence of light and temperature on growth of Ryegrass. (*Lolium* spp.) III. Pattern and rate of tissue formation. *Physiol. Plant.* **7**, 51

MITCHELL K.J. (1954b) Growth of pasture species. I. Short rotation and perennial ryegrass. *N.Z. J. Sci. Tech. A.* **36**, 193–206

MITCHELL K.J. & CALDER D.M. (1958) The light regime within pastures. *N.Z. J. Agric. Res.* **1**, 61–68

MONSI M. & SAEKI T. (1953) Uber den Lichtfaktor in den Pflanzengesellschaften und seine Bedeutung für die Staffproduktion. *Jap. J. Bot.* **14**, pp. 22–52

Nottingham (1961) Rept. Sch. Agric. University of Nottingham, 1961. *Plant growth* p. 23

OSWALT D.L., BERTRAND A.R. & TEAL M.R. (1959) Influence of nitrogen fertilization and clipping on grass roots. *Proc. Soil Science* **23**, 228–230

PERKS D.A. (1961) Some factors affecting the recovery of grassland after cutting. Unpublished Thesis Univ. Col. Wales, Aberystwyth

REID D. (1959) Studies on the cutting management of grass clover swards. I. The effect of varying the closeness of cutting on the yields from an established grass-clover sward. *J. Agric. Sci.* **53**, 299–312

ROBINSON R.R., SPRAGUE V.G. & LUECK A.G. (1952) The effect of irrigation, nitrogen fertilization and clipping treatments on persistence of clover and on total and seasonal distribution of yield in a Kentucky Bluegrass Sod. *Agron. J.* **44**, 239–244

SAEKI T. (1960) Interrelationships between leaf amount, light distribution and photosynthesis in a plant community. *Bot. Mag. Tokyo* **73**, 55–63

SAEKI T. (1961) Analytical studies on the development of foliage of a plant community. *Bot. Mag. Tokyo* **74**, 342–348

SINGH A. (1958) The reaction of different types of herbage plant to defoliation. Unpublished Thesis. Univ. Durham

STERN W.R. & DONALD C.M. (1961) Relationship of radiation, leaf area index and crop growth rate. *Nature* **189**, 597–598

SULLIVAN J.T. & SPRAGUE V.G. (1943) Composition of the roots and stubble of perennial ryegrass following partial defoliation. *Plant. Physiol.* **18**, 656–669

THORNE G.N. (1961) Dependence of photosynthesis on growth. *Rept. Rothamsted Exp. Sta.* 1961, pp. 90–91

TROUGHTON A. (1957) The underground organs of herbage grasses. *C.A.B. Bull.* No. 44

TROUGHTON A. (1960) Growth correlations between the roots and shoots of grass plants. *Proc. 8th Int. Grassl. Congr.* 280–283

WARD C.Y. & BLASER R.E. (1961) Carbohydrate food reserves and leaf area in regrowth of orchard grass. *Crop. Science* **1**, 366–370

WARREN-WILSON J. (1960) Influence of spatial arrangement of foliage area on light interception and pasture growth. *Proc. 8th Int. Grassl. Congr.* 275–279

WATSON D.J. (1947) Comparative physiological studies on the growth of field crops. I. Variation in net assimilation rate and leaf area between species and varieties, and within and between years. *Ann. Bot. N.S.* **11**, 41–76

WATSON D.J. (1952) The physiological basis of variation in yield. *Adv. Agron.* **4**, 101–145

WATSON D.J. (1958) The dependence of net assimilation rate on leaf area index. *Ann. Bot. N.S.* **22**, 37–54

WEINMAN H. (1961) Total available carbohydrates in grasses and legumes. *Herb. Abstr.* **31**, 255–261

WILLIAMS R.D. (1960) Nutrient uptake by grass roots. *Proc. 8th Int. Grassl. Congr.* 283–286

WILLIAMS R.D. & WALEDGE J. (1961) Physiological studies of grass roots (H. 107). *Grassl. Res. Inst. Exp. in Progr.* 1959–60, No. 13, 91–92

WILSON D.B. & McGUIRE W.S. (1961) Effects of clipping and nitrogen on competition between three pasture species. *Canad. J. Plant Sci.* **41**, 631–642

PRAIRIE, SAVANNA AND OAKWOOD ECOSYSTEMS AT CEDAR CREEK

J.D.OVINGTON

Department of Botany, University of Minnesota, U.S.A.[1]

ABSTRACT

On the upland, sandy soils of the Cedar Creek Natural History Area, Minnesota, examples of semi-natural prairie, savanna and oakwood occur in juxtaposition and present a unique opportunity to make ecological comparisons of ecosystems with different degrees of tree cover. Typical examples of each ecosystem type were studied intensively at monthly intervals from May to November, 1959. Although the inherent site conditions were not identical at all three study areas, it seemed that the form of the vegetation cover was of greatest importance in influencing the magnitude and pattern of ecosystem dynamics.

With increasing numbers of shrubs and trees present, the magnitude of the organic system and nutrient circulation increased greatly, suggesting that the presence of woody plants results in a greater utilization of the site and increased biological activity. The primary productivity of the oakwood was not greatly different from that of an intensively managed field of maize nearby; hence the woodland was probably making very full use of the site.

The savanna ecosystem, which was relatively rich in the plant nutrients nitrogen, potassium, calcium, magnesium and phosphorus, produced the largest mass of plant material at ground level.

THE STUDY AREA

The natural vegetation of eastern central Minnesota includes representative examples of (a) the northern conifer forests of spruce, fir, birch and pine, (b) the eastern and southern deciduous forests of oak, aspen, basswood, elm and sugar maple, and (c) the tall grass prairie of the western plains (Rosendahl and Butters, 1928). Within this general transition zone, a Natural History Area has been established at Cedar Creek near Minneapolis which, for its size of about 1,620 hectares (4,000 acres), contains a remarkably wide range of vegetation types. The varied nature of the plant cover at Cedar Creek can be attributed to several factors whose relative importance favours one or other vegetation type. The most noteworthy factors

---

[1] Now at the Nature Conservancy, Monkswood Experimental Station, Abbots Ripton, Huntingdonshire, England.

controlling the vegetation pattern are past differential burning by Indians and local differences in site conditions, particularly height of water table and the character of the soil which ranges from a deep base-rich sand to peat. The general character of the present day landscape, with its mosaic-like combination of forest, prairie and swamp, is probably not greatly different from that encountered by the early white colonists who arrived about 1856 but never settled in great numbers because of the relatively infertile soil. No doubt the detailed species composition and structure of the vegetation types have been modified to varying extents by selective logging, grazing and abortive attempts at cultivation. Nevertheless, since settlement was sparse and much of the area has been protected from human interference during the last two decades, it has retained much of its wilderness character.

On the upland sandy soils of the Cedar Creek Natural History Area, examples of natural prairie, savanna and oakwood occur in juxtaposition and present a unique opportunity to make ecological comparisons of natural ecosystems with different degrees of tree cover (Ovington and Heitkamp, 1963). Typical examples, one each of prairie, savanna and oakwood were selected for study in 1959. Each community changed greatly throughout the year and, to permit comparisons at different seasons, sampling was done at monthly intervals from May to November, thus covering the main growing period when the soil was not frozen. None of the ecosystems was being managed for any economic purpose and over many years grazing was allowed only by wildlife which freely wandered over the whole Natural History Area. Grazing by deer was not heavy in any of the three ecosystems.

In the prairie, forty two species of plants were recorded, grasses being dominant with *Andropogon gerardi*, *Stipa spartea*, and *Poa pratensis* most common. Trees were absent and, although the two shrubs *Rosa arkansa* var. *suffulta* and *Prunus pumila* were well distributed throughout the prairie, they did not form a dominant feature of the vegetation. In the savanna, the ground vegetation was more luxuriant than that of the prairie, with grasses again most common, but the two shrubs *Corylus americana* and *Prunus virginiana* were abundant, locally suppressing the forbs and grasses. Trees of both bur oak, *Quercus macrocarpa*, and northern pin oak, *Quercus ellipsoidalis*, were present in the savanna, the largest tree sampled being a bur oak 10 m. high and about 90 years old. In contrast to the prairie, tree seedlings occurred frequently in the savanna and the trees had a wide range of age. The trees of the oakwood were all northern red oak, *Quercus borealis*, the woodland having developed naturally, possibly after fire, so that the tree age distribution recorded was small compared to that of the savanna. The oldest oak tree felled was 58 years old with a height of 17 m and the tree crowns gave a dense, continuous over-storey canopy fairly uniform in height. The herbaceous layer of the oakwood was sparse but the shrub layer was the best developed of all the three ecosystems with *Corylus americana*, *Prunus virginiana*, *Rubus idaeus* and *Vaccinium angustifolium* very abundant.

It was recognized that although the inherent site factors of the three ecosystems were broadly similar, they were not identical despite the closeness of the study areas. However, it seemed that the site differences were probably of less ecological importance than the form of the vegetation cover in determining the relative annual magnitudes and patterns of the organic and nutrient systems. Although the three ecosystems formed a sequence of progressive dominance by woody plants in the order prairie, savanna and oakwood, they did not represent a natural time succession and it seemed unlikely that the prairie would develop naturally into a woodland similar to the oakwood. In fact, each community appeared remarkably stable. For example, there was no evidence of active colonization of the prairie by trees, even though the trees of the surrounding savanna produced abundant seed and the prairie had not been burnt for a number of years. Probably the most significant long term change taking place was that the amount of tree cover in the savanna and the abundance of shrubs in both the savanna and oakwood were increasing.

SAMPLING METHODS

Each ecosystem was sampled intensively at monthly intervals from April to November 1959. On each sampling occasion, plant organic matter, both living and dead, was collected in such a way that the monthly biomass of the different types of plant material could be expressed as oven dry weight per hectare of land surface and estimates made of the annual turnover of organic matter. So far as possible the same sampling techniques were used in each type area. Basically, a central square plot of 900 m² was pegged out for detailed sampling of the herbaceous layer. The living forbs and grasses were clipped from twenty quadrats (20 × 20 cm) selected according to an unbiased statistical procedure. All dead plant material on the soil was collected from the same twenty quadrats and the roots and subterranean stems were sampled by extracting soil cores at ten of the quadrats, and separating the plant material from the soil using a jet of water. The shrub and tree layers were sampled by harvesting a number of plants of each of the species present. After weighing the collected plant material when fresh, its dry weight was determined by oven drying sub-samples. A large sample of each type of plant material was ground down to a fine powder in a Wiley mill and analysed for total potassium, calcium, magnesium, phosphorus and nitrogen in order to provide data of the nutrient content of the plant biomass and cycling of these nutrients through each ecosystem.

THE ORGANIC SYSTEM

The most notable difference between the three ecosystems was in the amount of plant organic matter present. Taking into account the whole biomass of plant material, both living and dead, as well as above and below ground, the minimum and maximum values recorded as Kg per Ha were for the prairie, 6,100 and 9,700, for the savanna 54,400 and 63,200, and for the oakwood 224,200 and 257,100 (Table 1).   The ecosystems with trees were characterized by a relatively large accumulation of organic matter. At Cedar Creek this was not solely a result of the great mass of material contained in the tree trunks and branches, since the weight of dead plant material (litter plus dead branches on the trees) in the oakwood was about five times the weight of the total plant biomass of the prairie and approximately equal in weight to the biomass of the savanna.

The distribution and relative proportions of the different types of plant material collected varied greatly. The organic matter of the prairie was contained within a relatively narrow zone whereas in the oakwood it was distributed throughout a considerable depth because of the height of the trees. In the prairie, savanna and oakwood respectively the above ground herbaceous layer accounted, on average, for 6 per cent, 1 per cent and 0·03 per cent of the complete plant biomass, whilst the corresponding percentages for the tree layer above ground were 0, 54 and 69 and for dead plant material 35, 24 and 25. Although the proportion of the plant biomass represented by the herbaceous layer was greater in the prairie than in the savanna, more herbaceous material was present in the savanna, so that the effect of a partial overstorey of woody plants was to increase the amount of forbs and grasses. Where the over-storey was complete and dense, as in the oakwood, the herbaceous layer was greatly suppressed and the surface litter was exposed over much of the sample plot.

The monthly weights of the dead plant material and subterranean plant parts varied irregularly throughout the sampling period and no well defined annual pattern of change could be recognized. In the case of the roots and underground stems, this may have been due in part to the inadequacy

TABLE I

Oven dry weight of plant material (Kg $\times 10^3$ Ha^{-1})

Sampling month in 1959	April	May	June	July	August	September	October	November
Prairie								
Living plant material above ground	<0·1	0·1	0·5	0·7	1·0	0·9	0·4	0·2
Dead plant material above ground	2·9	2·0	2·5	3·0	2·7	2·4	3·0	3·8
Roots and subterranean stems	6·7	4·0	4·7	6·0	3·5	5·4	3·8	4·4
Total plant biomass	9·6	6·1	7·7	9·7	7·2	8·7	7·2	8·4
Savanna								
Living plant material above ground	30·2	30·3	32·5	32·8	35·0	33·5	31·0	30·9
Dead plant material above ground	11·1	12·2	10·9	12·9	14·3	14·8	16·6	16·5
Roots and subterranean stems	13·1	13·0	12·9	11·9	8·1	14·9	8·8	11·7
Total plant biomass	54·4	55·5	56·3	57·6	57·4	63·2	56·4	59·1
Oakwood								
Living plant material above ground	161·2	162·1	164·0	164·4	164·8	165·8	163·9	163·0
Dead plant material above ground	56·1	59·0	73·8	60·5	45·8	53·3	63·1	57·1
Roots and subterranean stems	13·0	15·5	19·3	20·7	13·6	15·9	11·9	10·1
Total plant biomass	230·3	236·6	257·1	245·6	224·2	235·0	238·9	230·2

of the sampling technique. In contrast, for all three ecosystems the monthly weights of the living matter above ground showed an increase from a minimum in April to a maximum in August or September before declining rapidly in October and November. This sequential change resulted from a series of similar changes in certain components of the living plant material above ground, notably the herbaceous layer and the new shoots produced in 1959 by the shrubs and trees (Figs. 1, 2 and 3). Generally most of the new shoot production of the shrubs and trees was foliar material but in the savanna the bur oaks were so heavily laden with acorns that the production of nuts was almost equal in weight to that of leaves.

The annual net production of above ground plant matter was estimated for the three ecosystems from the monthly dry weight data (Table 2) and, although for various reasons the estimates were probably too small, they showed the main differences of organic matter production between the three areas. As the degree of tree cover increased, the trees replaced the forbs and grasses as the primary producers of organic matter and a large and progressive increase in primary productivity resulted. The annual

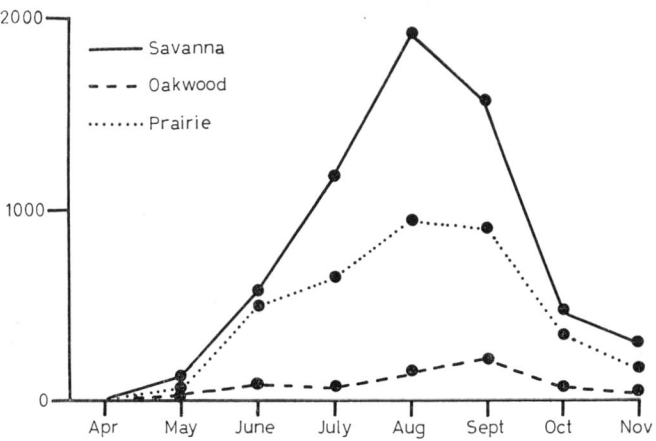

FIG. 1. Monthly oven dried weights in kg ha^{-1} of living herbaceous layers in 1959.

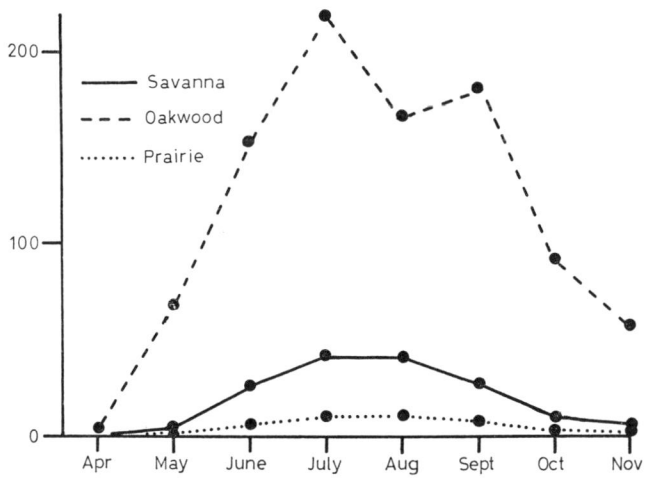

FIG. 2. Monthly oven dried weights in kg ha^{-1} of new shoots of shrubs in 1959.

production of above ground plant material in the oakwood was over eight times that of the prairie. In view of the greater weight of subterranean plant material present in the oakwood compared with the prairie, it seems probable that the annual production of roots was largest in the oakwood and that the increase in primary production due to the presence of the trees was even greater than appears from Table 2. The rate of organic matter production was not constant throughout the recording period and, in all

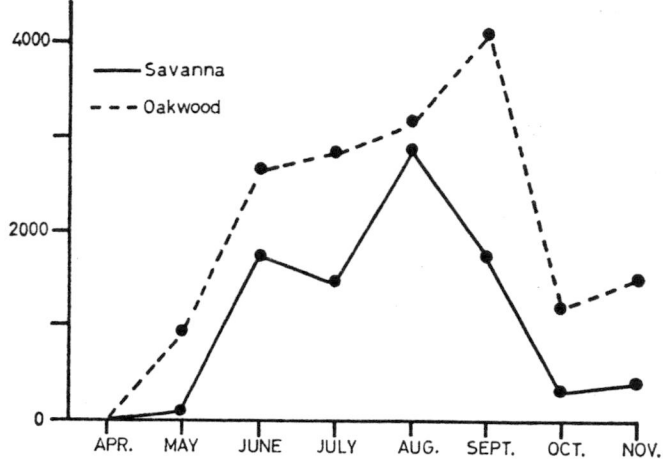

FIG. 3. Monthly oven dried weights in kg ha^{-1} of new shoots of trees in 1959.

three ecosystems, the bulk of the new organic matter above ground was produced within the four months from May to August.

A large proportion of the organic matter produced annually in stable semi-natural ecosystems disappears during the following twelve months,

TABLE 2

Annual net primary production Kg per Ha

	Prairie	Savanna	Oakwood
Herbaceous layer	920	1,886	182
Shrub layer	10	41	389
Tree layer			
Current year shoots	0	2,833	4,046
Older stems (branches and trunks)	0	503[1]	3,575[1]
Total	930	5,263	8,192

[1] Probably underestimated since these are mean, not current values.

5

mainly as a result of biological attack, so that there is little long term change in the biomass of plant material. In all three ecosystems studied at Cedar Creek, it seemed unlikely that the biomasses of the herbaceous layers and of the dead plant material were changing greatly from year to year so that the values given for the annual production of organic matter by the herbaceous layers can be assumed to give a reasonable estimate of the annual decomposition. Similarly, although some shrub and tree leaves might be blown from the ecosystems and the fruit removed by animals, on balance the annual production of leaves and fruit must be about equivalent to the amount decomposed yearly within each ecosystem. The greatest change in plant biomass from year to year was probably caused by thickening of the main stems and branches of the shrubs and trees but all of the plant material so formed would not be retained within the ecosystem indefinitely. Branches are frequently shed and over a period of time some shrubs and trees die. The breakdown of this woody material must contribute greatly to the turnover of plant material in the savanna and oakwood. However, if the decomposition of woody material and subterranean organs are not taken into account, the average annual turnover of organic matter represented by the herbaceous layer and the flowers, fruit and leaves of the shrubs and trees amounted in the prairie, savanna and oakwood to 0·9, 4·6 and 3·9 $Kg \times 10^3$ Ha^{-1} respectively. A greater and more rapid annual breakdown of plant material was clearly a characteristic feature of the two ecosystems having trees present. The higher value obtained for the breakdown of organic matter within the savanna compared to the oakwood resulted primarily from the presence of a relatively luxuriant herbaceous layer in the savanna. If allowance were made for the death of woody material the greater turnover of organic matter in the savanna compared to the oakwood would not be so pronounced.

Although the general patterns of organic matter production, accumulation and decomposition were similar for all three ecosystems, the magnitudes of these processes were greatly different being lowest in the prairie and greatest in the oakwood, with the savanna normally occupying an intermediate position. Under the prevailing natural conditions, the oakwood was remarkably efficient in exploiting the site conditions for the production of organic matter. This arboreal efficiency may be explained partly in such terms as relatively large amounts of chlorophyll, the vegetation depth above ground, the large number of buds in the tree crowns able to break rapidly into leaf in spring and the great root mass associated with the presence of trees. It is significant that the annual primary net productivity of the oakwood was at least equal and probably slightly greater than that of a field of maize nearby which had been cultivated intensively and had several applications of mineral fertilizer. The most efficient ecosystem for creating the greatest mass of potential food for domestic grazing animals would be the savanna since the shelter afforded by the scattered trees resulted in a greater primary production at ground level.

NUTRIENT CIRCULATION

The production of plant material by photosynthesis resulted in the uptake of plant nutrients (potassium, calcium, magnesium, phosphorus and nitrogen) from the soil, from precipitation and from the atmosphere. As organic matter accumulated or decomposed within the ecosystems the nutrient contents of the plant biomass increased or decreased.

Whilst the broad pattern of nutrient circulation resembled that of the corresponding organic system, the two were not exact replicas of one another since the percentage contents of nutrients per 100 g dry weight in the different types of plant material within each ecosystem varied greatly; for example, the tree leaves were much richer in nutrients than the tree trunks. In addition, the percentage nutrient contents of some types of plant material were not constant over the sampling period; thus as the year progressed, there was a general decrease in the percentages of potassium, phosphorus and nitrogen for all three living herbaceous layers. Differences were also found between ecosystems, the herbaceous layers of the savanna and oakwood, for instance, consistently had greater percentages of nutrients, particularly of potassium, magnesium, phosphorus and nitrogen, than the herbaceous layer of the prairie.

Large amounts of plant nutrients were contained in the plant biomass of all the three ecosystems, the weights increasing in the order prairie, savanna and oakwood for all five elements determined throughout the sampling period. In general, the nutrient content of the organic matter per hectare in the oakwood was about twenty five times that of the prairie, the ratio varying according to the nutrient concerned and the time of year. Seasonal changes in the plant biomass resulted in large differences in the nutrient capital it contained so that, during spring and early summer when organic matter production was high and the biomass was increasing rapidly, there must have been a considerable uptake of nutrients with a consequent drain on the soil reserves. Taking calcium as an example, the difference between the early spring figures and the summer maximum values of calcium in the plant biomass were for the prairie, savanna and oakwood 30, 99 and 202 Kg of calcium per hectare respectively. Much of the annual nutrient uptake was contained within foliar material and, when the leaves fall, would be returned to the soil to be released later by decomposition. On a long term basis, the nutrient capital of the plant biomass in the prairie probably did not differ greatly from year to year. In the savanna and oak-wood the amount of nutrients in the plant biomass must have increased, since woody material has accumulated over the years, but this would be only a small proportion of the annual circulation. Thus, taking calcium as an example, with an annual calcium uptake of 202 Kg Ha^{-1} in the oakwood in 1959 only about 15 Kg was retained as the result of increasing girth of tree branches and trunks.

Apart from soil weathering, the most important additions to the mineral nutrient capital would be derived from nutrients contained in the precipitation and in dust blown by the wind from the roads and surrounding agricultural fields. The three ecosystems probably differed little in the amount of nutrients supplied in the precipitation but differed greatly in their capacity to catch wind blown dust. The woodland with its dense and multistoried vegetation cover was probably very efficient in capturing and retaining wind blown dust, whereas the prairie on balance may have gained little since soil was observed blowing from small patches kept open in the prairie by rodents burrowing. No figures are available for the reduction of the nutrient capital by leaching as water drains through the sand but, at least during the summer months, this was not likely to be great since the soils of all three ecosystems became very dry.

DISCUSSION

The three types of essentially natural ecosystems studied at Cedar Creek Natural History Area differed greatly, not only in general appearance, but also in their functional dynamics. With increasing numbers of shrubs and trees present, the magnitude of the organic system and nutrient circulation increased greatly so that the presence of woody plants resulted in a greater utilization of the site by the plants and apparently an increased biological activity of the microflora and fauna. Whilst similar comparative studies will show to what extent these results are applicable on a wider geographical basis, they do appear typical of the general area around Minneapolis.

More intensive management, including seeding, regular mowing, the application of mineral fertilizers or heavier grazing of the prairie area would perhaps increase the productivity of the prairie at least on a short term basis but would also alter its natural status. Since the productivity of the natural oakwood was as great as that attained on nearby agricultural land, in which a crop of maize together with weed production was taken for comparison, it seems doubtful whether the productivity of a prairie type ecosystem in the area could be increased sufficiently by intensive management greatly to exceed that of the woodland. The savanna ecosystem was of particular interest in that the plants form a cover with attributes of both prairie and woodland types. The vegetation mass in the savanna varies irregularly and greatly in depth and must be effective in trapping solar radiation. From the point of view of the grazing animal the savanna produced the largest mass of plant material at ground level and this was also relatively rich in nutrients.

ACKNOWLEDGEMENTS

I am most grateful to the Louis W. and Maud Hill Family Foundation and the Graduate School of the University of Minnesota who provided funds for the investigation, and to the Governing Committee of the Cedar Creek Natural History area for permission to work at Cedar Creek. Professor D. B. Lawrence made many valuable suggestions and facilitated this research in numerous ways.

REFERENCES

OVINGTON J.D. & HEITKAMP D. (1963) Comparative studies of prairie, savanna, oakwood and maize field ecosystems (1) Plant biomass and productivity. *Ecology* **44,** 52–63
ROSENDAHL C.O. & BUTTERS F.K. (1928) *Trees and Shrubs of Minnesota* 385 pp. Minnesota

THE NUTRIENT-RECOVERY HYPOTHESIS FOR ARCTIC MICROTINE CYCLES

I. INTRODUCTION

FRANK A.PITELKA

Museum of Vertebrate Zoology and Department of Zoology,
University of California, Berkeley and Arctic Research Laboratory, Barrow, Alaska

Investigations of arctic microtine cycles, underway in northern Alaska more or less continuously since 1950, have centered on the brown lemming, *Lemmus trimucronatus*, in the Barrow region. By 1955, after the experience of one complete population cycle, the writer took the position that of all theories offered to explain microtine cycles, the most realistic are those attributing causal significance to periodic changes in quality and quantity of food. Since then, the guiding hypothesis for the northern Alaskan program has been that the cycle is a result of interaction between herbivore and vegetation mediated by factors of nutrient recovery and availability in the soil.

Three successive cycles witnessed since 1949 differ in several characteristics of timing. Those features considered primary to the pulse of the ecosystem will be distinguished from those considered secondary or minor. Patterns of cyclic fluctuation, even for high latitude or high altitude populations of *Microtus*, differ from those of *Lemmus*, but the cycle period is the same. The fact that this similarity extends into mid-latitudes for microtines living in dissimilar ecosystems raises the question whether the nutrient-recovery hypothesis can have general applicability. This difficulty stresses the need for further research on herbivore-vegetation interactions. For the time being at least, theories espousing controls extrinsic to ecosystems are not considered to be promising.

In 1960, the lemming population, then in peak phase, was sampled extensively for evidence of 'stress' signs. Analysis of adrenal weights, levels of circulating eosinophils, percentage of reticular erythrocytes in the circulating blood and blood sugar levels failed to support prevailing views regarding 'endocrine adaptive responses' in 'physiologic regulation of natural populations'. For the time being, theories seeking to explain population cycles in natural communities on the basis of intraspecific factors of physiology, behaviour, or genetics, without regard for spatial and temporal aspects of environmental requisites in normal habitats, are also not considered to be promising.

Observations of impact on vegetation by *Lemmus* in northern Alaska and by *Microtus* in central coastal California indicate that this impact is significant in both magnitude and variety. Complexities of the effects require detailed measurements presenting sampling problems that deter research. To provide a framework for such research, a current goal in the northern Alaskan program has been to establish whether or not there are vegetational and soil variables which correlate with phase of lemming cycle. The results of these studies, started in 1958, are presented by my colleague, A. M. Schultz, in the paper which follows.

Recent bibliography on Lemming ecology in northern Alaska

MAHER W.J. (1960) The relationship of the nesting density and breeding success of the pomarine jaeger to the population level of the brown lemming at Barrow, Alaska. *Proc. 11th Alaskan Sci. Conf.*, pp. 24–25

MAHER W.J. & PITELKA F.A. (1959) Comparison of breeding populations of the pomarine jaeger at Point Barrow, Alaska, in two successive lemming highs. *Bull. Ecol. Soc. Amer.* **40**, 78 (abstract)

MULLEN D.A. (1961) Use of physiologic indices in the study of population dynamics of brown lemming *Lemmus trimucronatus*. *Proc. 12th Alaskan Sci. Conf.*, pp. 28–30

PITELKA F.A. (1956) Sex ratio in relation to predation in lemming populations near Barrow, Alaska. *Bull. Ecol. Soc. Amer.* **73**, 78–79 (abstract)

PITELKA F.A. (1958a) Some characteristics of microtine cycles in the arctic. *18th Annual Biol. Colloq.* Oregon State College, pp. 73–88

PITELKA F.A. (1958b) Some aspects of population structure in the short-term cycle of the brown lemming in northern Alaska. *Cold Spr. Harb. Symp. Quant. Biol.* **22**, 237–251

PITELKA F.A. (1959a) Interrupted cycle of brown lemmings at Wainwright, Alaska, 1955–58. *Bull. Ecol. Soc. Amer.* **40**, 78–79 (abstract)

PITELKA F.A. (1959b) Population studies of lemmings and lemming predators in northern Alaska. *XVth Int. Congress Zool.*, Section X, No. 5, 3 pp.

PITELKA F.A., TOMICH P.Q. & TREICHEL G.W. (1955a) Ecological relations of jaegers and owls as lemming predators near Barrow, Alaska. *Ecol. Mono.* **25**, 85–117

PITELKA F.A., TOMICH P.Q. & TREICHEL G.W. (1955b) Breeding behavior of jaegers and owls near Barrow, Alaska. *Condor* **57**, 3–18

SCHULTZ A.M. (1964) The nutrient-recovery hypothesis for arctic microtine cycles. II. Ecosystemic variables in relation to arctic microtine cycles. This volume, pp. 57–68

THE NUTRIENT-RECOVERY HYPOTHESIS FOR ARCTIC MICROTINE CYCLES

II. ECOSYSTEM VARIABLES IN RELATION TO ARCTIC MICROTINE CYCLES

ARNOLD M. SCHULTZ

School of Forestry, University of California, Berkeley
and Arctic Research Laboratory, Barrow, Alaska

ABSTRACT

Correlated with the lemming cycle of northern Alaska, which is one of the best known and most readily observable features of the tundra, are fluctuations in primary production, forage quality, and decomposition rates. Also, a number of soil properties show year to year changes that appear to be linked with the microtine populations.

A four-year record of herbage yields, covering one complete lemming cycle, reflects the recovery of plant vigor that takes place from the time of overgrazing during the peak phase of the cycle to the last year of no grazing.

Chemical composition of green forage involving calcium, phosphorus, and protein, varies significantly during a lemming cycle. The change is in the direction of improving quality as the peak phase of the cycle approaches, and of a sharp reduction in quality during and following the decline phase. The variation may be explained partly by botanical composition changes resulting from selective grazing and partly by changes in the available soil nutrient pool.

In the soil system, important directional changes occur which can be attributed to two lemming activities, grazing and manuring. Grazing decreases the insulating ability of the vegetative cover; two or three years of no grazing allows the insulation to build up again. Thus, there is a 3-4 year cycle in depth of the active soil layer. Excreta produced during the 'high' years add a sudden dash of available nutrients to the substrate and perhaps modify the decomposer flora quantitatively as well as qualitatively.

The arctic tundra is supposed to be a simple ecosystem. The statement that it is simple is not only becoming trite but more and more untrue, it seems, the longer I study the tundra. In all fairness to students of complex ecosystems, however, I shall give some of the characteristics of the coastal tundra of northern Alaska to show how the idea of simplicity arose.

The vegetation near the coast of the Arctic Ocean has fewer than 100 species of vascular plants. Of these, grasses and sedges make up most of the plant cover and three species make up nearly all of the forage. The forage is grazed by one herbivore. The growing season is only two months long.

The active soil layer, seldom more than 16 inches deep, is underlain with permafrost, where no important biological or chemical activity takes place. Precipitation averages four inches per year. The topography is essentially level.

Though the variables of this ecosystem may be relatively few in number, and low in magnitude or range, they nonetheless present a real challenge to us, to identify them, measure them, and unravel their interrelationships. We are working on a frontier where we must pioneer the study of soil, vegetation, and microorganisms. Consequently any simplicity we encounter is welcome.

RATIONALE AND OBJECTIVES

Our approach in studying this ecosystem may be called the 'shotgun method' — a light spray at many conceivable targets. As the more fruitful leads emerge, they are studied intensively. The various phases of the investigation are presented schematically in Fig. 1.

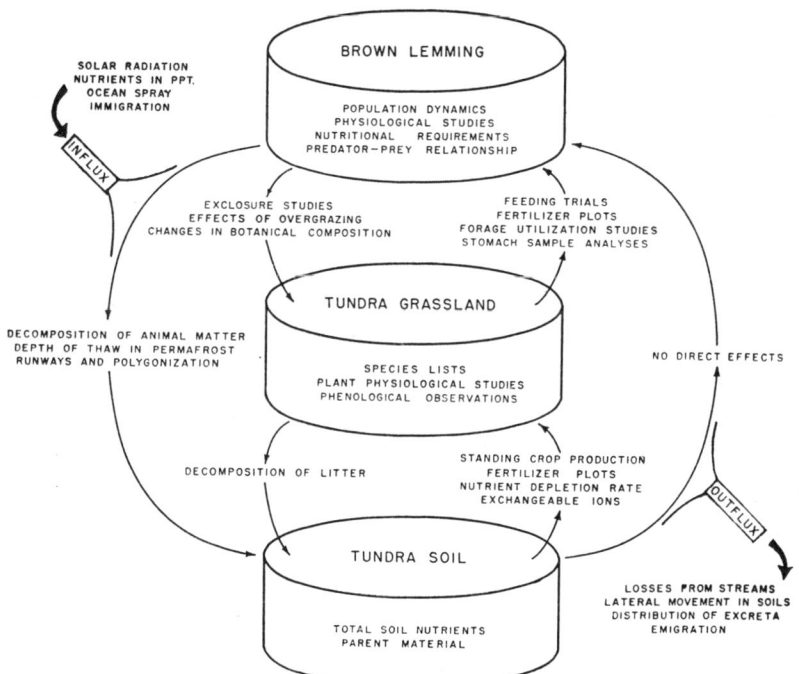

Fig. 1. Various phases of the investigation of an arctic tundra ecosystem.

We assume the tundra to be a homeostatically controlled system. First, there are independent external variables which we encounter as 'noise' within the system. They must be measured so that their effect can be removed, statistically, from the internal variables. Thus solar radiation, nutrients in snow and rainfall, and imports via ocean spray or migrating animals are being assessed. Not only gains but losses or outfluxes from the system are being considered.

Second, we must know something about the initial state of the system — the time-zero (T_0) properties. Here the concept of initial state is somewhat modified from the original (Jenny, 1961). Emphasis is placed on the three main components: the soil, the vegetation, and the animal. At a given time, how much total phosphorus, calcium, or nitrogen is in the parent material, the soil, the entire system? What are some of the basic characteristics of the plant and animal species, that is, the stable attributes we need to know in order to identify change?

Finally, we have to measure the changes that occur within the ecosystem. These include primary production and soil nutrient depletion, followed by litter decomposition and repletion of soil fertility; also grazing of vegetation by lemmings, followed by manuring and recovery of plant vigor. Essentially we have a series of feedbacks and servomechanisms, which are devices needed to maintain oscillations in any system.

This, then, is the rationale of the investigation. The ecosystem is dynamic, so variation is natural. But are the changes resulting from the biological and geochemical processes correlated? Is there a general cycle in the whole system?

The population dynamics and behavioral aspects of the lemming and its predators have been well documented by Pitelka (1964). I plan now to show evidence of cycling in the other components of the ecosystem, using the microtine cycle as a reference point. Our empirical data by no means make a complete story but they already make a long story, so that I can give only the highlights.

ECOSYSTEM SAMPLING REGIMEN

In the summer of 1958 an acre of wet meadow tundra was selected at Point Barrow for intensive study. It is a good lemming habitat and is situated adjacent to one of Pitelka's traplines. In addition, the acre was selected for its uniformity of vegetation and microrelief. This area, called the Gasline Site, has been used for an 'ecosystem sample' survey since 1958.

An ecosystem sample consists of a square-foot plot from which five types of collections are made: (1) green herbage clipped as closely as possible; (2) a litter sample consisting of dead but recognizable plant material; (3) fecal pellets when present; (4) a 6-inch diameter core of peat or organic soil, to a depth of 3 inches; and (5) a 4-inch diameter core of mineral soil beginning at the three inch level and extending to permafrost. Through the season the latter core may vary from 1 to 10 inches in length. This type of plot was designed to relate plant growth to soil fertility and to lemming activity on a specific spot without suffering the tempering influence of the statistical mean. However, in the data provided the statistical mean is given. Random clusters of such plots were taken at two week intervals between mid-June and mid-September.

Data from other sites will be presented. The Gasline plots, however, are our best basis for year to year comparison and for that site we have the longest record of lemming densities.

Another site for ecosystem samples is at Pitt Point. This is 100 miles east of Point Barrow, and also on the coast of the Arctic Ocean. The tundra on the two sites are very similar; the dominant forage plants are the same. The lemming cycle at Pitt Point has been one year out of phase with that of Barrow. This permits us to eliminate from the cycle the cosmic and broad meteorological effects, which are hardly different over such a short distance. Other study sites are at Wainwright, on the coast 100 miles southwest of Pt. Barrow, and at the Inaru River, 40 miles inland. Because of travel handicaps, the remote sites are not so frequently or intensively sampled and at this time little will be said about them.

HERBAGE PRODUCTION

The standing vegetative crop was sampled through the 1959, 1960, and 1961 growing seasons at frequent intervals. Comparative data from the Gasline Site give net production only, that is, gross production minus forage utilization and other losses. Only in 1960 was there any large difference between gross and net production. Standing crop values were highest in 1959, dropped sharply in 1960, the peak year of lemming activity, and rose slightly from 1960 to 1961.

The year 1959 was not exceptionally warm. Mean temperatures for June, July, and August were slightly below the 40 year averages. Yet production in late July and during August was very high. This represents the third year of recovery of the lemming range after the 1956 grazing period.

Summer temperatures in 1960 also were slightly lower than the long-term averages and the growing season was much like 1959. However, yields were from 100 to 200 pounds per acre lower throughout the summer of 1960 compared to corresponding dates in 1959. I will show later that this difference can be attributed to lemming activity.

The year 1961 was the first year of recovery from the peak lemming population of some 70 animals per acre. Spring yields were slightly higher than in 1960; summer yields about the same. Plots on more intensely grazed sites had lower yields in 1961 than in 1960.

Exclosures with paired plots open to grazing were used to measure the utilization by lemmings during the same time period. The open plots yielded 140, 80, and 95 per cent of the corresponding protected plots in 1959, 1960, and 1961, respectively.

Thompson (1955) had earlier measured forage production on nearby plots. His records start from 1950, the year after a peak phase of the cycle in 1949, and continue through 1954, the year after the peak phase of 1953. For the five years gross production was about 730, 870, 820, 820, and 760 pounds while net production was 730, 870, 570, 430, and 660 pounds per acre.

It is difficult for an untrained observer to tell how much forage is produced on the tundra from year to year. Grass is always present and a difference of 200 to 400 pounds per acre is not discernible without a control plot. For this reason the forage production cycle, although it should be expected, is not as well known in fact or legend as the lemming population cycle.

GRAZING AND RECOVERY

A special series of plots were used to study the effects of intensive grazing and recovery. On half of these the grass had been cut by lemmings in spring and early summer; on the other half the sod had been thoroughly uprooted. Clippings made in mid-August, the time of maximum standing crop, showed yields of 480 pounds per acre on the cut and 100 pounds on the uprooted areas. After one year no recovery had been made on either area. On the uprooted plots there was a 20 to 40 per cent decline in yield between 1960 and 1961. Recovery can be effected in much shorter time when nutrient availability is increased.

Observations by Thompson (1955) and Pitelka (1957) in 1953 and 1956 indicate that during the peak phases of a cycle, grass cutting is very general and rarely does a plant escape this form of grazing. In 1960 we observed this phenomenon on lemming habitats over the entire Point Barrow area; in addition, about 30 to 50 per cent of the area on these habitats were severely uprooted. Thus one half to two thirds of the tundra experienced a 50 per cent decrease in vigor and yield while one-third to half underwent close to a 90 per cent drop. The latter may not recover in time for the next lemming peak.

FORAGE QUANTITY AND REQUIREMENTS

At this point it might be well to speculate on the question whether the lemmings ever eat up their food supply. We have some evidence of daily intake requirements from a pilot feeding trial made at Point Barrow in 1961. The animals we had to work with weighed about 38 grams. They were fed rations of fresh *Dupontia fischeri* and *Eriophorum angustifolium*, two species most prevalent in the lemming's natural diet. Over the trial period the average daily intake of dry matter was 12 grams. One hyperactive individual weighing 30 grams took in 20 grams of dry matter daily! We do not know how much grass a large, 120 gram lemming would ingest. Nor do we know the intake difference between active animals in the field and captives in a laboratory. Grass intake increased 50 per cent one day when the electric current in the animal house failed. Thus we can assume our value of 12 grams to be minimal in a high population year.

The lemming density at Point Barrow in June, 1960 was estimated at 70 per acre. In many local places it was much higher. The density declined in early July and again was high in late July and August after new litters were born. Seventy lemmings each eating, conservatively, 12 grams per day require roughly two pounds of forage per acre per day. However this rate of herbage production is not reached until the end of June. It should be remembered that lemming densities already are high under the snow, at a time when little if any vegetative growth takes place.

A range manager would say that the lemmings consistently (that is, every 3 or 4 years) violate the principle of range readiness. By early August an acre of tundra would support about 800 animals on the basis of our assumptions. Our calculations are in good agreement with the measured utilization of 100–200 lb on the clipped plots and exclosures.

Now the question is – and we cannot yet answer it – how much food is taken from the perennating stem bases above the frost line and from roots and rhizomes in the thawing ground?

FORAGE QUALITY

Of the many chemical elements cycling within the ecosystems, phosphorus, calcium, and nitrogen will be singled out because they are abundant and are essential in the nutrition of plants, animals, and decomposer organisms. We shall assume that high quality forage is high in protein and the essential minerals.

All forage samples clipped for productivity studies have been analyzed for P, Ca, and N. We first concentrated our efforts on phosphorus and therefore I have more to say about this element than about the others. The phosphorus content, expressed as per cent of dry weight, of the 1959 Point Barrow samples were significantly higher than of those collected in 1958. An independent 1957 estimate was made; the phosphorus percentage was lower than in 1958. Forage samples from Pitt Point, one year out of phase with Point Barrow's lemming cycle, showed a similar trend of increasing phosphorus content as the population peak approached.

The phosphorus content of young plant tissues is always high and it decreases with maturity. This is not unique to arctic grasses. However, the rate of decrease – the slope of the curve – may vary. For this reason, individual points on a graph representing but one sampling date in a season, as we have seen for Pitt Point and for 1957 and 1958 Pt. Barrow samples, are not very reliable. Data for 1959–1961 for phosphorus in forage were therefore compared at corresponding dates. Early in 1960, the peak lemming year, the phosphorus values were high but they fell off rapidly. The 1961 values were generally lower than those of 1959.

Phosphorus values from forage in exclosures were more nearly the same year to year and the minor fluctuations were random.

Since phosphorus is quite stable in the ecosystem and not likely to be added from outside sources, as is nitrogen, for example, we must look for an 'internal' explanation to this apparent cycle. First, let us see if similar patterns are evident in calcium and nitrogen.

The normal trend in plant shoots is for calcium concentrations to increase with maturity, which is opposite to the behavior of phosphorus. In spite of this essential difference, the two elements showed the same year to year relationships. Nitrogen in the plant shoot decreased in concentration with maturity as did phosphorus but again, the year to year trend was the same as for the other elements. In contrast, magnesium showed neither clear cut seasonal trends nor the cyclic pattern.

ROLE OF PHOSPHORUS IN THE LEMMING CYCLE

The importance of phosphorus and calcium, separately and together, is well known to animal nutritionists. But the significance of these minerals to reproduction and growth in wild populations has not yet been demonstrated. Until we know more about the specific requirements of *Lemmus*, we will have to rely on experimental work with other mammals. For example, the phosphorus requirement for reproduction in the white rat is 0·45 per cent of its diet (McCoy, 1942). There may not be as much similarity between the microtine rodents and the laboratory rat as between microtines and other grazing mammals such as sheep or cattle. This would be fortunate because we have much reliable information on domestic livestock. The lower limits of feeding standards for sheep have been given as 0·17 per cent P for gestation and 0·24 per cent for lactation (Cook, 1956). Mineral requirements for cattle are generally considered higher than for sheep (Stoddart and Smith, 1955).

In addition to the role phosphorus plays in the processes associated with reproduction, it is also vital in bone building and growth processes in the young animal. Recent experiments have shown that the phosphorus requirement of young pigs 2 to 7 weeks of age was 0·44 per cent of the ration ; a diet with less than that resulted in bone abnormalities and low weight gains (Combs et al., 1962).

These minimum limits in phosphorus requirements lead to one possible explanation for the slow build-up of the lemming population. If the observed 'phosphorus cycle' in the forage is real, the P level must reach a certain threshold before reproduction in the population can begin. This threshold may be at or above the minimum requirement ascertained experimentally for the species.

The same type of evidence is available for calcium and the same arguments apply. It would seem that a similar case could be made for protein.

It is difficult to fit a nutritional hypothesis to the other 'end' of the cycle, the population decline. All three elements reach their highest concentration during the peak phase and while the decline in P and N is steeper than in other years, they do not become limiting until after the 'crash' has occurred. From a nutritional standpoint, the only undesirable condition obtaining during the actual population decline is a widening of the Ca : P ratio.

A recent essay on lemmings in a popular book (Sanderson, 1961) states that the cycle is directly dependent on vitamins A and E which fluctuate for mysterious reasons. We cannot afford to dismiss the suggestion entirely. I am thinking about the period in spring when the densest lemming population is forced to subsist on rhizomes, roots, dry grass and stem tissues with little if any carotene. This is the period when 'stressed' behavior occurred in 1960. After green grass appeared in early July, the population recovered and a summer generation was produced which lived into the winter (Pitelka, 1964).

A simply conceived experiment is now in progress. It is nothing more than a six acre fertilizer plot where N, P, K, Ca, and S are supplied in extravagant amounts every year. This will 'break' the nutrient cycle in the forage and, theoretically, it should stabilize the lemming population, providing that the experimental area is large enough.

'EXPLANATIONS' FOR CYCLES IN FORAGE QUALITY

Hypotheses for explaining the cyclic fluctuations in phosphorus and calcium content of the forage are not as neat as those proposed for the animal cycle. This may be attributed to a dearth of information about chemical processes in arctic soils and to our difficulty in making the proper measurements. Concepts concerning mid-latitude soils may not apply at all. In spite of this low degree of confidence, two good hypotheses are suggested and we have experiments in progress which are designed to test them. One is concerned with depth of the active soil layer, the other with animal excreta and their decomposition. Each will be taken up in a separate section of this paper.

DEPTH OF ACTIVE SOIL LAYER

Every spring after melt-off, the soil gradually begins to thaw, reaching a maximum depth in late August. The permafrost 'line' is a zone ranging several inches in thickness from one year to the next. The part of the profile above permafrost is called the active layer. On wet meadow tundra, its thickness ranges between 12 and 16 inches. Three principal environmental factors determine the depth of thaw, two external to the ecosystem, the other internal. The first is total solar radiation in summer; when radiation is high, the active layer reaches its maximum depth. The second extrinsic factor is moisture. Rainfall in summer speeds up the thawing process and depresses the frost line. The third factor, a dependent one, operates within the system.

That lemmings have a significant effect on the freezing and thawing process of the tundra might not be readily admitted by the geophysicists or even the cryopedologists. At least, to my knowledge, no serious proposals along these lines have been suggested. In our soil core sampling we had noticed that in exclosures the active layer was always shallow compared to that of the outside paired plots. A check of the sample data back to 1958 was made which formed the basis for the following interesting hypothesis: due to their foraging, nesting, and run-way building activities in a high population year, lemmings remove or so change the distribution pattern of vegetation and litter that there is a minimum of insulating material on the ground. The next year, when lemmings are largely absent, the plants begin to recover their vigor and litter begins to build up. This build-up of insulating material continues until the next peak lemming year.

6

It is apparent, from our data that the thawed zone became shallower in successive years 1958 and 1959, following the 1956 lemming high. Then in 1960 this accumulated insulation was removed, only to start building up again in 1961. To eliminate the possibility that weather alone may have coincidentally produced the sequence of results that fits our hypothesis perfectly, depth of thaw was measured in a set of exclosures where in over 10 years litter-fall and decomposition is now close to equilibrium. Here it is seen that the year 1960 was actually a poor year for rapid thawing.

To test the hypothesis further, we have now established long transects across several tundra types to be sampled regularly every summer.

As the active layer fluctuates in depth, so does the pool of nutrients available to plants. Let us look at values for total phosphorus, calcium, and magnesium (Table 1). Phosphorus and calcium are more concentrated in the upper layers. Because of the volume-weight gradient from the light peat layer to the heavy mineral soil near permafrost, the potentially available source of these nutrients may increase downward. Pot tests to measure available rather than total nutrient elements will be set up this summer.

Is it possible that when absorption by plant roots is confined to the top, nutrient-rich layers of soil, uptake of these minerals per unit weight of plant would be greater than when the roots occupy a larger, more dilute zone? This seems to be suggested by the fact that magnesium, which is

TABLE 1

Concentration of three minerals in the top
six inches of wet meadow tundra soil

Soil depth (in.)	% P	% Ca	% Mg	Vol. wt. (T/acre in.)
0–1	0·206	0·502	0·514	5·4
1–2	0·153	0·513	0·396	7·6
2–3	0·101	0·400	0·549	16·6
3–4	0·064	0·067	0·943	33·5
4–5	0·047	0·057	0·855	61·3
5–6	0·048	0·050	0·930	98·2

uniformly distributed throughout the profile, did not show the cyclic effect as did P and Ca.

We have a greenhouse at the Arctic Research Laboratory; with this facility we hope next summer to find an answer to the question posed above.

DECOMPOSITION OF ORGANIC MATTER

Only a small part of the total nutrients are in the organic part of the eco-system. But the readily available nutrients, which we have not yet measured, are more important. To what extent are they tied up by the more stable components of the ecosystem and at what rate are they mineralized and re-used?

The ecosystem samples mentioned earlier provided data for current production (green grass) and litter (dead grass, etc.) on the same plots. Calculating decomposition constants

$$k = \frac{\text{green grass}}{\text{green} + \text{dead}}$$

for different years and different seasons is a rough approach to the problem. From a limited number of k values we have concluded that the greater the production, the faster the rate of decomposition. Thus, as the grasses recover from grazing, production accelerates, mulch accumulates, and the rate of decomposition accelerates also.

On the basis of this hypothesis, let us reconstruct what happens to organic matter over one complete cycle. Starting the year after the peak phase, production is low, not much litter has built up, and the decomposition of plant material is slow. As decomposition speeds up, more minerals are made available, naturally in the top-most layers of the soil profile. Theoretically the maximum should be reached the year before the next peak lemming year. Oxidation takes a different route the following year. Here the current production goes through the animal, lemming and predator, and about 80 per cent is returned rapidly to the tundra as urine and faeces. Urine especially is easily broken down and its products readily taken up by plants. This explains the high initial values for P and N in the forage produced early in 1960.

As a result of the sudden splash of animal excreta, there may be a drastic change in microfloral populations. During late summer of the peak year and the season after, when the preponderance of organic matter is again of plant origin, another shift must be made in the microbial population. This could well influence the year to year variability in soil fertility and a corresponding variability in forage quality.

We are testing most of these ideas with experiments. For example, we are comparing decomposition of such materials as peat, green grass, litter, faeces, and dead lemmings against a pure cellulose standard. We are attacking the problem from several angles with bacteriological techniques, resin exchange columns and radioactive isotopes. Some day we shall be able to present more than theory about this important ecosystem function.

CONCLUSION: THE INTEGRATED ECOSYSTEM

In an investigation of this kind there is always the question of how much evidence must be on hand and how much testing need be done before a theory can rest. The stress theorist may think we have taken in too much territory and the cosmologist thinks not enough. I have presented only such hypotheses as can be tested experimentally. Should most of these be proven by experiment, broad problems at different levels will be solved. First, the pragmatic question, why do lemmings cycle? and the broader one, why do microtines cycle? On a more theoretical level, is there demonstrable homeostasis in the ecosystem? And in between are many isolated questions concerning the integration of the various parts of the system.

If it should turn out that lemmings can get along with no phosphorus at all . . . then we have a new problem to study.

REFERENCES

COMBS G.E., VANDEPOPULIERE J.M., WALLACE H.D. & KOGER M. (1962) Phosphorus requirement of young pigs. Jour. Animal Science **21**, 3–8

COOK C.W. (1956) Range livestock nutrition and its importance in the Intermountain Region. Utah State Agr. Coll. Monog. Series **5**, 1–28

JENNY H. (1961) Derivation of state factor equations of soils and ecosystems. Proc. Soil Sci. Soc. of Amer. **25** (5), 385–388

McCOY RICHARD H. (1942) Dietary requirement of the rat. In The Rat in Laboratory Investigation. Ed. by Griffith and Farris. Lippincott and Co., Philadelphia, 488 pp.

PITELKA F.A. (1957) Some characteristics of microtine cycles in the arctic. Eighteenth Annual Biology Colloquium: Arctic Biology. Corvallis, Oregon, pp. 73–88

PITELKA F.A. (1964) The nutrient-recovery hypothesis for arctic microtine cycles. I. Introduction. Pp. 55–56, this volume.

SANDERSON I.T. (1961) The continent we live on. Random House, New York, 299 pp.

STODDART L.A. & SMITH A.D. (1955) Range management. 2nd Ed. McGraw-Hill Book Co., Inc. New York, 433 pp.

THOMPSON D.Q. (1955) The role of food and cover in population fluctuations of the brown lemming at Point Barrow, Alaska. Trans. 20th North American Wildlife Conf., Montreal, Quebec, pp. 166–174

GRAZING AND RANGE MANAGEMENT

A HISTORY OF BIOTIC AND CLIMATIC CHANGES WITHIN THE NORTH AMERICAN GRASSLAND[1]

RALPH L. DIX

Department of Plant Ecology, University of Saskatchewan, Saskatoon, Canada

ABSTRACT

The many causes or influents which were and are responsible for the origin and maintenance of the North American Grassland are discussed according to the following categories: physiographic, climatic, biotic, and historical. Emphasis is placed on the Great Plains and Central Lowlands regions of this vegetation type and the time scale is that of the geologist and archeologist.

Physiographic and climatic changes in the North American Grassland through Tertiary, Pleistocene and Recent time are briefly outlined, and the origins and time sequences of the development of the major vegetational units are treated. The original grassland is believed to have formed *in situ* in the Central Great Plains area from Arcto-Tertiary and Neotropical-Tertiary stock in late Oligocene or Miocene. Changes in physiography, and more particularly in climate, encouraged the rapid evolution of plant species in this area and many modifications in this grassland occurred through late Tertiary, Pleistocene and Recent time, particularly in the woodland-grassland tension zones. The origins of the Mid-western prairie, coastal prairie, desert plains grassland and Northern Plains grassland are traced.

A brief review of the historical period in the North American Grasslands, up to the present century, is presented.

A universal characteristic of grassland vegetation is changeability. This characteristic may be attributed in part to factors inherent in the nature of grassland vegetation, such as its susceptibility to frequent burning, or to conditions imposed on the vegetation by forces external to it, such as climatic fluctuation or change. An expression of the former in North America is illustrated by the encroachment in historical time of forest into the grassland of Mid-western United States with the cessation of fire (McComb and Loomis, 1944; Curtis, 1956). The hypothesis (Sauer, 1950) which holds the origin and maintenance of all, or most, of the world's grasslands to be primarily due to fire appears untenable, however, since the sensitivity of at least some grasslands to climatic change is well documented (Albertson and Weaver, 1942; 1945). Grasslands compete with forests in

[1] Contribution No. 331 from the Department of Plant Ecology, University of Saskatchewan.

71

mesic, and with deserts in xeric, regions and the existence of chaparral, savannah, parkland and other woody vegetation having a grassland matrix attests to an incomplete victory for either grassland or woody species. Further, there seems no *a priori* physiological reason why groups of plants should not exist whose ecological optima occur within an area intermittently too dry to support forest growth but with sufficient available moisture to sustain plants other than desert xerophytes. In the present paper it will be assumed that some grasslands exist due almost entirely to fire, that other grasslands exist due almost entirely to external causes and that in many, or most, cases both fire and external factors are operative at the same or different times, and to differing degrees, within the same grassland.

The many causes or influents which may be responsible for the origin and maintenance of grassland any be somewhat subjectively grouped into the following categories, all of which interact with each other and operate through time: physiographic, climatic, biotic and historical. This paper will discuss the principal factors which have contributed to the origin and maintenance of the North American Grassland and will attempt to place these factors in historical perspective. Emphasis throughout the paper will be placed on the grassland occurring on the Great Plains and the western portions of the Central Lowland Provinces (Fenneman, 1931), since such an emphasis will permit the drawing of a clearer, though simplified, image of the major changes which have occurred in the North American Grassland through time. Further, since several excellent reviews dealing with changes during the past half-century have recently appeared, the time scale of the geologist and archaeologist will be emphasized.

PHYSIOGRAPHIC INFLUENTS

The North American continent has been compared to a bowl turned rightside up, a rim around the outside and a great valley, cut off from free atmospheric circulation, in the interior (Gilpin, 1860). The Appalachian Mountains, the eastern rim of the bowl, are ancient (Permian), much eroded and forested mountains and are not directly concerned in the present discussion. The great valley at the centre of the bowl is drained by the Mississippi River system which has carried, deposited, sorted and resorted the debris from both the Rocky Mountain and Appalachian systems throughout this valley. The western rim of the bowl, the Rocky Mountains, is of particular concern to the present discussion since it has contributed the major physiographic features to our area and plays an important part in atmospheric circulations across it.

Crustal upwarpings in the present Rocky Mountain region, a local expression of a trans-world period of mountain building, brought the Mesozoic Era to a close. Even as they were being constructed, these mountains were eroded rapidly and debris was transported, deposited and reworked by east-flowing streams which built coalescent sheets of alluvial detritus so as to form gently east-sloping aggradational plains of vast extent across the area now supporting the North American Grassland. By Oligocene times, these mountains were peneplained, but the Miocene witnessed a renewal of the Rocky Mountain uplift and the initiation of a second and still current erosional cycle which has continued the formation of the Great Plains and those parts of the Central Lowlands which lie west of the Mississippi River. Thus, by the close of Miocene, the major physiographic features of the area now occupied by the North American Grassland were essentially established.

The surface of this vast plain has been reworked in Pleistocene and Recent times by glaciation, wind and water. The northern portions were subjected to four major glacial advances and retreats, the most extensive of which overran virtually all of the area north and east of the present Missouri River. As the successive ice sheets retreated, veneers of glacial drift were deposited over the surface, previous drainage patterns were modified and shallow lakes were left stranded. Great volumes of melt water flooded southward carrying heavy loads of glacial debris which were deposited in extensive beds along the major spillways. At a later date, particularly during the dry Hypsithermal period, these deposits lost much of their vegetative cover, were reworked by wind action and served as source regions for the great eolian deposits found throughout the Great Plains and Central Lowlands. Loess deposits having this origin commonly reached thicknesses of 60 to 125 feet along the Mississippi and Missouri River drainage channels. Similar loessal deposits in the plains of eastern Colorado, western Kansas and Nebraska were probably derived from silt brought eastward by streams, such as the Platte River, which carried melt water from Pleistocene glaciers in the Rocky Mountains.

CLIMATIC INFLUENTS

In contrast to physiography, climate is by far the most fickle element in the make up of the area. This is true despite the paradox that basic planetary air flow has been relatively constant through at least the latter portion of geologic time and that the major source regions for the mass flow of surface air have wandered but little. Nevertheless, climatic change during historic time is recorded; in fact it is the personal experience of millions of people now living. But historic time is less than a moment in geologic time and, since climate is not subject to fossilization, all evidence upon which estimates of past climates are based must come from inferences drawn from the geologic record.

The physiological factor most often limiting to plant growth in nature is moisture, and the frequency and duration of water stress in plants is determined by various combinations of temperature and precipitation; thus, a decrease in temperature without any change in precipitation tends to increase the supply of growth water. This relationship is useful, though not universally applied, in simplifying the postulation of ancient climates from the fossil record. It permits explanations based on temperature changes alone, for which evidence is more abundant and reliable. To take but one example from the Northern Plains, Moir (1958) radiocarbon dated *Picea glauca* wood excavated in an area now supporting steppe and removed by 200 miles from present *Picea* forests. His samples indicated an age of 11,480 years ± 300 B.P. and a climate cooler and moister than present was postulated for that time. However, precipitation records from near the excavation site (Kidder County, North Dakota) show that the present annual precipitation is 16 inches, which compares with an annual precipitation of 15·4 inches for The Pas, Manitoba, a station more than 200 miles within the present *Picea* forest. Thus, the present precipitation of Kidder County is probably sufficient to support *Picea* and its presence 11,000 years ago necessitates only the assumption that temperatures were lower at that time; the difficult task of accounting for precipitation change is made unnecessary. Of course, when independent evidence is present, such as for the creation of a new rain shadow by mountain building, the assumption of a change in precipitation regime is demanded.

Willett (1950) has presented evidence from weather records which show that at least the present temperature rise is not uniform over the earth. Rather, the rise appears to be pronounced towards the poles and at high altitudes while the tropics have experienced no appreciable change. There is no obvious reason why such differential warming should not have characterized earlier climatic change. It would appear reasonable to assume, therefore, that distributional adjustments of vegetation at high latitudes in response to temperature change are not necessarily paralleled by sympathetic adjustments in remote subtropical regions. In the North American Grassland, for example, an invasion of forest into the grasslands of Canada would not necessarily be paralleled by an invasion of mixed prairie into desert grasslands.

Precipitation values are more difficult to derive from the geologic record than are temperature values because temperature is less susceptible to local influences. Nevertheless, some generalities are required for our purposes. Flint (1957), in a review of Pleistocene precipitation, suggests that secular cooling can be expected to reduce precipitation because of reduced evaporation from the ocean surface. He concludes that 'precipitation in and near the chief glacier-covered regions was less during major glacial maxima than it is in the same regions today'. If this conclusion be accepted, an inverse and proportional correlation can be assumed between secular precipitation and temperature. Thus, for a given location, a warmer geological period suggests an increase, while a cooler geological period suggests a decrease in precipitation.

The following historical discussion will be restricted to the Cenozoic Era, since this is the period in which most of the modern occupants of the North American Grassland came into prominence and for which evidence is most abundant. Emphasis will be increased with the approach of present time, since this is the period of greatest interest to the subject of this symposium.

At the end of the Cretaceous, the high temperatures which had prevailed throughout the Mesozoic began to decline. This reduction was not of great magnitude, however, and by mid Paleocene the trend had reversed. Through late Eocene and continuing into early Oligocene, a time of rapid evolution of modern plant and animal forms, the earth enjoyed the warmest period in its history (Brooks, 1951). Since the early Rocky Mountains had been peneplained by this time, moist Pacific air flowed freely over the Great Plains and central lowland regions creating a climate which was not only warm but humid. The renewal of the Rocky Mountain uplift, which began in late Oligocene and persists to the present, isolated this area from the moist Pacific air and it was at this time that the climate began to take on its present arid to sub-humid character (MacGinitie, 1953). The late Oligocene, Miocene and Pliocene periods were characterized by a relatively steady decrease in temperature. Even the Pliocene, however, appears to have had temperatures somewhat higher than present and about the same precipitation pattern (Dorf, 1960).

From the high temperatures of Eocene and early Oligocene, a rapid and persistent decline was initiated which plunged the earth into a period of severe cold from which it has not yet fully recovered. During Pleistocene, the northern portions of Europe and North America were subjected to four massive glaciations, each glaciation being interrupted by a correspondingly long period of warming and ice retreat. These inter-glacial periods were, on the average, warmer than the present climate, which Dorf

(1960) believes to be perhaps two-thirds of the way out of the last glacial stage. The last ice sheet retreated from the northern fringe of the area now occupied by the North American Grassland approximately 10,000 years ago (Kupsch, 1960). This ice retreat was followed by a warming trend which lasted from about 8000 B.C., to the beginning of the Christian era — the Hypsithermal of Deevey and Flint (1957). A period of moderate cooling followed which reached a minimum about the first century A.D., at which time temperatures again began to increase, and the period from 1000 to 1300 A.D. appears to have been the warmest in historical time. It was at this time that Norsemen farmed in Greenland and grapes were grown in southern England (Ahlmann, 1949). The climate began to change toward relatively cooler conditions beginning about 1600 A.D. and this cool period lasted until 1850; since that time the general climatic trend has been toward warmer conditions. Since there is no evidence to the contrary, temperatures in the North American Grassland are assumed to have followed these world trends through geologic time.

In his classic paper on the present climate of the North American Grassland, Borchert (1950) described the area as being primarily under the influence of three air masses: a cold and dry mass descending into the area from north-western Canada; a warm moist mass flowing north from the Gulf of Mexico; and a Pacific mass which, after being forced to rise over the Rocky Mountains, reaches their eastern slopes as a dry cool front. The quantity and distribution of the precipitation received by the Grassland is determined, for the most part, by the frequency and geographic location of the collisions of these air masses. Borchert found the periods of low precipitation in the Grassland to be well correlated with the force of the westerlies. 'The stronger the westerlies over the United States, the more extensive the drought area east of the Rockies. This has been shown for short periods and for long periods; it is a phenomenon observable in the climatic records for periods of a few days or for many years; and it has been shown in a variety of studies of weather and climate'.

Thus, a characteristic climatic feature of the North American Grassland appears to be periodic drought. Thornthwaite (1941) reports that drought periods of 35 or more consecutive days may be expected annually and periods of between 60 and 70 days once in ten years. Prolonged drought periods of 90 days in the Northern Great Plains and 120 days in the Southern Great Plains are less frequent. Malin (1956) has reviewed the early historical reports of drought in the North American Grassland while Weakly (1943) has shown, by the analysis of tree rings from western Nebraska, that over a period of 400 years, 154 were 'drought' years and

237 'wet' years. Drought years were markedly aggregated and 13 drought periods of five or more years occurred during this time. Their average duration was 12·8 years while wet periods had an average span of 20·6 years. Drought periods are more frequent and more severe in the south and western portions of the Grassland and less frequent and less severe towards the north and east (Borchert, 1950).

BIOTIC INFLUENTS

By the beginning of the Cenozoic Era, most of the North American continent was free of marine seas and the Great Plains and central lowland regions were emerging as low aggregating plains formed by debris brought east from the Rocky Mountains. With the retreat of Cretaceous seas, the newly emerging land was subject to invasion by two floral elements (Fig. 1) which had differentiated in late Cretaceous time from a generalized, mostly angiosperm, flora of tropical origin (Axelrod, 1952). This was a warm period in the earth's history and a temperate, mesophytic forest occupied most of the eastern United States, Canada, Asia and northern Europe. This flora, the Arcto-Tertiary flora, contained such familiar genera as *Acer*, *Fagus*, *Picea*, and *Tilia*, and persisted more or less unchanged until the close of Eocene time. The cooling temperatures of the Oligo-Miocene period caused the members of this forest to be redistributed on the basis of temperature tolerances and the forest divided into a sub arctic unit, dominated mostly by coniferous evergreens, and a temperate unit, dominated mostly by broad leaved deciduous trees and shrubs. Continued differentiation and development of these forest types eventually gave rise to the present forest patterns (Fig. 1) of temperate and sub-arctic North America (Braun, 1947; 1950; Mason, 1947; and Chaney, 1947). In western United States, Mexico and Central America, the luxuriant Neotropical-Tertiary flora, containing such plants as *Ficus* and *Percea*, occupied an area as far north as latitude 55° in western North America. Lower Oligo-Miocene temperatures and the rain shadow created by the rising Rocky Mountains forced this flora to retreat southward where it survives almost undifferentiated in parts of Central America, northern South America and Mexico (Chaney, 1947).

The increasing aridity of the Great Plains, Central Lowlands, and Rocky Mountain Lowlands during late Oligocene and Miocene forced the Arcto- and Neotropical-Tertiary floras to retire to the north and south, respectively, and only their more drought tolerant members, which were presumably the grasses and other herbaceous plants, were able to survive and remain behind. The retreat of the canopy and shrub species decreased competition which permitted an increase in the survival of new genetic forms of the drought tolerant members of the parent floras. In this way, a great central grassland was formed *in situ*. Presumably, the retreating forests left in their wake transitional regions varying from closed forest to open grassland. It is interesting that Bews (1929) suggested such forest margins as the habitat of many early grasses.

Evidence for this early grassland is mostly indirect. Elias (1942) confirmed the identification of two early fossil grasses (*Clementsiela* and *Muhlenbergia*) from late Tertiary beds in the Colorado High Plains but the most convincing evidence is from studies of the dentation and skeletal structure of fossil horses and other herbivores (Kowalewsky, 1873–1874; and Osborn, 1910). These studies show a gradual development from teeth originally generalized to those highly specialized for the grinding of hard vegetation. Correlated with dental modifications are the elongation of a jaw and neck suitable for grazing purposes and the development of anatomical characteristics which adapted the mammals for escape and rapid travel in open country. This fossil series suggests that, while the open grassland apparently began to appear in Eocene, the development of modern grassland types must have taken place in late Miocene or Pliocene (Osborn, 1910). The species composition of these grasslands is unknown, although Elias (1942) has identified *Stipa, Panicum, Setaria* and several other modern genera from Miocene deposits in Nebraska. Similarly, evidence of fire has not appeared in the fossil records of the grassland and its role is therefore unknown. The tension zones between the grassland and neighboring woody vegetation probably varied greatly in physiognomy and species composition. A few of these tension zones may have been relatively narrow and well defined but most were probably broad and indistinct or locally imperceptible.

Concomitant with, but independent of, the development of this grassland, a new xeric flora developed to the south which was probably effective in isolating the grassland from further invasion from that direction. On the Mexican Plateau, following the retreat of the Neotropical-Tertiary flora into eastern and southern Mexico during early Oligocene, the Madro-Tertiary flora differentiated from xeric savannah (Fig. 1). The xeromorphic types of this new flora, particularly the shrubs and small trees, appear to have been ancestral to the present desert, chaparral and live oak vegetation of northern Mexico and adjacent arid lands of southwestern United States (Axelrod, 1950; 1958).

The meagre fossil record from late Tertiary grassland precludes any serious discussion of its species composition, regardless of the temptation created by Elias' fossils of living (and ecologically important) grass genera. It does permit the assumption, however, that the major vegetational units of North America had reached their present relative positions by Pliocene. A great grassland occupied the centre of the continent. This grassland was composed of members which had survived the retreat of forest. A northern unit remained from the retreat of the Arcto-Tertiary flora and a southern unit remained from the withdrawal of the Neotropical-Tertiary flora (Fig. 1). To the north, and separated by a narrow band of deciduous savannah, a conifer forest extended for some unknown distance to be replaced by Arctic tundra at high latitudes. To the west, a Rocky Mountain conifer forest, a derivative of the Arcto-Tertiary flora, probably maintained a narrow tension zone with the grassland. To the east, a narrow tension zone separated the grassland from a deciduous forest of Arcto-Tertiary origin. The southern unit of the grassland formed a broad, almost imperceptible, tension zone with the now expanded (Axelrod, 1950) Madro-Tertiary flora.

Tertiary ended when the major cooling trend, begun in Oligocene, permitted the formation and spread of continental glaciers over the lowlands of higher latitudes. The Pleistocene was a period of continuous and sharp fluctuations in northern climates, and consequently it was also a period of mass, though not necessarily long, migrations of vegetational units. Opinion differs greatly as to the magnitude of these vegetational migrations; some (Braun, 1950; Love, 1959) believe the migrations to have been short while others (Deevey, 1949; Dorf, 1960) suggest migrations over great distances. There is considerable evidence to show that the displacement of vegetation was much greater in the east than in the west, possibly due to the warm summers of the latter region (Love, 1959; Deevey, 1949). Manley (1955) suggests a steeper thermal gradient, north to south, during the glacial maximum than at present and this suggestion is consistent with the previously discussed conclusions of Willett (1950) that recent weather records show that the present warming trend is more pronounced toward the poles than toward the equator.

The entire Pleistocene period was one of continuous flux. There were four major ice advances and retreats and each inter-glacial period appears to have been warmer than the present (Dorf, 1960). The major vegetational units had reached their present relative position by the beginning of the Ice Age and they responded to the secular cooling and warming by migration and evolution. It seems unlikely, however, that all species present were equally successful in this since the inherent potential for rapid migration

and evolution varies greatly in plants (Stebbins, 1947). Thus, when a vegetational unit (or species) migrated into new territory, or returned to territory it had previously occupied, new plant associations were established
and species had often undergone significant changes in germplasm.

Since the grassland occupied the centre of the continent, it received the
greatest stimulation during the Ice Age. As temperatures waned or intensified, its frontiers withdrew or expanded; with each withdrawal or
expansion it competed across tension zones with conifer forest, deciduous
forest or desert scrub. Within the grassland itself, members of the two
principal floral elements migrated, mingled, competed and evolved, and,
undoubtedly, many members were lost even as new taxa came into
existence. Throughout the Pleistocene, the great central plain of the continent was, in effect, a giant palimpsest on which these events were recorded,
however illegibly. Whatever we know, or hope to know, of the recent
vegetational history of this grassland must come from interpretations of
the perplexing scrawl of living distributional patterns of both vegetation
and taxa, with occasional assistance from the fragmentary fossil record.

By the end of Tertiary, a sub-humid 'oak-opening' type of vegetation
had developed along the eastern frontier of the grassland in response to
minor fluctuations in critical soil moisture levels. The grassland matrix of
this assemblage was composed, in the north, of genera of Arcto-Tertiary
origin, such as *Agropyron*, *Koeleria* and *Poa*, while to the south, *Bouteloua*
Sporobolus, *Stipa* and *Hilaria*, of Neotropical origin, dominated the grassland. During interglacial time and during the warm parts of climatic
cycles, such as the recent Hypsithermal period, the deciduous forest retreated eastward, permitting the western grassland to occupy the abandoned area. Some members of the forest flora, particularly the grasses, were
able to withstand the climatic change and survived to integrate with the
grassland flora. Prominent genera of this group include *Andropogon*, *Liatris*,
Panicum and *Sorghastrum*. Gleason (1923) has pointed out that the four most
important grasses of the Illinois prairie belong to this group. With cooling
temperatures and the subsequent increase in growth water, the forest re-
occupied its former area and the grassland again moved west, taking with
it newly evolved drought tolerant forms of forest species. The present
ubiquitous distribution of *Andropogon scoparius* is but one illustration of
such differentiation and migration.

The Mid-western prairie is now composed mostly of contributions from
the deciduous forest and northern steppe (Fig. 1), but a few species originally from the southern steppe (e.g., *Bouteloua curtipendula*) have ecological
importance. The Mid-western prairie was first recognized as a vegeta-

tional unit by Pound and Clements (1898) (their 'prairie-grass formation') but Gleason (1923) appears to have been the first to decipher its origin. Gleason's original hypothesis has stood the test of further study, although his apparent assignment of the entire developmental period to the specific warm period which occurred immediately after the retreat of Wisconsin ice, now seems questionable. It is more likely that the Mid-western prairie developed through a long series of warm periods which must have occurred throughout the inter-glacial periods of the Pleistocene (Flint, 1957). The occurrence of relict tall-grass prairie in Colorado (Livingston, 1952) suggests that the Mid-western prairie migrated to the western edge of the Great Plains sometime before the recent Hypsithermal, perhaps during a period of ice advance. The recent work of Hartley (1958a and 1958b) on the origin, evolution and distribution of the tribes *Andropogoneae* and *Paniceae* lend weight to the history of the Mid-western prairie outlined above. Similarly, this work tends to discourage the view that these tropical genera migrated into the North American Grassland by way of Mexico.

The origin of the coastal prairie was similar to that of the Mid-western prairie discussed above, except that it originated from an intermingling of southern, rather than northern, steppe and deciduous forest. The genera of forest origin (e.g., *Andropogon* and *Panicum*) are much the same for the two areas, the differences being mostly at the species level. The principal genera of grassland origin are *Bouteloua*, *Hilaria* and *Stipa*, which are elements from the southern steppe. Weaver and Clements (1938) have pointed out the relationships between the coastal prairie and its western neighbor. The eastern elements in this grassland are replaced by the more xeromorphic western species under the influence of overgrazing. The coastal prairie grades imperceptibly into the Mid-western prairie in north eastern Texas.

The desert plains grassland (Clements, 1936) forms the southern periphery of the North American Grassland and is dominated by species formed *in situ* as the ancient forests retreated from the Southern Great Plains and, to a lesser extent, by scrub species of Madro-Tertiary origin (Fig. 1). The dominant grasses belong to the genera *Bouteloua*, *Hilaria* and *Aristida*, which are all of Neotropical origin. The southern steppe was least affected by the climatic fluctuations of the Pleistocene, although concomitant mountain building to the west undoubtedly influenced local precipitation patterns and the generally lower temperatures of the glacial, and higher temperatures of the inter-glacial, periods probably caused local changes in distributional patterns. The extent of the exchange of germplasm between the southern steppe and the Madro-Tertiary desert flora is

7

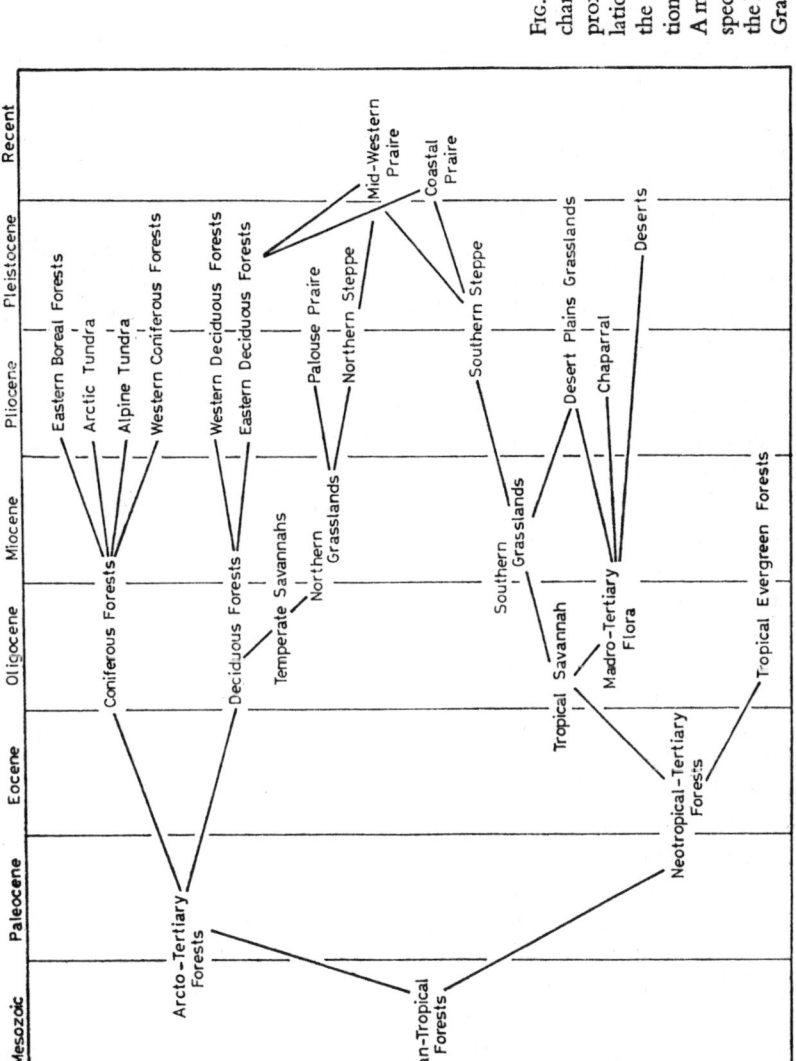

Fig. 1. A provisional chart showing approximate time relationships between the major vegetational units of North America, with special reference to the North American Grassland.

not known but the broad tension zone between them has been uninterrupted since its formation in early Miocene. The desert plains grassland is probably the oldest grassland type still present and its comparative stability probably was not disturbed until European man began to exert his influence on the area.

The grassland of the Northern Great Plains was closest to the Pleistocene glaciers but, paradoxically, was probably not as much influenced by them as was the Mid-western prairie. Love (1959) concluded from her studies in Manitoba that the ice 'reached right out on the bare grassland' and, therefore, the mingling of its species with other vegetation types was not possible. Love suggests that, as the last ice sheet retreated, the wasteland was first re-occupied by a marsh-grassland vegetation and later, as drainage improved, by an upland grassland from the west, and, still later, by deciduous and coniferous forests. At present, grassland vegetation forms a great north-facing convex semi-circle and extends 300 miles beyond the glacial border where it is replaced by Boreal Forest. The outer shell of this semi-circle is dominated by a *Festuca scabrella* grassland (Moss, 1944; Moss and Campbell, 1947; and Coupland and Brayshaw, 1953). This grassland is of an upland type and appears not at all related to the 'marsh-grassland' of Love (1959). The vegetation of the Northern Great Plains is not sufficiently known to justify any more than speculation concerning the existence or location of fescue grassland in glacial times, but its compositional similarity (Moss, 1955) to the Palouse Prairie of British Columbia (Tisdale, 1947) suggests that it may have survived in or near the ice-free corridor which is thought to have existed in the foothills of the Rocky Mountains in Alberta and Montana (Hansen, 1950). As the last ice sheet retreated, this grassland may have migrated eastward into the Great Plains, forming a relatively narrow northern fringe of the North American Grassland. *Festuca scabrella* itself extends into the Great Plains as far south and east as north-western North Dakota, but most of its associated species in the Rocky Mountain foothills are limited to Alberta and western Saskatchewan. The mixed grass vegetation (Coupland, 1960) to the centre of the fescue fringe appears to be relatively undifferentiated northern steppe and is of ancient Arcto-Tertiary derivation.

Man appears to have reached the New World about 20,000–30,000 B.P. by way of the Bering Strait. It is not known what baggage he carried, but a crossing of this Arctic region even during an inter-glacial period necessitates the conclusion that he must have been in control of fire (Wedel, 1961). This means that in the New World man witnessed the retreat of the last ice sheet and climatic and biotic changes which accompanied it. Indeed, the presence of man in possession of fire at such an early date opens the possibility that he may have influenced the development of vegetation over a very wide area and for a very long period of time. Stewart's (1956) review of primitive man's use of fire would make this seem likely.

The first evidences of man in the North American Grassland are the occurrences of spear points in association with the mammoth. This association, which is widespread throughout the Great Plains from Saskatchewan to New Mexico, indicates that man was present in some numbers and that the Great Plains vegetation at that time was more luxuriant than at present, for the mammoth could not have survived on the existing steppe. The latter offers a possible connection with the tall grass relict prairie from Colorado described by Livingston (1952). There is no evidence from archaeological sites, however, that the elephant or other large grazing animals were victims of fire drives. Wedel (1961), in considering the possibility that man may have contributed in a major way to the destruction of that group of large grassland mammals which became extinct near the end of Pleistocene, found no positive evidence to support such a view. He points out that the archaeological record of that time shows no evidence that fire was used as a tool for the control of vegetation. This is surprising, since the earliest historical records describe the use of fire for this purpose by the American Indian throughout the continent.

Archaeological evidence does suggest, however, that the aborigines were victims of climatic fluctuations. Sites dating before 7000 B.P. and containing fragmentary skeletons of the mammoth, native horse, and now extinct species of bison, are fairly common. Sites between this date and 4000 B.P., however, are rare. This gap corresponds to the Hypsithermal period discussed in a previous section and it may well be that this warm period drove primitive man from the Plains. After about 4000 B.P., traces of man became more abundant, although the evidence suggests that he depended more on food gathering that upon the hunt, which may be a reflection of a lingering semi-arid climate. In late prehistoric time, probably during the twelfth and thirteenth centuries, there appear to have been major adjustments in the distribution of populations in the Plains. The population appears to have moved into villages, commonly situated on streams, and it was here that European man made early contact with the Plains Indian. The time of this population shift coincides with the warm period from A.D. 1000 to 1300, which is well documented for Europe. This appears to have been the warmest in historical time. Wedel (1961) describes aboriginal man in the Great Plains at this time as follows: 'The picture in general, from the

Dakotas to Texas, seems to be one of innumerable small, widely scattered communities, probably not often exceeding a few score inhabitants, the women tilling their gardens in the nearby creek bottoms and the men hunting along the valley margins and on the adjacent uplands'.

CHANGES IN HISTORICAL TIME

This section deals with the changes in the North American Grassland which are documented, however sketchily, by written records. There is no suggestion that such changes are different in kind from those discussed previously, but it is certain that they differ in intensity and distribution. Recent discussions of climatic change in the North American Grassland during the past century have been presented by Borchert (1950); Weaver (1954); Weaver and Albertson (1956); and Coupland (1958), while the effects of grazing during the same period have been reviewed by Weaver (1954); Weaver and Albertson (1956); Dyksterhuis (1958); Humphrey (1958); and Ellison (1960). The discussion which follows is, therefore, restricted to a brief review of the historical period up to the turn of the century.

Historical records from early travellers are consistent in describing the universal use of fire by the North American Indian to control vegetation (Day, 1953). By the time of arrival of European man on the North American continent, the Indian had achieved remarkable success in the domestication of plants, but he had been notably unsuccessful in domesticating food animals. Thus, he depended upon the hunt, and, to improve his kill, used fire as a tool in hunting and in the 'management' of vegetation. The principal object of the chase was the bison, although deer, an animal of the forest edge, was also a staple. The burning of vegetation had the universal effect of favoring grassland over woodland. The evidence is clear that, in North America, the Indian had, by A.D. 1500, greatly expanded the area of grassland (Gleason, 1923). This was particularly true in the tension zone areas. The biotic changes which have occurred in the various tension zones since the sixteenth century have been remarkably similar in kind, although the changes have been most striking in the South-west and Mid-west, and least spectacular in Canada.

European man brought with him domesticated sources of animal protein and power and, wherever he dominated, these soon replaced the game mammals. The forage value of the grassland was recognized by European man but he failed to appreciate the role of fire in its maintenance. In fact, he looked upon grassland fire as catastrophic, since it tended to destroy forage, and did all in his power to bring about its control. More important, his culture was primarily agricultural and it was necessary to protect his fields from fire. With the cessation of fire, grassland immediately began to give way to woodland, scrub and forest and this situation was exaggerated considerably by heavy grazing, which left insufficient litter and mulch to carry a fire. This, in turn, prevented even an occasional wild fire from sweeping back the woodland invasion. The details of this story have been presented in recent reviews (Moss, 1955; Humphrey, 1958; Curtis, 1956, 1959; and Ellison, 1960) and they need not be considered here.

Existing evidence strongly indicates that the Great Plains steppe is a climatic grassland (Albertson and Weaver, 1942, 1945; and Borchert, 1950). This was the last grassland to come under the domination of European man, although he was operating along its fringes soon after his arrival on the continent. The horse became available to the Plains Indian through escape and capture soon after its arrival in Mexico about 1520 and it was easily and enthusiastically adapted into his culture pattern (Roe, 1955). This new combination created a relatively affluent, highly war-like Indian culture which dominated the Plains for over three centuries (Webb, 1931). Ecologically, the effects of this were not great. While it permitted the Plains Indian the highest development of his culture (Wedel, 1961), the period ended before he could increase his numbers to challenge the productivity of the vast bison herds or the grazing lands on which they fed. The temporary affluence of the Plains Indians at that time discouraged his acceptance of agriculture, but his picturesque culture soon withered before the advance of European man.

The reports of explorers sent into the Great Plains by the United States and Canadian governments had pronounced them a desert. Partly because of this, and partly because they were not yet needed, this area long appeared unattractive for European settlement and remained under the control of the Indian. Expansion pressures soon after 1865, however, changed this view and within 15 years from that date the bison and Indian were swept from the Plains. The first European occupants of the Plains were cattlemen, operating a giant open-range cattle industry which itself had but a short history (Webb, 1931; Osgood, 1929). They were, in turn, replaced by the grain farmer. By chance, an unusually wet period (Weakly, 1943) occurred concomitantly with the arrival of European man on the Plains, and this, coupled with the inherent optimism of the frontiersmen, led to the widespread belief that agriculture was bringing a more favorable climate. But drought returned in the late 1880's and the cattlemen and agriculturalists learned their first bitter lessons of living in this changeable, and seldom charitable, environment.

Fortunately, pioneer workers around the turn of the century in both Canada and the United States proved beyond question the value, or, more accurately, the necessity, of research on the ecology, soil science, climatology and economics of the Great Plains environment. While much has since been accomplished toward understanding the ever changing environment of the North American Grassland, we are still insufficiently aware of its basic nature to predict the limits of its potential and productivity.

REFERENCES

AHLMANN H.W. (1949) The present climatic fluctuation. *Journ. Geog.* **112**, 165–193

ALBERTSON F.W. & WEAVER J.E. (1942) History of the native vegetation of western Kansas during seven years of continuous drought. *Ecol. Monog.* **12**, 23–51

ALBERTSON F.W. & WEAVER J.E. (1945) Injury and death or recovery of trees in prairie climate. *Ecol. Monog.* **15**, 393–433

AXELROD D.E. (1950) Studies in late Tertiary paleobotany. *Carnegie Inst. Wash. Pub.* **590**, 320 pp.

AXELROD D.E. (1952) A theory of angiosperm evolution. *Evolution* **6**, 29–60

AXELROD D.E. (1958) Evolution of the Madro-Tertiary Geoflora. *Bot. Rev.* **24**, 434–509

BEWS J.W. (1929) *The world's grasses.* Longmans Green and Co. London–New York–Toronto, 408 pp.

BORCHERT J.R. (1950) The climate of the central North American grassland. *Ann. Assoc. Amer. Geog.* **40**, 1–39

BRAUN E.L. (1947) Development of the deciduous forests of eastern North America. *Ecol. Monog.* **17**, 211–219

BRAUN E.L. (1950) *Deciduous Forests of Eastern North America.* Blakiston Co., Philadelphia. 596 pp.

BROOKS C.E.P. (1951) Geological and historical aspects of climatic change. In *Compendium of Meteorology.* T.F. Maline, ed. Boston: American Meteorological Society, pp. 1004–1018

CHANEY R.W. (1947) Tertiary centers and migration routes. *Ecol. Monog.* **17**, 139–148

CLEMENTS F.E. (1936) The origin of the desert climax and climate. In *Essays in geobotany* in honor of William Albert Setchell. (T.H. Goodspeed, ed.) Univ. Calif. Press, pp. 87–140

COUPLAND R.T. (1958) The effect of fluctuations in weather upon the grasslands of the Great Plains. *Bot. Review* **24**, 273–317

COUPLAND R.T. (1960) A reconsideration of grassland classification in the Northern Great Plains of North America. *J. Ecol.* **49**, 135–167

COUPLAND R.T. & BRAYSHAW T.C. (1953) The fescue grassland in Saskatchewan. *Ecology* **34**, 386–405

CURTIS J.T. (1956) The modifications of mid-latitude grasslands and forests by man. In Thomas W.L. (ed.) *Man's Role in changing the face of the earth.* Univ. of Chicago Press, pp. 721–736

CURTIS J.T. (1959) *The vegetation of Wisconsin.* Univ. of Wisconsin Press. Madison. 657 pp.

DAY G.M. (1953) The Indian as an ecological factor in the northeastern forests. *Ecology* **34**, 329–346

DEEVEY E.S. Jr (1949) Biogeography of the Pleistocene. Pt. 1. Europe and North America. *Bull. Geol. Soc. Amer.* **60**, 1315–1416

DEEVEY E.S. & FLINT R.F. (1957) Postglacial hypsithermal interval. *Science* **157**, 182–184

DORF E. (1960) Climatic changes of the past and present. *American Scientist* **48**, 341–364

DYKSTERHUIS E.J. (1958) Ecological principles in range evaluation. *Bot. Review* **24**, 253–272

ELIAS M.K. (1942) Tertiary prairie grasses and other herbs from the high plains. *Geol. Soc. Amer. Special Paper* **41**, 1–176

ELLISON L. (1960) Influence of grazing on plant succession of rangelands. *Bot. Review* **26**, 1–78

FENNEMAN N.M. (1931) *Physiography of Western United States*. McGraw-Hill Book Co., Inc. New York

FLINT R.F. (1957) *Glacial and Pleistocene geology*. John Wiley and Sons, Inc. New York, 553 pp.

GILPIN W. (1860) *The central gold region: the grain, pastoral and gold regions of North America*. Philadelphia: Somer, Barnes & Co. 194 pp.

GLEASON H.A. (1923) The vegetational history of the Middle West. *Anns. Assoc. Am. Geog.* **12**, 39–85

HANSEN H.P. (1950) Postglacial forests along the Alaska Highway in British Columbia. *Proc. Amer. Philos. Soc.* **94**, 411–421

HARTLEY W. (1958a) Studies on the origin, evolution and distribution of the gramineae. 11. The Tribe Paniceae. *Australian J. of Bot.* **6**, 343–357

HARTLEY W. (1958b) Studies on the origin, evolution and distribution of the gramineae. 1. The Tribe Andropogoneae. *Australian J. Bot.* **6**, 116–128

HUMPHREY R.R. (1958) The desert grassland — a history of vegetational change and an analysis of causes. *Bot. Review* **24**, 193–252

KOWALEWSKY W. (1873–1874) Monographie der Gattung *Anthracocherium* Cuv. *Palaeontographica. n.s.*, vol. 2 (22)

KUPSCH W.O. (1960) Radiocarbon-dated organic sediment near Herbert, Saskatchewan. *Amer. Jour. of Science* **258**, 282–292

LIVINGSTON R.B. (1952) Relict true prairie communities in central Colorado. *Ecology* **33**, 72–86

LOVE D. (1959) The post-glacial development of the flora of Manitoba: a discussion. *Canadian Jour. Botany* **37**, 547–585

McCOMB A.L. & LOOMIS W.E. (1944) Subclimax prairie. *Bull. Torrey Bot. Club* **17**, 46–76

MACGINITIE H.D. (1953) Fossil plants of the Florissant beds. Colorado. *Carnegie Inst. Wash., Pub.* **599**, 188 pp.

MALIN J.C. (1956) The grassland of North America: its occupance and the challenge of continuous reappraisals. In Thomas W.L. (ed) *Man's role in changing the face of the earth*. Univ. of Chicago Press, pp. 350–366

MANLEY G. (1955) A climatological survey of the retreat of the Laurentide ice sheet. *Amer. Jour. Sci.* **253**, 256–273

MASON H. L. (1947) Evolution of certain floristic associations in western North America. *Ecol. Monog.* **17**, 201–210

MOIR D. R. (1958) Occurrence and radiocarbon date of coniferous wood in Kidder County, North Dakota. *N. Dak. Geol. Survey. Misc. Ser. No.* 10, 108–114

MOSS E. H. & CAMPBELL J. A. (1947) The fescue grassland of Alberta. *Canad. Jour. Res. C.* **25**, 209–227

MOSS E. H. (1944) The prairie and associated vegetation of southwestern Alberta. *Canad. Jour. Res. C.* **22**, 11–31

MOSS E. H. (1955) The vegetation of Alberta. *Bot. Rev.* **21**, 493–567

OSBORN H. F. (1910) *Age of mammals.* Macmillan and Co. New York, 635 pp.

OSGOOD E. S. (1929) *The day of the cattleman.* The Univ. of Chicago Press. 285 pp.

POUND R. & CLEMENTS F. E. (1898) *The phytogeography of Nebraska.* Jacob North & Co., Lincoln

ROE F. G. (1955) *The Indian and the horse.* Norman, Univ. of Oklahoma Press. 472 pp.

SAUER C. (1950) Grassland climax, fire, and man. *J. Range Mangt.* **3**, 16–21

STEBBINS G. L. Jr (1947) Evidence on rates of evolution from the distribution of existing and fossil plant species. *Ecol. Monog.* **17**, 149–158

STEWART O. C. (1956) Fire as the first great force employed by man. In Thomas W. L. (ed.) *Man's role in changing the face of the earth.* Univ. of Chicago Press, pp. 115–133

THORNTHWAITE C. W. (1941) Climate and settlement in the Great Plains. *U.S. Dept. Agr. Yearbook 1941*, 177–187

TISDALE E. W. (1947) The grasslands of the southern interior of British Columbia. *Ecology* **28**, 346–382

WEAKLY H. E. (1943) A tree ring record of precipitation in western Nebraska. *J. Forestry* **41**, 816–819

WEAVER J. E. (1954) *North American prairie.* Johnsen Publishing Co. Lincoln. 348 pp.

WEAVER J. E. & ALBERTSON F. W. (1956) *Grasslands of the Great Plains.* Johnsen Publishing Co. Lincoln, 395 pp.

WEAVER J. E. & CLEMENTS F. E. (1938) *Plant ecology.* McGraw-Hill Book Co. Inc. N.Y. and London. 601 pp.

WEBB W. P. (1931) *The Great Plains.* Grosset and Dunlop. New York. 525 pp.

WEDEL W. R. (1961) *Prehistoric man on the Great Plains.* Univ. of Oklahoma Press. Norman. 355 pp.

WILLETT H. C. (1950) Temperature trends of the past century. *Centenary Proc. Royal Meteorol. Soc.*, pp. 195–206

RANGE DYNAMICS CONTROL—AN ECOLOGICAL URGENCY

David F. Costello

Pacific Northwest Forest and Range Experiment Station
Forest Service, U.S. Department of Agriculture
Portland, Oregon

ABSTRACT

Range management in the United States is founded principally on the application of ecological principles and processes.

The guiding principle is manipulation of secondary succession with the objective of maintaining or improving productivity of ranges, with due regard for the impact of grazing on other land uses.

The history of the range in western America is one of progressive deterioration in the nineteenth century, recognition of the need for management principles in the first quarter of the twentieth century, followed by the rise of the conservation movement, and great expansion of research in recent years.

Ecological research has contributed especially to: Methods of artificial revegetation; eradication of poisonous plants; grazing rates under systems of season-long, deferred, and rotation grazing; rangeland erosion control; and classification of range condition in terms of potential production.

Pressure on range lands now has reached a critical point. The impacts of increasing industrial development, urbanization, population increases, and multiple use of land is causing ecological reactions and changes in natural vegetation almost faster than we can measure them. Especially needed are: A nationwide appraisal of the range resource; guidelines for ecosystem management; increased emphasis on autecology; more ecological study of the interactions between land uses; and establishment of production goals which are within the biological capability of the range.

Change, through ecological processes such as invasion, competition, ecesis, and succession, is a constant and universal characteristic of vegetation. Control of change, therefore, is the main essential of range management, which has as its principal objective habitat management for sustained optimum production of forage for grazing animals. Since changes in range vegetation are occurring at an ever increasing rate, as a consequence of increasing demands for meat, wool, wild game, and other products of the land, it is imperative that ecology be looked to for ever greater contributions to a knowledge of proper range management.

Since range dynamics control is the basic ingredient of management, it now seems appropriate to outline the major changes which have occurred on range lands in the western United States, to examine modern practices and concepts as they apply to present range management, and to explore some of the possibilities for ecological contributions to range management in the future.

THE ORIGINAL WESTERN GRASSLANDS

In the beginning a magnificent vegetation resource awaited the coming of white man and his grazing animals to western America. Two-fifths of the 1·904 billion acres of the continental United States, exclusive of Alaska, were grassland.

No adequate description of the original western range has been written. Historical records and ecological studies of relict areas and of sites protected from grazing for experimental purposes indicate that the major grazing types were highly productive. Probably the most comprehensive description is contained in the classical paper 'Natural Vegetation', by Shantz and Zon (1924). Numerous descriptions of specific range communities have been written (Aldous and Shantz, 1924; Weaver and Fitzpatrick, 1934; Daubenmire, 1942; Humphrey, 1958; and others).

The original western range was an enormous untapped natural resource of apparently never ending prairies, plains, deserts, and mountain lands (U.S. Dep. Agric., Forest Service, 1936). The tall-grass prairies occupied more than 40 million acres in an area which extended westward from Illinois to the 100th meridian and from Canada on the north to Texas on the south. Acre for acre, the prairie was the most productive of all the range types. The dominant grasses, which included the bluestems (*Andropogon* spp.), needlegrasses (*Stipa* spp.), switchgrass (*Panicum virgatum*) and many palatable grasses, forbs, and shrubs of lower stature, were most valuable for summer grazing. They did not cure well on the stalk for winter grazing.

Short-grass range covered 280 million acres lying between the prairies on the east and the Rocky Mountains on the west. The principal grass species were the gramas (*Bouteloua* spp.), buffalograss (*Buchloe dactyloides*), bluestem wheatgrass (*Agropyron smithii*), and needle-and-thread (*Stipa comata*). These provided nutritious forage throughout the summer growing season. When well cured, they also furnished excellent winter forage.

Pacific bunchgrass occurred on a total area of 61 million acres in Montana, the Pacific Northwest, and in central California. The characteristic species were Idaho fescue (*Festuca idahoensis*) and bearded bluebunch wheatgrass (*Agropyron spicatum*) in the Northwest, and California needlegrass (*Stipa pulchra*) in the great central valley of California. These grasses were palatable when green but of minor value in the cold wet winter season. California needlegrass was especially vulnerable to overgrazing.

Semidesert grasslands in the Southwest occupied 93 million acres, chiefly in Arizona and New Mexico. In the warm dry climate forage was available throughout the year from low growing grasses such as tobosa grass (*Hilaria mutica*), alkali sacaton (*Sporobolus cryptandrus*), black grama (*Bouteloua eriopoda*), and various three-awns (*Aristida* spp.). In this region of little rainfall, overgrazing easily denuded the range and permitted the invasion of undesirable weeds and shrubs.

Sagebrush-grass occurred on 90 million acres of semiarid lands in the west, particularly in the Great Basin of Utah, Nevada, and Idaho. A great variety of grasses, forbs, and other shrubs grew among the sagebrush (*Artemisia* spp.) plants which formed open diminutive forests. Grazing capacity was moderately high on the better soils. The type was susceptible to overuse because of its accessibility to grazing animals throughout the year and because of sporadic rainfall in the semiarid climate.

Ranges of low value were found in other arid and semiarid parts of the west. Two principal types were the southern desert shrub, characteristic of the dry desert lands of Arizona, Nevada, and southeastern California and salt desert shrub of Wyoming and the Great Basin. The predominant vegetation was low shrubs with scattered grasses. Together these types covered about 67 million acres.

Open forests of pinon pines (*Pinus* spp.) and Junipers (*Juniperus*) characterized the foothills of many mountain ranges from Colorado to Oregon and California. The principal value of the type, which covered 74 million acres, was derived from the numerous palatable grasses and shrubs which grew between the trees and furnished forage in spring and fall for migratory game animals.

In the mountains, open forest types of ponderosa pine (*Pinus ponderosa*), Douglas-fir (*Pseudotsuga menziesii*), aspen (*Populus tremuloides*), and spruce (*Picea* spp.) fir (*Abies* spp.) supported highly productive stands of grasses, forbs, and shrubs. Grass and sedge meadows occurred in non-forested areas in the mountains. Above timberline, alpine tundra occupied over 4 million acreas. In all, the open forests occupied more than 130 million acres, valuable for summer forage in the yearlong grazing cycle for both game and livestock.

MAN'S PAST USE OF THE GRASSLANDS

Expansion of the grazing industry began early in America. Columbus brought the first livestock on his second voyage in 1493. Coronado introduced horses, mules, cattle, sheep, and hogs into the Southwest in 1540. Later introductions of livestock were made in Florida, California, and northern Mexico (Barnes, 1926). From these early beginnings, grazing animals quickly occupied the 'inexhaustible' range in the interior of America.

The major grazing expansion in the West, 1865–1890 was accompanied by important biological, social, and economic changes. The bison of the Great Plains were slaughtered by the millions. Subjugation of the Indians proceeded rapidly, permitting settlement by homesteaders who brought their plows and barbed wire fences. Sheep were driven into the Inter-mountain and Northern Plains areas from California and Texas, resulting in competition for cattle forage. Overexpansion, lack of biological know-ledge, the urge for riches, and absence of management guidelines contri-buted to widespread depletion. Within half a century grazing capacity of the original range was reduced by one-half. By the end of the nineteenth century, planning and improved management had become imperative.

In the period, 1900–1930, many economic and social adjustments occurred. A start also was made in the development of range management principles on an ecological basis. Major changes in land use resulted from population increase, economic growth, transportation improvement, and shifts in land ownership (Clawson et al., 1960). In 1890, most of the western range was still open public domain. By 1900 the area of Indian reservations had been cut in half, thus opening the land to use by white men. By 1920 most of the prairies of the mid west, the Palouse grasslands of the North-west, and the Pacific prairie in the central valley of California, had been plowed. Most of the public domain had disappeared from the Great Plains. Throughout the West the earmarks of forage depletion were evident. The cover of palatable species had been reduced, their vigor and productivity had been decreased, noxious and undesirable shrubs had invaded the range, and accelerated erosion was rampant. Lack of balance in seasonal forage supplies, and drought, made economic livestock production hazardous or impossible on millions of acres in the early 1930's. In view of these drastic changes in the original range it was a propitious time for the rise of the conservation movement in America.

ECOLOGICAL INFLUENCE ON RANGE MANAGEMENT

Happily, a start had been made early in the twentieth century in the development of range management principles. The classic studies of Cowles (1899, 1901), Sampson (1919), Clements (1928), Shantz and Zon (1924), and other workers had laid the foundation for application of the succession concept to range management in America. Sampson (1919) described range degeneration in terms of 'stages' which were interpreted by later workers as condition classes. Although various classifications of condition were proposed, depending on the climatic regions and plant associations where they were developed, most were built on the concept that range recovery is accomplished through secondary succession.

Range condition is generally defined as the status of the range at a given time in terms of its ultimate potential under good livestock management and under the prevailing edaphic and climatic conditions. Four condition classes have commonly been recognized: poor, fair, good, and excellent (Pickford and Reid, 1942; Costello and Turner, 1944; Humphrey, 1947; Dyksterhuis, 1949). These four stages are not necessarily synonymous with secondary succession stages. In most vegetation types it is possible to re-cognize many ecological stages in the progression from bare ground to highly productive vegetation.

The 'climax' is not necessarily the excellent condition sought after by practical range managers since even the relicts of Clements (1934) are difficult or impossible to find in many thousands of square miles of western range. We do not always need climax communities in order to establish degrees of range condition. In actual practice, we use the best and most productive stands that are available to represent excellent condition. If, in time, these best stands become still better, we adjust our series of more or less arbitrary conditions to fit the new facts at hand.

In the long run, of course, it will be desirable to have a resolution of the conflict among proponents of the monoclimax, polyclimax, and prevailing climax theories (Malin, 1952; Whitaker, 1953; Egler, 1951). As Sellick (1960) points out, 'The development, verification and acceptance of a unified ecological philosophy would provide the basis for a firm establish-ment of plant ecology as a world science.'

A point of further ecological interest is that many of the original plant communities were not in climax condition when occupation by white man began. Humphrey's (1953) investigation of the desert grassland, for exam-ple, suggests that this community was a subclimax maintained by fire. Now, with fires largely controlled, the true climax of low trees, brush, and cacti is developing on areas formerly dominated by grass. Habeck (1961) found evidence that, originally, the Willamette Valley in western Oregon was largely covered with oak openings and prairie. Earlier workers had believed that the valley was covered with coniferous forest. Again, control of fire has permitted the development of dense oak forests while the prairies were being plowed.

Larson (1940) suggested that buffalo, antelope, and other animals on the Plains maintained the short-grass 'disclimax' before domestic livestock were introduced. Since that time, numerous studies have shown that mixed prairie develops under light grazing and that mid-grasses such as *Agropyron smithii* are especially encouraged by deferred and rotation grazing. It is significant that most of the workers who have studied the mixed-grass prairie have given more attention to the effects of grazing intensity and available soil moisture in their establishment of range condition standards than they have to a pristine or past climax condition which they have never seen.

It seems, then, that the practical approach for the range manager and the ecologist is to determine what each plant community, whatever its present condition, can become under different environmental influences and under different systems of management. To do this we need many controlled grazing experiments of long time duration involving grazing animals, better permanent plots, more photographs, and vastly improved skill in integrating and interpreting the factors that produce vegetation change.

WHAT PROGRESS HAVE WE MADE?

Research in the last 50 years has accumulated a large store of knowledge applicable to many uses of range lands, including the restoration of depleted forage, development of grazing systems for optimum livestock production, and integration of grazing with other land uses, including big game production, forestry, and outdoor recreation (Costello, 1957). Few studies, other than those dealing with the discovery and description of range plants, were made before 1900. Early intensive studies were reported for the mountainous West by A. W. Sampson (1919). Grazing experiments, directed from permanent headquarters stations, were started in the northern Great Plains and in Utah and Arizona from 1910–1926. But the formal establishment of forest and range experiments occurred only after the creation of a research branch in the U.S. Forest Service and passage of the McSweeney-McNary Forest Research Act in 1928. This marked the beginning of a period of greatly expanded research, dealing with the western range, in which various federal agencies, state experiment stations, colleges and universities have taken part.

Research accomplishments in the 25 year period from 1930 to 1955 have been summarized by Sampson (1955). His discussion highlights progress made in the fields of range reseeding, natural reseeding through deferred and rotation grazing, range fertilization, eradication of poisonous plants, rangeland erosion control, and wildland management on areas used for livestock grazing and timber production.

We have made progress in other ways in our understanding of the role of plant ecology in range research and range management. At least some of us have become aware of the complexity of natural phenomena facing the range manager. Allee and Park (1939), Cain (1939), Billings (1952), Sampson (1952), and others have depicted the interrelations of biotic and physical factors which must be considered in the solution of grazing problems. The growing belief is that many of these problems can be solved only through total ecology (Griggs, 1945) and through application of such fundamental concepts as energy relations, ecological balance, competition, and ecologic patterns (Dice, 1955).

In general, we have accumulated an enormous body of literature relating to range management and western grazing lands. The bibliography by Renner et al. (1938), contains 8,274 citations. Many thousands of bibliographic references have since been published in Herbage Abstracts, which is generally available to American researchers. Recently, hundreds of articles have been published in *Ecology, Ecological Monographs, The Journal of Range Management*, and in state experiment station bulletins. A number of excellent textbooks relating to ecology and range management also are generally available (Stoddart and Smith, 1955; Sampson, 1952; Weaver and Clements, 1938; Hanson and Churchill, 1961; Odum, 1959; and Clarke, 1954). In spite of this vast reservoir of knowledge, no one insists that we should not continue to add new knowledge through ecological research.

Some progress has been made in synthesis of research, but not enough. Hanson (1950) and Weaver (1954), for example, have reviewed the nature of western grasslands. Ellison (1960) has reviewed the application of studies of secondary succession to range management. Weaver and Albertson (1956) have summarized the results of many years of investigation of vegetation on the Great Plains. Three summaries dealing with vegetation analysis and measurement techniques have been published recently (Cain and Castro, 1959; Brown, 1954; and Mosby, 1960). These are extremely useful since they abstract much literature not readily available to many range technicians.

Many more syntheses of important phases of ecological research are needed. No one, for example, has reviewed the very extensive literature

8

on antelope bitterbrush (*Purshia tridentata*), one of the most important deer foods in the West. Nor has anyone given monographic treatment to all information available on effects of grazing intensity on vegetation response. Examples could be multiplied. It would be desirable to have assembled in one place all that is known about range condition classification, plant competition, systems of grazing, and standards of utilization. Where diversity of opinion exists, as it does in recommendations for the proper per cent of grazing use in different localities, the one who synthesizes should be impelled to discover the common theme of all the findings. Only through such broad understanding can we achieve a firm basis for effective range management.

THE RANGE TODAY

Three-fourths of the range area of the United States still lies west of the 100th meridian. It is still a renewable resource of great economic importance. But many changes have occurred since white man came to America.

The tall-grass prairies have mostly been converted to farm lands. The 20 million acres which remain have been greatly modified by grazing, drought, and the introduction of exotic grasses and weeds. Millions of acres of mixed-prairie have been plowed for wheat production in the Great Plains. The Pacific prairies have all but vanished in favor of wheat and other cultivated crops. In the foothills, where remnants remain, the bunchgrasses have been extensively replaced by annual grasses and weeds. Much of the original sagebrushtype still exists but annual cheatgrass brome (*Bromus tectorum*) instead of perennial bunchgrasses, now constitutes its principal understory. In the mountainous areas other millions of acres have been eroded, the meadows denuded, and palatable grasses replaced by undesirable or poisonous weeds.

Many factors, other than the direct factor of grazing, have affected the western range. The area of grazing and forest land now is only half of what it was in 1850. This enormous decrease in the rangeland base had many causes: cultivation; timber cutting; industrial development; dam building and water impoundment; road construction; land withdrawal for military use, air strips, and power lines; reservation for campgrounds and other recreational use; closure for national parks and national monuments; and urban expansion.

Will this shrinkage of the range area continue? Clawson *et al.* (1960) believe that we are reaching a point where further major change is unlikely. Some possible subtractions from the present grazing area are possible. Additional semiarid lands may be changed to irrigated farms, but extensive development is limited by water supplies. Brush invasion may decrease some acreages now available to grazing, but chemical and mechanical control may more than compensate by making other areas grazeable. Urban expansion will take more land. But on the whole the total area of land removed from grazing will be small.

Additions to grazing area are likely. Large areas in the Great Plains may be regrassed. In the West, Renner (1954) estimates that 80 to 125 million acres might ultimately be regrassed, although the necessary seed supplies are not now available, nor have the economics been explored. Increases in productivity of existing rangelands can also have the effect of adding new land. Most of these increases will have to be made through the application of the ecological knowledge we now have and which we can develop in the future. In view of an estimated population of 310 million people in the United States in the year 2000 (Clawson et al., 1960), it seems imperative that we begin now to apply our intelligence, skill and technology to the land we have.

WHAT CAN THE ECOLOGISTS DO?

The western range is important. It provides forage for millions of cattle, sheep, and game animals. It is the source of most of the water used for irrigation of cultivated crops, for hydroelectric power, for industrial processes, for fishing and other forms of recreation, and for domestic consumption in our ever-expanding urban areas. And it is the connecting link in a vast cycle of animal production in which livestock are grazed for a portion of their lives on the relatively inexpensive forage of natural grasslands and finished for market on more expensive supplements, pastures, and crops produced on intensively cultivated lands.

Because of its importance, the range must be maintained and improved through management. But management is not possible without knowledge, guidelines, and means of control. Since we now are living in a physical and natural world which is changing almost more rapidly than we are able to measure, an accelerated program of ecological research is needed.

Here are some of the recent changes we have caused. We plowed 18 million acres of mixed prairie in the Great Plains in approximately 10 years. No one visualized the dust storms that were to follow. We sprayed chemicals on millions of acres of forests, ranges, and croplands to control destructive insects and noxious plants. But no one is sure of the effects on wildlife, including beneficial birds, small game animals, and fish. We lowered our water tables through gully erosion and by pumping ground water from ever deeper and deeper wells. No one is able to say what major vegetation changes ultimately will follow. We cut timber from millions of acres and converted the land to vast brushfields, which must be cleared by spraying or burning before they can be replanted to trees. No one knows what the effect will be on future game populations, water production, or human recreation.

Many of these activities on the land have been useful and necessary. Possibly the very magnitude of the change man has wrought on the land-scape is the basis for our modern recognition of the beneficial and practical aspects of an ecological approach to future management. In the field of range management, the task ahead for research and administration is to develop guides which will assure that grazing use is in balance with the full potentialities of the site, including the potential for forest growth, water production and recreational use, where these are applicable.

Among our ecological needs for the future, the following are worthy of emphasis:

An appraisal of the range resource

We need an inventory of what is on the ground in order to establish a base from which to measure what happens in the future. A timber resource review (U.S. Dep. Agric., Forest Service, 1958) and a recreation resource review (Outdoor Recreation Resources Review Commission, 1962) are now available. But no comparable review of the range resource has been made. Such a comprehensive review should be made periodically, '... especially in our Western states, where watershed, range, timber, wildlife, and recreational values are so closely intermingled and so impor-tant to this nation's future welfare and economy' (Parker, 1952).

Ecosystem management

If we are to realize the potentialities of the western range, our management practices will have to be intensified. One way to do this is to manage each major ecological community for itself. Essentially, this is ecosystem management.

For example, Branson and Weaver (1953) point out that almost every square mile of mixed prairie studied in Nebraska included three very different communities, each presenting a separate problem in its seral his-tory. Each community had a different history of degeneration from the climax under excessive grazing. Each had a still different history during recovery.

It is not uncommon to find meadows, sagebrush stands, bunchgrass areas, and forested range in a single pasture or grazing unit. The origin and successional sequence is different for each of these communities. The meadow may have originated from a lake; by overgrazing and erosion it can be converted into a weed community. The sagebrush stand may have replaced an original grassland. The bunchgrass type may in time be invaded by shrubs or forest trees. In such a complex we cannot expect unmanaged livestock to give proper use to all these vegetation types. If left to their own devices, sheep may concentrate their grazing on shrubs and neglect the forested range; cattle will denude the meadow and underutilize the bunchgrasses.

Only through fencing, herding, salting, riding, deferred and rotation grazing, and with proper numbers of animals applied separately to each of these types, can we expect to achieve optimum returns for the livestock operator and maintain or improve the range at the same time. And in order properly to apply these management practices we must understand and apply knowledge attained through studies of dynamic ecology on specific seres.

Autecology

The very existence of vegetation depends upon the completion of the life cycles of individual plants. All changes and reactions which occur in structure and development of vegetation can be traced to reactions of individual plants. Because of the wide range of palatabilities among different plants and because of differences in the sensitive stages in the development of individual species, a sound knowledge of the autecology of important species is necessary.

Relatively few exhaustive studies of this kind have been made for important native forage plants. Poisonous plants such as *Helenium hoopesii* and *Halogeton glomeratus* have received attention because they have created immediate economic problems (Doran and Cassady, 1944; Tisdale and Zappetini, 1953). The rewards from such studies have been great, since they have revealed weak points in the plants' life cycles and have suggested points of attack for successful control measures.

The reward from study of the autecology of perennial grasses and palatable shrubs should be equally great when findings are applied with the positive objective of improving chance of survival of these desirable species. Autecological studies should include all developmental phases of the plant, internal physiological relations, the competitive ability of the species, its associations with other plants, its reactions to soil conditions, its response to clipping or grazing at different intensities and in different seasons, and its physical requirements in the microenvironment.

Multiple use ecology

Characteristic of the western range is the complex relationship between grazing and other land uses. Even where grazing is the primary use, other uses are widely advocated, either at the same time or at different times. Some uses are compatible with grazing; some are not. Protection of mountain watersheds to produce water for irrigation and urban consumption, for example, may exclude both grazing use and timber cutting, Competition between game animals and livestock frequently results in conflicts in management. Siltation from overgrazed ranges affects the quality of fishing and other forms of recreation on streams and reservoirs. Timber cutting affects wildlife production.

The problem thus becomes one of obtaining optimum returns from the major use of a given area with least disturbance to subordinate uses. We must give increased attention to the ecological impacts of different uses and to the interactions between uses, even on lands primarily suitable for grazing. Team research will be necessary since this broader ecology is beyond the scope or capability of the individual research worker or of any specialized agency.

Multiple factor experiments

The range manager is always faced with multiple decisions and the principle of diminishing returns. He must, for example, ask himself: What is the best balance between numbers of grazing animals per unit area and time to begin grazing? Seasons of grazing and rates of grazing are closely related. Obviously, the longer livestock are on the range, the fewer the number of animals which can be grazed to attain a given degree of utilization. Likewise, the earlier the season opens, the greater the impact on new growth of vegetation. Furthermore, the later the closing date, the less vegetation cover left on the ground for photosynthetic activity, soil moisture retention, and erosion prevention. Also, heavier grazing rates or earlier opening dates can result in early use of all current herbage production in poor growing seasons.

In spite of the need for answers which will resolve these multiple decisions, most of our intensive grazing studies have been designed around single factors, namely, rate of grazing, season of use, deferred and rotation systems, or class of animal. We need grazing experiments in which each of these factors is superimposed upon the other. Obviously, more replications and more record taking will be required, but the returns will justify the cost of doing this more complex research. With modern statistical design and electronic data processing the task should be entirely feasible.

At the same time, we need more multiple correlation studies of physical factors and biotic reactions on the range. By this means we may be able to assess the relative importance of factors in the holocoenotic environment described by Billings (1952), Sampson (1952), and others, instead of merely theorizing about them.

Biological goals

Since the early work of Sampson (1919), it has been believed that, in general, highest forage productivity is characteristic of seral stages near the climax and lowest productivity is characteristic of the pioneer stages of succession. There are exceptions to this rule. Some of the grass-weed stages in the early succession on abandoned fields in the Great Plains are more productive, in terms of forage weight and botanical diversity, than the ultimate mixed-grass prairie. The same is true of some secondary succession stages which precede the attainment of the bunchgrass stage beneath ponderosa pine forests in the Rocky Mountains. Also, evidence exists (Costello and Turner, 1941; Weaver and Albertson, 1936; Tomanek, 1948) that under certain climatic conditions the range is more productive when it is grazed moderately or lightly than when it is not grazed at all.

In view of these findings we need ecological studies to determine at what step on the succession ladder the range can be maintained on a sustained-yield basis and at the same time maintain optimum soil stability and achieve optimum economic returns.

A choice of succession level has been made already by some ranchers and by some ecologists. Many ranchers, for example, have accepted cheatgrass brome (*Bromus tectorum*) as a disclimax in the sagebrush-grass association with which they are willing to live. They do this with the thought that reseeding may be too expensive and that natural revegetation to perennial bunchgrasses may take a lifetime, or even centuries. Their realistic economic horizon is nearer than the theoretical ecological horizon of return to reliable yearly yields of forage. In California, even the ecologists agree that the annual vegetation in the central valley is more productive than the former climax, dominated by *Stipa pulchra*, which is too unstable to maintain under modern grazing pressure.

We therefore have the problem of determing which disclimaxes we wish to maintain. We will have to determine how near the climax they should be. And we will have to test whether or not they can be maintained economically in the face of fluctuating weather, flexible ranching management practices forced on the livestock operator by the consuming public, and a dynamic vegetation which constantly reacts to all physical and biotic causes.

Energy relations in ecosystems

Little attention has been given by range researchers to energy production, energy utilization, and energy accumulation on areas used by grazing animals. Most of us have been content to use weight, density, composition, frequency, and other indices for estimating productivity. Lately there is a tendency to generalize our estimates of productivity in more or less intangible terms of range condition classes or in terms of the theoretical climax. All of these criteria are at best only approximate measures of what the grazing animal uses in growth and other metabolic processes. And they certainly do not measure what goes on in the ecosystem as a whole.

We could profitably devote some of our future research effort to obtaining more precise knowledge of the maximum productive potentials of different sites. We need to test the possibility of estimating biological capability of our rangelands in terms of gram calories per acre and as percentages of available radiation.

We already have some general principles to serve as a basis for planning studies of energy relations. There is evidence that some ecosystems are more efficient as photosynthetic units than others. The rate of energy accumulation varies as a plant association matures. Also, the growth form of plants is an important factor in the rate of organic matter production. Since vegetation can be changed through manipulation, it is evident that the imaginative range researcher could devise numerous studies of theoretical and practical value in the field of energy relations. Such experiments might even produce a measure of energy transformation in terms that would be interchangeable between plants and grazing animals.

FROM THE PAST TO THE FUTURE

The past is important. It has given us what we have today. The livestock industry in America began with the introduction of grazing animals to a new continent. For 200 years occupation of a vast unspoiled grazing territory progressed slowly. Then suddenly enormous expansion of the grazing industry resulted in complete occupation of the western range. Competition for grass began. Deterioration of the range resource rapidly followed as a result of mismanagement, lack of knowledge, and the desire for quick riches. And recently, conversion of grazing lands to other uses reduced the grazeable acreage to half of what it was in 1850.

The present rests upon a notable heritage of conquest, experience, and knowledge of what was done and what could have been done in the past. We now possess a large body of practical information on management of the range resource. We have many guidelines for management of which none is perfect and certainly not all of which are being used. We are gaining support in the conservation movement and an ecological conscience is apparent in many individuals and organizations. The speed of the forces of destruction has been slowed. But deterioration of the value of vegetation, soil, and other resources is still proceeding faster in many areas than is the speed of recovery in other places.

The future poses the picture of need for more rapid accretion of ecological knowledge. We cannot continue to allow changes in the productivity of the land without knowledge of how to direct and control those changes. We must solve one of the fundamental questions of our age — how to operate within natural laws instead of disrupting them.

Man must realize that he is not beyond nature but that he is a part of it. He cannot escape from the biological requirement that he must eat. But he must also live and recreate. This he cannot do without vegetation, and soil, and water, and the guidance of the ecologist.

REFERENCES

ALDOUS A.E. & SHANTZ H.L. (1924) Types of vegetation in the semi-arid portion of the United States and their economic significance. *J. Agric. Res.* **28** (2), 99–128

ALLEE W.C & PARK T. (1939) Concerning ecological principles. *Science* **89**, 166–169

BARNES W.C. (1926) The story of the range. *69th Congr., 1st Sess., Hearings on S. Res. 347 before Subcom. of Com. on Pub. Lands and Surveys*, Part 6, 1579–1640

BILLINGS W.D. (1952) The environmental complex in relation to plant growth and distribution. *Quart. Rev. Biol.* **27**, 251–265

BRANSON F. & WEAVER J.E. (1953) Quantitative study of degeneration of mixed prairie. *Bot. Gaz.* **114** (4), 397–416

BROWN DOROTHY (1954) *Methods of surveying and measuring vegetation.* Bull. 42. Commonwealth Bureau of Pastures and Field Crops, Hurley, Berks.

CAIN S.A. (1939) The climax and its complexities. *Amer. Midl. Nat.* **21**, 146–81

CAIN S.A. & CASTRO G.M. DE O. (1959) *Manual of vegetation analysis.* Harper & Brothers, New York. 325 pp.

CLARKE G.L. (1954) *Elements of Ecology.* John Wiley & Sons, Inc. 534 pp.

CLAWSON MARION, HELD R.B. & STODDARD C.H. (1960) *Land for the future.* The Johns Hopkins Press, Baltimore

CLEMENTS F.E. (1934) The relict method in dynamic ecology. *J. Ecol.* **22**, 39–68 illus.

CLEMENTS F.E. (1928) *Plant succession and indicators.* The H.W. Wilson Co., New York. 453 pp.

COSTELLO D. F. (1957) 'Grasslands' in America's natural resources. The Ronald Press Company, New York. 211 pp.

COSTELLO D.F. & TURNER G.T. (1941) Vegetation changes following exclusion of livestock from grazed ranges. J. For. 39, 310–315

COSTELLO D.F. & TURNER G.T. (1944) Judging condition and utilization of short-grass ranges on the Central Great Plains. U.S. Dep. Agric. Farmer's Bull. 1949, 1–21

COWLES H.C. (1899) The ecological relations of the vegetation on the sand dunes of Lake Michigan. Bot. Gaz. 27, 95–116, 167–202, 281–308, 361–391

COWLES H.C. (1901) The physiographic ecology of Chicago and vicinity; a study of the origin, development, and classification of plant societies. Bot. Gaz. 31, 73–108, 145–182

DAUBENMIRE R.F. (1942) An ecological study of the vegetation of south-eastern Washington and adjacent Idaho. Ecol. Monogr. 12 (1), 53–79

DICE L.R. (1955) What is Ecology? Sci. Monthly 80, 346–351

DORAN C.W. & CASSADY J.T. (1944) Management of sheep on range infested with orange sneezeweed. U.S. Dep. Agric. Circ. No. 691, 28 pp.

DYKSTERHUIS E.J. (1949) Condition and management of rangeland based on quantitative ecology. J. Range Mgmt. 2 (3), 104–115

EGLER F.E. (1951) A commentary on American plant ecology based on the textbooks of 1947–1959. Ecology 32, 673–695

ELLISON L. (1960) Influence of grazing on plant succession of range lands. Bot. Rev. 26 (1), 1–78

GRIGGS R.F. (1945) Biology and agriculture in the post war world. Science 101, 235–239

HABECK J.R. (1961) The original vegetation of the Mid-Willamette Valley, Oregon. Northw. Sci. 35 (2), 65–77

HANSON H.C. (1950) Ecology of the grassland. The Bot. Rev. 6, 283–360

HANSON H.C. & CHURCHILL E.D. (1961) The plant community. Reinhold Publ. Corp., New York. 218 pp.

HUMPHREY R.R. (1947) Range forage evaluation by the range condition method. J. For. 45 (1), 10–16

HUMPHREY R.R. (1953) The desert grassland, past and present. J. Range Mgmt. 6 (3), 159–164

HUMPHREY R.R. (1958) The desert grassland: a history of vegetational change and an analysis of its causes. Bot. Rev. 24, 193–252

LARSON F. (1940) The role of the bison in maintaining the short grass plains. Ecology 21, 113–121

MALIN J.C. (1952) Man, the state of nature, and climax: as illustrated by some problems of the North American grassland. Scientific Monthly 74 (1), 1–8

MOSBY H.S. ed. (1960) Manual of game investigational techniques. Edwards Brothers, Inc., Ann Arbor, Michigan

ODUM E.P. (1959) Fundamentals of ecology. 2nd Ed. W.B. Saunders Co., Philadelphia. 546 pp.

Outdoor Recreation Resources Review Commission (1962) Outdoor recreation for America. U.S. Govt. Printing Off., Washington D.C. 246 pp.

PARKER K.W. (1952) The role of plant ecology in range research and range management. Proceedings of the Sixth International Grassland Congress. Pennsylvania State College, State College, Pa. Vol. I., 618–624

PICKFORD G.D. & REID E.H. (1942) Basis for judging subalpine grassland ranges of Oregon and Washington. *U.S. Dep. Agric. Circ.* **655**, 1-37

RENNER F.G., CRAFTS E.C., HARTMAN T.C. & ELLISON L. (1938) A selected bibliography on management of western ranges, livestock, and wildlife. *U.S. Dep. Agric. Misc. Publ. No.* 281, 468 pp.

RENNER F.G. (1954) The future of our range resource. *J. Range Mgmt.* **7** (2), 55-6

SAMPSON A.W. (1919) Plant succession in relation to range management. *U.S. Dep. Agric. Bull.* **791**, 76

SAMPSON A.W. (1952) *Range management: principles and practices.* John Wiley & Sons, New York. 570 pp.

SAMPSON A.W. (1955) Where have we been and where are we going in range management. *J. Range Mgmt.* **8** (6), 241-246

SELLICK G.W. (1960) The climax concept. *Bot. Rev.* **26** (4), 534-545

SHANTZ H.L. & ZON R. (1924) Natural vegetation. *U.S. Dep. Agric. Atlas of American Agriculture*, I (E), 1-29

STODDART L.A. & SMITH A.D. (1955) *Range Management.* 2nd Ed. McGraw Hill Book Co., Inc. 433 pp.

TISDALE E.W. & ZAPPETINI G. (1953) *Halogeton* studies on Idaho ranges. *J. Range Mgmt.* **6**, 225-236

TOMANEK G.W. (1948) Pasture types of western Kansas in relation to the intensity of utilization in past years. *Kans. Acad. Sci., Trans.* **51**, 171-196

U.S. Dep. Agric., Forest Service (1936) The western range. *74th Congress 2nd Session, Senate Document* 199, U.S. Govt. Printing off., Washington, D.C. 620 pp.

U.S. Dep. Agric., Forest Service (1958) Timber resources for America's future. *Forest Resource Report No.* 14. U.S. Govt. Printing Off., Washington, D.C. 713 pp.

WEAVER J.E. (1954) *North American prairie.* Johnsen Publishing Company, Lincoln, Nebraska. 348 pp.

WEAVER J.E. & ALBERTSON F.W. (1936) Effects of the great drought on the prairies of Iowa, Nebraska, and Kansas. *Ecology* **17**, 567-639

WEAVER J.E. & ALBERTSON F.W. (1956) *Grasslands of the Great Plains.* Johnsen Publishing Company, Lincoln, Nebraska. 395 pp.

WEAVER J.E. & CLEMENTS F.E. (1938) *Plant ecology.* McGraw-Hill Book Co., Inc., New York. 601 pp.

WEAVER J.E. & FITZPATRICK J.T. (1934) The prairie. *Ecol. Monogr.* **4**, 100-114

WHITAKER R.H. (1953) A consideration of climax theory: the climax as a population and pattern. *Ecol. Monogr.* **23**, 41-78

UTILIZATION OF THE FRONT RANGE TUNDRA, COLORADO

John W. Marr

Institute of Arctic and Alpine Research and Department of Biology,
University of Colorado

ABSTRACT

Alpine tundra is conspicuous in the Front Range. On level, winter snow-free sites with stable soils having a 6–12 in. layer rich in humus, *Kobresia* meadow is the climatic climax ecosystem. Conspicuous species in other common stands are *Deschampsia caespitosa, Silene acaulis, Trifolium spp., Carex elynoides, Carex scopulorum, Artemisia scopulorum, Polygonum bistortoides, Oreoxis alpina, Hymenoxis grandiflora, Paronychia sessiliflora* and *Phlox pulvinata.*

Elk, mountain sheep, ptarmigan, marmots, pocket gopher, voles and mice are common animals.

At one time domestic sheep spent several weeks each summer in the Front Range tundra and a few areas are still heavily grazed. Data are not sufficient to determine the damage brought about by grazing, but greater dispersal of sheep would probably reduce its effect.

Mountain sheep, elk and deer graze the tundra in summer and the first two mentioned now sometimes remain all winter. The pocket gopher has an important influence on vegetation and its tunnels are used by actively grazing microtines. Other processes than animal activities, notably ice heaving and churning, are active in reducing plant cover. Despite reproduction by seedlings in some tundra plants, revegetation of cleared areas is very slow.

The importance of basic ecological knowledge is emphasized as a necessary foundation for conservationist policies at a time when the pressure of human activities is increasing.

INTRODUCTION

Alpine tundra, the ecological region which lies above upper altitudinal tree-limit, occupies nearly one-half million acres of landscape in the Front Range. This tundra is interrupted by forest only twice in an eighty mile segment along the Continental Divide, the backbone of the Range. The tundra region's lower limit is at an average altitude of about 11,500 feet and it includes the tops of the highest peaks, some above 14,000 feet. Topography varies from sharp peaks and ridges with precipitous slopes hundreds of feet high to gently rolling expanses of hundreds of acres. Igneous and metamorphic rocks predominate. Cryopedological processes,

110   JOHN W. MARR

some currently active, have produced a variety of patterned-ground (Washburn, 1956). Some soils are thin and rocky, but stable areas of deep weathered mantle occur with well developed soil rich in humus. Soil moisture is usually deficient in late June, late summer and fall.

Kobresia meadow in almost level, winter snow-free sites with stable soil having a 6 to 12 inch layer rich in humus is the climatic climax ecosystem.

PLANTS OF THE FRONT RANGE

There are approximately three hundred species of phanerogams in the Front Range tundra. Sedges, grasses, cushion plants, and several flowering herbs are conspicuous; terrestrial mosses and lichens are present, but they are never as conspicuous as they are in arctic tundra. Rock lichens are common.

The ecosystem concept (Tansley, 1935) provides the most effective and efficient basis for research activities in mountains, notably in the Front Range (Marr, 1961). An ecosystem may be defined as a relatively homgeneous segment of the landscape made up of a characteristic set of eco-system components; organisms, environmental factors, and ecological processes. The ecological organization of alpine tundra baffled many early American botanists probably because their experience had been with relatively large plants and large landscape units of temperate forest or grassland regions, whereas the tundra land is often fragmented into a myriad of small units. Osburn (1962), identified twenty stands of ten stand-types in a single four acre snowfield area on Niwot Ridge.

Our knowledge of the different stand-type ecosystems of the Front Range tundra is meagre in comparison with the detailed information available on tundra areas in some countries. The more common stand-types in several different parts of the range have been described by Cox (1933), Marr (1961), Kiener (1939), Osburn (1958, 1963) and Willard (1960). I shall summarize here, the more important stand-types.

Kobresia meadow stand-type (Plate 1)

This stand-type is especially interesting because it is the climatic climax unit. Since this type is snow-free most of the winter, its plants are exposed to rigorous extremes of alpine winter weather. It is a paradox that the Kobresia meadow requires long intervals of stability, yet thrives in a region where soil instability is common. Retzer (1956) described the soil of Kobresia meadow as 'alpine turf soil'. Kobresia meadow is most common in almost flat windswept areas. It also occurs on gentle slopes where winds

PLATE 1. *Kobresia* meadow at 12,300 feet close to the Institute's Laboratory on Niwot Ridge.

are strong enough to prevent snow from accumulating all winter, and where soils have been stable for hundreds of years. *Kobresia myosuroides* (Vill.) Fiori and Pohl was present in all stands of this type sampled on Niwot Ridge and Trail Ridge. Other species with high frequencies were *Arenaria obtusiloba* (Rydb.) Fern., *Artemisia scopulorum* Gray, *Campanula uniflora* L., *Carex rupestris* All., *Carex scopulorum* Holm, *Eritrichium aretioides* (Cham.) DC., *Gentiana prostrata* Haenke, *Geum rossii* (R. Br.) Ser., *Lloydia serotina* (L.) Sw., *Oreoxis alpina* (Gray) C. and R., *Phlox pulvinata* (Wherry) Cronquist, *Polygonum viviparum* L., *Ranunculus pedatifidus* Smith, *Selaginella densa* Rydb., *Trifolium dasyphyllum* T. and G.

Deschampsia caespitosa (L.) Beauv. meadow

This is a true grassland stand-type. It is a topographic climax type on slopes and concave surfaces that have snow cover persisting all winter but melting in early summer, with relatively high soil moisture throughout most of the summer. The individual bunches of grass almost overlap, leaving little space for other species. *Artemisia arctica* Less. *ssp. saxicola* (Rydb.) Hulten, *Geum rossii*, *Ranunculus adoneus* Gray, and *Polygonum bistortoides* Pursh., are the most common species associated with hairgrass in this stand-type. Retzer (1956) called the soil of this stand-type 'alpine meadow soil'.

Dryas stands

These are characterized by a mosaic of small terraces a few inches high and a few feet in depth and held in place by mats of *Dryas octopetala* ssp. *hookeriana* (juz.) Hulten. These stands occur in sites that are exposed to strong winds that keep them snow-free most of the time. The soil is coarse and is moving downslope in a mass-wasting process. The steps of the terraces are largely bare, and few plants other than *Dryas* occur in the stand.

Other stand-types

There is a series of stands whose character is influenced by the period when snow cover is present. *Trifolium parryi* Gray meadow occurs in shallow depressions where a thin cover of snow lies all winter but melts early in the spring, and where there is no source of ground water. *Geum rossii*, *Polygonum bistortoides* and *Artemisia scopulorum* are common in this type. Where snow remains until early summer, *Ranunculus adoneus* impatiently pushes its flowers up through the last layers of melting snow and provides a beautiful contrast of white and yellow. *Polygonum bistortoides, Trifolium parryi*, *Artemisia scopulorum*, *Festuca brachyphylla* Schultes and *Trisetum spicatum* (L.) Richt. appear in this stand later in the season.

In sites where snow does not melt until late summer, the vegetation cover is sparse. Lichens, mosses and liverworts are the only plants in the stands with the latest melting snow. *Sibbaldia procumbens* L., *Juncus drummondii* Mey., *Carex pyrenaica* Wahl, and *Carex incurviformis* Mack are common vascular plants near the centre of snowbank areas. Moving outward from these areas of sparse plant cover, the density of plants increases. At the well-watered lower periphery of the snowbank area, a dense cover of vigorous sedges and grasses occurs.

A cushion plant stand occurs on sites whose surface is tipped into the strong westerly winds but where the soil is relatively stable. Conspicuous species are *Silene acaulis* L., *Arenaria obtusiloba*, *Eritrichium aretioides*, *Lloydia serotina*, *Oreoxis alpina*, *Paronychia sessiliflora* Nutt., *Phlox pulvinata*, *Trifolium nannum* Torr., *T. dasyphyllum* and *Luzula spicata* (L.) DC.

ANIMALS OF THE FRONT RANGE

The most striking aspect of the animals in the front range tundra is that one rarely sees any of them. It is unusual to pass near a boulder area without hearing the penetrating high-pitched whistle of a pika (*Ochotona princeps saxatilis* Bangs), but the animal itself is usually invisible, either because it blends with a jumble of rocks, or because it is hidden in a labyrinth of spaces between the boulders. Ptarmigan (*Lagopus leucurus leucurus* Swainson) are often seen by visitors who traverse the tundra throughout the year, but inexperienced hikers may walk within a few feet of these birds without disturbing them.

Deer (*Odocoileus hemionus hemionus* Rafinesque), elk (*Cervus canadensis nelsoni* Bailey), mountain sheep (*Ovis canadensis canadensis* Shaw), coyote (*Canis latrans latrans* Say), red fox (*Vulpes fulva macroura* Baird), yellow-bellied marmot (*Marmota flaviventris luteola* Howell), voles and mice (*Microtus* sp., *Peromyscus* spp. and *Phenacomys* sp.) and shrew (*Sorex* spp.) are also tundra inhabitants in the Front Range. Seasonal residents are the long tailed weasel (*Mustela frenata longicauda* Bonaparte), white tailed jack rabbit (*Lepus townsendii townsendii* Backman) and bob cat (*Lynx rufus uinta* Merriam). Deer move beyond the tree limit only in the warm season but have been seen in the tundra in early spring. Elk may remain on the tundra of Trail Ridge in the Rocky Mountain National Park over the winter. In other areas mountain sheep probably visit the tundra in winter. Ives (1942) reports that mountain sheep were plentiful on Niwot Ridge until 1890.

The most influential tundra animal is probably the pocket gopher (*Thomomys talpoides fossor* Allen). Its presence is made conspicuous by the soil it leaves on the surface, or the tubes of soil that it deposits in its snow tunnels and which are revealed on the melting of the snow in spring. Research on terrestrial invertebrates of the Front Range has been advanced by collections made by our Institute staff, by Alexander (1951) on grasshoppers, Gregg (1947) on ants, and by Taussig (1962). Publications on tundra aquatic ecology and taxonomy include those of Pennak (1955), Neldner and Pennak (1955), Schmitz (1959) and Baker (1961).

GRAZING IN THE TUNDRA OF THE FRONT RANGE

As trails and wagon roads developed in the Front Range at a rapid pace in the late nineteenth century, ranchers ranged their stock higher and higher in the mountains. Winters are far too severe for wintering of stock, even in the subalpine forest, but summers are congenial for domestic animals. Cattle and horses often stray up into the tundra for pasturage, but they have rarely been herded there deliberately. The grazing of cattle is discouraged by a high-altitude induced disease, high mountain or brisket disease, resulting from congestive failure of the right side of the heart (Alexander and Jensen, 1959).

Domestic sheep do very well in the tundra, and large flocks once spent many summer weeks in the Front Range. Some areas are still heavily grazed, but the last herd on Niwot Ridge was in 1946. Willard's (1960) extensive investigation has not produced any evidence of grazing by domestic animals on Trail Ridge, one of our best tundra areas. In other areas of the Front Range, grazing by domestic sheep has influenced the character of the tundra, though data are not adequate to assess the magnitude of this process. Paulsen (1960) made a survey of thirty-three alpine areas, including ecotone sites, in Wyoming, Colorado, and New Mexico. He lumped the different stands into two categories, turf and meadow. The turf category includes *Kobresia* stands, *Carex elynoides* Holm stands and several other types, while his meadow consists of hairgrass and several other stand-types. He found evidence of considerable damage to tundra ecosystems due to trails cut in the tundra and severe trampling in bedding areas. Otherwise, he detected little effect, and considers that the damage observed could have been avoided by herding practices that would keep the sheep dispersed rather than concentrated. Paulsen found an average herbage production of 263 pounds per acre, air dried, in turf stands, and 626

9

pounds in meadow sites. Continuing with an analysis of utilization, he found that where sheep grazing was light, average utilization in all stands studied in terms of percent of herbage production removed by the sheep was only 7 per cent.

Mountain sheep (*Ovis canadensis canadensis* Shaw), elk (*Cervus canadensis nelsoni* Bailey), and deer (*Odocoileus hemionus hemionus* Rafinesque) all graze the Front Range tundra in summer. Elk and mountain sheep have remained in the Trail Ridge tundra all winter for many years, a behaviour that may be of recent origin resulting from pressure of the human population on their previous ranges at lower elevation. Although no studies have been made of the effects of these animals on the tundra, it seems likely that they would have had a significant influence.

The activities of the pocket gopher (*Thomomys talpoides fossor* Allen) initiates some of the most interesting and important processes in the tundra (Osburn, 1958) and creates a situation in which there is a definite control of vegetation by an animal. Osburn found tundra areas on Niwot Ridge in 1956 where microtines had grazed so heavily that the vegetation appeared to have been mowed. Willard (1960) pursued this observation on Trail Ridge and found that the microtines use and enlarge gopher tunnels for runways and that they often shred cushion plants into minute fragments. Paddock (1961) described the effect of the pika's 'hay' harvesting on the vegetation.

PLANT SUCCESSION

It is difficult to distinguish the effects of grazing from other natural phenomena since the same type of stand may result from both. A stand in which activities of the pocket gopher have left remnants of *Kobresia* sod interspersed with patches of bare gravel and cushion plants probably resembles closely a stand produced by over-grazing. In any event it is clearly evident that sod is susceptible to erosive destruction, but the mineral soil is relatively free from erosion because it is so porous.

The occurrence in tundra of ecosystem change, the replacement of one system by another in time in one site, or plant succession in a general sense, has been questioned by several ecologists. It is obvious, however, that some types of change do occur; they certainly do not have the same characteristics as the process of plant succession in temperate regions, but this is not surprising since the other components of the ecosystem are also different.

Plant reproduction is essential if there is to be any change or recovery in vegetation. Cox (1933) appears to have assumed that seed germination and plant establishment was a regular event in his study area, but Holch et al. (1941) and others have stated that tundra species rarely reproduce by seed, depending almost entirely on vegetative reproduction. Osburn (1961), however, has found a super-abundance of seedlings in each of five successive years in six stands. On Trail Ridge, Willard (1960) found that an abundance of seedlings became established in any stand that became open due to disturbance.

Many processes can cause the soil to be bare and to remain plant-free as long as they are active: such processes are the modification and destruction of plant cover by ground ice heaving and churning, animal grazing and other animal activities. Even after the initial process has ceased, for reasons that are usually obscure, revegetation is inhibited by another process, that of needle-ice activity. In this process (Schramm, 1958) 'combs' of ice crystals up to several inches long form at night in the soil surface. Their elongation pushes a thin frozen crust upward; seedlings held tight in this crust are broken or uprooted. The ice melts, usually the next day, and as the soil particles collapse into the spaces left by the melting ice, many seedlings and young plants are left prostrate on the churned soil surface with their roots stretched, damaged, or broken. Needle ice does not form every night because it requires rather precise conditions of water and rate of temperate change. Eventually, if it fails to occur for a sufficiently long interval, plants can become established. These plants then change the micro-environment enough to prevent needle ice formation. In time a complete plant cover may develop.

The only real time scale we have for ecosystem development is on Trail Ridge. After the earliest road across the tundra was abandoned, engineers scraped the borders and attempted to obliterate all signs of the road. Plants have not worked as fast as the engineers. Today, twenty-six years after the attempt to erase the road, it is still clearly visible. Griggs (1956) studied this road bed for several years and documented the course of revegetation minutely. The only part of the road approaching stability is a segment of hairgrass meadow. Attempts made to revegetate the cut-banks along the new Trail Ridge Road by transplanting strips of sod (Harrington, 1946) have not met with spectacular success. Even after twenty-five years, most of the sod strips are still separated by almost bare soil.

Cox (1933) dealt with the question of succession and climax. He described a variety of vegetation types and believed that many, if not most, of the communities formed successional series that would eventually achieve the *Kobresia* meadow climatic climax. His data do not document positive evidence of change from one community to another, however, and it seems possible that his diagram of successional tendencies is an ordination of climax units separated by various complexes of environmental factors with soil moisture probably being paramount. My own observations provide little reason to expect eventual convergence of the vegetation of many sites through succession to a single climax. It is difficult to interpret some of Cox's data because there is no evidence that he recognized the importance of the activities of the pocket gopher in controlling the nature of the vegetation of a given area.

FUTURE

Any consideration of the Front Range tundra leads to the recognition of the striking fact that it is a relatively natural landscape, a region still free from conspicuous modification by man. There is little doubt that human pressure on this landscape will increase in the future. Grazing pressure will probably decrease still more for a time as the commendable policies of the Forest Service follow conservative lines and reduce grazing until more research has been carried out so that policies will be based on solid foundations. It is likely that pressure for grazing permits will then increase, and there may eventually be even more sheep on our tundra in the future than now. If the Forest Service has its way, however, I believe we can be confident that future grazing will not modify the tundra very much.

It appears to be inevitable that large-scale hydrological engineering will some day take place in our tundra. This tundra rests atop mountains surrounded by relatively arid lowland, parts of which have growing populations and reasonably rich soils. The water needs of both the agriculture and the urban areas are already making close to maximum use of water available from natural runoff and transmountain diversions. Larger amounts of water can be made available during the middle and late summer drought periods, when it is now most deficient, by holding more snow in the tundra that now blows down to a lower elevation, and perhaps by controlling melting of accumulated snow so that some of that which falls in years of plenty can be held over for years of deficiency. One can imagine vast basins of snow and ice, or artificial glaciers, whose melting is controlled by man. Such operations will require considerable changes in the landscape. Let us hope that by that time our basic ecological knowledge will be adequate to enable the engineer to achieve his ends and still leave relatively stable ecosystems.

ACKNOWLEDGMENTS

I am grateful to the United States Army Quartermaster Research and Development Command, the United States Atomic Energy Commission, the University of Colorado, and a long list of graduate and undergraduate research assistants whose contributions have made it possible for me to visit the area periodically in all seasons of the year for the past ten years. I am grateful to William H. Bradley, Eilif Dahl, William S. Osburn, Markley Paddock, and Beatrice Willard for helpful criticisms of the manuscript.

REFERENCES

ALEXANDER A. F. & JENSEN R. (1959) Gross cardiac changes in cattle with high mountain (Brisket) disease and in experimental cattle maintained at high altitudes. *Amer. Jour. Veterinary Research* **20**, 680–689

ALEXANDER G. (1951) The occurrence of orthoptera at high altitudes with special reference to Colorado Acrididae. *Ecol.* **32**, 104–112

BAKER M. M. (1961) The altitudinal distribution of mosquito larvae in the Colorado Front Range. *Trans. Amer. Ent. Soc.*, **87**, 231–246

COX F. (1933) Alpine plant succession on James Peak, Colorado. *Ecol. Monog.* **3**, 299–372

GREGG R. E. (1947) Altitudinal indicators among the Formicidae. *Univ. Colo. Stud. Series D.* **2**, 385–403

GRIGGS R. F. (1956) Competition and succession on a Rocky Mountain fellfield. *Ecol.* **37**, 8–20

HARRINGTON H. D. (1946) Results of a seeding experiment at high altitudes in the Rocky Mountain National Park. *Ecol.* **27**, 375–377

HOLCH A. E., HERTEL E. W., OAKES W. O. & WHITWELL H. H. (1941) Root habits of certain plants of the foothills and alpine belts of the Rocky Mountain National Park. *Ecol. Monog.* **11**, 327–345

IVES R. L. (1942) Early human occupation of the Colorado Headwater Region. *Geographical Review* **32**, 448–462

KIENER W. (1939) Sociological studies of the alpine vegetation on Long's Peak. Unpublished Thesis. Univ. of Nebraska, Lincoln, Nebraska

MARR J. W. (1961) Ecosystems of the east slope of the Front Range in Colorado. *Univ. Colo. Stud. Series in Biology No. 8. Institute of Arctic and Alpine Research Contribution No. 4.*

NELDNER K. H. & PENNAK R. W. (1955) Seasonal faunal variations in a Colorado alpine pond. *Amer. Midl. Nat.* **53**, 419–430

OSBURN W. S. Jr (1958) Ecology of winter snow-free areas of the alpine tundra of Niwot Ridge, Boulder County, Colorado. Unpublished thesis. Univ. Colo. Boulder, Colorado

OSBURN W. S. (1961) Successional potential resulting from differential seedling establishment in alpine tundra stands. (Abstract.) *Bull. Ecol. Soc. Amer.* **42**, 146–147

JOHN W. MARR

OSBURN W. S. (1963) The Dynamics of fallout distribution in a Colorado alpine tundra snow accumulation ecosystem. In *Radioecology*. Schultz, V. and Klement, G.W. Jr. (editors), pp. 51–71. Reinhold Publishing Corporation and American Institute of Biological Sciences.

PADDOCK M. W. (1961) The food habits of the pika, *Ochotona princeps saxatilis* Bangs. Unpublished thesis. Univ. Colo. Boulder, Colorado

PAULSEN H. A. Jr (1960) Plant cover and forage use of alpine sheep ranges in the Central Rocky Mountains. *Iowa State Jour. Sci.* **34,** 731–748

PENNAK R. W. (1955) Comparative limnology of eight Colorado mountain lakes. *Univ. Color. Stud. Series Biology* **2,** 1–75

RETZER J. L. (1956) Alpine soils of the Rocky Mountains. *Jour. Soil Sci.* **7,** 22–32

SCHMITZ E. H. (1959) Seasonal biotic events in two Colorado alpine tundra ponds. *Amer. Midl. Nat.* **61,** 424–446

SCHRAMM J. R. (1958) The mechanism of frost heaving of tree seedlings. *Proc. Amer. Phil. Soc.* **102,** 333–350

TANSLEY A. G. (1935) The use and abuse of vegetational concepts and terms. *Ecology* **16,** 284–307

TAUSSIG W. H. (1962) An ecological study of *Formica neorufibarbis gelida* Wheeler in the alpine tundra of Colorado. Unpublished thesis, Univ. Colo. Boulder, Colorado

WASHBURN A. L. (1956) Classification of patterned ground and review of suggested origins. *Geol. Soc. Amer. Bull.* **67,** 823–866

WILLARD B. E. (1960) The ecology and phytosociology of the tundra curves, Trail Ridge, Colorado. Unpublished thesis, Univ. Colo. Boulder, Colorado

RANGE RELATIONSHIPS OF SOME UNGULATES NATIVE TO BANFF AND JASPER NATIONAL PARKS, ALBERTA

Donald R. Flook

Canadian Wildlife Service, Edmonton, Alberta

ABSTRACT

The range relationships of five ungulate species native to Banff and Jasper National Parks in the Rocky Mountains of Alberta are discussed: mountain goats (*Oreamnos americana*), bighorn sheep (*Ovis canadensis*), mule deer (*Odocoileus hemionus*), moose (*Alces alces*), and elk (*Cervus elaphus*).

The Parks lie almost entirely within the Subalpine and Alpine Phytogeographic Zones. Alpine forage includes grasslike plants, forbs, and browse. Although the Subalpine Zone is characterized by closed canopy coniferous forest, it contains a number of subclimax types which produce herbaceous and browse forage. Fire-produced habitats are prominent. Limited areas of stable grassland occur on arid, low elevation, valley bottoms.

Browse forms the major part of the diet of mule deer and moose whereas mountain goats and bighorn sheep graze predominantly. Elk are intermediate in foraging habits, having demonstrated their ability to thrive on diets predominating in either grasslike plants, or browse and forbs. For that reason, combined with an ability to use a variety of types of terrain and a high fecundity, elk have been a very vigorous competitor in Banff and Jasper Parks and have adversely affected mule deer, bighorn sheep, and moose. Goats, because of their choice of high elevations and very rugged terrain have not been affected by interspecific competition.

INTRODUCTION

Included in the fauna native to Banff and Jasper National Parks in the Rocky Mountains of Alberta, are the five ungulate species: mountain goats (*Oreamnos americana*), bighorn sheep (*Ovis canadensis*), mule deer (*Odocoileus hemionus*), moose (*Alces alces*), and elk (*Cervus elaphus*).

Various environmental factors influence the available forage supply and thus affect the welfare of the animals. Conversely, foraging activities affect the plant cover and result in some cases in intraspecific and interspecific competition.

The purpose of the paper will be to point out the ecological relationships resulting from the foraging activities of the ungulates. In order to do so it will be necessary first to describe the forage producing types of the area, and the niches occupied by the ungulates.

The writer's studies and observations in the area have included parts of each year during 1955-62. Information has been drawn from published and unpublished reports of government fostered studies in the parks as well as studies in other comparable areas.

GEOGRAPHY OF THE AREA

Banff and Jasper Parks together occupy 6,764 square miles, entirely within the Rocky Mountains. The Continental Divide forms their western border and is also the boundary between Alberta and British Columbia. Elevations in the Parks vary from 3,232 feet to 12,294 feet. The mountain ranges run north and south and are bisected by 'U' shaped valleys of several east flowing rivers. Precipitation varies from a low of about 15 inches in eastern valleys to over 30 inches on the Continental Divide. In the eastern valleys, about half the precipitation is rain while in the west, more precipitation falls as snow. Extremes of temperature between summer and winter are characteristic of the area.

VEGETATION IN GENERAL

The two parks lie almost entirely within two phytogeographic zones, the Alpine and the Subalpine Zones. Small areas on the east boundary are in the Boreal Cordilleran Transition Zone (Moss, 1955).

Alpine vegetation occurs between elevational treeline at about 7,000 feet and permanent snow. As the Rockies are very rugged, a large proportion of land surface in the Alpine Zone consists of bare rock and scree. However, much of the vegetated area in the Alpine Zone produces forage including grasslike plants,[1] forbs,[2] and shrubs.

In the Subalpine Zone, climax spruce-fir forest is the most extensive vegetation. In that type *Picea engelmanni* shares the higher elevations with *Abies lasiocarpa* while *Picea glauca* characterizes lower elevations. Two subclimax tree species follow fire in the Subalpine Zone: *Pinus contorta* and aspen, *Populus tremuloides*. *Pinus contorta* occurs extensively over a wide range of elevations. *Populus tremuloides* is restricted to limited stands on better developed soils at lower elevations. Both *Pinus contorta* and *Populus tremuloides* are followed by spruce in plant succession.

---

[1] Grasses, sedges and rushes.
[2] Non grasslike herbs.

FORAGE PRODUCING TYPES OF
THE SUBALPINE ZONE

The aspect of the Subalpine Zone of the Parks is one of a closed canopy coniferous forest which produces very little forage. However, there are in the Subalpine Zone various subclimax types which produce grass and browse forage. For simplicity I have categorized them in five main types: open stands of conifers, fire-produced grass and browse areas, aspen stands, moist shrubby meadows, and avalanche slopes. A brief description of the five types follows.

Open conifer stands

Following removal of climax spruce-fir forest by fire, natural reforestation by conifers is often slow. Until the tree canopy closes, grasses, particularly *Elymus innovatus* and the shrub *Sheperdia canadensis* occupy the area between the trees.

Fire-produced grass and shrub ranges

Reforestation of arid south-facing slopes which have been stripped of tree cover by fires is particularly slow. Such slopes carry a cover of grasses and sedges, in some cases intermixed with shrubs, in particular *Juniperus horizontalis* and *Arctostaphylos uva ursi*. Those slopes which have been burned repeatedly remain in grass-sedge cover for prolonged periods.

Similar conditions occur on burned-over flats, where a gravel substratum under a shallow soil causes arid conditions.

Aspen stands

Young stands of *Populus tremuloides* produce palatable browse if not over-utilized. After the trees have increased in height so that the branches are above the reach of browsing animals, sprouts from the roots continue to produce forage. Palatable shrubby browse species such as *Prunus melanocarpa, Amelanchier alnifolia, Cornus stolonifera,* and certain species of *Salix* are associated with *P. tremuloides.*

Moist shrubby meadows

Characteristic of this type are valley bottom lands with a high water table, carrying stands of *Salix* spp., and *Betula glandulosa,* with a mat of sedges and grasses. Some such areas have resulted from siltation of old beaver dams. Of similar status are flood plains, subject to water table fluctuations and disturbance by changes in stream channels. They frequently support both *Populus tremuloides* and *Populus balsamifera* near the stream banks.

Avalanche slopes

The last range type in the Subalpine Zone results from avalanches. They prevent trees from becoming established on certain slopes, and thus maintain a cover of shrubs and herbaceous plants. Such slopes are of some importance as summer range for large mammals.

STABLE GRASSLAND

In addition to the forage types found in the Alpine and Subalpine Zones, there are isolated areas of grassland in low elevation valley bottoms along the east side of the parks which appear to be stable. The valleys are completely surrounded by wooded slopes which receive moderate precipitation. The grassy valley bottoms themselves, however, probably receive less than 15 inches of precipitation per year. The dominant plants are *Koeleria cristata* and *Carex* spp. Those are low-growing tufted species which tolerate heavy grazing. Their position of dominance over the taller grass species may result from heavy grazing.

NICHES OCCUPIED BY UNGULATES

Mountain goats

Mountain goats are associated with rugged, rocky, escape terrain. The ranges, both summer and winter, are predominantly in the Alpine Zone. However, they also use some habitat in the Subalpine Zone. Those can be grouped in four categories: grassed rockslide slopes; rocky slopes and ledges, with a sparse grass and sedge cover; avalanche slopes and grassed slopes stripped of forest by fire. Fire produced habitat is of less significance to goats than to the other ungulates discussed.

The diet of goats is largely grass-like plants at all times of the year, with forbs and browse of secondary importance (Saunders, 1955).

Goats are well distributed throughout the parks including the heavy snow zone near the Continental Divide. They survive the winter by using exposed ridges or slopes kept relatively snow-free by wind. Their seasonal movements tend to be quite local.

Bighorn sheep

Bighorn sheep are found on grassed slopes close to rough terrain. They use less rugged escape terrain, however, than that usually selected by mountain goats. They graze some areas where the only escape terrain within a half-mile is steep banks of shale or clay.

In summer they range extensively in both the Alpine and Subalpine Zones. However, for winter range, absence of snow depths greater than a few inches is essential, as their diet at that time of year is largely low-growing forage plants. As a result, most bighorn winter ranges have a southern exposure, where the direct sunlight rapidly dissipates the snow cover. Some sheep winter in the Alpine Zone, but at least half the population winters in the Subalpine Zone. Most of the subalpine range has been produced by fire. However some sheep forage in winter on grasses under restricted open stands of *Pseudotsuga menziesii*.

The summer diet of bighorn sheep is quite variable, but on the average, grasslike plants make up slightly less than half the total, followed by forbs and browse in that order of importance. Legumes are grazed commonly in summer, particularly *Hedysarum mackenzii*, *Astragalus* spp., and *Oxytropis* spp. The winter bighorn diet is largely grasslike plants, with forbs and browse of secondary importance (Cowan, 1947; Wishart, 1958).

Mule deer

Mule deer occur in the valley bottoms and on slopes of moderate gradient. They are predominantly browsers, and use forest cover for escape. As a result, they are associated with shrubby areas and forest edges.

Snow influences mule deer survival by reducing the availability of the lower browse plants and, particularly if crusted, by impeding their travel. To avoid deep snow some mule deer exhibit local seasonal movements from extensive summer ranges in the upper Subalpine Zone to restricted winter ranges in the lower valley bottoms. Some deer remain in the lower valley bottoms throughout the year.

The summer diet of mule deer in the area is largely browse and forbs. Grasses are used early in the season when their new growth is the only succulent forage available. Forbs are important until August. As they become withered at that time, browse becomes the main component (Shepherd, 1960).

The winter diet of mule deer is predominantly browse, with smaller amounts of forbs, and grasslike plants. The preferred browse species are *Prunus melanocarpa*, *Amelanchier alnifolia*, *Cornus stolonifera*, *Populus tremu-*

loides, and *Salix* spp. (Shepherd, 1960). In earlier periods, fire converted climax coniferous forest to productive deer range dominated by *P. tremuloides* with the other aforementioned preferred browse species. However, on most light snow winter ranges in the parks, those species have since been depleted or eliminated by elk. On depleted winter ranges the deer diet is still predominantly browse, but the animals have turned to the low palatability browse species: *Arctostophylos uva ursi, Sheperdia canadensis, Juniperus horizontalis*, and *Pseudotsuga menziesii* (Cowan, 1947).

Moose

Moose, throughout the year, are frequently associated with Subalpine moist shrubby meadows which support stands of willow and dwarf birch. They also utilize' fire-produced aspen ranges throughout the year, and avalanche slopes in the summer. In summer they favour ranges near streams and shallow lakes. They wade into the water to forage upon aquatic vegetation, and also to seek refuge from biting flies (Flook, 1959).

Moose are predominantly browsers at all times of the year, preferred species being: *Populus tremuloides, Salix* spp., *Betula glandulosa, Cornus stolonifera, Amelanchier alnifolia*, and *Prunus melanocarpa*. In summer, aquatic plants are highly preferred, but because their supply is limited, they make up a small part of the total diet. They include such emergent plants as sedges, and *Equisetum* spp. and such submergents as *Potamogeton* spp. and *Hippuris* spp. (Mair, 1952; Millar, 1953). In winter, coarse grasses and sedges are used to a minor extent.

Moose show selectivity as to species of *Salix* as was noted at a fenced exclosure in a moose wintering area in Banff Park. Inside the exclosure the species *S. glauca* and *S. macalliana* were of about equal height. As the moose prefer *S. macalliana*, it was suppressed outside the exclosure to the point of being shorter than *S. glauca* which was browsed very little.

Moose tolerate greater snow depths than the other cervids. They are solitary, and one or two animals can browse all winter in a limited area.

Elk

Elk in Banff and Jasper Parks are found in the widest variety of habitats of any of the ungulates. They are associated with grassland and shrubby areas interspersed with forest on both valley bottoms and mountain slopes. For escape, they make use of both forest cover and hilly terrain. In summer they occur throughout the Subalpine Zone, and occasionally in the lower Alpine Zone. Those elk which summer at high elevations migrate as far as forty miles to winter ranges at lower elevations to the east. Others remain at fairly low elevations throughout the year.

Where browse is adequate, elk are better able to cope with deep snow than are mule deer, but not as well as moose. They are sometimes forced by deep snow to evacuate areas in which moose, sharing the same range, may remain.

Elk in Banff and Jasper Parks now subsist primarily on grass-like plants throughout the year. Browse is of secondary importance in summer, and of very minor importance in winter. *Populus tremuloides*, and other preferred browse species were depleted by an overpopulation of elk in the 1930's and 1940's. Before that time, they no doubt made up a significant portion of the diet. The browse used now is mainly *Salix* spp. and species of lower palatability such as *Sheperdia canadensis*, and *Arctostaphylos uva ursi*.

Elk are able to adjust their foraging habits to a marked degree. In Elk Island Park, Alberta (Holsworth, 1960), and in Riding Mountain Park, Manitoba, elk food habits are quite different from those of elk in the Rocky Mountains. In those parks, *P. tremuloides* is the dominant species. Other browse plants are abundant, and there is a well developed forb layer under the tree canopy. In both those areas, browse and forbs together comprise the major part of the summer diet, and browse alone makes up most of the winter diet.

ECOLOGICAL RELATIONSHIPS

The food habits of mountain goats are similar to those of bighorn sheep. However, because of the goats' choice of higher elevations and more rugged terrain their ranges overlap only slightly and competition for food is of little significance. As most goat range is perpetuated by climatic conditions, or by geological erosion, fire is of little importance in creating habitat. Information on goat population trends is scanty, but no marked fluctuations are known to have occurred within the history of the area.

Elk have been the most vigorous competitors in the parks and have adversely affected mule deer, moose and bighorn sheep. That can be best demonstrated by briefly reviewing a chain of events over the past eighty years.

Shortly before 1880, elk were abundant in the foothills of the Rockies, and occurred in the eastern parts of what is now Banff and Jasper Parks. They disappeared from most of that area in the 1880's. The causes were not documented but it seems likely that severe winters were implicated. A very small relic herd survived in the Brazeau watershed in Jasper Park (Millar, 1915).

Banff Park was established in 1885, and Jasper Park in 1907. In 1915 goats were apparently numerous, bighorn sheep, mule deer, and moose, less so, and only the one small herd of elk was present (Millar, 1915).

There are records of widespread forest fires in the parks in the period from about 1880 until 1935. While forest fires were no doubt a regular occurrence before that time, they apparently increased in the interval of railroad construction and settlement. They extended the grassland and browse ranges.

Releases of elk from Yellowstone Park were made in Banff and Jasper Parks between 1918 and 1920 (Lloyd, 1927). From those animals, together with the relic herd in Jasper and elk emigrating from British Columbia, elk in the parks increased as did moose, deer, and sheep, and began to occupy the new ranges created as a result of fires. By 1939, elk and moose were still dispersing to fill new ranges. All four species were numerous, with elk probably being present in greatest numbers. Signs of damage to aspen were noted in the main valleys (Clarke, 1940).

For the next few years elk continued to increase and range conditions became more critical. The low elevation, light snowfall browse ranges were damaged most. There the preferred shrubs were severely hedged or killed, lower branches of *P. tremuloides* trees were removed and their sprouts were cropped to snow level.

Because their winter range was restricted to the depleted, low snowfall, browse areas, mule deer suffered in particular.

Moose as well as deer were directly affected by elk through reduction in the supply of winter browse. Elk have affected moose in another less significant way through their effect on beaver (Mair, 1952). Beaver, by damming streams, created ponds which produced aquatic plants preferred by moose. *P. tremuloides* is the key food for beaver. Elk, by selective browsing on it, have prevented replacement of the trees cut by beaver. As the *P. tremuloides* supply near the streams has become exhausted, the beaver have abandoned them, the dams have fallen into disrepair, the water levels have dropped, and the ponds are no longer favourable for moose. Thus, directly and indirectly moose numbers in the lower valleys have been limited as a result of the browsing activity of elk.

Elk have damaged some grassland ranges although to a lesser extent than is the case in the aspen stands. The south facing grassed slopes in the Subalpine Zone have been most affected. Elk use those slopes at all times of the year, but particularly in winter, when they are one of the few types of range that is relatively free of snow, and in spring when they are the first areas on which grasses have produced new growth. Spring grazing is especially damaging to the grass cover and top soil. On those slopes there is a large range of overlap between elk and sheep, and where the grass and sedge cover has been depleted there has been direct competition for food. For example in 1948, a winter of excessive snowfall, range depletion is thought to have contributed to a heavy winter mortality of both sheep and elk in Jasper Park. Elk reached a peak of population in the two parks in the early 1940's. The problem of range depletion was recognized at that time, and programmes of herd reduction were begun. Since that time elk harvests have been carried out annually by park wardens, as many as 700 animals having been removed in Jasper Park, and 400 in Banff Park, in a single winter. The elk population was effectively reduced and is now being held at a fairly stable level. In the past few years 200 elk have been removed annually in Banff Park. In Jasper Park the elk population has remained at a moderate level over the past four years without any harvest. There, timber wolves (*Canis lupus*) have recently increased under protection and are accounting for much of the annual increment of elk.

Grassland ranges have shown improvement following the reduction of elk numbers, whereas the aspen stands have never recovered sufficiently to tolerate continued use.

Concerning the relative abundance of the five ungulate species in the two parks, elk, bighorn sheep, and mountain goats are all fairly numerous and probably rank in that order of abundance. Moose are less common, and mule deer are present in the smallest numbers.

Spruce is gradually becoming established on the ranges which have been created by forest fires, and those areas will eventually revert to a climax forest. A well implemented policy of forest fire control in the parks is now preventing the creation of any extensive new ranges. Thus if total forest protection is continued, we must expect a reduction in range land and in the numbers of elk, moose, deer and bighorn sheep.

In conclusion, browse forms the major part of the diet of mule deer and moose whereas mountain goats and bighorn sheep graze predominantly. Elk are intermediate in foraging habits, having demonstrated their ability to thrive on diets predominating in either grasslike plants, or browse and forbs. For that reason, combined with an ability to use a variety of types of terrain and a high fecundity, elk have been a very vigorous competitor in Banff and Jasper Parks and have adversely affected mule deer, bighorn sheep, and moose.

REFERENCES

CLARKE C.H.D. (1940) *Wildlife Investigation in Banff National Park*, 1939. Mimeo. report to Dept., Mines and Resources, Ottawa

COWAN I. McT. (1947) Range competition between mule deer, bighorn sheep, and elk in Jasper Park, Alberta. *Trans. Twelfth North Amer. Wildl. Conf.*, pp. 223–227

FLOOK D.R. (1959) Moose using water as refuge from flies. *J. Mamm.* **40**, 455

HOLSWORTH W.N. (1960) Interactions between moose, elk, and buffalo in Elk Island National Park, Alberta. Unpublished thesis, Univ. British Columbia, Vancouver

LLOYD H. (1927) Transfers of elk for re-stocking. *Can. Field Nat.* **41**, 126–127

MAIR W.W. (1952) The impact of an introduced population of elk upon the biota of Banff National Park. Unpublished thesis, Univ. British Columbia, Vancouver

MILLAR J.B. (1953) An ecological study of the moose in the Rock Lake area of Alberta. Unpublished thesis, Univ. Alberta, Edmonton

MILLAR W.N. (1915) The big game of the Canadian Rockies. In *Proceedings of Meeting of Committee on Fisheries, Game, and Fur-bearing Animals*, pp. 100–124. Commission of Conservation, Canada. Ottawa

MOSS E.H. (1955) The vegetation of Alberta. *Bot. Rev.* **21**, 493–567

SAUNDERS J.K. (1955) Food habits and range use of the Rocky Mountain goat in the Crazy Mountains, Montana. *J. Wildl. Mgnt.* **19**, 429–437

SHEPHERD D.H. (1960) The ecology of the mule deer of the Sheep River Region. Unpublished thesis, Univ. Alberta, Edmonton

WISHART W.D. (1958) The bighorn of the Sheep River valley. Unpublished thesis Univ. Alberta, Edmonton

THE EFFECTS OF GRAZING ON THE BOGONG HIGH PLAINS, VICTORIA[1]

STELLA G.M. CARR

Department of Botany, Queen's University, Belfast

A quantitative study was begun in 1945 involving comparison of grassland communities which have been protected from stock with others on which grazing has continued.

The results obtained to date show that selective grazing of the herb component of the swards and trampling of shrubs prevent regeneration in the communities studied and in some cases completely alters their character. In areas protected from stock, improvement in the physical properties of the soil has been recorded. Bulk density has decreased, the percentage content of organic matter and field capacity have increased.

The area discussed is an important alpine catchment in S. E. Australia, latitude 37° S and elevation 5,400–6,200 ft. Although the greater part of the area appears to be well vegetated, the vegetation shows degenerative changes which are identified as the early stages of accelerated erosion. Some of the deterioration is due to past fires but, as much of the area has never been burnt, grazing is thought to be responsible for the observed damage. The area has been used for summer grazing for 100 years but before European settlement the fauna was insect dominated.

The major plant communities of the area are:

(*a*) Those associated with a high water table, viz., peat bogs around springs and along water-courses. The vegetation of these areas consists of shrubs and sedges rooted in an acid peat and has one species of sphagnum as its major component.

(*b*) Those associated with well-drained soils. These are mainly communities dominated by *Poa caespitosa* to which shrubs and herbs make variable contributions. Some shrub communities occur on shallow soils.

[1] Summary only.

SHEEP GRAZING

FACTORS WITHIN PLANT ASSOCIATIONS AFFECTING THE BEHAVIOUR AND PERFORMANCE OF GRAZING ANIMALS

G. W. Arnold

C.S.I.R.O. Division of Plant Industry, Canberra, A.C.T.

ABSTRACT

Grazing animals select leaf in preference to stem, and green in preference to dry material either because the selected material is higher in nitrogen, sugar and phosphate and lower in fibre, or because the differences in chemical composition are associated with physical characteristics of selected parts of the plant. The reasons for a high preference ranking for one species may be quite different from those for another species.

The total available dry matter and that available so far as the animal is concerned may differ. Selective grazing of pastures may result in the animals restricting their grazing to a small proportion only of the total area available and thus limit animal production from the pasture as a whole.

The interrelationships between pasture on offer, grazing time, bites per minute and intake per hour of grazing by sheep are discussed. Decreasing pasture availability results in increased grazing time and rate of eating; eventually a point is reached where total intake begins to decrease. On *Phalaris* – annual grasses – subterranean clover pasture this point would appear to be at about 850 lb dry matter per acre. On this pasture type intake was found to decrease at high levels of pasture availability because, it is suggested, the structure of the pasture prevented normal grazing.

Finally, the results of a sheep grazing experiment are described and the reasons for seasonal changes in animal production are discussed in the light of the reactions of the grazing animal to the particular pasture type used.

INTRODUCTION

In the past fifty years a considerable fund of knowledge on how to grow better quality, higher producing pastures and on the digestion and metabolism of ruminants, has been established. Various systems of grazing management have been devised for the better utilization of herbage and for higher animal production. On mesophytic pastures none of these have proved significantly superior to continuous grazing (Wheeler, 1960). This lack of success in improving the utilization of herbage under grazing conditions indicates a weak link in our knowledge of the response of grazing animals to plant communities. An understanding of the mechanisms oper-

ating in the selection and harvesting of food by grazing animals is surely
basic to the study of their nutrition and productivity.

The principal reasons for this lack of knowledge are the complexity of
the relationships between grazing animals and plant communities, the
virtual impossibility of controlling more than a few of the variables, and

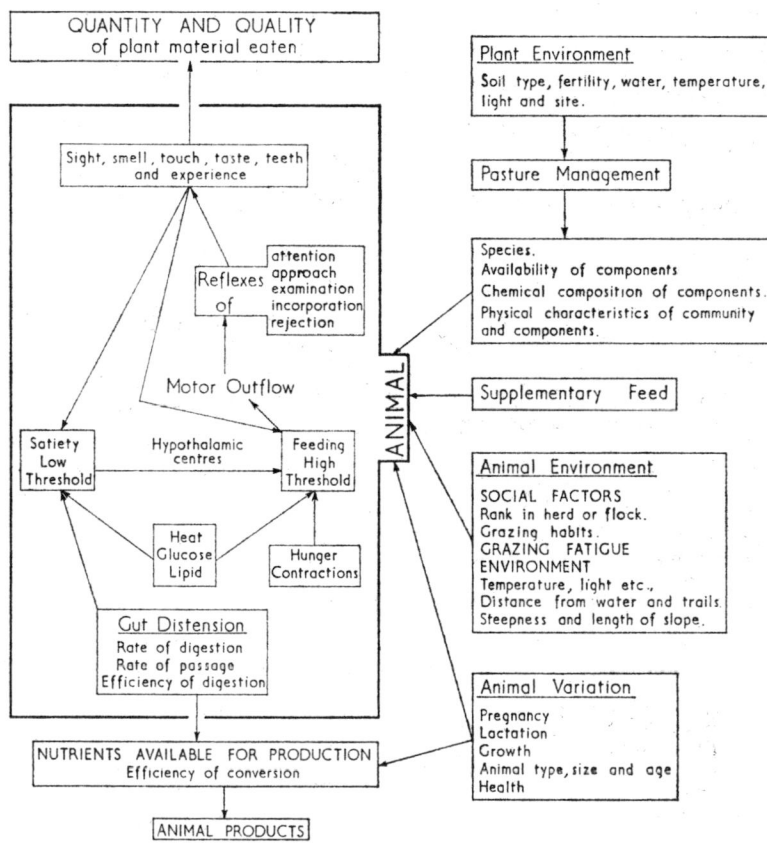

FIG. 1. The complexity of soil-plant-animal relationships (source — Arnold,
1962a).

lack of techniques. The development of oesophageal fistulation in both
sheep and cattle and the use of electronic apparatus on grazing animals
have opened the way to more precise and detailed study of the diet and
behaviour of grazing animals in the future. It is, therefore, important to
review what is known at present.

Figure 1 summarizes the many factors that can influence the quantity and quality of plant material eaten by grazing animals. The diet of the grazing animal will finally be controlled by its brain centres. This central control of diet has been summarized by Brobeck (1957)—'The function of the central nervous system is to gather all these reactions (to environmental and metabolic conditions) up into a common denominator, viz., the excitability of neurons having to do with all of the several components of feeding behaviour—everything from searching for food to discrimination among possible sources of nourishment and on to the actual processing of the diet within the digestive tract.'

However, this paper will be restricted to the plant environment and factors within it that affect the diet and productivity of the grazing animal; animal factors will only be discussed where they have a direct bearing on the animals' reaction to plants. Emphasis will be on recent work with sheep in temperate Australia.

II. SELECTION OF PLANT MATERIAL

It has long been recognized that grazing animals eat particular plants or graze particular plant communities with relish but reject others. There has been general agreement that sheep and cattle select leaf in preference to stem (Arnold, 1960a; 1962a; Cook and Harris, 1950; Reppert, 1960) and green (or young) material in preference to dry (or old) material (Arnold, 1962a; Cook, Stoddart and Harris, 1956; Cowlishaw and Alder, 1960; Milton, 1953; Reppert, 1960; Stapledon, 1934). Physiologically younger material, may be preferred because it is generally shorter or because it differs in chemical composition from older material.

The selected material, compared with the material from which it is selected, is usually higher in nitrogen (Arnold, 1960a; Cook et al., 1956; Hardison, Reid, Martin and Woolfolk, 1954; Weir and Torell, 1959), phosphate (Cook et al., 1956; Plice, 1952; Staten, 1949), sugars (Plice, 1952) and gross energy (Cook et al., 1956). Fibre is lower (Hardison et al., 1954; Weir and Torell, 1959) as would be expected since nitrogen is higher. Opinions differ whether selected material is higher in minerals.

The question arises whether green and leaf materials are preferred *because* they contain more nitrogen, soluble carbohydrate and phosphate and less fibre than older materials and stem, or whether the differences in chemical composition merely *associated* with physical characteristics of the selected plant parts.

The numerous experiments carried out either to test plant species for acceptability or to study the causes of preferences have been reviewed recently by Arnold (1962a). The evidence available indicates that preferences of animals for particular strains or species are rarely associated with their nitrogen or fibre contents but that dry matter, phosphate and soluble carbohydrate contents may influence preferences. Even where there is little difference between species in chemical composition or stage of growth, distinct preferences by sheep are frequently found. Preferences amongst a number of grass species, studied in the vegetative stage of growth by Arnold, Bush and Chapman (unpublished data) are given in Table 1. None of the chemical or physical attributes of the species studied was related to the marked preferences shown by sheep.

TABLE 1

Differences in preferences by sheep for grasses in the vegetative stage of growth

Species	Number of Strains	Initial leaf length (in.) 3.5.61	N % in herbage DM 3.5.61	N.A.F. % in herbage DM 3.5.61	% reduction in leaf length in 4 weeks
Dactylis glomerata	15	7·4	2·78	29·3	40·0
Arrhenatherum spp.	4	7·5	2·83	23·9	39·8
Hordeum bulbosum	8	6·6	2·94	29·5	34·8
Bromus inermis	9	7·0	2·41	27·6	32·1
Phalaris spp.	9	7·1	2·44	28·9	29·4
Festuca spp.	12	8·8	2·35	27·0	24·4
Bromus spp.	4	8·8	2·52	27·6	24·3
Lolium spp.	7	5·8	2·45	24·9	20·8
Phalaris tuberosa	14	7·9	2·57	26·5	19·2
Other species	9	7·1	2·64	29·3	12·5

Note: N.A.F. %=normal acid fibre. The experiment was carried out in late autumn to winter when growth was very slow and thus would not have been likely to influence the results.

Roe and Mottershead (1961) extracted an unknown compound from preferred strains of Phalaris arundinacea which increased the consumption of disliked strains of this species when they were sprayed with it. However, the frequently found inter- and intra-specific variation in preferences can rarely be tied down to a specific factor. This is not really surprising since preferences will be determined through the animal's special senses. The animal will receive stimuli from the various attributes of a plant and make a comparison of its favourable and unfavourable characteristics with that of another species. Thus the reasons for a high preference ranking for one species or strain may be quite different from those for another species. Preferences will be modified by the animal's previous experience and food requirements.

What can be said is that there are certain characteristics that increase the chances of a species being liked and others that have the reverse effect. It is important to establish the influence that these characteristics have on the diet, and hence the productivity of the animal, and the effects that the animal has on a plant community.

III. AVAILABILITY OF PLANT MATERIAL TO THE ANIMAL

The discussion, so far, has been restricted to selection of plant materials where animals have a simple choice to make between species or plant parts. Under normal grazing conditions however, the situation is more complex; plant species will be intermingled and the animal, by its selective grazing, may alter the composition of the plant community and thus be forced to alter its choice of material. One of the most important aspects of selective grazing is that it will influence the plant material actually 'available to the animal' and thus affect not only the quantity and quality of plant material eaten but also the utilization of total material available.

Because of the differential acceptability of the components of a plant community the total amount of herbage on offer is rarely, as far as the animal is concerned, the amount apparently available. Also, the very presence of some disliked species can strongly influence the utilization of liked species. This has been demonstrated for a wide variety of plant associations (*Ann. Rep. Rocky Mt. For. Range Exp. Sta.*, 1955, 1956, 1959; Glendenning, 1944; Milton, 1933, 1953; Phillips and Pfeiffer, 1958).

In pastures the presence of dry material has an important effect on utilization and on what is selected. The diet is selected almost exclusively from the green components (Arnold, 1962a) when pastures are mainly green. As the percentage of dry material in the pasture increases the animals are unable to eat an entirely green diet without decreasing their total intake. In a recent experiment we found that even with a high grazing pressure on a pasture containing 50 per cent dry material, the sheeps' diet contained 70 per cent green components. There was, however, an almost complete suppression of preferences amongst green components as a result. The greatest amount of green dry matter (DM) was removed from those species mixtures that had initially the greatest amount of DM (Arnold, 1962a). When the grazing pressure is low the amount of dry material present in a pasture can prevent the utilization of green components. This is particularly the case when the green grass leaves are 'protected' by the dry stubble and thus are not grazed.

When grazing, sheep and cattle move in a horizontal plane and select in a vertical plane (Arnold, 1960a). This fact is basic to an understanding of selective grazing. The actual structure of a pasture can influence the diet by preventing normal grazing and thus affecting selection. It is much more difficult for sheep to graze on a tall dense stand of forage than on a short dense stand. In late spring and in summer the structure of *Phalaris*—annual grasses (*Bromus* spp.; *Hordeum* spp.)—subterranean clover pastures, which are widely grown in S.E. Australia, is frequently unsuited to sheep grazing. In summer when understocked the green *Phalaris*, which would normally be preferred, was enmeshed in dry grass and although there may be 500 lb green DM per acre available in this pasture, virtually none is eaten. In February 1961 the mean organic matter intake (OMI) of sheep grazing such a pasture was significantly lower than that of sheep grazing similar pastures at higher stocking levels (see Table 2). It is suggested that since the quality of the diets of all groups of sheep was similar, as evidenced by

TABLE 2

Intake of sheep grazing dry *Phalaris* – annual grasses – subterranean clover pastures
(February, 1961)

	Sheep per acre			
	2	4	6	9
Mean N per cent in faecal OM	2·05	1·96	1·98	1·98
Mean daily OMI (g)	465	600	727	694
DM per acre (lb)	3406	2634	1917	853
Per cent green grass	19·1	9·4	8·6	9·1
Per cent dry grass	80·8	83·9	79·0	79·4
Per cent dry clover	0·1	6·7	12·4	11·0
N per cent in pasture DM	1·20	1·77	1·81	1·81

Source of data — Arnold and McManus (unpublished)
OM = Organic matter
OMI = Organic matter intake
DM = Dry matter

the faecal nitrogen values, and since the botanical compositions of the pastures were not greatly dissimilar, the differences in intake were largely caused by pasture structure and its effect on the sheeps' ability to graze properly.

Figure 2 shows the mean changes in the amounts of each component of the available DM and the botanical composition of the diet of sheep

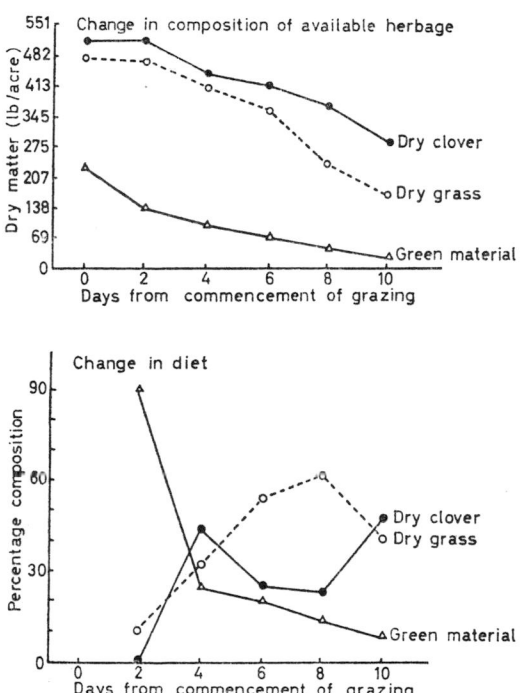

FIG. 2. Selective grazing of dry pasture (source—Arnold, 1962a).

rotationally grazing a pasture similar to that described above; the grazing period was ten days. The amount of green material and dry grass initially declined more rapidly than that of dry clover, and the diet contained progressively more dry clover and less green material. It is also apparent that the sheep did not consume all the available green material before eating other components. The clover formed a layer close to the ground below any green shoots with the dry grass forming an almost enveloping web around the other components; the dry grass was thus the most readily available plant material. Some of the green material and much of the dry clover only became readily available when some of the dry grass had been eaten. It is probable, therefore, that the dry clover made little contribution to the diet initially because of the structure of the pasture and not because it was disliked.

The position of a plant in relation to the topographical and physical features of the country can also exert considerable influence on the degree to which it is utilized. Glendenning (1944) demonstrated that distance from a watering place, distance from a trail, and steepness and length of slope can have an important effect on the utilization of a plant community. He might have added distance from shade, which is important in much of Australia. Aspect can also be important: Hercus (1961) found that grazing pressure in winter on Otago hill country is concentrated on sunny faces no matter what quantity and quality of herbage is available on adjoining shaded aspects.

It follows that the amount of plant material 'available' to the grazing animal may be determined as much by the animal as by climate and soil fertility and it need not in any way be related to the total DM per acre on offer. By selective grazing the animal will frequently reduce the area of pasture that it will graze because uneaten areas become progressively less attractive. As pasture growth slows, the amount present on the grazed areas of pasture rapidly decreases and, unless previously neglected areas are eaten, food intake must decline. All too frequently the latter occurs. Thus, as a result of highly selective grazing in winter on heavily stocked *Phalaris* —annual grasses—subterranean clover pastures in Canberra, intake was reduced because the sheep refused to eat what appeared to be highly nitri tious herbage on the ungrazed areas. This phenomenon has, of course, important effects on animal production. In a study of management systems for fat lamb production (Arnold and Bush, 1962), we have found that any advantage accruing from restricting ewes to a proportion of the total available area, in order to provide a creep grazing area of pasture for the lambs, was frequently lost because the lambs selectively grazed the creep area. Table 3 gives the percentage of the creep areas that were being grazed, and the DM available on grazed and ungrazed areas, in October 1961 when the lambs had been grazing the areas for eight weeks. At the high stocking rate the lambs were grazing predominantly on 33 per cent of the total area available. The grazed areas by 16.10.61 had only 609 lb DM per acre, at which level intake was insufficient to maintain rapid weight gains, whilst ungrazed areas had 2,714 lb DM per acre.

TABLE 3

Selectivity of grazing by lambs (October, 1961)

	Low stocking rate	High stocking rate
Per cent of total area being grazed	16·6	33·0
Yield of DM on grazed areas (lb/ac.)	1260	609
Yield of DM on ungrazed areas (lb/ac.)	2215	2714
Mean DM yield (lb/ac.)	2056	2019

Note: Each value is the mean of 4 plots; data from Arnold and Bush (unpublished).

IV. THE HARVESTING OF FORAGE

Availability implies that the plant material can readily be removed by the grazing animal. Their preference for leaf rather than stem could be explained in these terms. In grazing uniform rows of herbage the sheep moves across the herbage and, providing it is acceptable, removes the uppermost parts. Having done this the process is repeated until the rows of grass are tightly grazed. This process rarely operates on a pasture since it is usually uneven and the acceptability of the herbage varies. The sheep will remove material from favoured areas but in doing so reduces the depth of herbage gradually. A favoured area is not usually eaten from six inches to ground level at once, but gradually becomes more tightly grazed. It is rare for sheep to graze from the bottom of a pasture upwards in the sense of biting whole grass or clover leaves off at their bases.

When grazing short green pasture each bite encompasses a number of leaves and part of each is consumed. On pasture where the green herbage present was enveloped by dry grass and therefore was not being eaten, it could not be selected and grazed upon in the normal way, since each bite would have taken in few leaves and intake per hour of grazing would have been extremely low. In order to satisfy the appetite in such situations, it is possible that normal preferences must be abandoned and material chosen that will provide a reasonable intake per hour of grazing.

In fairly short green pasture conditions Arnold (1960b) has shown that grazing time on green *Phalaris*—annual grasses—subterranean clover pasture increased linearly as the amount of pasture on offer decreased. Grazing time was more closely related to the green DM than to the total DM on offer. As green DM per acre decreased from 2,200 lb to 700 lb, grazing time increased from 7·0 to 10·3 hours. Individual grazing times of 13 hours were recorded on very scant pasture. But there must be a limit beyond which the increase in grazing time does not compensate for the shortage of pasture and intake cannot be maintained. We have some evidence that grazing time begins to decline when there is less than 500 lb green DM per acre on offer on this type of pasture.

The relationships between intake per hour, bites per minute and the amount of pasture on offer will of course vary. Animal condition and food

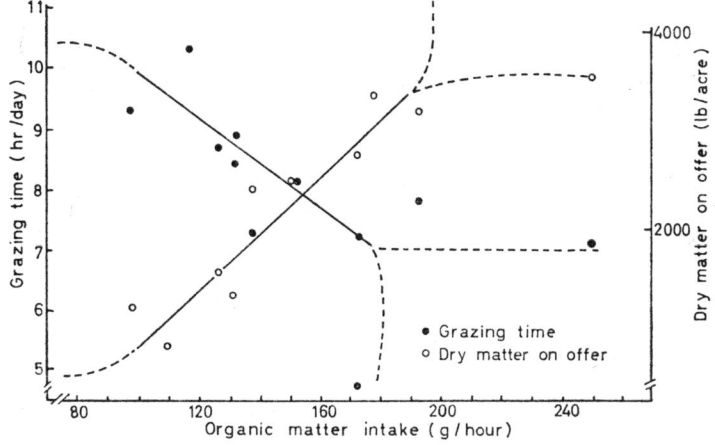

FIG. 3. Relationships between grazing time, pasture yield and intake per hour of grazing.
Note: The solid lines have been fitted to the points by eye. The dotted lines indicate the possible direction of the curves the reasons for which are discussed in the text.

requirement as well as the type of pasture will be variables that need consideration. On *Phalaris*—annual grasses—subterranean clover pastures we have found that the number of bites per minute changes with both the quantity and quality of pasture on offer, being highest on short green pasture in winter (60–80) and lowest on abundant dry pasture in summer (25–40).

Intake per hour of grazing increases rapidly as the amount of pasture on offer increases so that 200 g OM per hour are consumed when the pasture on offer amounts to 2,500 lb DM per acre. Above this level the relationship will be strongly influenced by animal demand because grazing time will plateau out around seven hours per day and by adjusting bites per minute the animal can alter intake per hour of grazing. This is shown in Fig. 3 (black circles). The point for 250 g OMI per hour was for lactating ewes; had wethers been presented with 5,000 lb DM per acre, intake per hour of grazing would possibly have remained at 200 g. Allden (1962) recently reported very similar relationships for sheep grazing ryegrass— subterranean clover pasture; the maximum rate of intake of DM occurring at values greater than 2,000 lb green DM per acre.

The relationship between grazing time and intake per hour of grazing is also shown in Fig. 3 (open circles). Intake per hour of grazing decreases rapidly as grazing time increases because high grazing time is associated with low pasture availability, and lower intake per bite is not fully com- pensated by increase in bites per minute. On abundant pasture a high food requirement could be met by maintaining grazing time at a minimum (7 hr) and increasing bites per minute; it may be possible for animals with a low food requirement to maintain bites per minute and decrease grazing time.

The data presented in Fig. 3 are scant and derived from one type of pasture; however, the suggested interrelationships of pasture on offer, grazing time, bites per minute and intake per hour of grazing appear to be supported by Allden's (1962) findings. They are summarized in Table 4.

TABLE 4

Interrelationships of four variables of grazing behaviour

P = Pasture on offer	L	<1000			
(lb/acre)	M	1000–2500			
	H	>2500	$P_L \rightarrow G_H$	B_H	I_L
G = Grazing time (hr)	L	$<7 \cdot 5$			
	M	$7 \cdot 5 – 8 \cdot 5$	$P_M \rightarrow G_M$	B_M	I_M
	H	$>8 \cdot 5$			
B = Bites per minute	L	<45	$P_H \rightarrow G_L$	B_L	I_H
	M	45–65			
	H	>65			
I = Intake per hour of grazing (g OM)	L	<120			
	M	120–150			
	H	>150			

Note: Pasture on offer is not necessarily the amount the animal considers 'available'. The effect of Low (L) Medium (M) and High (H) levels of pasture on offer on the other three variables are shown in the box.

V. HERBAGE INTAKE

The quantity of herbage eaten by grazing animals has been only briefly mentioned so far. It will be influenced not only by the food demand of the animal, grazing behaviour and the structure and amount of pasture on offer but also by the effects of the chemical characteristics of the herbage eaten on rumen physiological processes.

High moisture content herbage can reduce voluntary intake. Both Arnold (1962b) and Lloyd Davies (1961, 1962) have reported this for sheep with cut herbage fed in pens. There appears to be a linear relationship

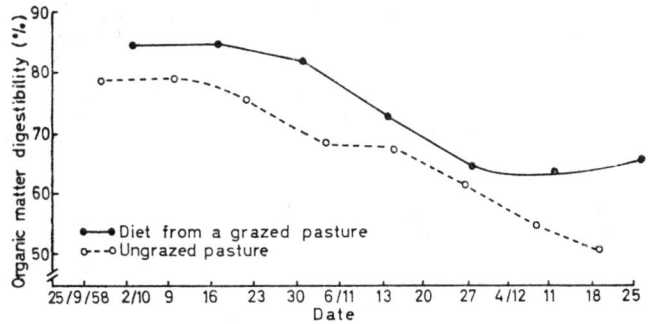

FIG. 4. Changes in the digestibility of *Phalaris* — subterranean clover pasture with advancing maturity (source — Arnold, 1962b).

between voluntary DM intake and the DM content of herbage from 10 to 28 per cent. Above this level Arnold (1962b) found no relationship between these two variables. Milford (1960) reported that the DMI of tropical grasses was negatively correlated with their DM content but suggested that this was probably due to leaching of nutrients from dead tissue. Paltridge (1955) found that the weight gain of sheep grazing sown pastures in south-eastern Queensland was fairly closely associated with the moisture content of the pasture available and suggested that sheep made low weight gains on high moisture content green pasture because they were unable to consume sufficient dry matter. Intake may have been restricted because of limitations, (a) in the bulk capacity of the rumen, or (b) in the elimination of water from the system. Nevertheless, the animal can greatly increase voluntary DMI, even of forage of extremely low DM content, in response to the increase nutrient demand of lactation (Lloyd Davies, 1961).

Low mineral content forage frequently depresses appetite and this has received considerable attention by workers in the United States in recent years. It is also well established that prolonged grazing of forage low in cobalt leads to extreme inappetence (Underwood, 1956). Excessive or low levels of various other trace elements in forage (copper, molybdenum and selenium) can also derange metabolism and forage intake.

The rate and extent to which the DM digestibility of herbage declines with advancing maturity varies with the species and the environment, but there appears to be a well-defined pattern for nearly all species in that digestibility remains high until the onset of flowering (Arnold, 1962b; Minson, Raymond and Harris, 1960). The change in digestibility for a

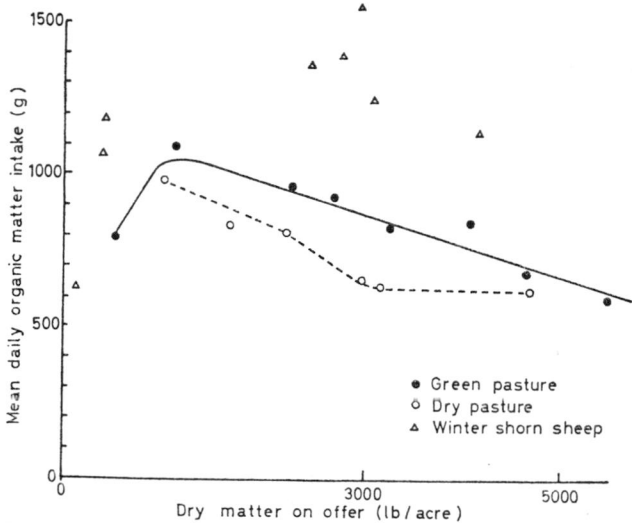

FIG. 5. Relationship between pasture on offer and intake (source — Arnold, 1962a).
Note: Considerably higher intake of sheep following winter shearing at all levels of pasture on offer.

Phalaris—annual grasses—subterranean clover pasture with advancing maturity is shown in Fig. 4. The digestibility of the diet of sheep grazing a similar pasture did not decline at the same time nor to the same extent as that of ungrazed pasture. This is due to (a) selective grazing of more digestible components and (b) grazing maintaining the herbage in a younger stage of growth.

With advancing maturity there is an increase in the amount of structural tissues in the plant. The cellulose cell walls become coated with lignin which is virtually indigestible. McCullough (1956), Brannon, Reid and

11

Miller (1954), Spahr, Kesler, Bratzler and Washko (1961), and Blaxter, Wainman and Wilson (1961) all found that the voluntary DMI of forages is related to the apparent digestibility of the DM or energy content of the forage.

At Canberra we have investigated the relationship between the amount of pasture on offer and the intake of sheep grazing *Phalaris*—annual grasses —subterranean clover pastures. The relationship was found to differ for green and dry pasture (see Fig. 5). On green pasture of this type, intake increases rapidly up to 900 lb DM per acre but from there on declines steadily. The curve is not of the expected asymptotic form. Low intake when there are very large quantities of pasture on offer can be partially attributed to the structure of the pasture. The increase in intake as the amount on offer declines from 3,000–1,000 lb DM per acre has been attributed by Arnold (1962a) to an increased grazing time which increases maintenance requirement (Lambourne, 1961) and thus food demand. The cause of the increased maintenance requirement has not been determined. At about 850 lb DM per acre grazing time is probably at its maximum (>10 hr per day) and even if rate of eating were to be increased a limit must soon be reached beyond which intake cannot be maintained as the amount of pasture on offer decreases. This relationship was altered, however, by animal demand. Cold stress following mid-winter shearing of wethers stimulated an increase in intake by 350–400 g OM daily. Even when the sheep were grazing scant feed, intake was substantially increased by cold stress or lactation.

VI. RELATIONSHIPS BETWEEN PLANT COMMUNITIES AND ANIMAL PRODUCTION

Willoughby (1959) reported the results of an experiment in which weaner Merino sheep were grazed on *Phalaris*—subterranean clover pasture. He summarized his findings as follows:

'Availability of dry pasture did not affect animal production so long as green pasture was present. Small increases in green pasture in the period of slow growth (winter) gave large increases in liveweight and wool production. Large increases in green pasture in the period of rapid growth (spring) had no effect on the animal. Increasing the amount of dry pasture reduced liveweight loss only slightly.'

Roe, Southcott and Turner (1959) in a long term grazing experiment on native pasture at Armidale, N.S.W. reported that in green periods Merino sheep ate virtually no dry material and that an increase of 1 cwt of green forage DM per acre increased liveweight gain by 0·8 lb per month. Wool fibre diameter also increased with increased green DM yield.

From his data Willoughby (1959) obtained an asymptotic relationship between availability of green pasture and animal production, the asymptote occurring at about 1,400 lb DM per acre (Fig. 6, upper curve). There was only a narrow scatter of points around the curve which is rather surprising because the curve was derived from data for both winter and summer green feed. It has been pointed out already that in summer, although green feed is present, it may not be available as far as the animal

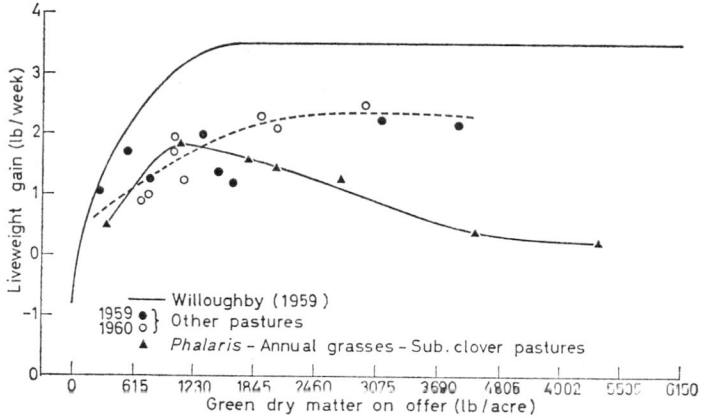

FIG. 6. Relationships between green dry-matter on offer and liveweight gain of sheep.

is concerned. Also, as has been shown, selective grazing in both winter and spring frequently results in less than the total green herbage being available to the animal.

Analysis of the data from a long term experiment on *Phalaris*—annual grasses—subterranean clover pasture grazed by Merino wethers, recently completed by Dr McManus and myself, has yielded quite different results. Considering winter and spring periods for three consecutive years the curve shown in Fig. 6 was obtained. This was arrived at by pooling data for pasture DM on offer as follows: 0–500, 500–1,000 lb green DM per acre, etc. There was tremendous variation in weight change for any one level of green DM per acre. Nevertheless there was a definite trend for weight gain to decrease as the amount of green pasture on offer increased; this agreed with the observed effects on intake shown in Fig. 5.

The essential differences between Willoughby's and our experiment were (a) that Willoughby used growing animals which had a much greater potential for weight gain than the wethers we used and, (b) our pastures contained a considerable amount of annual grasses that produce a very dense tall sward in late spring. This sward hampers grazing, whereas Willoughby's pastures were much more open and contained more clover, so that even in late spring there was a dense layer of readily available herbage close to the ground.

Another experiment (Bush and Arnold unpublished data), on eight different pastures other than Phalaris—annual grasses—subterranean clover

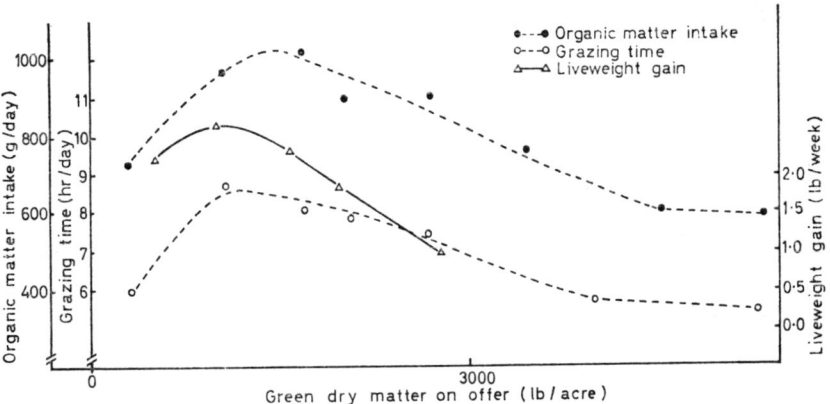

FIG. 7. Relationships between grazing time, liveweight change and intake, and green dry-matter on offer for Phalaris – annual grasses – subterranean clover pasture.

gave the results also shown in Fig. 6. Most of these pastures provided fairly short dense herbage in late spring and were grazed by Merino wethers. The data for the spring periods of 1959 and 1960 gave little indication of a decline in weight gain on green pasture as the quantity on offer increased. Maximum weight gains were about 2·4 lb per week compared with 3·5 lb per week obtained by Willoughby from weaner sheep; both from pastures yielding over 1,500 lb green DM per acre. Scott-Young (1960) found that young Merino wethers gained maximum weight when the green herbage yield was 600 lb DM per acre.

There are therefore quite different relationships between green pasture on offer and liveweight gain for different pastures and different animal conditions. This, and the variability of our results, is not surprising when it is remembered that a relationship like this can be influenced by so many factors. Trying to relate animal production to a single parameter of the pasture is of questionable validity. In any pasture situation it is important to know what the animal's reactions are in order to explain the resultant animal production. Figure 7 summarizes our findings on the reactions of wether sheep grazing *Phalaris*—annual grasses—subterranean clover pasture. There would seem to be a fairly simple explanation of the relationship between green DM on offer and liveweight change if we look at the intake curve but we must seek what determines the intake curve before we can expose the roots of the problem.

VII. THE CONTINUOUS CYCLE OF PASTURE— ANIMAL RELATIONSHIPS

The changes in the diet of sheep during the year and their causes, together with the effects of these changes on the animal's productivity, are best described by taking one example. This is the experiment already referred to in various parts of this paper; the initial results of which have been reported by Arnold and McManus (1960). Plots of *Phalaris*—annual grasses—subterranean clover pasture were set stocked at 2, 4 and 6 sheep per acre. This range of stocking level was such that at 2 sheep per acre the pasture would almost never become heavily grazed, but at 6 sheep per acre a shortage of pasture might be expected in winter and possibly in late summer. Only the first year's results covering the period from May 1958 to July 1959 will be considered.

On the intake side we found that increasing stocking level, and thus decreasing the amount of pasture on offer, increased mean daily OMI. This was particularly noticeable between 4 and 6 sheep per acre. Intake was high in late winter, decreased through spring and summer and increased again in autumn, although this pattern of intake is not necessarily true every year. The important fact is that intake varied through the year even at low stocking level. The reasons for this and its effect on animal production must be considered.

The digestibility of the diet showed large seasonal fluctuations, which, coupled with those of OM intake, brought about large variations in digestible organic matter intake (DOMI). In general the sheep at the highest stocking levels had the highest diet digestibility and highest DOMI.

Liveweight changes fluctuated considerably during the year: the changes were greatest at the highest stocking level where sheep gained 15 lb in 6 weeks in spring but lost 13 lb in 6 weeks in late summer. Wool production showed fluctuations similar to those of liveweight with almost twice as much wool being produced in a 6 week period in spring as in a similar period in winter or summer. Sheep at the highest stocking level produced least wool.

Sheep at the highest stocking level, because they had the highest DOM intake and lowest wool production, required much more DOM per unit of wool than sheep at the lowest stocking level. Efficiency of wool production was lowest in winter and summer, when from 2 to 4 times more DOM was required to produce a gram of wool than in spring. Even at the lowest stocking level there were large differences between 6 week periods in the efficiency of wool production.

A number of factors were involved in these seasonal and stocking level differences in production, and in the efficiency of production; two of these were probably most important. First, the amount of pasture on offer in winter affected OM intake; as the amount of pasture on offer decreased grazing time and the energy cost of grazing probably increased so that although intake was maintained or increased, the maintenance requirements of the animals increased. This is in line with the findings of Coop (1961) and Lambourne (1961). Secondly, OM intake declined with the fall in diet digestibility in late spring and summer and this was associated with changes in the quality of the diet other than digestibility. Although protein intake declines considerably in summer, it is unlikely, on these pastures, that it limits production (Arnold, McManus and Ball, unpublished data). There is, however, the strong possibility that the diet yielded a greater proportion of acetic acid and a lesser proportion of propionic acid in the rumen in summer than in spring. This would result in an increased heat increment from the utilization of the end products of digestion (Armstrong and Blaxter, 1956), and, therefore in a decreased efficiency of production.

The results of this experiment indicate the problems associated with animal production from *Phalaris*—annual grasses—subterranean clover pasture; the two principal ones being shortage of pasture in winter and the low quality of the pasture in summer. A further problem, encountered in other years, is that of the structure of the pasture in summer. Certain of these problems can be overcome by management procedures and conservation, although the latter is liable to be uneconomic where wool production is concerned. Control over the botanical composition of pastures can be an important aid in reducing seasonal fluctuations in animal production, particularly with the species used in improved pastures in south-eastern Australia. Preliminary findings (Bush and Arnold, unpublished data) on this aspect are summarized in Table 5. Highest animal production has come from balanced grass–clover pastures because grass dominant or clover dominant pastures have serious limitations at particular seasons of the year; clover growth is poor in winter and grass pastures decline badly in quality in summer and may also limit intake by their structure. However, clover dominant pastures (leaving aside the advantages and disadvantages of their oestrogen content) remain of relatively high nutritional value in summer and also allow normal grazing by sheep in late spring and summer.

TABLE 5

Animal Production from pastures of different botanical composition

	Period	Native pasture (short grass)	Clover dominant	Grass dominant (long grass)	Balanced grass–clover pasture
Spring	2.9.59–19.11.59	$13 \cdot 0^a$	$21 \cdot 5^b$	$11 \cdot 8^a$	$14 \cdot 1^a$
Summer	4.12.59–10.2.60	$0 \cdot 8$	$-0 \cdot 5$	$-2 \cdot 2$	$1 \cdot 2$
Autumn	10.2.60–10.5.60	$-3 \cdot 5^a$	$-5 \cdot 5^a$	$-4 \cdot 2^a$	$4 \cdot 1^b$
Winter	10·5·60–6·9·60	$-8 \cdot 6^a$	$-4 \cdot 2^a$	$10 \cdot 4^b$	$9 \cdot 4^b$
Greasy wool (lb/sheep)	19.11.59–6.9.60	$8 \cdot 2^a$	$8 \cdot 8^a$	$10 \cdot 7^b$	$10 \cdot 9^b$
Spring	6.9.60–15.12.60	$19 \cdot 7^b$	$31 \cdot 5^c$	$19 \cdot 6^b$	$14 \cdot 1^a$
Summer	15.12.60–3.3.61	$3 \cdot 1^c$	$-3 \cdot 8^b$	$-9 \cdot 8^a$	$-2 \cdot 5^b$
Autumn	3.3.61–6.6.61	$-0 \cdot 3^a$	$9 \cdot 6^{bc}$	$8 \cdot 5^b$	$13 \cdot 0^c$

Notes: Values with different superscripts in the same row are significantly different at the 5 per cent level.
2.9.59 to 6.9.60   Native pastures stocked at 1 sheep per acre
                    All other pastures stocked at 4 sheep per acre
6.9.60 to 6.6.61   Native pastures stocked at 2 sheep per acre
                    All other pastures stocked at 6 sheep per acre.

By grazing grass dominant and mixed swards in winter and early spring and clover dominant pastures in late spring and summer, it might be possible to improve production in both unproductive seasons. The increased grazing pressure on grass dominant pastures in spring would slow the rate of maturity of plants and reduce the height and number of seed heads produced; both would lead to higher food intake.

By applying our knowledge of the animals' reactions to a particular pasture situation it should be possible to devise systems of grazing management that *will* improve animal production from our pastures by taking into account the effects of the pasture on the animal as well as the effects of the animal on the pasture. Also, the various factors within plant communities that affect the diet of the grazing animal, discussed above, all need to be considered in the development of new pasture plants.

ACKNOWLEDGEMENT

It is a pleasure to acknowledge the co-operation of Dr W. R. McManus of the School of Wool Technology, University of New South Wales, in some of the projects described.

REFERENCES

ALLDEN W. G. (1962) Rate of herbage intake and grazing time in relation to herbage availability. *Proc. Aust. Soc. Anim. Prod.* **4**, 163–166

Ann. Rep. Rocky Mt. For. Range Exp. Sta. 1955, 1956 and 1959

ARMSTRONG D. G. & BLAXTER K. L. (1956) The heat increment of a mixture of steam volatile fatty acids and of glucose in the fasting sheep. *Proc. Nutr. Soc.* **15** *Abstracts* pp. i–ii

ARNOLD G. W. (1960a) Selective grazing by sheep of two forage species at different stages of growth. *Aust. J. agric. Res.* **11**, 1026–1033

ARNOLD G. W. (1960b) The effect of the quantity and quality of pasture available to sheep on their grazing behaviour. *Aust. J. agric. Res.* **11**, 1034–1043

ARNOLD G. W. (1962a) The diet of the grazing sheep. Unpublished thesis. London University

ARNOLD G. W. (1962b) Effects of pasture maturity on the diet of sheep. *Aust. J. agric. Res.* **13**, 701–706

ARNOLD G. W. & BUSH I. G. (1962) The effects of stocking rate and grazing management on fat lamb production. *Proc. Aust. Soc. Anim. Prod.* **4**, 121–129

ARNOLD G. W. & MCMANUS W. R. (1960) The effect of level of stocking on two pasture types upon wool production and quality. *Proc. Aust. Soc. Anim. Prod.* **3**, 63–68

BLAXTER K. L., WAINMAN F. W. & WILSON R. S. (1961) The regulation of feed intake by sheep. *Anim. Prod.* **3**, 51–61

BRANNON W. F., REID J. T. & MILLER J. I. (1954) The influence of certain factors upon the digestibility and intake of pasture herbage of beef steers. *J. Anim. Sci.* **13**, 535–542

BROBECK J. R. (1957) Neural basis of hunger, appetite and satiety. *Gastroenterology* **32**, 169–174

COOK C. W. & HARRIS L. E. (1950) The nutritive content of the grazing sheep's diet on summer and winter ranges in Utah. *Bull.* 342 *Utah agric. Exp. Sta.*

COOK C. W., STODDART L. A. & HARRIS L. E. (1956) Comparative nutritive value and palatability of some introduced and native forage plants for spring and summer grazing. *Bull. 385 Utah agric. Exp. Sta.*

COOP I. E. (1961) The energy requirements of sheep. *Proc. N.Z. Soc. Anim. Prod.* **21**, 79-91

COWLISHAW S. J. & ALDER F. E. (1960) The grazing preferences of cattle and sheep. *J. agric. Sci.* **54**, 257-265

GLENDENNING G. E. (1944) Some factors affecting cattle use of northern Arizona pine-bunchgrass range. *SW For. Range Exp. Sta. Res. Rep.* 6

HARDISON W. A., REID J. T., MARTIN C. M. & WOOLFOLK P. G. (1954) Degree of herbage selection by grazing cattle. *J. Dairy Sci.* **37**, 89-102

HERCUS J. M. (1961) What do sheep eat on tussock grassland? *N.Z. J. Agric.* **103**, 73-76

LAMBOURNE L. J. (1961) Relative effects of environment and liveweight upon the feed requirements of sheep. *Proc. N.Z. Soc. Anim. Prod.* **21**, 92-101

LLOYD DAVIES H. (1961) Plant fluids as intake depressors in ruminants. *Symposium on Ruminant Metabolism Prospect N.S.W.* 1961

LLOYD DAVIES H. (1962) Intake studies in sheep involving high fluid intake. *Proc. Aust. Soc. Anim. Prod.* **4**, 167-171

McCULLOUGH M. E. (1956) A study of techniques for measuring differences in forage quality using dairy cows. *Tech. Bull. N.S.4 Georgia agric. Exp. Sta.*

MILFORD R. (1960) Criteria for expressing nutritional values of subtropical grasses. *Aust. J. agric. Res.* **11**, 121-137

MILTON W. E. J. (1933) The palatability of the self-establishing species contributing to different types of grassland. *Emp. J. exp. Agric.* **1**, 347-359

MILTON W. E. J. (1953) The palatability of herbage on undeveloped grasslands in west-central Wales. *Emp. J. exp. Agric.* **21**, 116-122

MINSON D. J., RAYMOND W. F. & HARRIS C. E. (1960) The digestibility of grass species and varieties. *Proc. 8th Int. Grassl. Congr.* pp. 470-474

PALTRIDGE T. B. (1955) Sown pastures for South-Eastern Queensland. *Bull.* 274. C.S.I.R.O.

PHILLIPS J. D. & PFEIFFER R. K. (1958) An example of the relation between palatability of pastures and selective butter-cup control. *Proc. 4th Brit. Weed. Contr. Conf.* pp. 15-17

PLICE M. J. (1952) Sugar versus the intuitive choice of foods by livestock. *J. Range Mgmt.* **5**, 69-74

REPPERT J. N. (1960) Forage preference and grazing habits of cattle at the Eastern Colorado Range Station. *J. Range Mgmt.* **13**, 58-65

ROE R. & MOTTERSHEAD B. E. (1962) Palatability of *Phalaris arundinacea. Nature, Lond.* **193**, 255-257

ROE R., SOUTHCOTT W. H. & TURNER H. N. (1959) Grazing management of native pastures in the New England region of New South Wales. 1. Pasture and sheep production with special reference to systems of grazing and internal parasites. *Aust. J. agric. Res.* **10**, 530-554

SCOTT-YOUNG (1960) Unpublished Thesis. University of Adelaide

SPAHR S. L., KESLER E. M., BRATZLER J. W. & WASHKO J. B. (1961) Effect of stage maturity at first cutting on quality of forages. *J. Dairy Sci.* **44**, 503-510

STAPLEDON R. G. (1934) Palatability and the management of the poorer grasslands. *J. Minist. Agric.* **41**, 321-328

STATEN H. W. (1949) Palatability trials of winter pasture crops and effect of phosphate fertilisers on palatability. *Tech. Bull. T-35. Okls. agric. Exp. Sta.*

UNDERWOOD E. J. (1956) *Trace elements in human and animal nutrition.* New York: Academic Press. Inc. 430 pp.

WEIR W. C. & TORELL D. T. (1959) Selective grazing by sheep as shown by a comparison of the chemical composition of range and pasture forage obtained by hand clipping and that collected by oesophageal-fistulated sheep. *J. Anim. Sci.* **18,** 641–649

WHEELER J. L. (1960) Field experiments on systems of management for mesophytic pastures. *C.S.I.R.O. Div. Plant Industry. Rep.* No. 20, 50 pp.

WILLOUGHBY W. M. (1959) Limitations to animal production imposed by seasonal fluctuations in pasture and by management procedures. *Aust. J. agric. Res.* **10,** 248–268

HOME RANGE BEHAVIOUR IN HILL SHEEP

R. F. HUNTER

Hill Farming Research Organization

ABSTRACT

At intervals throughout one day in each week in the period May–November, 1961, the location of the members of a flock of 160 sheep grazing a ring-fenced 350 acre hill pasture was recorded on a vegetation and topographic map of the pasture. The sheep could be individually recognized, their pedigrees and live weights being known.

The 350 acre pasture was not a common environment for the sheep who split themselves into sub-flocks, composed of families of sheep, the sub-flocks being restricted to parts of the pasture which differed in altitude, aspect and vegetation.

While the possibility cannot be excluded that the differences among the sub-flocks in both lamb and hogget weights was of genetical origin, it is more likely that these differences arise from the home ranges, adopted by the sub-flocks, being different and contrasting and not either similar or common environments.

Phenotypic selection of ewe lambs for stock ewe replacements resulted in more lambs being retained from some sub flocks and less from others.

The relevance of home range behaviour in hill sheep to hill sheep management and to experimental work with hill sheep is discussed.

INTRODUCTION

Hill sheep in Scotland are maintained throughout the year on their pasture with little or no supplementary feeding. The flock breeds its own replacements; the rams, however, are bought in from other farms. The extensive pastures are in the main unfenced, hence the sheep could range for many miles. It is known, however, that sheep do not range extensively but, to use a term advanced by Burt (1949), adopt home ranges. Burt describes a home range as an area shared by a group of animals of the same species, thus distinguishing it from a territory which applies to any area defended against other members of the same species. The adoption of an area of hill pasture by a group of sheep is the basis of the 'hefting' system practised in much of Scotland's hill pastures, the term 'heft' describing both the group of sheep and the area of pasture to which they restrict themselves or are restricted by shepherding.

155

Fraser and Stamp (1957) have commented on the family group's being the basis of the hefting system and they understood that family groups tended to remain within the same area of pasture. Milner (unpublished data), studying a Cheviot heft which was common to numerous unrelated sheep, showed that related sheep were found within approximately the same parts of it. Similar behaviour has been noted by Burns (1962) in the Herdwick and Swaledale breeds. In addition to such behaviour within a group of sheep of the same breed, Peart (1961) and Munro (1962) noted that mixed stocking of the so-called sub-breeds of the Cheviot and Black-face breeds resulted in the sub-breeds occupying different home ranges within a common pasture.

That hill sheep adopt home ranges is therefore a well-known phe-nomenon and one which it was thought might repay a detailed study.

The sheep whose behaviour was studied comprised a Scottish Blackface flock of ewes and hoggets which grazed the Alderhope heft at Sourhope, the Hill Farm Research Association's [H.F..R.O.'s] farm in the Cheviots in south-east Scotland. The flock was on this heft when the farm was acquired for experimental purposes in 1947 and had been for as long as local farmers could remember. Prior to 1955 the heft was unfenced. The 350 acre (142 ha) heft is ring-fenced and extends from an altitude of under 1,000 ft (304 m) to an altitude of 1,985 ft (604 m). The vegetation and topography of the heft is shown in Fig. 1.

In order to identify the sheep number plates were hung round their necks, it being possible to read the number without appreciably disturbing the sheep. Variously coloured fence posts were sited on the heft and the position of these posts marked on a gridded map. The observer, carrying a copy of the map, walked over the heft noting on it the position of individual sheep. For each observation period the observer employed a fresh map.

From 25 May until 29 August 1961, four observations were made per day on one day per week, each observation taking two people about 2 hours, with a break of 1–1½ hours between observations. After 29 August the day was too short to permit four observations being made and until 14 November, two per day were made. Observations were not made while the rams were with the ewes (21 November until 29 December) as the sheep during this period are herded daily and are kept together in one group. Observations restarted in January 1962; these observations have not been included in this paper, they do not however contradict conclu-sions based on the observations which are reported. A copy of the map of the heft was allocated to each ewe or hogget and the position where each sheep had been recorded on the field maps was copied on these separate maps. Thus a picture of the home range of each sheep was built up by accumulating on one map its locations as recorded at successive periods within a day and on successive days of observation at approximately weekly intervals.

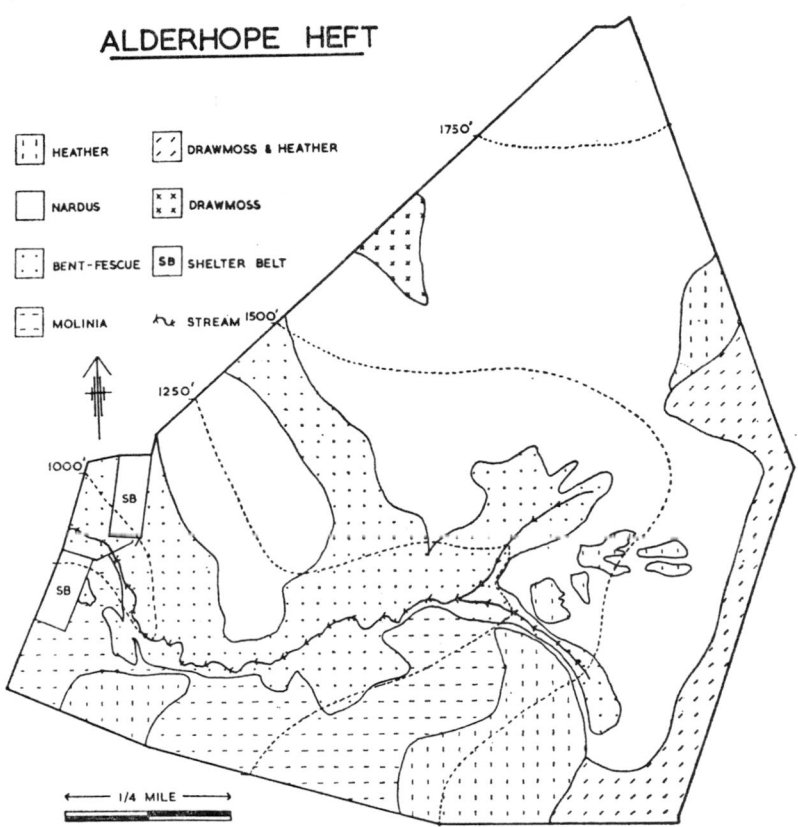

FIG. I. The vegetation and topography of the Alderhope heft.

PARTITION OF THE FLOCK INTO HOME RANGE GROUPS

During the period 29 May to 14 December the location of the sheep was recorded on 22 days, 62 observations were made during these days and 75 per cent of the possible number of sheep–location–records (approximately 11,500) were collected. Failure to collect 25 per cent of the records was caused by number plates falling off or breaking, the sheep's wool obscuring the plate or its being impossible to view the sheep from the correct angle in order to see the number plate. In all 8,684 records were collected and the location of these is shown in Fig. 2A in which each dot represents two records. The distribution of these records is not uniform

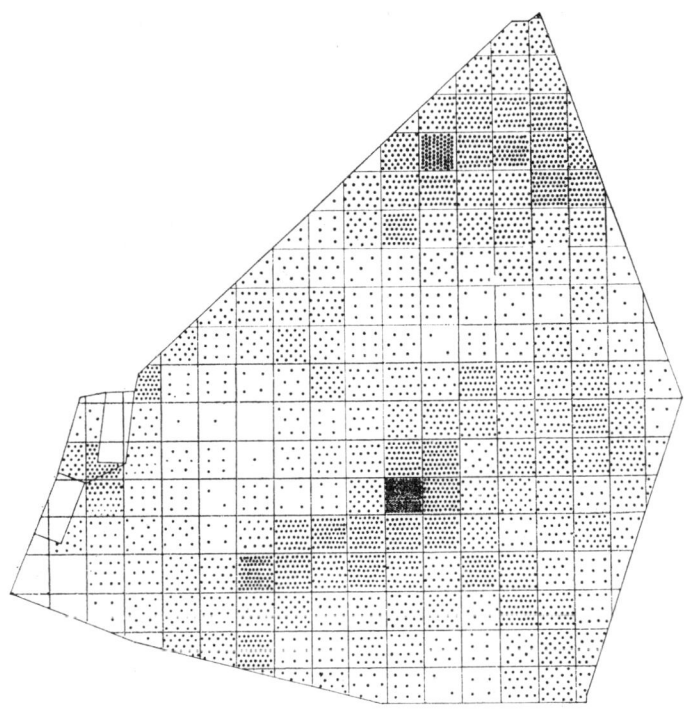

FIG. 2A–F. Distribution maps of the different groups of sheep on the Alderhope heft.

FIG. 2A. Distribution of all the sheep comprizing the Alderhope heft.

over the pasture, a result which would be expected from the sheep's known preference for certain types of vegetation and of certain areas for resting (Boulet, 1939; Hunter, 1954a; 1962).

The distribution of the records for individual sheep did not form a continuous series of partially overlapping distributions but occurred in more or less clearly defined groups. Two of these groups were very clearly defined, the Top, 40 sheep (Fig. 2B) and the Fence, 20 sheep (Fig. 2C). The Middle, 52 sheep (Fig. 2D) and Bottom, 38 sheep (Fig. 2E), home range groups were less clearly separated. It would have been possible to have treated these two groups as one large group composed of a series of partially overlapping distributions or to have split it into four sub-groups. The

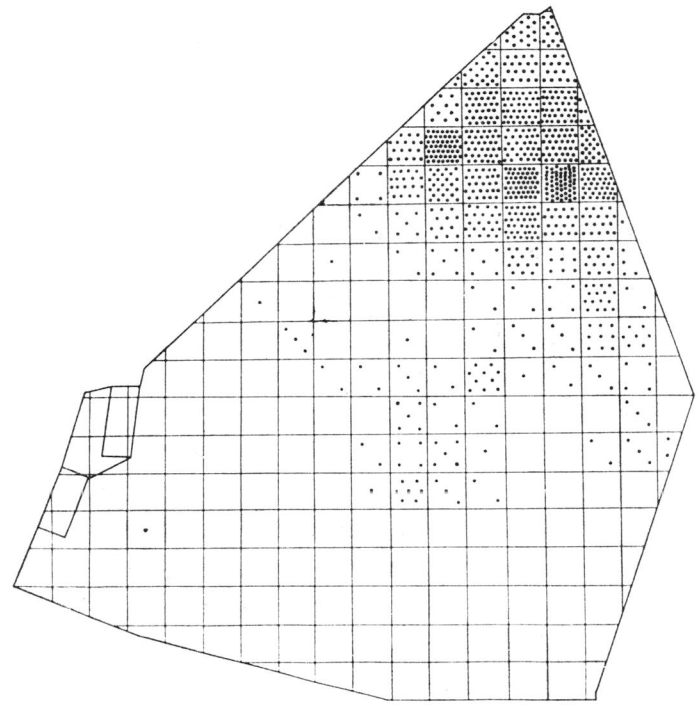

FIG. 2B. Distribution of the Top home range group.

recognition of these two groups is therefore somewhat arbitrary. It should not be thought, however, that the degree of overlap is as large as it shows when Figs. 2D and E are compared. Part of the Bottom group's resting area, to which many members of the group went at night, was within the Middle group's range. The degree of overlap of the areas within which these two groups grazed is much less. During winter these two groups tend to join. This results from the topography of the bottom range, much of which faces north and may remain covered after the rest of the pasture is free of snow or frost. The Bottom group then moves into the Middle group home range, presumably to find grazing free of snow or frost or to find warmer unshaded conditions. The home range of the remaining group, Central, 16 sheep (Fig. 2F) is not clearly defined, sufficient records not being available. It has affinities with both Middle and Bottom but the

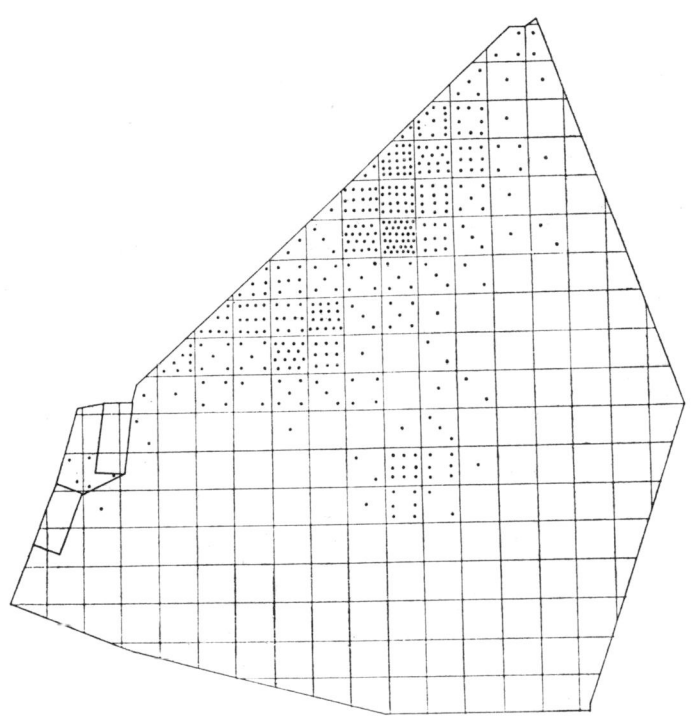

FIG. 2C. Distribution of the Fence home range group.

sheep composing it have a daily pattern of movement distinguishing them from both groups. The recognition of home range groups presents no great difficulty. However, using the data available, it is difficult to decide if the members of a home range group have identical grazing patterns. The indication is that this is not so but each sheep establishes a proprietorship over certain patches within the home range sharing different patches with different sheep.

The sheep were not herded on the days of observation and observations have not yet been made on the days when they are. They are not herded into home ranges but the shepherd gathers them together within the lower area of the heft. It must therefore be assumed that the sheep adopt home ranges of 80–100 acres (32–40 ha) in extent in spite of their being shep-herded and that the degree of herding is insufficient to overcome this tendency as it is manifest on days when they are not herded.

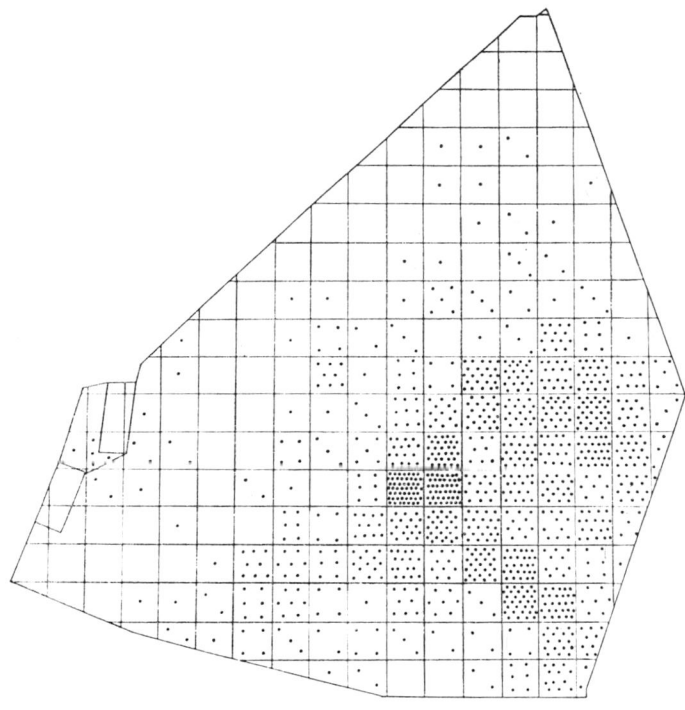

FIG. 2D. Distribution of the Middle home range group.

In mapping the heft six sward types were recognized: *Nardus* on pod-solic soils with associated *Deschampsia flexuosa, Festuca ovina, Anthoxanthum odoratum, Agrostis tenuis* and *A. canina*; bent-fescue, occurring on the freely-drained mull and podsolic brown earth soils occasionally flushed or infested with bracken (*Pteridium acquilinum*) and comprised principally of *A. tenuis, F. ovina* and *F. rubra*; *Molinia* on wetter podsolic soils with a 12 in. (30·5 cm) peat horizon accompanied by *N. stricta, D. flexuosa, Juncus squar-rosus* and *Vaccinium myrtillus*; heather (*Calluna vulgaris*) on soils similar to

12

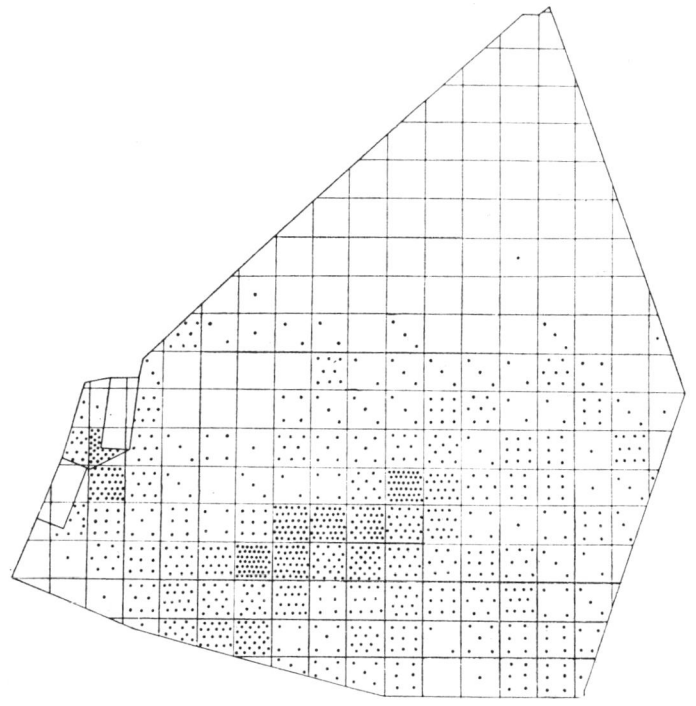

FIG. 2E. Distribution of the Bottom home range group.

either the *Molinia* or *Nardus* types, draw moss (*Eriophorum vaginatum*) and heather on deep peat; and draw moss on deep peat.

The proportion of these six types within the various ranges is shown in Table 1.

TABLE 1

Composition of home ranges, percentage of area occupied by different sward types.

	Nardus	Bent-fescue	Molinia	Heather	Draw moss	Draw moss and heather
Top and Fence	76	18	—	1	2	3
Middle	47	20	14	10	—	9
Bottom	39	28	18	10	—	5

Both the Top and the Fence home ranges contain less bent-fescue and more *Nardus* than either Middle or Bottom. The home ranges therefore differ in altitude, aspect and in the proportion of the different pasture types present within them. They do not however differ, to a noticeable extent, in their respective stocking rates.

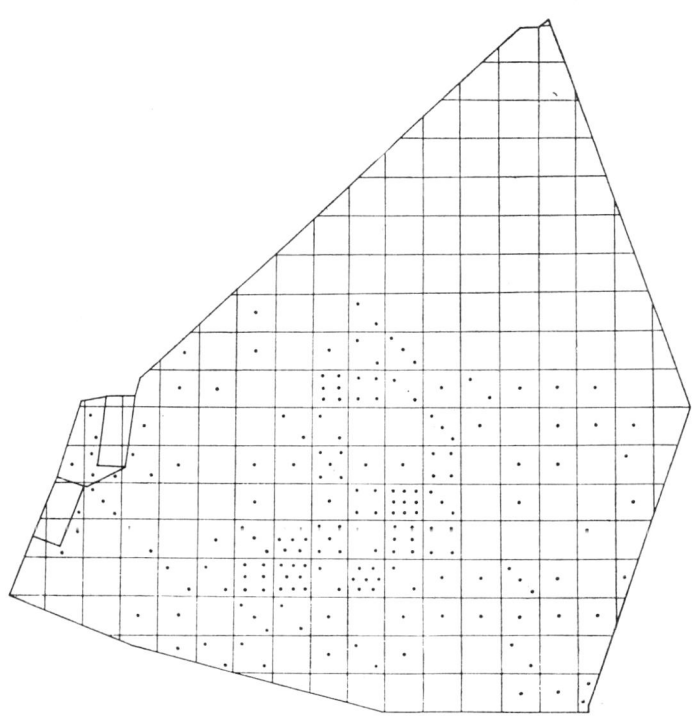

Fig. 2F. Distribution of the Central home range group.

RELATED SHEEP WITHIN HOME RANGE GROUPS

Since 1956 the lambs born on Alderhope have been ear-tagged soon after birth and hence the relationships of the sheep within the flock have been known since that date. This makes it possible to determine whether groups of related sheep occur more frequently within home range groups than split between different home ranges. The degrees of relationship studied are sister/sister and dam/daughter pairs. The dam/daughter pairs are divided into two classes: (1) the daughter born not later than 1959 and (2) the daughter born in 1960. Lambs born in 1960 were hoggets in 1961 and it is well-known that they continue to follow their mothers at this age. It was therefore thought necessary to separate this class of daughters from older daughters if a fair test were to be made of the persistence of dam/daughter relationships within home ranges. The sisterhood relationships are also split into two classes, pairs of sisters and groups of three sisters. Owing to the low values for both the observed and the expected frequencies χ^2 has not been calculated for the data given in Table 2. As the

TABLE 2

Numbers of groups of related sheep occurring in the same or split among different home ranges

			Numbers of groups				
			Home range		3 in same	2 in same 1 in different home range	all in different
Relationship			Same	Different			
Sisterhood	Pair of sisters	observed	7	10	—	—	—
		expected	3·9	13·1	—	—	—
	Three sisters	observed	—	—	4	2	1
		expected	—	—	0·4	3·6	3·0
Dam/ daughter	Daughter born before 1960	observed	9	6	—	—	—
		expected	3·4	11·6	—	—	—
	Daughter born in 1960	observed	10	2	—	—	—
		expected	2·7	9·3	—	—	—

records do not go back further than 1956 the full extent of family relationship within a home range group cannot be examined, nevertheless, it is clear that related sheep show a marked tendency to graze the same area of a hill pasture and that home range groups are to a large extent composed of groups of related sheep.

PERFORMANCE OF THE SHEEP COMPRISING DIFFERENT HOME RANGE GROUPS

The sheep are weighed at five, more or less regular, intervals throughout the year. As the weight of an adult sheep is a function of its size and condition, for which characteristics separate estimates are not available, a comparison of the weights of adult sheep is perhaps of less value than a comparison of the weights of juvenile sheep, whose weight reflects the rate of growth as affected by the level of nutrition.

HOGGET WEIGHTS

Table 3 shows the mean weight (lb) of the hoggets at various dates in the period November 1960–August 1961. In the analysis of variance of these data the dates of weighing were grouped into seasons, a winter season comprising the November, January and March weighings and a summer season comprising the June and August weighings.

TABLE 3

Mean weight of hoggets (lb) at different dates (1960–61)

Home range group	Date of weighing					No. of hoggets
	Nov.	Jan.	Mar.	June	Aug.	
Top and Fence	68·5	65·3	58·9	72·1	82·2	12
Middle	70·7	66·0	61·3	78·7	90·3	6
Bottom	71·5	69·6	61·1	79·4	86·9	12

Comparison of differences between mean winter and summer weights

Mean summer weight
—mean winter weight

Top and Fence	12·88
Middle	18·50
Bottom	16·78

S.E. of difference between Top and Fence and Bottom mean differences

$$= 1·45$$

S.E. of difference between Middle and either of other differences

$$= 1·77$$

The analysis showed that the Top and Fence range was significantly poorer than the other two. The interaction between range and season is of special interest (Table 3), the hoggets on the Top and Fence range having a lower growth rate than those on the other two ranges whose performance was similar.

WEIGHT OF LAMBS AT WEANING

The weight of a lamb at weaning (mid-August) is influenced by sex, age of mother (1st crop lambs being lighter than 2nd and subsequent crops) and whether the lamb was a single or a member of a pair of twins.

The comparison of the lambs from the various groups is therefore complicated by the different number of lambs within each range not being balanced for sex, age of mother or single or multiple birth and this has been taken into account in the analysis. Estimates of the mean differences between groups, adjusted individually to take into account this imbalance, are shown in Table 4 together with their S.E.'s. Taking twice the S.E. as

TABLE 4

Difference (lb) and S.E. of the difference in weaning weights of lambs reared on different home ranges

Ranges compared	Middle minus Bottom	Bottom minus Top and Fence	Middle minus Top and Fence
Difference	3·00±1·55	1·91±1·59	4·30±1·50

a difference of significance the lambs from the Middle home range are therefore heavier than those from the combined Top and Fence home ranges. The comparison of the performance of both the hoggets and the lambs from the different home ranges indicates that the Alderhope heft is not composed of a single group of sheep, or of sub-groups living in a common nutritional environment, but is composed of sub-groups living in different environments.

RETENTION OF EWE LAMBS FOR STOCK EWE REPLACEMENT

The stock ewes first lamb when two years old and, after five lamb crops, are sold. Thus in August of each year approximately one-fifth of the ewe stock is sold and the number of ewes is maintained by retaining an adequate number of ewe lambs. These ewe lambs are then called ewe hoggets or ewe hoggs. The selection of ewe hoggets is by their appearance, the larger lambs being preferred and the selection being made among all the ewe lambs available on the heft.

Table 5 shows that the ewe lambs from the Top and Fence home ranges have not been preferred. By assuming that the ewes composing the groups found in the various home ranges in 1961 were in these ranges in 1960 and in 1959 the degree of retention of the ewe lambs from these ranges in these previous years is also tabulated. If this assumption is correct and gives a true picture of a long-term trend then the gene fund in the Top and Fence home range sheep is gradually being replaced by that found in the other home ranges. A similar process may be taking place in many hill flocks. It is not known if the poorer performance of the Top and Fence range sheep is due mainly to genetical or to nutritional causes so the consequences of this long-term trend, if it obtains, cannot be predicted.

TABLE 5

Number of ewe lambs retained as hoggets (1959–61) from the various groups

K = Kept   R = Rejected   T = Total available for selection

Home range group	1959			1960			1961			1959–61		
	K.	R.	T.	K.	R.	T.	K.	R.	T.	K.	R.	T.
Top and Fence	4	9	13	5	14	19	11	11	22	20	34	54
Middle	9	5	14	7	8	15	24	8	32	40	21	61
Bottom	3	3	6	5	4	9	13	6	19	21	13	34
Totals	16	17	33	17	26	43	48	25	73	81	68	149

χ^2 for the summation table (1959–61) 10·38 with 2 d.f. (P<0·01).

THE BEHAVIOUR OF THE RAMS IN RELATION TO THE HOME RANGE GROUPS

The rams are generally kept apart from the ewes except during the mating period when they run with the ewes on the hill. The practice, which varies slightly from farm to farm, is to allocate one ram to 40–60 sheep, the ewes and rams being herded together once or twice a day.

On Alderhope, three rams ran with the ewes for the first 17 days of mating (the oestrus period in the sheep is 17 days) and two other rams were allocated for the second period. Mating began on 21 November and finished on 29 December. During the first period two two-year-old and a four-year-old ram were employed, each ram being fitted with a harness and a keel block, the two-year-olds carrying red and yellow keel respectively and the four-year-old blue keel. At the end of the second oestrus period the sheep were gathered and the colour of keel marks each ewe bore was recorded, these records showing by which ram or rams she had been served.

The distribution of the rams among the ewes comprising the various groups is shown in Table 6. Excluding the central group whose numbers are small and whose affinities are uncertain (it could perhaps be joined with the Middle group) the χ^2 ($\chi^2 = 3\cdot82$ with 6 d.f. P$<0\cdot7>0\cdot5$) indicated that the rams were distributed at random among the groups.

TABLE 6

Home ranges and mating behaviour

Home range group	Ram			Total number of matings	Number of sheep in home range group
	Red	Blue	Yellow		
Bottom	16	33	15	64	38
Middle	20	44	21	85	52
Top	22	28	13	63	40
Fence	12	15	6	33	20
Totals	70	120	55	245	150

$\chi^2 = 3\cdot82$ with 6 d.f. P$<0\cdot7>0\cdot5$.

It had been thought that the tendency of the ewes to split up into home range groups might lead to different rams following different groups and hence cause a non-random distribution of the rams among the flock as a whole. The practice of herding the ewes together and the sexual drive which causes rams, as also the ewes when in heat, to seek each other have in this case entirely counteracted this tendency. If the differences in performance among different groups is genetically determined, it therefore appears unlikely that this results from different male parentage as the management practice during mating, as described here for 1961, is that traditionally followed in the flock.

DISCUSSION

The development of home range groups

In the sheep's social life the basic unit appears to be the family group which has its origin in the need of the lamb to follow its mother. The persistence of this behaviour into adult life is an obvious, though not necessarily correct, explanation for the formation of the family group.

The development of the home range group is less readily explained, for, while the family may graze as a group, there is no obvious cause which stops it from ranging widely as a group and restricts it to grazing within a home range in a more or less loose association with other families. The explanation which is now suggested is based on the interaction of two factors: the social behaviour of the sheep and the preference the sheep show among different types of hill pasture sward.

Sheep show a marked preference for swards growing on a mull soil type, these on a hill pasture being the bent-fescue and bracken infested bent-fescue swards. If on a hill pasture all the sheep were to crowd on to the bent-fescue areas, they would find themselves at a high density per unit area competing for grazing in short supply. The level of competition and of social tension among the sheep would rise and at a certain level this tension and competition might be sufficient for the more aggressive sheep to drive out those less aggressive. The increase in social tension may arise from the difficulty of establishing a recognized pecking order as the number of the group increases, as suggested by McBride and Foenander (1962) in the case of domestic fowls. This social relationship might then become formalized by the formation of home range groups and maintained by the behaviour pattern of the family group. This argument requires that as the stocking rate is changed then the poorest area of the pasture, as measured by the preferences of the sheep, is the first to be emptied and the last to be filled. There is some evidence that this is in fact the case (Hunter, 1960).

Relationship of behaviour to flock management

The farmer is interested in both the quality and the quantity of his stock but these two features are not independent as an increase in numbers may often be offset by a decline in quality and vice versa.

The effect of changing the stocking rate cannot be predicted by assuming that there will be a proportionate change in the stocking rate over the pasture as a whole since the pasture is not a common pasture but a series of home ranges. If these ranges vary greatly in quality, a decrease in the sheep population will empty the poorest range and raise the mean performance of the flock. If the ranges approach equal quality a decrease in the population may empty a range but may not lead to an appreciable improvement in the mean performance of the flock. Should all the ranges be fully occupied and overstocked then it follows that a decrease in the population will improve stock performance.

It would appear therefore that while there are gross relationships with over- or under-stocking, within these limits the consequences of minor variations in the stocking rate, of the order of ± 20 per cent, may vary from pasture to pasture. Thus dogmatic assertions that an increase or a decrease in the stocking rate will lead to this or that consequence should be viewed with suspicion.

If we are to regard a hill pasture as a series of home ranges in which each range is fenced from the others by the social behaviour of the sheep, then the problem of improving an open hill pasture becomes the problem of deciding which home ranges within it might best be improved. While the argument requires the test of experiment, it appears that a few acres of improved pasture within the Top range on Alderhope might be the best policy if there were limited monies available for the purpose of improvement.

In selecting his hoggs for stock ewes, the farmer has the choice of two procedures. He can select the best from the pasture as a whole or the best within home ranges. The first procedure has been followed at Alderhope, the second is followed by some farmers (Roberts, 1947). Neither procedure is informed by a knowledge of the reasons for the different level of performance of the sheep from different home ranges. Are the sheep on the Top range poorer because they are genetically poorer or is their range nutritionally poorer or indeed are they genetically superior but this superiority is masked by a lower nutritional level? It would seem of importance for research to determine if the assortment of sheep into home ranges is based on genetic characteristics of agronomic importance. If it were, then it would form a basis for the selection of the ewe stock.

Relationship of behaviour to experimental studies

In research work with hill sheep the experimenter is faced with the same problem that faces other research workers in that the more effectively he can reduce the variability of his material, or allocate the variation to its various sources, the more readily he can examine the effect of experimental treatments. Some of the variation among the Alderhope sheep can be allocated to the variation among home range groups. If the Alderhope heft were to be used for a simple test of, for example, an anthelmintic, it would be an advantage to randomize the allocation of treatments not among the members of the heft as a whole but among the members of the home range groups. Thus a knowledge of the behaviour of the sheep would aid the precision and the information to be gained from such a trial.

Research with hill sheep is complicated by the problem of deciding what is the best unit to use for experimental work. One solution is to divide the hill into relatively large units by fencing, the Alderhope heft being an example of this procedure. It would appear, however, that the home range group might form a better experimental unit though this would require further study before it could be accepted.

It has been clearly shown that the Alderhope heft is not a common environment for the flock of sheep maintained on it, but that the inter-action of the sheep's social behaviour with the vegetational and topo-graphic variation of the heft has produced groups of sheep in different environment. These differing environments have brought about differ-ences among the members of the flock which are not only of statistical significance but are also of practical significance. A hill pasture should not be assumed to be a common environment for the sheep on it and the assumption that it is should not be accepted in experimental studies. While the behaviour of the sheep on Alderhope may not be repeated in detail, or indeed may not be similar, on other pastures, the worker conducting studies of hill sheep on their natural pasture cannot ignore the possible influence of home range behaviour on their performance.

ACKNOWLEDGEMENTS

The writer is glad to acknowledge the help given by Mr G. E. Davies B.SC., Mr P. S. Reid and Mr J. Barrington in collecting the data in the field, for advice, and for carrying out some of the statistical analysis, he is indebted to Dr M. R. Sampford of the A.R.C. Unit of Statistics, Aberdeen Uni-versity.

REFERENCES

BOULET L.J. (1939) The ecology of a Welsh Mountain sheep walk. Unpublished Thesis, University College of Wales, Aberystwyth

BURNS MARCA (1962) Observations on Fell sheep and their crosses. Unpublished paper to B.S.A.P., Edinburgh 1962

BURT W.H. (1949) Territoriality and home range concepts as applied to mammals. *J. Mammalogy* **24** (3), 346–353

FRASER A. & STAMP J.T. (1957) *Sheep Husbandry and Diseases.* pp. 274–275. Crosby Lockwood and Son

HUNTER R.F. (1954a) The grazing of hill pasture sward types. *J. Brit. Grassl. Soc.* **9,** No. 3, 195–208

HUNTER R.F. (1960) Aims and methods in grazing behaviour studies on hill pastures. *Proc. 8th Int. Grassl. Congress*

HUNTER R.F. (1962) Hill sheep and their pasture. *J. Ecol.* **50,** 651–680

MCBRIDE G. & FOENANDER F. (1962) Territorial behaviour in flocks of domestic fowls. *Nature* **194,** 102

MUNRO JOAN (1962) A study of the milk yield of three strains of Scottish Blackface ewes in two environments. *Anim. Prod.* **4,** 343–349

PEART J.N. (1961) *2nd report Hill Farming Research Organisation*

ROBERTS E.J. (1947) Re-building our hill flocks. *Agriculture, Lond.* **54,** 213–217

ANALYSIS OF SHEEP DIET UTILIZING PLANT EPIDERMAL FRAGMENTS IN FAECES SAMPLES

DAVID J. MARTIN

Botany Department, West of Scotland Agricultural College, Glasgow

ABSTRACT

The self-selected diet of Blackface ewes and their lambs on free range on hill pasture in Argyllshire has been investigated using the technique of identification of epidermal fragments in faecal samples. These fragments are the only specifically identifiable constituents of ingested material which are available without recourse to fistular sampling methods.

The results of analysis of 254 faecal samples taken over a four-year period indicate that there is a recurrent annual pattern of grazing shown by the animals. Correlation between grazing intensity of sward types and faecal sample analyses is good. The seasonal and yearly use of the more important sward components is considered. The ewes and lambs tend to select the same type of diet although grazing on ecologically different hirsels and must be able to exercise a preference depending on the available grazing.

INTRODUCTION

The most characteristic feature of epidermal walls is the presence of the fatty substance cutin as an impregnation of the walls themselves and as a separate layer, the cuticle, on the outer surface of the cells (Esau, 1953). The cuticle varies in thickness and is continuous except at the stomata. It is resistant to biochemical macerating agents such as digestive enzymes and can be recovered from rumen and faecal material.

The epidermis of monocotyledonous plants consists of (a) undifferentiated cells, frequently elongated, which make up the bulk of the surface, and (b) various types of differentiated cells such as stomatal guard cells, cork cells, silica cells and asperities. The undifferentiated cells and stomata occupy most of the inter-costal regions of the leaf whilst the cork cells, silica cells and asperities are frequently restricted to the costal regions.

The frequency and distribution of these elements vary from species to species and may be utilized in identification. Prat (1932) and Metcalfe (1960) have shown the value of the epidermal characters in generic and

173

specific identification, whilst Prat (1948) and Borrill (1957) have shown, respectively, that varieties of *Zea mays* and ecotypes of *Dactylis glomerata* were separable on epidermal characteristics.

The epidermis of dicotyledonous plants consists of undifferentiated cells, stomata and asperities. The undifferentiated cells are much less regular than those of the monocotyledons. Sufficient criteria exist in the dicotyledon epidermis to allow of identification to species level, as has been shown by Winton and Winton (1932) and by Accorsi (1949).

The plant fragments of diagnostic value in rumen and faecal samples are those composed of cuticle with the contiguous epidermal cell wall attached. The frequency and distribution of the epidermal cell types can be seen in such fragments. Most fragments consist of inter-costal material and thus the costal characters are of limited value in this context. In fragments where costal material is present the underlying vascular tissue is usually still adherent and renders the costal areas opaque.

About 30 per cent of the weight of ruminant faecal material is composed of the residue of the plants eaten and consists of cuticle with attached epidermal cell walls, vascular tissue and fibrous tissue (Phillipson, 1952). Vascular and fibrous tissues have no characteristics which make them of value in determining the species of plant from which they came.

Analyses of rumen samples from sheep fed a known diet have been carried out by Norris (1943) and Tribe (1950a). Accurate qualitative results were obtained but quantitative results were misleading and no constant correction factor could be applied.

In 1952 the Scottish Hill Farming Research Committee suggested a study of 'the cuticular remnants in sheep faeces, in order to examine the possibilities of utilizing faecal examination as a means of specific recognition of the plant components of the diet' (Anon, 1953). A preliminary study on this basis was carried out by the present author utilizing rumen samples which were available. The results of analysis of monthly samples from 1950 and 1951 were presented (Martin, 1955). It was pointed out that faecal samples would be equally useful, contained material which was more easily identifiable and were more freely obtainable.

Hercus (1959), basing her work on Martin's (1955) findings, utilized faecal samples from sheep on free range on New Zealand hill pasture. She showed the method to be of promise in evaluating the diet of animals on free range.

The work to be described in the present paper is an extension of the previous work carried out by the present author (Martin, 1955) in this case utilizing faecal samples throughout.

MATERIALS AND METHODS

The experimental animals were part of the Blackface hill flock at Lephin-more Hill Farm, Argyll (56° 5' N; 5° 14' W). Half of these animals were able to graze a full range of the flora available from sea level to about 1,100 ft. The other half were on a restricted range, due to afforestation, fencing and natural barriers. These latter animals could only graze on the plants available between 600 and 1,500 ft. There was a difference in the flora of the two hirsels, the full range hirsel (Barnacarry) being predomin-antly a *Festuca/Molinia/Juncus* community while the restricted range hirsel (Low End) was *Calluna/Eriophorum/Juncus* in type.

On each hirsel two ewes were selected for investigation of their diet. These ewes were chosen at random from amongst those which could reasonably be expected to remain part of the flock during the period of investigation, and which would lamb each year. Each ewe bore a single lamb in each year of the investigation, and the diet of these lambs was similarly investigated.

Faecal samples were taken direct from the rectum at times of normal flock handling for dipping, worming and other gatherings.

The diet of the ewes was followed by continuous analysis of faecal samples from May 1957 until September 1960. Lamb diet was investigated from birth in May until weaning in October for the years 1957-9.

These faecal samples were supplemented by others taken at times of visits to the area. On such occasions, faeces seen to be freshly voided were collected and analysed. This was particularly the case with lamb samples early in the sampling period, as occasionally no sample could be obtained from the lambs at the time of gathering.

The samples were stored in formalin-acetic-alcohol after being shaken to induce a separation of the fragments. For purposes of analysis the samples were further separated by agitation and separation with a rubber-covered stirring rod. It was found that the plant fragments did not break into smaller pieces with this treatment but did separate easily from one another.

The prepared sample was then diluted and an aliquot examined under a binocular microscope.

To enable accurate identification of the epidermal fragments in the faeces samples, check material from sixty of the plant species growing on the grazing areas was prepared by one or more of the following methods.

Maceration in (*a*) dilute nitric acid (Martin, 1955) or (*b*) bleaching solu-tion and subsequent scraping (Metcalfe, personal communication) or (*c*) lactic acid (Clarke, 1960) or (*d*) ethylene diamine tetra-acetic acid (Letham, 1958). Other methods used were maceration by bacteria (Louw, Williams and Maynard, 1949; Skoss, 1955) or by stripping off a cellulose acetate film impression (North, 1956).

From the epidermal preparations, photomicrographs and camera lucida drawings were made showing the characteristic features of the abaxial and adaxial leaf surfaces and, where applicable, of the stem surface.

Typical examples of these photomicrographs are shown in Plate 1, from a grass, a rush and a dicotyledonous herb.

RESULTS AND DISCUSSION

1. Yearly grazing pattern

The results obtained from the analysis of faecal samples from the experimental ewes and lambs on Barnacarry hirsel are presented in Fig. 1. These show the fragment percentage as an average over the whole period of study compared with the fragment percentage for each year of study. Ewe results are shown at bimonthly intervals; lamb results are shown at monthly intervals.

It can be seen that there is a close parallel in each year to a set pattern of grazing, indicating that there is an annual grazing cycle. This is particularly the case with the ewe results.

The analyses show that the lambs do not show as regular a grazing sequence as do the ewes, particularly on *Agrostis stolonifera*. The reasons for this are: (1) there is a greater variability between the results for each lamb; (2) the lambs have a different type of diet from that of the ewes; and (3) the lambs are as yet unfamiliar with the grazing area (Martin, in preparation).

It can be concluded that, for the species shown, which were chosen for their importance in the overall diet, the sheep exhibited a grazing pattern which was repeated in its essentials each year. The same is true for most of the species investigated but not illustrated.

It can also be concluded from further results that, apart from a grazing sequence at species level as shown, there is an annually recurring resemblance in the grazing of groups of plants, e.g. grasses, sedges and rushes (see also Table 1).

Essentially similar results were obtained from the samples taken from Low End ewes and lambs.

Hunter (1954a, b) has shown that sheep tend to have an annual cycle of

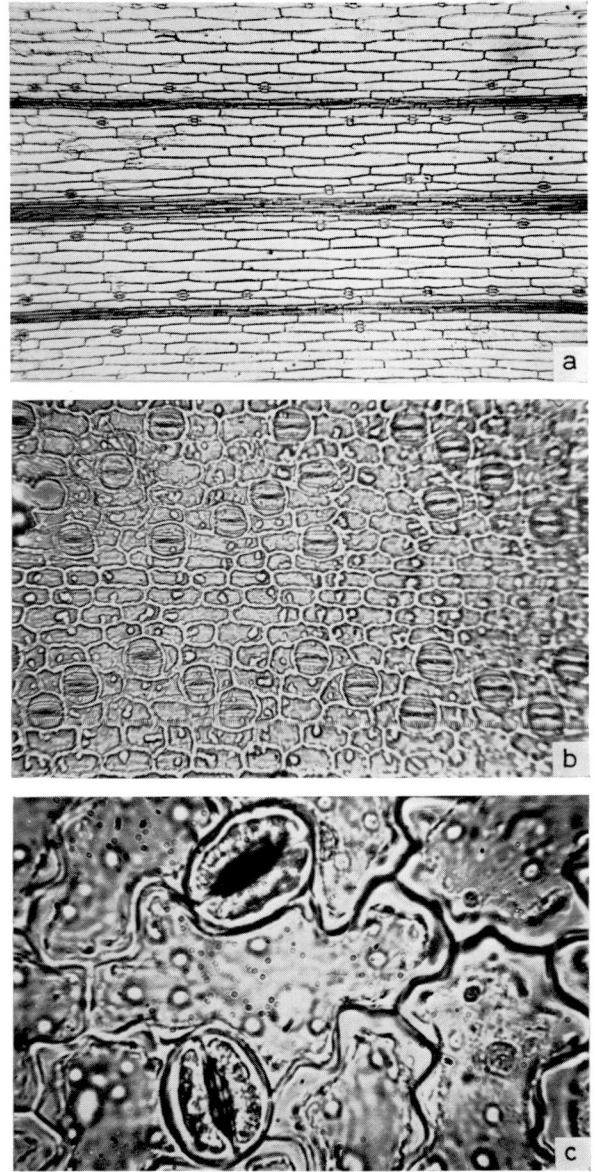

PLATE 1. Characteristic appearance of epidermal material.

(a) *Poa annua:* Adaxial surface of leaf, magnification 40;
(b) *Juncus effusus:* Surface of stem, magnification 160;
(c) *Trifolium pratense:* Abaxial surface of leaf, magnification 400.

Facing p. 176

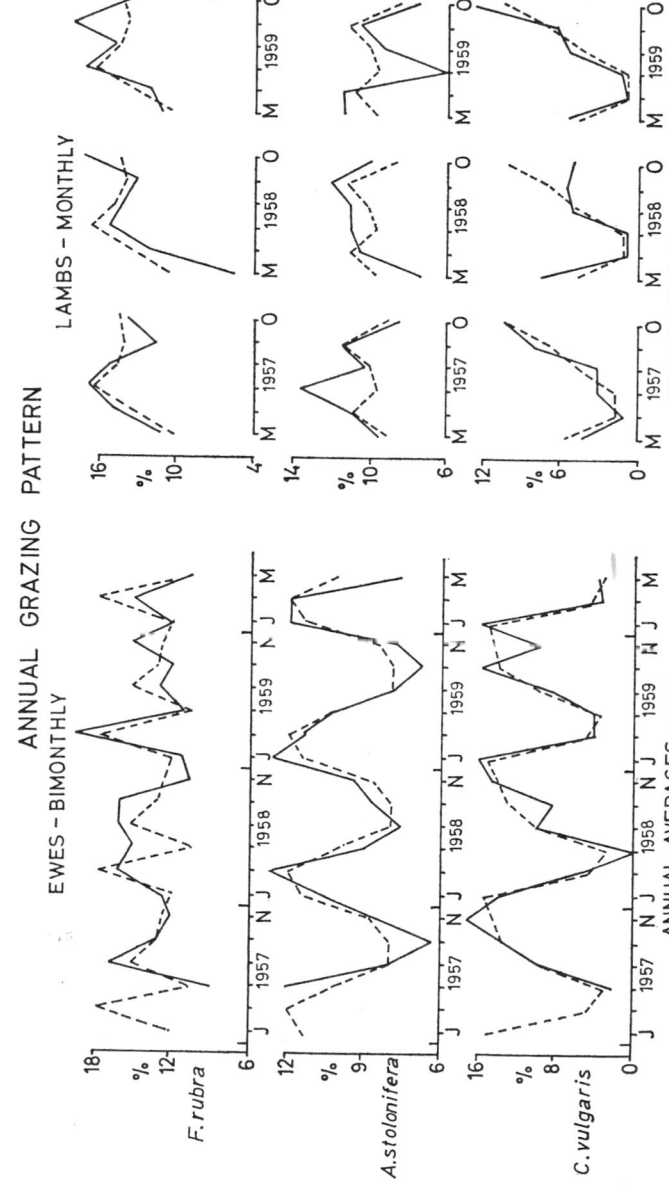

FIG. 1. Annual grazing patterns for ewes (left) and lambs (right). The long term average, based on the whole period 1957–59, is shown as a thrice repeated dotted line with which the results for each particular year, shown as a full line, can be compared.

13

DAVID J. MARTIN

TABLE I

Comparison of fragment counts — average monthly percentage

| | BE — Barnacarry Ewes | | | | BL — Barnacarry Lambs | | | | | | | |
| | LE — Low End Ewes | | | | LL — Low End Lambs | | | | | | | |
	Jan.	Feb.	Mch.	Apl.	May	Jun.	Jul.	Aug.	Sep.	Oct.	Nov.	Dec.
1. *F. rubra*												
BE	12	13	21	15	9	12	17	13	14	13	12	13
LE	10	12	19	16	13	13	17	14	13	12	11	13
BL					10	13	16	15	14	14		
LL					13	15	18	15	13	14		
2. *A. stolonifera*												
BE	11	12	13	12	10	9	7	6	6	7	8	7
LE	9	10	11	7	9	6	5	6	7	7	8	9
BL					10	11	10	10	11	9		
LL					8	8	6	5	5	6		
3. *Juncus* species												
BE	13	12	7	4	3	3	2	3	4	7	11	13
LE	14	13	10	8	6	4	5	4	4	8	12	15
BL					1	1	0	1	2	4		
LL					5	3	3	3	3	6		
4. *Eriophorum* species												
BE	8	7	7	10	12	8	4	4	3	2	2	5
LE	9	8	9	8	9	9	6	5	5	2	3	7
BL					11	10	8	5	4	2		
LL					9	8	8	6	4	3		
5. *Carex* species												
BE	5	5	7	10	7	4	3	4	3	4	7	8
LE	6	6	6	9	7	4	4	5	4	7	9	7
BL					4	5	4	5	4	4		
LL					8	9	7	8	8	8		
6. *N. stricta*												
BE	0	1	1	3	2	3	2	1	1	1	1	2
LE	0	0	1	2	2	1	1	1	0	1	0	0
BL					0	0	0	0	0	0		
LL					1	1	1	1	0	0		
7. *M. caerulea*												
BE	4	8	8	6	7	5	1	2	1	1	1	2
LE	4	6	7	7	6	6	4	3	3	2	2	4
BL					7	7	5	2	1	1		
LL					6	6	4	2	1	1		

TABLE I contd.

	Jan.	Feb.	Mch.	Apl.	May	Jun.	Jul.	Aug.	Sep.	Oct.	Nov.	Dec.
8. C. vulgaris												
BE	17	19	6	3	2	3	5	14	13	12	13	15
LE	19	21	11	8	6	4	7	13	13	10	14	16
BL					5	1	2	4	7	10		
LL					4	3	3	3	5	9		
9. Trifolium and Lotus species												
BE	0	1	2	2	3	5	6	3	5	7	5	1
LE	0	0	1	1	2	6	7	10	10	7	1	0
BL					4	8	10	9	8	9		
LL					3	6	6	10	11	9		
10. Gramineae, Juncaceae and Cyperaceae												
BE	54	64	74	79	73	64	57	43	55	49	53	50
LE	64	65	76	78	74	66	52	56	55	59	60	65
BL					68	74	68	60	57	53		
LL					71	72	70	56	58	60		
11. Forage Herbs												
BE	28	27	15	11	15	23	27	31	33	37	33	31
LE	29	29	20	18	21	27	29	38	39	32	26	26
BL					17	17	20	23	28	36		
LL					20	24	24	33	38	33		

movement over different types of swards. The present results confirm such a cycle on the basis of the plants eaten.

There is some variation between individual sheep, greatest in the case of the lambs, which cannot be shown in Fig. 1. Over the period of study, however, the average diet of each sheep was remarkably alike, as Hercus (1959) has also found. Variation in diet preferences between sheep leads to such variation, as does the flock factor, suggested by Hunter (1958) by which the movements of a sheep, and hence the species which it grazes, are influenced by the distribution of the flock and by the close proximity of other members of the flock.

2. Seasonal use of selected species

The fragment counts of certain species in the faecal samples are shown in Table 1; 1–11. The results are expressed to the nearest percentage and are the average monthly percentages over the four-year sampling period.

Festuca rubra (Table 1; 1)

Red fescue fragments were, at almost all times of the year, the most frequent component of sample counts. On both hirsels the intake was highest in March when young fresh growth of this plant was appearing. This selection disappeared to some extent from April till June, rising again to a peak in July. This sequence of fragment count values was found in both ewe and lamb samples; in the latter the values tended to be higher at almost all times of the sampling period.

The low intake period of May–June is not solely a reflection of decreasing palatability of red fescue at this time of the year but rather an indication of the presence of other species becoming available in a general spring flush. In particular, plants such as *Molinia caerulea*, *Nardus stricta*, *Carex* spp. and *Eriophorum* spp. were eaten more commonly during this period and thus contributed to the spring decline in the grazing of red fescue.

Agrostis stolonifera (Table 1; 2)

In this species a tendency was shown towards major use at only one period of the year, from February to April, with intake decreasing to a very low value in autumn samples. The spring use coincides with the start of yearly growth in this species, and the autumn minimum is at the time of an increasing amount of dying leaf blades, while there is still a relative abundance of more palatable species, particularly forage herbs, available to the animals.

The two ewe groups follow an essentially similar pattern of grazing. On the other hand, the lamb grazing results differ considerably from one another. The Low End lambs follow the Low End ewe pattern fairly closely whereas the Barnacarry lambs show an *Agrostis* intake which is considerably higher than any of the other three groups. The reasons for this are not clear. There is a difference in the amount of *Agrostis* available to the animals on each hirsel, the greater proportion being on Barnacarry. Since the ewe samples for each hirsel are similar in content throughout the year, allowing for the variation in amount available on each hirsel, it follows that the lambs on Barnacarry have a grazing pattern on *Agrostis* which is not determined solely by availability of the species or by imitation of the ewe, as are the patterns for some other species. The results were obtained from lambs in successive years, thus the variation cannot be due to any extent to sampling error.

Juncus spp. (Table 1; 3)

These species were shown to be very valuable in the period October–March. They are winter-hardy and are easily found in severe weather conditions; *J. squarrosus* in particular can be pulled from the ground to give succulent basal material in the winter. *J. effusus* was the most frequent in samples over the whole sampling period, but in January and February samples *J. articulatus* and *J. squarrosus* were present in the same frequency as *J. effusus*.

Eriophorum spp. (Table 1: 4)

These species (*E. vaginatum* and *E. angustifolium*) occurred most frequently in sample counts from April–June but also formed an important part of the December–April samples. The material eaten in this latter period must have been rather unpalatable, much of it being of dead leaves from the previous growing season, although *E. vaginatum* shows a few green shoots at almost all times of the year.

Carex spp. (Table 1; 5)

In these species the most frequent sample counts were found in the periods March–May and October–December. At such times they formed an appreciable part of the diet. Even during spring and summer they were by no means a negligible factor in the diet analyses. As with *A. stolonifera* it can be seen that one group of animals, in this case Low End lambs, showed an appreciably higher intake of *Carex* spp. than any other group of animals. On Low End hirsel the *Carex* spp. tend to occur in larger communities than on Barnacarry and this is the probable factor influencing their higher intake by the Low End lambs.

Nardus stricta (Table 1; 6)

At no time of the year did this species form an important part of the diet, and indeed it was only in the period April–July that it was grazed to any extent. This corresponds with its major growth period for the year; after this period it becomes wiry and more or less completely unpalatable. The lambs consistently ate less of this species than did the ewes, particularly on the Barnacarry hirsel.

Molinia caerulea (Table 1; 7)

From January–June this species appeared to be readily grazed by the sheep. For part of this period, until March, they must have been grazing mainly on old leaves of the previous year's growth or, by intensive selection, grazing on early growth of the current year.

It is of interest to note that the lambs showed a higher preference for this species than did the ewes, until about August.

Calluna vulgaris (Table 1; 8)

Considerable importance has always been attached to this plant as a component of the diet of hill sheep and the results obtained showed a high incidence of it in the samples.

The highest counts were found in the November–February samples, corresponding to the time when there is little other herbaceous material available. Heather intake quickly declined as other plants became available in the spring, but showed a slight increase after the heather had flowered.

The lambs consistently ate less heather than did the ewes, and the analyses of the lamb samples showed a more marked fall in heather intake during the April–June period than did the ewe samples. Gradually thereafter the lamb intake approached that of the ewes, until in October the fragment counts in lamb and ewe samples were almost the same.

Trifolium spp. and Lotus spp. (Table 1; 9)

The intake of these species followed very closely to their pattern of growth and availability throughout the year. A considerable increase in fragment count was evident from April onwards, when their growth starts in quantity, until a rapid fall in September, after they had flowered and fruited.

These species are infrequent over the grazing areas in question and the present results must be considered as showing a definite selection process for them, particularly by the lambs.

Gramineae, Juncaceae and Cyperaceae (Table 1; 10)

At all times of the year, these, the narrow-leaved plants of importance on the hill, formed the greater part of the diet. The period March–May corresponds to the spring flush of many of the components of this group and the decline shown later reflects, in part, the lesser attractiveness of the maturing plants and the greater availability of forage herbs. As the autumn approached the intake of grasses, rushes and sedges again increased.

It was noted that, almost consistently, the lambs had a higher intake of this group of plants than did the ewes.

Other forage herbs (Table 1; 11)

This group comprises the herbaceous Dicotyledons and the petalloid Monocotyledons. In April, during the period of least intake of forage herbs, the grasses and their allies are at their most palatable while the herbs are few in number and small in bulk. This position is gradually reversed as the year progresses and by October maximum intake of the herbs is found, at a time when many of the grasses have flowered and become less attractive to the grazing animals.

3. *Diet analyses and comparative grazing intensity*

Hunter (1954a, b) has investigated the movement of sheep over an ecologically well-marked hillside in Midlothian. His results were expressed as Comparative Grazing Intensities (C.G.I.) (Boulet, 1939) which show the relative incidence of grazing on any particular area, and also the pattern of grazing throughout the year.

In some cases the present results can be compared with those of Hunter in order to show whether or not the animals, when grazing in, for example, a Festucetum, are in fact grazing mainly on *Festuca*.

Fig. 2; 1–5 shows the comparison which can be made from the two sets of results. Hunter's results were obtained from observation of Blackface ewes on an unrestricted hill, and for the purposes of comparison the results from Barnacarry ewes in the present study have been used.

It can be seen that the sequence of grazing throughout the year as shown by the two methods is quite similar. Hence it can be concluded that when the animals are in a particular plant community they graze mainly on the dominant species; it can also be concluded that the analysis of faecal samples can assess the past movements of sheep over various communities, provided that the communities are reasonably pure.

Variations between results obtained by the two methods indicate that the sheep were ignoring the main constituent and selectively grazing some minor member. This would be particularly so where the faecal counts for a particular species were consistently below the C.G.I. assessment for the same period of the year. Where the faecal counts were consistently above the C.G.I. assessment the implication would be that much of the species under consideration was being grazed from impure stands.

It must be noted that, in the present instance, correspondence of faecal sample and C.G.I. values do not imply that the same amount of the plant, in terms of weight, was grazed at the two centres, but solely that the same pattern of grazing was exhibited by the two sets of animals.

In the comparisons for *Calluna vulgaris* Hunter's results do not include

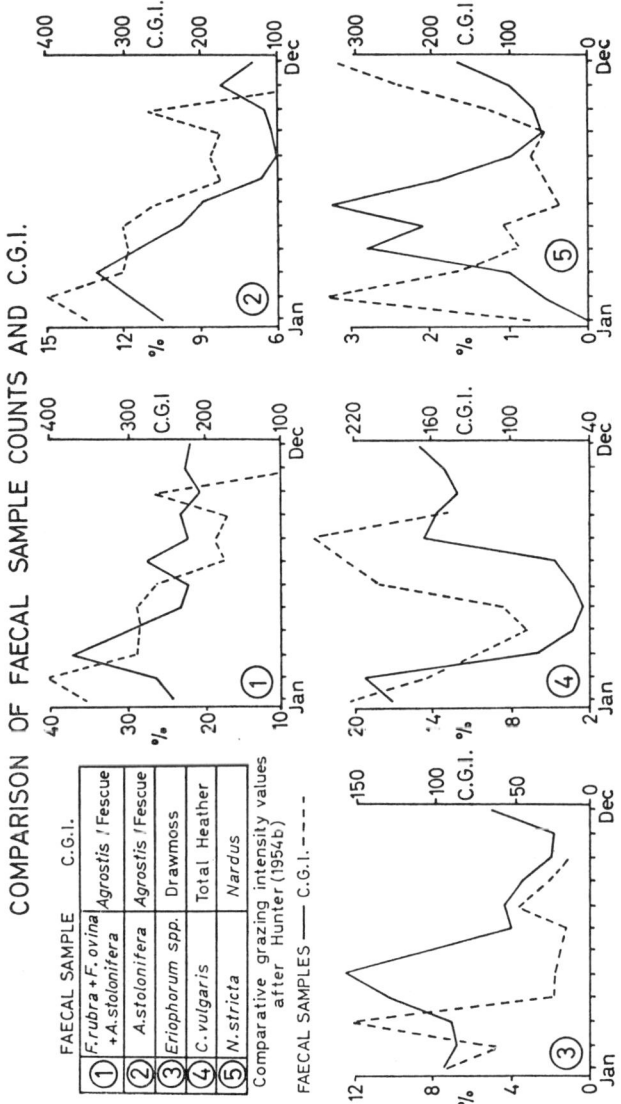

Fig. 2. Comparison of annual grazing pattern found from faecal analysis and comparative grazing intensities.

those days in which snow cover was so heavy as to interfere with the sheeps' choice of sward types, and he notes that if these days had been added the C.G.I. of heather would have been increased. This would influence the C.G.I. results in the period November–March.

In the case of *Nardus stricta* it can be seen that in the period April–September the faecal counts were much higher than the C.G.I. values. The spring values may well be high due to the fact that spring droughts have a more severe effect at Lephinmore than in Midlothian, leading to a higher intake of those plants, including *Nardus*, which can withstand such conditions.

It can also be seen from the comparison of these results that the maxima and minima from the present result are frequently one month later than those shown by Hunter's work. A probable explanation for this is that the two sets of results were obtained under different climatic conditions which would affect the rate of growth and time of maturity of the plants.

4. *Ewe and lamb diet*

From a statistical analysis of the results of this study it can be shown that, despite a difference in the amount of the major components of the diet available on each hirsel, the diet of the sheep on Barnacarry hirsel was essentially the same as that of the sheep on Low End hirsel. Exceptions to this were found in the case of *N. stricta*, of which, in ewe samples, significantly less was eaten by the Low End ewes, and in the case of *C. vulgaris* of which significantly more was eaten by the Low End ewes.

Nardus is of more or less equal occurrence on both hirsels, whereas Low End hirsel carries much more *Calluna* than does Barnacarry. It is probable, therefore, that the Low End ewes ate more *Calluna* because there was more available, but it must be borne in mind that no significant difference was evident in the amount eaten of other species which vary in quantity between the two hirsels, for example *Festuca* spp., *Eriophorum* spp. and *Juncus* spp.

When a similar analysis is applied to the lamb diet results it is found that the Low End lambs ate significantly more of the *Juncus* spp. and *Carex* spp. and significantly less *A. stolonifera* than did the lambs on Barnacarry. The probable factors influencing these differences are availability and quantity of the three species on the hirsels.

It can be concluded that, apart from a few exceptional cases, both ewes and lambs on each hirsel selected an essentially similar diet from a differing flora, to the extent of intense selection for infrequent species or the rejection of abundant species.

From the above results and comparisons it can be deduced that sheep show a definite pattern of grazing throughout the year on the species available to them, and as a result also vary the intensity of their grazing on types of plants, for example on herbs or on grasses.

Almost without exception, maximum intake of a species was found to be at the time of the year when it is most palatable, with secondary maxima occurring at times when there was little or no choice of grazing material available to the animals. Fenton (1949), Tribe (1950a, b), Davies (1925) and Arnold (1961) are in agreement that sheep prefer the finer, younger and more succulent herbage; Arnold extends this to selection by the sheep for the leaf or stem material which contains the most nitrogen as protein at any given time.

F. rubra and *C. vulgaris* were the most common plant fragments in the samples at almost all times of the year. At the present stage of this method of investigation, frequency of a particular species is not a guide to the amount eaten in terms of weight. MacLeod (1955), however, has shown that the consumption of heather by sheep is greater than might generally have been realized, and that they graze on entire shoots up to two inches long in the winter. The present results bear out his contention that heather is an extremely important and valuable part of the diet.

The *Juncus* spp. and *Carex* spp. formed an important part of the diet in winter and spring. Dougall (1951) regards *C. panicea* as an important feature of the winter feed of sheep whilst Braid (1954) places the Cyperaceae as the third most important group of plants on hill pasture, after the grasses and heather.

The results from *Molinia caerulea* indicated that this plant might be more widely grazed than is generally realized, although Wallace (1884) commented that sheep fatten and do well on *Molinia* 'living on little else for a month or more, and continuing all summer to eat a part'. As with so many other hill pasture plants, its usefulness is of limited duration. An increase in the amount of this plant available on the hill would not necessarily lead to better grazing conditions in general.

As mentioned above, the results for *Trifolium* spp. and *Lotus* spp. indicated that there had been intensive selection for them, particularly by the lambs. One of the most pressing hill pasture problems is the production of legume species which will grow and nodulate successfully under such conditions, producing strong vegetative growth available to the animals for long periods of the year and supplying a higher protein intake than is currently available.

Hercus (1960) has shown that it might be possible to correlate qualitative investigations of the type described here with quantitative data. Such an extension would be extremely valuable, since the present work, while indicating the relative amount of a species grazed at any time of the year, does not define the weight of this species nor its weight relative to another species. Little is at present known of the relations obtaining among weight ingested, digestibility and faecal fragment counts. Further intensive work on stall-housed animals fed a weighed and known diet will be necessary to find the required correlations.

ACKNOWLEDGEMENTS

The author wishes to express his thanks to Professor John Walton of the University of Glasgow, and to Dr William Fletcher of the West of Scotland Agricultural College, for their interest and encouragement during this investigation.

Thanks are also due to the Director of the Hill Farming Research Organization and to the Manager and Staff of Lephinmore Hill Farm for their help and advice.

REFERENCES

ACCORSI W.R. (1949) Caracteristicas morfologicas, anatomicas e citologicas de epidérmê iñteriôr dâ fôlhâ daš Rublaceae. *Lilloa* 10, 5–39

ANON (1953) *Hill Farm Research, 2nd Report.* H.M.S.O., Edinburgh

ARNOLD G.W. (1961) Diet of sheep. *Nature, Lond.* **192,** 113–114

BORRILL M. (1957) A morphologically distinct ecotype of *Dactylis glomerata* L. *Nature, Lond.* **179,** 544–545

BOULET L.J. (1939) The ecology of a Welsh mountain sheep's walk. Unpublished Thesis, U.C.W., Aberystwyth (Cited by Hunter 1954b)

BRAID K.W. (1954) Make up of hill and marginal land grazings. *Scot. Fmr.* **62,** 1463, 1499

CLARKE J. (1960) Preparation of leaf epidermis for topographic study. *Stain Tech.* **35,** 35–39

DAVIES W. (1925) Relative palatability of pasture plants. *J. Minist. Ag.* **32,** 106–116

DOUGALL B.M. (1951) Carnation sedge (*C. panicea*) and sheep. *Agriculture, Lond.* **62,** 348–349

ESAU K. (1953) *Plant Anatomy.* Chapman and Hall, London

FENTON E.W. (1949) Vegetation changes in hill grazings. *J. Brit. Grassl. Soc.* **4,** 95–105

HERCUS B.H. (1959) A method of estimating the botanical composition of the diet of sheep. *N.Z.J. agric. Res.* **2,** 72–85

HERCUS B.H. (1960) Plant cuticle as an aid to determine the diet of grazing animals. *Proc. Int. Grass. Cong.* 1B

HUNTER R.F. (1954a) Some notes on the behaviour of hill sheep. *Brit. J. an. Behaviour* **2,** 75–78

HUNTER R. F. (1954b) The grazing of hill pasture sward types. *J. Brit. Grassl. Soc.* **9,** 195–208

HUNTER R. F. (1958) Hill land improvement. *Advanc. Sci.* **59,** 194–196

LETHAM D. S. (1958) Maceration of plant tissues with ethylene-diamine tetra-acetic acid. *Nature, Lond.* **181,** 135–136

LOUW J. G., WILLIAMS H. H. & MAYNARD L. A. (1949) A new method for the study *in vitro* of rumen digestion. *Science* **110,** 478–480

MACLEOD A. C. (1955) Heather in the seasonal dietary of sheep. *Proc. Brit. Soc. An. Prod.* **13,** 13–17

MARTIN D. J. (1955) Features on plant cuticle. *Trans. Proc. Bot. Soc. Edin.* **36,** 278–288

METCALFE C. R. (1960) *Anatomy of the Monocotyledons I. Gramineae.* Clarendon, Oxford

NORRIS J. J. (1943) Botanical analysis of stomach contents as a method of determining forage consumption of range sheep. *Ecol.* **24,** 244–251

NORTH C. (1956) A technique for measuring structural features of plant epidermis using cellulose acetate films. *Nature, Lond.* **178,** 1186

PHILLIPSON A. T. (1952) The passage of digesta from the abomasum of sheep. *J. Physiol.* **116,** 84–97

PRAT H. (1932) L'epiderme des graminees. *Ann. Sci. nat.* **10,** 14

PRAT H. (1948) General features of the epidermis in *Zea mays. Ann. Mo. bot. Gdn.* **35,** 341–352

SKOSS J. D. (1955) Structure and composition of plant cuticle in relation to environmental factors and permeability. *Bot. Gaz.* **117,** 55–72

TRIBE D. E. (1950a) The composition of a sheep's natural diet. *J. Brit. Grassl. Soc.* **5,** 81–91

TRIBE D. E. (1950b) The behaviour of the grazing animal. *J. Brit. Grassl. Soc.* **5,** 209–224

WALLACE R. (1884) The natural and artificial food of Scotch hill sheep. *Trans. Highl. agric. Soc. Scot.* **16,** 250–273

WINTON A. L. & WINTON K. B. (1932) *The Structure and Composition of Foods.* Wiley and Sons, New York

SELECTIVITY IN GRAZING

R. Elfyn Hughes, C. Milner and J. Dale

The Nature Conservancy,
Headquarters for Wales and Bangor Research Station,
Penrhos Road, Bangor, North Wales

ABSTRACT

The possible factors determining 'palatability' or 'acceptability' of plants to grazing animals have been considered in the light of recent work on the chemical composition and the nutritional value of the plants.

Particular attention has been given to studies dealing with the energy value of herbage in the regulation of food intake by ruminants. The wider significance of this factor in the study of plant herbivore relationships and the flow of energy in such systems is emphasized.

Work on the broader aspects of selective grazing at present in progress in Snowdonia, North Wales, by the Nature Conservancy has been described. The voluntary sheep population density borne by a range of plant communities sited along a rainfall gradient of from 40 in. (101·6 cm) to 200 in. (508 cm) mean annual has been shown to have an inverse relationship to altitude, rainfall and the trend towards soil podsolization.

A preliminary experiment tends to show that voluntary sheep population density is related to sheep body weight increment on a per acre but not on a per capita basis. It is suggested that the increased population density on acceptable plant communities may limit body weight gain so that it is little different from that which accrues from less acceptable vegetation.

I. INTRODUCTION

The voluntary selection by grazing animals, particularly by sheep, of broad categories of vegetation, has been investigated in Britain in recent years (Boulet, 1939; Hunter, 1954; Hughes, 1954; 1958a; 1958b; 1960). Within this broad pattern of grazing, there is a finer selection of individual species and parts of plants. Investigations into this aspect of selectivity in grazing can be subdivided into three categories:

(a) The determination of the degree of selection of plant species and their parts by different herbivores.
(b) The factors determining selective grazing.
(c) The nutritional value of the selected species and components to the animal.

Some of the results which have accrued from such investigations are of basic significance, particularly in relation to the study of the flow of energy in plant-herbivore systems.

II. SELECTION OF SPECIES AND FACTORS DETERMINING SELECTION

It is not proposed to review in detail the earlier work on selective grazing, as several reviews already exist (Davies, 1925; Milton, 1933; Tribe, 1950; Ivins, 1952), but to consider the factors which may determine selectivity and its nutritional significance.

From earlier work, it was generally considered that nutritional value and its specific and seasonal variation was an important factor in determining the acceptability of plants or parts of them to animals. It was, however, considered that when animals, particularly sheep, were given free choice between the more succulent, and apparently more nutritious, grassland and the rough, more fibrous vegetation, the sheep alternated its grazing between the two. Many weeds were regarded as being acceptable to the grazing animal because of their high mineral content. In more recent years these views have been re-examined. Tribe (1950), for instance, concludes that animals have no instinct as to what is best for them and, in an analysis of Linnaeus' early work on the acceptability of different plants to animals, he found no common features which determined acceptability. Ivins (1952) considered that selective grazing was not determined by the chemical composition of the plants though he did record intra-specific variations in the acceptability of certain species and strains to cattle. The most acceptable species was rib grass (*Plantago lanceolata*), and the least was trefoil (*Medicago lupulina*). This is of interest, since rib grass is known to have high mineral content and the economic productivity recorded from this species is considerable (Fagan and Watkins, 1932; Milton, 1943).

In this connection, recent work in mid-Wales by Davies, Jones and Milton (1959) is of interest. They have shown that, in the case of poor hill vegetation of *Molinia*, *Agrostis* and *Festuca* grassland, the calcium status of the vegetation plays an important role in determining palatability and yield of living material and its digestibility. Addition of calcium carbonate to the diet of sheep improved their growth.

Attempts have been made to correlate 'palatability' or acceptability with specific qualities of the herbage. Tribe and Gordon (1950) have considered the effect of colour and smell on the grazing habits of sheep, and concluded that neither were of very great significance, although the sense .

of smell is of importance in the initial stimulation of appetite. Investigations by Bell (1959) into the significance of taste showed interesting variations in response amongst herbivore species to compounds of quinine. Such variations in response might provide some explanation of the different grazing habits of the animals studied. For example, rabbits and oxen rejected quinine compounds at concentrations of 1·6 and 1·9 mg per 100 ml of water, respectively; goats did not reject a solution until it contained 125 mg of quinine per 100 ml.

Taste is possibly concerned in differences noted by Roe and Mottershead (1962) in the palatability of strains of *Phalaris arundinacea*, since the 'factor' reducing the palatability of a strain could be extracted and, by addition, used to change the palatability of other strains. It is of interest in this connection that silkworm larvae appear to react to specific substances in mulberry leaves which attract them and stimulate biting and swallowing (Hamamura and Naito, 1961; Hamamura, Hayashiya and Naito, 1961).

Citral, linalol acetate and lanalol attract silkworm larvae; beta-sitosterol stimulates biting and a so far unknown substance stimulates swallowing.

It is evident that this is a field for further enquiry and significant to the basic studies in plant-herbivore relationships and productivity.

III. NUTRITIONAL VALUE OF SELECTED SPECIES AND THEIR PARTS

Two important lines of enquiry in the field of nutrition have developed in recent years which are of significance to studies in plant-herbivore relationships.

These lines are:

(*a*) The *digestibility* of the organic matter of the herbage and its constituents.

(*b*) *Energy flow* in the plant-grazing animal system.

(*a*) The *digestibility of the herbage grazed by animals*

Raymond (1959) considers that the nutritive value of the food eaten by the animals is directly related to its digestibility rather than to its chemical composition. It is also believed to be related to the amount of food voluntarily ingested, which when related to particular plant species and parts of them, is a measure of selectivity in grazing.

He shows seasonal inter- and intra-specific variation in the percentage of digestible material in three strains of grass, namely S.37—Cocksfoot (*Dactylis glomerata*), S.23 and S.24—Perennial Rye Grass (*Lolium perenne*), which is related to the stage of growth. Similarly, Reid (1959) has shown that digestibility of forages decreases from 30 April onwards according to a relationship that could be expressed in the form of a linear equation.

The significance of the amount of voluntary intake of food is also stressed by Crampton (1959) and Blaxter (1960). Ivins (1960) suggests that the amount of herbage, expressed as dry matter, eaten by the animal is closely related to its digestibility. The acceptability and digestibility are said to be closely related and complementary. Therefore Ivins suggests that the nutritive value of herbage can be regarded as being proportional to the square of its digestibility. The digestibility of herbage has been shown to be related to milk production in cattle (Brundage, 1960; Blaser et al., 1959).

Grazing animals appear to select from the individual plant those organs of highest digestibility. The preference for leaves rather than for the stem has been shown for instance in the case of lucerne (Meyer et al., 1957) and the grass, Phalaris tuberosa (Arnold, 1960). Arnold's work showed that there was selection of the tissue of highest nitrogen content. Sheep were more effective than cattle in the selection from lucerne of forage higher in digestible nutrients (Meyer et al., 1959). Hardison et al. (1954) have shown that the material selected by steers is of higher digestibility than the vegetation as a whole. Cattle selected herbage from the tops of plants (Blaser et al., 1960) higher in digestibility, protein and fat, and lower in crude fibre, than did the animals grazing the bases of plants left after an earlier grazing. It has been suggested (Crampton, 1959) that the digestibility of grass is limited by that of the cellulose and hemi-cellulose present, although the digestibility of the latter may be influenced by internal factors such as the rumen environment, particularly its micro-flora and the amount of lignin ingested. It is clear that the whole problem of the causation of selective grazing by herbivores is complex and needs much further elucidation, particularly with regard to small mammals.

(b) The energy considerations

The relationship between the energy value of herbage to the grazing animal and its digestible nutrients is of significance in relation to the foregoing (Crampton et al., 1957; Crampton, 1959). In the case of ruminants, theoretically, this means that, since voluntary intake of food is linked with digestibility, the energy implications are considerable. A significant contribution has been that of Blaxter et al. (1961) on the regulation of food intake by the sheep. In this work, an attempt was made to place on a quantitative basis the generalization that the voluntary food intake of ruminants increases with the quality of the fodder they are given.

The voluntary intake of fodders of varying quality was related to their apparent digestible energy, increasing rapidly as digestibility increased from 38 to 70 per cent and, thereafter, more slowly. An increased digestibility in the range between 40 and 60 per cent resulted in a considerable increase in the total amount of apparently digestible energy and an increase in daily gain in weight. Blaxter's findings are summarized in Table 1.

The results and conclusions of the studies discussed in previous sections are of importance to ecology and the study of energy flow in ecological systems grazed by ruminants. It appears that animals such as sheep tend to graze plants or parts of them of high digestibility and, from the studies of Blaxter *et al.* (1961), this can lead to a considerable increase in the energy available to the animal and an enhanced rate of growth. It is concluded, for example, that an increase in the digestibility of a fodder from 50 to 55 per cent (10 per cent increase in the value of the food) increases body gain by 100 per cent. Similar considerations may be of significance to the study of the dynamics of ruminant animal populations and their application to that of small mammals is of immediate importance. Golley (1960) in his work on the energy dynamics of a food chain of an old field community records very high digestibility of lucerne (90 per cent) and other food materials to *Microtus*. In the case of blue grass, the dominant species of the environment studied, the *Microtus* feeding on it lost weight or died. It is possible that, in the field, the *Microtus* were highly selective in their feeding, and parts of the plants of high digestibility in terms of energy may have been selected. Clearly the application of the kind of work developed by Blaxter to problems of this kind is most important, though the regulation of energy intake of other animals may be different from that of sheep. In poultry and rats for example, food intake is regulated so that a constant energy intake is maintained, this being the reverse of the regulating mechanism in ruminants.

IV. THE BROADER ASPECTS OF SELECTIVE GRAZING

The more general selection by sheep of particular plant communities for grazing has already been mentioned. Work in this field has been pursued from the Nature Conservancy's Research Station at Bangor, N. Wales. Its main areas of investigation are in Snowdonia; the slopes of Snowdon and the uplands of the Conway Valley (Hughes, 1958a and b and 1960). Since 1956 a weekly census has been made of selective sheep grazing

14

TABLE I

The regulation of food intake by the sheep from Blaxter *et al.* (1961)

(Incorporating Tables 3, 4 and 7 of Blaxter)

Fodder Quality	Crude protein = total nitrogen × 6·25	Apparent digestibility of energy as % energy ingested	Voluntary intake of dry matter $\frac{g/24\ hr}{[kgW]^{0.734}}$	Intake digestible energy $\frac{k\ cal/24\ hr}{[kgW]^{0.734}}$	Digestible energy available above estimated maintenance $\frac{k\ cal/24\ hr^{1}}{[kgW]^{0.734}}$	Gain or loss in weight $\frac{g/24\ hr}{[kgW]^{0.734}}$
Poor	7·5	44·7	50·5	101·9	1·1	−1·5
Medium	9·5	58·8	77·2	206·3	105·5	+6·5
Good	17·8	74·8	94·0	318·9	218·1	+11·4

[1] The maintenance requirement of the trained adult sheep has been estimated to be $108 \cdot 8 \pm 2 \cdot 2$ k cal digested energy/24 hr/[kgW]$^{0.734}$

kgW = Body weight in kg

0·734 = Exponent relating basal energy metabolism to body weight (Brody, 1945) within seventy plots, which incorporate various kinds of communities, the dominants being *Agrostis* spp., *Festuca* spp., *Calluna vulgaris*, *Nardus stricta*, *Ulex gallii* and *Pteridium aquilinum* on acidic brown earths and podzols derived respectively from basic and acidic igneous rocks. They occur at altitudes of from 800 ft (244 m) to 3,000 ft (914 m) O.D. and traverse a rainfall range of 40 in. (101 cm) to 200 in. (508 cm) mean annual. The sheep population densities characteristic of the communities have been taken as a crude index of the yield of living material from them. Population densities generally show an inverse relationship to altitude, rainfall and to the trend of the soil to podzolization (Hughes, 1954, 1958a and b and 1960).

During the past year (1961), a preliminary attempt has been made to find whether these voluntary population densities reflect a real difference in the increment of animal material per unit area. Two sites, dissimilar both ecologically and in the sheep population densities they bear, were enclosed. The body weight changes in 12 ewes and 12 lambs were followed between mid-May and early July 1961. Both sites were at an altitude of 1,500 ft (457 m) o.d. and had a mean annual rainfall of approximately 160 in. (460 cm). Fig. 1 sets out the weekly variation throughout the year in sheep population densities on these two plots (*a*) and (*b*). A description of each follows.

(a) *Agrostis–Festuca grassland*

On an acidic brown earth derived from colluvium consisting mainly of basic igneous rock, the normal voluntary sheep population densities during the growing season varied from approximately 2·25 to a maximum of 4·1 ewe units[1] to the acre (or approximately 7·5 to 13·66 units/hectare).

The experimental plot was 2·4 acres (0·98 ha) in size and, therefore, bore a population density of approximately 7 ewe units/acre (19 ewe units/ha).

(b) *Nardus stricta grassland*

On a peaty podzol soil derived from acidic igneous rocks and acidic drift, the sheep densities varied between 1·5 to 2·5 units to the acre (4·9 to 8·33 units/ha) during the growing season.

The experimental plot was 6·50 acres (2·63 ha) in size and the population density would be approximately 2·75 ewe units/acre (7·4 ewe units/ha).

Since the voluntary sheep population densities differed, the enclosures

---

[1] The number of ewe units expresses the number of ewes considered equivalent to the actual stock grazing the pasture. Thus 1 lamb = ½ ewe unit.

were made so that the experimental densities were proportional to the densities observed under conditions of free grazing. The growth of vegetation might, therefore, tend to be limiting. Ivins (1960) stressed the importance in pasture productivity studies for these circumstances to prevail. The results of these experiments are set out in Table 2. The gain in body weight of lambs on a *per capita* basis did not differ on the two classes of land (10·42 lb on the *Agrostis-Festuca* and 8·25 lb on the *Nardus* plot), although the *per capita loss* in weight of ewes is significantly greater on the *Agrostis-Festuca* plot (3·1 as opposed to 0·58 lb on the *Nardus* site). However, the body weight increment of lambs per unit area is substantially

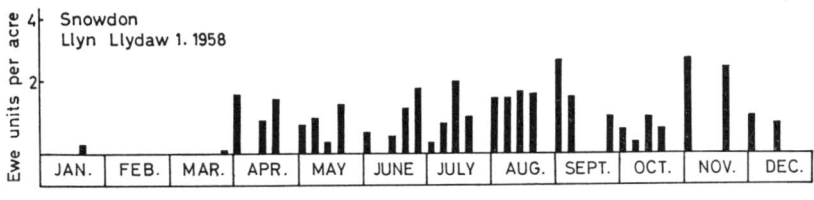

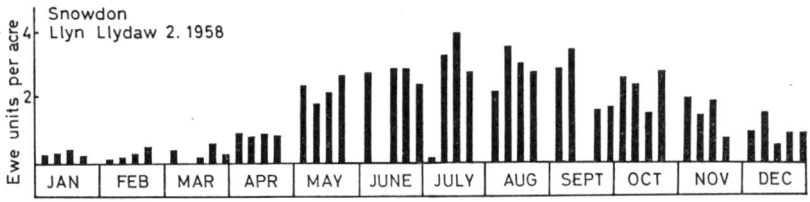

FIG. 1. Variation in population densities of sheep on two sites at Llyn Llydaw in 1958.

(a) Vegetation, *Nardus stricta*. 1500 ft (457 m) O.D. 160 in. (406 cm) mean annual rainfall. Area 7·5 acres (3·04 ha). Soil parent material–Rhyolite. Aspect N.E.

(b) Vegetation, *Agrostis-Festuca* grassland. 1500 ft (457 m) O.D. 160 in. (406 cm) mean annual rainfall. Area 22·8 acres (9·42 ha). Soil parent material – Pumice Tuff.

different (*Agrostis-Festuca* a gain of 49·61 lb/acre and *Nardus* a gain of 15·23 lb/acre), as is the loss of weight of ewes (*Agrostis-Festuca* a loss of 14·88 lb/acre and *Nardus* a loss of 1·08 lb/acre).

At present no data are available concerning the digestibility of organic matter or energy in the dry matter available in the vegetation at the start of the experiment. The estimated available dry matter per acre on the *Agrostis-Festuca* plot was twice as great as that on the *Nardus* site. It is of interest that according to the data available which are set out in Table 3

TABLE 2

Llyn Llydaw Experimental Area – Snowdon 1,500 ft (457 m) – Rainfall 160 in.
(406 cm) mean annual. Duration of experiment 24.5.61–2.7.61 (40 days).

1 Soil and Vegetation	Brown Earth *Agrostis/Festuca* grassland. 2·43 acre (0·98 ha) Plot	Peaty Podzol *Nardus stricta* grassland. 6·45 acre (2·61 ha) Plot
2 Mean sheep population ewe units/acre	4–7 (10–17 ha^{-1})	1·5–3 (3·7–7·4 ha^{-1})
3 Mean gain in weight of Individual lambs in lb	10·42 (4·62 Kg)	8·25 (3·74 Kg)
4 Mean loss in weight of individual ewes in lb	3·1 (1·4 Kg)	0·581 (0·264 Kg)
5 Gain in weight of lambs in lb/acre	49·61 (55·6 Kg ha^{-1})	15·23 (17·06 Kg ha^{-1})
6 Loss in weight of ewes in lb/acre	14·88 (16·65 Kg ha^{-1})	1·08 (1·208 Kg/ ha^{-1})
7 Net gain of animal material in lb/acre	34·73 (38·91 Kg ha^{-1})	14·15 (15·86 Kg ha^{-1})
8 Dry matter in lb/acre at beginning and end of Experiment	510 (570 Kg/ha) 67 (75 Kg ha^{-1})	206 (230 Kg ha^{-1}) 246 (275 Kg ha)

The calculated value of 't' (students' t test) for the differences on the two plots in the mean gain in body weight of lambs was 1·168, which, for a value of $n = 21$ degrees of freedom is not significant.

The calculated value of 't' for the differences in the mean gain of body weight of ewes was 6·137, which for a value of $n = 21$ shows that the differences between the means are significant at a level $P < 0·001$.

Metric equivalents are shown in brackets.

R. ELFYN HUGHES, C. MILNER AND J. DALE

TABLE 3

Nutrient Constituents of Vegetation

Llyn Llydaw experimental area — Snowdon

1,500 ft (457 m) O.D. — Rainfall 160 in. (406 cm) mean annual

All results expressed as a percentage of dry matter except for Cu & Mo.

Analyses carried out by D. E. Morgan, Esq., National Agricultural Advisory Service Centre, Bryn Adda, Bangor.

	Agrostis-Festuca Plot (Llyn Llydaw 2)		*Nardus* Plot (Llyn Llydaw 1)	
	24.5.61 Inside plot before 1st grazing	2.7.61 Inside plot after 1st grazing	24.5.61 Inside plot before 1st grazing	2.7.61 Inside plot after 1st grazing
Dry matter %	28·6		39·2	
Dry matter lb per acre	510·0	67·7	206·0	246·0
C. protein	14·1	10·7	12·1	11·1
C. fibre	23·9	27·9	25·3	28·2
Oil	2·7	1·9	1·9	2·0
Tot. ash	5·3	5·1	3·4	3·6
Nitrogen free extract	54·0	54·4	57·3	55·1
Ca	0·39	0·34	0·17	0·18
P	0·21	0·25	0·16	0·11
K	1·66	0·98	0·92	0·82
Mg	0·25	0·25	0·12	0·14
Na	0·16	0·10	0·09	0·09
Cu[1]	7·8[1]	7·8[1]	7·8[1]	7·7[1]
Mo[1]	0·30[1]	0·17[1]	0·82[1]	1·20[1]

[1] — parts/million.

there are no basic differences in the vegetation revealed by gross analyses for crude protein, fibre, oil, total ash, nitrogen-free extracts and mineral elements, except that the vegetation of the more productive site contains more calcium than that of the poorer site. This may be an important factor amongst others determining their relative yield of living material. This closely parallels the findings of Davies, Jones and Milton (1959). No herbage cobalt data are available but it is known that its concentration in the soil is greater on the more productive plot (20 parts per million as opposed to 3 parts per million total cobalt in the soil of the poorer plot (Table 4)). It is possible that these differences are reflected in the vegetation.

The conclusions that can be reached now, are that two ecologically dissimilar areas bearing different voluntary populations of sheep:

SELECTIVITY IN GRAZING 199

TABLE 4

Chemical data for two soils of the Llyn Llydaw experimental area — Snowdon 1,500 ft (457 m) O.D. — Mean annual rainfall 160 in. (406 cm).

Vegetation	(a) *Agrostis/Festuca* grassland					(b) *Nardus stricta* grassland		
Soil parent material and soil group	Pumice tuff colluvium (brown earth)					Rhyolitic drift (peaty Podzol)		
Horizon	0·4 in. (0–10 cm) A	4–7 in. (10–17 cm) A(B)	7–14 in. (17–35 cm) (B)	14–26 in. (35–66 cm) C	26–33 in. (66–84 cm) C	1–8 in. (2·5–20 cm) Ao	8–27 in. (20–68 cm) B	27–33 in. (68–84 cm) C
pH	6·6	6·5	6·0	6·2	6·0	4·9	5·1	5·2
[1]CaO	168	108	66	62	53	6	6	6
[1]K$_2$O	6·7	6·3	3·8	3·8	2·4	20·3	1·9	1·9
[1]P$_2$0$_5$	8·8	4·8	2·0	2·4	0·1	0·4	<0·1	0·1
% organic carbon	4·1	1·9	1·3	1·2	1·4	32·2	3·6	1·5
Cu p.p.m.	10	10	10	10	—	20	10	10
Co p.p.m.	20	20	20	20	—	3	3	Tr.
Mo p.p.m.	Trace	Trace	Trace	Trace	—	1	1	1

[1] mg/100 gr air-dry soil.

(a) have contrasting outputs of plant dry matter and net gains in body weight of sheep per unit area which appear to be related,

(b) the calcium levels in the vegetation may have a direct bearing on body weight gains of the sheep.

Differences in the digestibility of the organic material of the two kinds of vegetation may exist, and also differences in their nutritive value in terms of digestible energy, but no data of this kind have so far been obtained.

Assuming that the *Agrostis-Festuca* site has greater digestible organic matter and energy, it is possible to speculate that the voluntary intake of herbage by sheep grazing on it may be greater than that from the *Nardus* site. There is possibly some evidence that this may be so, since at the termination of the experiments the dry matter product of the herbage per acre on the former site was 67 lb (75 kg ha^{-1}) and on the latter 246 lb (275 kg ha^{-1}). The loss in weight of ewes on the *Agrostis-Festuca* plot is significantly greater than is that of the ewes on the *Nardus* plot (i.e. 3·1 in contrast to 0·58 lb) and suggests that the total experimental population density of sheep on the former plot is nearer the limit of its carrying capacity, than is the density imposed upon the *Nardus* site. It is evident also that voluntary intake of herbage from the *Agrostis-Festuca* site is not sufficient to enable *per capita* gains in weight of the lambs to be greater than those on the *Nardus* site. Under conditions of free grazing Blaxter's interpretation of the regulation of food intake in the sheep may operate. Increase in the voluntary intake and energy available to the animal may mean a mounting population density. The latter may ultimately limit body weight gains so that they are little different from those accruing from vegetation less acceptable to sheep, though increment per unit area may be greater. These considerations parallel those of Mott (1960).

At lower rainfalls in northern Snowdonia, higher sheep population densities (Hughes, 1958a, 1960) prevail, particularly on certain soils derived from basic igneous rock. Thus at 1,200 ft (365 m) O.D. with 70 in. mean annual rainfall, an *Agrostis-Festuca* site on soil derived from glacial drift with local pumice tuff colluvium supported a summer sheep population density of 10–12 ewe units per acre compared with the *Agrostis-Festuca* site illustrated in Fig. 1 where the summer sheep population density never exceeded 4 ewe units per acre. The possibly greater input of energy from solar radiation through the plant-herbivore system there may imply that not only will there be a greater increment of living material per unit area but also on a *per capita* basis. The foregoing hypothetical considerations will determine the course of enquiry in the future. The energy relationships of the sheep and vegetation will be investigated insofar as field conditions permit and these will be taken against the background of major gradients of soil, rainfall and solar radiation.

VI. ACKNOWLEDGEMENTS

The authors wish to thank Mr Evan Roberts, the Conservancy's Chief Warden for its Snowdonian Reserves for his invaluable help in the recording of sheep populations in the census work referred to, and in many other ways. Thanks are also due to Mr D. E. Morgan, for making available the data incorporated in Table 2, to Mr D. F. Ball for the soil data in Table 4 and to Dr D. F. Perkins for the dry matter data incorporated in Table 2.

The authors also wish to acknowledge the considerable support given by Sir Richard Williams Bulkeley, Bt. of Baron Hill, Beaumaris; Mr David Jones, of Gwastadannas, Beddgelert; the Central Electricity Generating Board and Mr Thomas Williams of Tan yr allt, Talybont, near Conway on whose land the work reported on in Section IV was carried out.

REFERENCES

ARNOLD G. W. (1960) Selective grazing by sheep of two forage species at different stages of growth. *Aust. J. Agric. Res.* **6**, 1026–1033

BELL F. R. (1959) Preference thresholds for taste discrimination in goats. *J. Agric. Sci.* **52**, 125–132

BLASER R. E., HANMES R. C., BRYANT H. T., HARDISON W. A., FONTIENOT J. P. & ENGEL R. W. (1960) The effect of selective grazing on animal output. *Proc. VIII. International Grassland Congress, Reading*, pp. 601–606

BLASER R. E., KINCAID C. M., BRYANT H. T. & ENGEL R. W. (1959) Effects of full and restricted winter rations on dams and summer dropped suckling calves fed on different rations. *J. Anim. Sci.* **18**, 21–34

BLAXTER K. L. (1960) Energy utilization in the ruminant. *Proc. VII. Easter School in Agric. Sci.* Butterworth, London, pp. 185–197

BLAXTER K. L., WAINMAN F. W. & WILSON R. S. (1961) The regulation of food intake by sheep. *Anim. Prod.* **3**, 51–61

BOULET L. J. (1939) The ecology of a Welsh Mountain sheepwalk. Unpublished thesis. University of Wales.

BRODY S. (1945) *Bioenergetics and growth.* Reinold Publishing Corp., New York.

BRUNDAGE A. L. (1960) The relationship of daily milk production to herbage digestibility and intake. *Proc. VIII. International Grassland Congress, Reading*, pp. 450–453

CRAMPTON E. W. (1959) Inter-relations between digestible nutrient and energy content, voluntary dry matter intake, and overall feeding value of forages. *Grassland Symposium, American Association for the Advancement of Science, Washington D.C.*, pp. 205–211

CRAMPTON E. W., LLOYD L. E. & WILSON R. S. (1957) The Caloric value of T.D.N. *J. Anim. Sci.* **16**, 541–549

DAVIES W. (1925) The relative palatability of pasture plants. *J. Minst. Agric.* **32**, 106–116

DAVIES R. O., JONES D. T. H. & MILTON W. E.(1959) Factors influencing the composition and value of herbage from fescue and *Molinia* areas. *J. Agric. Sci.* **53**, 268–285

FAGAN T. W. & WATKINS H. T. (1932) The chemical composition of the miscellaneous herbs of pastures. *Welsh J. Agric.* **8**, 144–151

GOLLEY F. B. (1960) Energy dynamics of a food chain of an old field community. *Ecol. Monogr.* **30**, 187–206

HAMAMURA Y. & NAITO K. (1961) Food selection by silkworm larvae (*Bombyx mori*) *Nature. London* **190**, 879–880

HAMAMURA Y., HAYASHIYA K. & NAITO K. (1961) Beta sitosterol as one of the biting factors. *Nature. London* **190**, 880–881

HARDISON W. A., REID J. T., MARTIN C. M. & WOOLFOLK P. G. (1954) Degree of herbage selection by grazing cattle. *J. Dairy Sci.* **37**, 89–102

HUGHES R. E. (1954) The ecology of some North Wales sheepwalks. *European Grassland Conference Report, Paris, June 1954 (O.E.E.C. Project No. 224)*, 53–60

HUGHES R. E. (1958a) Sheep population and environment in Snowdonia (North Wales) *J. Ecol.* **46**, 169–190

HUGHES R. E. (1958b) *Report of the Nature Conservancy for year ended 30th September 1958.* H.M.S.O. London, pp. 63–65

HUGHES R. E. (1960) *The ecological approach to problems of land-use in upland Wales.* Memo. 3rd Symposium in Agricultural Meteorology, University College of Wales, Aberystwyth

HUNTER R. F. (1954) The grazing of hill sward types. *J. Brit. Grassland Soc.* **9,** 195–208

IVINS J. D. (1952) The relative palatability of herbage plants. *J. Brit. Grassland Soc.* **7,** 43–54

IVINS J. D. (1960) Personal Communication

MEYER J. H., LOFGREEN G. P. & HULL J. L. (1957) Selective grazing by sheep and cattle. *J. Anim. Sci.* **16,** 766–772

MILTON W. E, (1933) The palatability of self-establishing species in grassland. *Emp. J. Exp. Agric.* **1,** 347–360

MILTON W. E. (1943) The yields of ribwort plaintain (ribgrass), when sown in pure plots and with grass and clover species. *Welsh J. Agric.* **17,** 109–116

MOTT L. O. (1960) Grazing pressure and the measurement of pasture production. *Proc. VIII. International Grassland Congress, Reading,* pp. 606–611

RAYMOND W. F. (1959) The nutritive value of herbage. *Proc. VI Easter School in Agric. Sci.* Butterworth, London, pp. 156–164

REID J. T. (1959) The evaluation of energy in forage. *Grassland Symposium, American Association for the Advancement of Science, Washington, D.C.,* pp. 213–223

ROE R. & MOTTERSHEAD B.E. (1962) Palatability of *Phalaris arundinacea. Nature, London* **193,** 255–256

TRIBE D. E. (1950) The behaviour of the grazing animal—a critical review of present knowledge. *J. Brit. Grass Soc.* **5,** 209–214

TRIBE D. E. & GORDON J. G. (1950) An experimental study of Palatability. *Agric. Progress* **25,** 94–101

PART III

GRAZING IN THE MARINE ENVIRONMENT

GRAZING BY PLANKTONIC
ORGANISMS

THE WORK OF GRAZING IN THE SEA

D. H. Cushing

Fisheries Laboratory, Lowestoft

ABSTRACT

Savage's (1937) data are used to make an estimate of the grazing efficiency of the herring on zooplankton. It is likely that the best increment in weight is obtained when the herring feeds on animals of the size of *Calanus*.

The grazing by planktonic herbivores is discussed, using the experiments of Monakov and Sorokin (1959, 1961). From them the nature of superfluous feeding is described.

From observations at sea in the spring of 1954, the duration of *Calanus* stages is estimated. An estimate of specific growth rate is obtained. From estimates of algal productive rate, measures of apparent grazing and superfluous feeding are obtained. It appears that the spring outburst in 1954 was controlled predominantly by grazing, nutrients having no effect.

The fish do not show superfluous grazing. *Calanus* shows superfluous feeding when the density of algae is sufficient to allow the animal to feed without swimming. This situation cannot arise with the herring, since the fish must swim actively to find its food by aggregation.

INTRODUCTION

Algae are eaten by herbivorous copepods in the sea and these copepods are eaten by pelagic fish such as herring. The processes at each trophic level differ, but here we examine similarities. In both cases, the prey is distributed in the water in a patchy manner. Herring do not merely filter their food from the water, they select it (Battle *et al.*, 1936); if this is so, the fish must use their senses in order to make the greatest numbers of attacks on prey of the selected size. It is sometimes thought that copepods do not select their algal prey, but Harvey (1937) showed clearly that *Calanus* took *Lauderia* in preference to *Ditylum*; Petipa (1959a, b) has shown that *Acartia clausi* will select that algal species with the largest rounded cells. Because of the likeness between the two predator/prey systems, data on the feeding of herring on zooplankton will be used to illuminate the grazing of copepods on algae.

207

THE FEEDING EFFICIENCY OF THE HERRING

Savage (1931, 1937) has published much information on the gut contents of herring caught off Shields in summertime. On two occasions, the quantity in the gut was compared with the quantity found in the water on the same night; the plankton was caught in a vertical haul, and can be expressed as numbers or as mm^3/m^3. The gut material expresses two sorts of information; the number of animals found is the number of attacks made and the volume is the quantity of food taken. Battle *et al.* (1936) have measured the digestion rates for herring at different temperatures and so it is possible to convert the gut material into number of attacks *per day* and volume of food eaten *per day*.

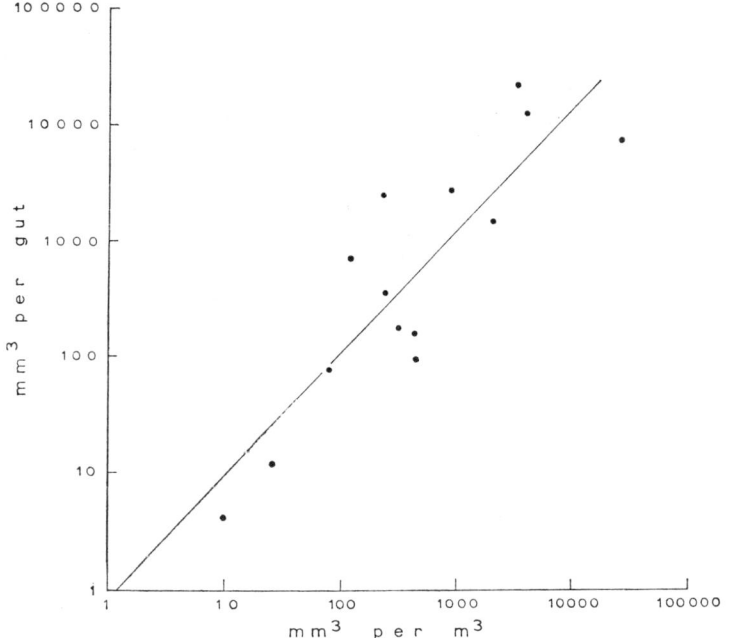

FIG. I. The relationship between volume in the gut and volume in the sea.

The lengths of copepods were raised to volumes with the use of Kamshilov's formulae (1951) to give total values of mm^3/m^3; Fig. I shows the volume of each category found in the gut plotted against the values of mm^3/m^3 in the sea; the quantity in the gut is dependent on the quantity in the sea. The plankton net had 60 meshes to the linear inch (roughly the mesh size of the herring's gill rakers), so the retention range of net and fish were about the same. Fig. 2 shows the relation between the number of organisms in the gut per day (or number of attacks made per day) and the quantity in the sea in mm^3/m^3. So the number of attacks also depends on the quantity in the water. However, the important point is that the scatter in Fig. 2 is very much greater than that in Fig. 1. There is thus plenty of scope for the selection of food particles, the animal needing to find the greatest quantity of food of the right size. One interesting point in Fig. 2 is that below a level of 100 mm^3/m^3, very few attacks are made, and the herring must starve.

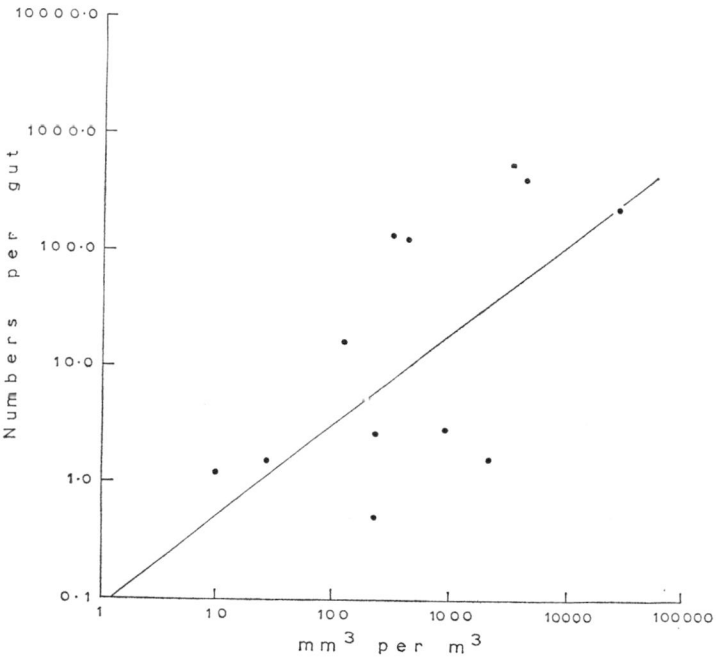

FIG. 2. The relationship between numbers per gut/day (number of attacks made per day) on volume in the sea.

The largest quantity of Savage's data comprises gut contents of about 100 herring for each ten-day period from May to September for each of five years, 1930–4. Fig. 3 shows the relationship between the number of attacks made per day and the daily volume found in the gut; Figs. 3(a), (b), (c), (d) and (e) give the relationship for each of the five years. The weight in the gut increases, dependent on the number of attacks made. In

15

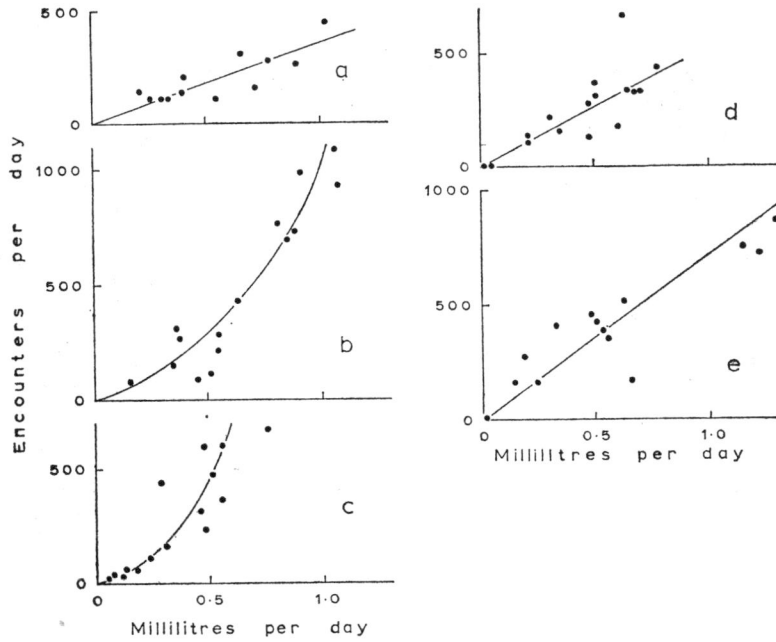

FIG. 3. The relationship between number of attacks made per day and the daily volume in the gut (from Savage's 1937, data). (a), (b), (c), (d), (e): the relationship for each year, 1930, 1931, 1932, 1933, and 1934.

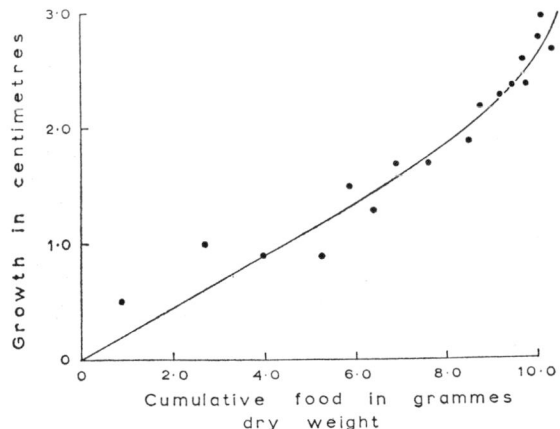

FIG. 4. The relation between food taken as g dry wt/gut summed through the season and the increment of length (cm) as measured on the scale of the herring.

some years a curvilinear relation is found in the number of attacks. Ivlev (1960) has formulated this problem as: $r = R(1-e^{-\alpha p})$, where r is the daily ration, R the ration at infinite concentration, p the prey density and α a constant. If we consider that the number of attacks made is proportional to prey density, the relations given in Fig. 3 are those expected from Ivlev's formulation, i.e. $\log_e(1-r/R) = -\alpha p$.

Fig. 4 shows the relation between the food taken as g dry wt/gut summed through the summer and the increment of length as measured from the scale of the herring and proportioned to the fish's length; this work was carried out by Mr B. C. Mumford during the Shields fishery in 1956. From this figure it is concluded that 10 g dry weight of food produced

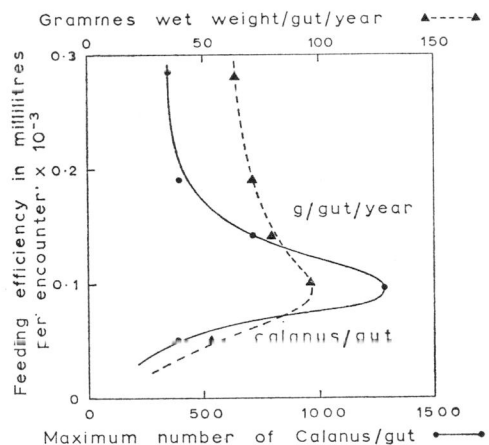

FIG. 5. The relation between grazing efficiency (ml/encounter × 10⁻³ and g wet wt/gut/yr between May and September only) and maximum numbers of *Calanus*/gut.

2·2 cm in length. $W = 0·0085\ l^3$ (where W is wt in g and l is length in cm). The average length of herring in the samples used at the start of the period was 24·82 cm; that after an increment of 2·2 cm was achieved was 27·02 cm. The increment in wet weight during the period was 14·75 g or 2·95 g dry weight. The cumulative quantity of food taken was 10 g dry weight. The time for digestion at the temperatures observed in 1956 was 14 hours (using the data from Battle *et al.* 1936). Hence the quantity of food taken should be raised by 24/14. From Fig. 4, we conclude that increments of growth are proportional to the quantity of food eaten. We also conclude that the coefficient of conversion of food taken to the increment of growth is 17·2 per cent.

D. H. CUSHING

The number of attacks or encounters made per ml of food as an average for the year is a measure of grazing efficiency. The measure of grazing efficiency is taken from Fig. 3, which gives the relationship between volume in the gut and the number of attacks or encounters made. Each point on Fig. 5 represents an average for each of the five years studied by Savage. Savage's data as g/day wet weight may be added for each year from May to September. Table 1 gives the quantity eaten in each yearly period, May to September, the maximum number of *Calanus* in each gut and the grazing efficiency.

Fig. 5 shows the relationship between grazing efficiency and the quantity of food taken in each year from May to September. It will be seen that

TABLE I

Grazing efficiency of the herring

	g wet wt/gut/yr*	Max n. Calanus/gut	Grazing efficiency (ml/encounter)
1930	65·9	352	0·00286
1931	96·3	1,280	0·00098
1932	53·2	391	0·0005
1933	71·6	399	0·00192
1934	79·7	706	0·00141

* From May to September.

maximum weight in the gut is found at about 1,000 encounters per day (Fig. 3(b)). In terms of feeding efficiency (ml/encounter) the value of 1,000 encounters per day is comparatively low (0·1 ml/encounter). Growth is proportional to the quantity of food in the gut (from Fig. 4) and the best growth is found when the greatest weight is found in the gut. We may assume that the number of encounters is proportional to the density of the prey captured; we may further assume from Fig. 1 that the weight of food taken is proportional to the size of the prey and to its density in numbers. In general, size is inversely proportional to density in numbers and so it is likely that there is an optimum size of prey for each predator. The wet weight of the individual food organism attacked by the herring appears to be about 1 mg (1 g wet wt of food taken per day at 1,000 encounters per day), which is the size of a large *Calanus*, the largest prey for its density in unit volume searched; hence the search for *Calanus* by herring will yield the greatest weight in food. It is most interesting that there is a physiological basis for the close connection found between the abundance of *Calanus* and the growth and recruitment to the herring fisheries (Burd and Cushing, 1962).

Ivlev (1960) studied the energy expenditure in grazing with *Alburnus alburnus* L., a plankton eating fish feeding on *Cyclops* sp., by measuring the resting and active metabolism with respirometers. He found that the fish consumed 38·3 cal/d from food (7·7 cal/d were not assimilated) and lost 25·6 cal/d in metabolism, and gained 5·0 cal/d in weight. Ivlev's first coefficient of efficiency k_1 (energy of gain in weight/energy in food) was 12·1 per cent:

$$\left(\frac{5 \cdot 0 \text{ cal/d} \times 100}{38 \cdot 3 \text{ cal/d}}\right)$$

and his second coefficient of efficiency (energy of gain weight/total transformed energy) was 16·4 per cent:

$$\left(\frac{5 \cdot 0 \text{ cal/d} \times 100}{38 \cdot 3 - 7 \cdot 7 \text{ cal/d}}\right).$$

There were 73,450 *Cyclops*/m³ and the fish took 363/hr, or 4,166 attacks per day in a twelve hour day. The herring appears to make 500–1,000 attacks per day which is considerably less. In high densities of food, in a tank, the number of attacks made will be high, little energy being lost in searching.

Winberg (1956, Table 30, p. 229) has summarized many experiments for a range of efficiencies and a range of weights (see Table 2, which is part of Winberg's table).

TABLE 2

Daily rations and daily gains in weight for animals of different weights

Wet wt (g)	Daily ration as % wt			Daily wt gain as % wt		
	k_2 60% k_1 48%	20% 16%	5% 4%	k_2 60% k_1 48%	20% 16%	5% 4%
0·001	89·5	44·7	37·6	43·0	7·1	1·50
0·01	56·3	28·2	23·7	27·0	4·5	0·95
0·1	35·4	17·7	14·9	17·0	2·8	0·59
1·0	22·5	14·8	9·5	10·8	2·4	0·38
10·0	14·4	7·2	6·0	6·9	1·15	0·24
100·0	9·1	4·5	3·8	4·4	0·72	0·15
1000·0	5·6	2·8	2·4	2·7	0·45	0·09

The figures given in this table are based on measurements of oxygen consumption (or metabolism) in a respirometer reported as ml O_2/g wt/hr at 20°C. A very large number of published observations were used for a wide range of fish species, both marine and freshwater. It was shown that
$Q = 0.3w^{0.8}$,

where Q is rate of oxygen consumption per unit time,
   „ w is the weight of the animal in g,

In the analysis of the published data,
   let R be the daily ration,
   „ P be the daily increment in weight,
   „ T be the daily expenditure in metabolism (oxygen consumption per unit weight per unit time).

Then $$k_1 = \frac{P}{R} \cdot 100 \text{ and } k_2 = \frac{P}{0.8R} \cdot 100 = 1.25\, k_1.$$

It is assumed that the calorific equivalent of food and the body of fish do not differ.

The ratio of the weight of food in the gut to the weight of the animal for an extensive range of data is given for the following fish from Blegvad (1917):

Wt of food in gut/wt of animal	
Pleuronectes platessa	1/36
„ *limanda*	1/37
„ *flesus*	1/28
Gadus callarias	1/35
Gobius sp.	1/36
Gasterosteus sp.	1/37

The digestion correction used for herring might increase this ratio from about 1/35 to about 1/29 per day, which is of the order of 3·0–3·3 per cent/day, as daily ration. Combining this with Winberg's table, the herring weighing about 130–140 g, it implies that the appropriate value of k_1 in the field is low, 4 per cent rather than 16 per cent. With a conversion efficiency of food to growth of 17·2 per cent, the daily ration of 3·0–3·3 per cent/day would be expected to produce 0·52 per cent of body weight/day in growth which is rather higher than that expected from a value of k_1 in Winberg's table. Perhaps the true value of k_1 lies between 4 and 16 per cent.

THE FEEDING OF *CALANUS*

We may turn to the grazing by planktonic herbivores on algae. Cushing (1959) developed an encounter theory of grazing, formulated as $S_o = S_m/(1 + vxy)$, where S_m is the 'mechanical' volume swept clear in barren water, S_o is the 'operational' volume swept clear, v is S_m/sec, x is the time in secs to eat one algal cell and y is the number of algal cells/litre. If we equate $1/S_m$ to Ivlev's R and vx to his α, it will be seen that the two expressions, if not formally the same, are alike. It is characteristic of either formulation that the quantity filtered will decrease with increasing density. The work of Monakov and Sorokin (1959) on the grazing of *Chlorococcus* by *Daphnia*

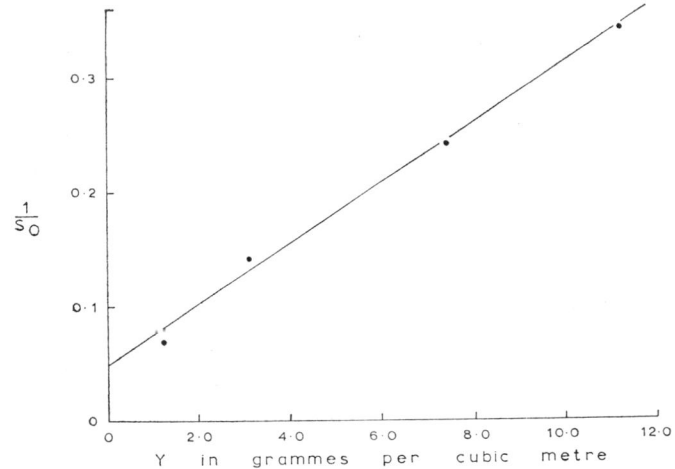

FIG. 6. The reciprocal of S_o, the volume filtered per day, on algal density y (from the data of Monakov and Sorokin, 1959); *Daphnia longispina* is fed upon *Chlorococcus*.

longispina shows just this form of relation. Fig. 6 shows the reciprocal of the volume filtered $(1/S_o)$ on the algal density, y. The intercept is $1/S_m$ and S_m, the volume swept clear in barren water, is 20·9 ml/day; the slope, vx, could be estimated if the algal density were expressed in numbers/litre. Thus we may conclude that the grazing of *Daphnia* on *Chlorococcus* may be described in the same manner as the grazing of *Alburnus* on *Cyclops*.

If we may extend Winberg's table (Table 2) for fish to copepods (the wet weight of *Calanus* copepodite stage V is <0·001 g), the daily ration as percentage of the wet weight would probably be greater than 37·6 per cent. Winberg suggests that the oxygen consumption of fish is well expressed in the equation:

$$Q = 0 \cdot 3 w^{0.8},$$

where Q is ml O_2 respired/hr (at 20°C)

,, w is wet weight in g.

For crustacea he found,

$Q = 0 \cdot 165 w^{0.81}$ (at 20°C); in freshly caught material,
$Q = 0 \cdot 236 w^{0.81}$ (at 20°C).

Using these results, Winberg considered that the metabolic rate (ml O_2 respired/g wet wt of animal) of fish might be 35–90 per cent higher than that of crustacea. Zeuthen (1947) made careful measurements of the respiration of small marine animals, and from his results the metabolic rate of *Calanus* (1 mg) would be about ten times that of an animal of 100 g. In this range, the measurements of Zeuthen and Winberg are comparable. Thus, it is likely that the daily ration as percentage of weight is perhaps 30–40 per cent.

Beklemishev (1961) has quoted Lucas' (1936) experiments on *Eurytemora hirundoides* Nordquist and the work of Harvey, Cooper, Lebour and Russell (1935) and Riley (1947) at sea showing that the herbivorous zooplankton in general can destroy about 20–30 per cent of its own weight per day. Harvey et al. showed that the number of copepod faecal pellets in the sea rises during the spring increase, depending on the standing stock of algae, rather than upon the number of copepods. This suggested that some superfluous feeding had taken place, which Beklemishev (1957) defines as destruction without use to the herbivores. From Winberg's work it is possible that feeding at a rate of 30–40 per cent of the animal's weight per day is necessary and so any rate in excess of this would be described as superfluous feeding. Fig. 7 shows an inverse relationship between daily ration/body weight and food assimilated/daily ration; as the daily ration increases (which was the algal quantity destroyed as the difference in radioactivity in the algae at the start and end of the experiment), the proportion of food assimilated (as active carbon in the daphnids) decreases. The material used in this experiment is the same as that shown in Fig. 6; the quantities (1–10 mm³/litre) are those that might be found in the sea. It is likely from Winberg's table that the animal needs between 30 and 40 per cent of its body weight per day. So most of the range shown in Fig. 7.

50–200 per cent, represents superfluous feeding. As superfluous feeding increases, the proportion of food assimilated decreases—as if the herbivores were uselessly killing the algae. There is no evidence that the herring grazes on *Calanus* in this way, because the ratio of daily ration to body weight rarely rises above 3 or 4 per cent. This appears to be a profound difference between the fish grazing on copepods and the herbivorous copepod grazing on algae.

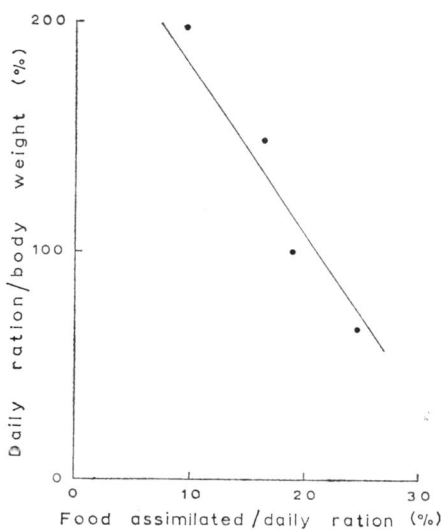

Fig. 7. Inverse relationship between the ratio of daily ration to body weight and the ratio of food assimilated to daily ration (from the data of Monakov and Sorokin, 1961). The daily ration is given by the difference in activity between the beginning and the end of the experiment in the concentration of C^{14} in the culture measured by radioactive tracer methods.
Food consumption is given by the concentration found in the daphnids.

During the spring of 1954, a patch of *Calanus* was followed continuously for two and a half months. The patch, which was about 30–50 miles across, was identified from cruise to cruise by its abundance only; as one ship entered port, having charted the patch, a second sailed to chart it again. Variations in abundance due to diffusion are likely to be small during such short time intervals of five to eight days between the midpoints of cruises (Cushing and Tungate, 1963). Fig. 8(a) shows the numbers/m³ of *Calanus* copepodite stages in the patch for the thirteen observations in two and a half months; it provides some evidence that the patch retained its identity during the period of examination. Fig. 8(b) gives the volume of algae (mm³/litre) and the weight of herbivores during the period; the former was estimated from counts and size measurements made on water bottle samples and the latter were derived from length measurements using Kamshilov's formulae (1951). Fig. 8(b) shows that the spring outburst was described fully during the period. Fig. 8(c) gives the percentage by weight of the population of *Calanus* copepodite stages and naupliar stages, separately, which of course were mainly *Calanus* nauplii. It must be pointed out that all molluscan larvae, ciliates and euphausiids were ignored; the numbers were very low, the sampling instruments being the water bottle, fine international silk net, Hensen net and Gulf III sampler. Fig. 8(c) shows that the herbivore population was predominantly a *Calanus* population. Fig. 8(d) gives the wet weight of algae, as mm³/litre (= mg/ litre wet weight) and the concentration of nutrients, phosphate-phosphorus, silicate and nitrate-nitrogen in μg-at/litre; it will be seen that there was no sharp decline in nutrients during the spring outburst (Cushing and Nicholson, 1963). Fig. 8(e) shows the algal productive rate as calculated theoretically (using the method in Cushing (1959)) and that as observed using the method of cell width decrease across the pervalvar axis (Cushing, 1955 and Cushing, 1963); the algal productive rate increased after the spring increase died away. The results shown in Fig. 8(a)–(g) are treated more extensively in the papers quoted.

From the estimates of algal numbers in the *Calanus* patch made from cruise to cruise and the estimates of algal productive rate, it was possible to determine the total algal mortality, Z from

$$Z = R - 1/t. \log_e P_1/P_0,$$

where P_0 is the algal quantity in one cruise, P_1 is the algal quantity in the subsequent cruise, R is the daily algal productive rate, Z is the total algal mortality rate and t is the time in days.

In order to find the quantity eaten, we must separate the algal mortality due to grazing from mortality due to other causes. It is assumed that grazing mortality is generated by the weight of herbivores, because they search a volume of water for food which they convert to weight. Fig. 8(f) shows the relationship between the total algal mortality, Z, and the weight of herbivores. The regression is significantly different from zero and the intercept provides a measure of the non-grazing mortality. It is clear that grazing is the major source of mortality. It is likely that the non-grazing mortality is composed of death by causes other than grazing, sinking and

TABLE 3

The quantity apparently eaten by *Calanus* stage V as compared with its daily requirement and the number of eggs produced per day

Cruise	Average Standing stock of algae mm³/l	Production mm³/l	n/litre Calanus V	Weight[1] of Calanus V per litre (mg)	Daily requirement[2] of Calanus V populat on in mg/litre	Daily requirement as % of standing stock	Daily quantity eaten by 1 Calanus V mg (mm³)	Quantity eaten by Calanus V as % body wt	Daily volume swept clear by 1 Calanus V	No. eggs/ Calanus ♀ / day	Calanus lengths/ cell
4–5	0·167	0·198	0·001	0·00059	0·00022	0·01	—	—	—	62·5	—
5–6	0·588	3·736	0·008	0·0047	0·00177	0·30	5·307	349·9	4380	23·0	0·85
6–7	0·501	1·603	0·021	0·0124	0·00466	0·43	3·714	390·3	7018	14·0	0·90
7–8	0·201	0·391	0·033	0·0195	0·00733	3·60	0·661	26·8	965	2·0	1·22
8–9	0·160	0·558	0·085	0·0502	0·01888	11·80	0·463	46·3	2948	2·5	1·33
9–10	0·011	0·022	0·128	0·0755	0·02838	9·90	0·036	4·3	4174	1·5	3·23
10–11	0·003	0·003	0·168	0·0991	0·03726	1242·0	0·0034	0·05	128	0·0	4·73
11–12	0·004	0·003	0·133	0·0785	0·02952	738·0	0·015	1·15	1624	0·0	4·33
12–13	0·004	0·0019	0·119	0·0702	0·02640	660·0	0·012	1·23	1564	0·0	4·33

[1] 1 *Calanus* V weighs 0·59 mg wet wt.
[2] Daily requirement is 37·6 per cent of body weight, wet wt from Table 2.

diffusion. We cannot distinguish these causes save to suggest that diffusion (using an adaptation of the Joseph and Sendner equation (1958) by my colleague J. A. Gulland) reduced the planktonic concentrations by as much as 15 per cent on one occasion.

The intercept on the ordinate in Fig. 8(f) is 0·447, so the best estimate of G, the algal non-grazing mortality, is Z–0·447. The total quantity apparently eaten is estimated from $(P_0 \cdot G/R–Z)$ $(e^{(R–Z)t}–1)$, calculated separately for each cruise interval. This quantity is divided amongst the herbivore categories by weight. Table 3 gives the quantities apparently eaten by *Calanus* stage V as compared with its daily requirement and the number of eggs produced per day. The daily requirement is taken at 37·6 per cent of body weight/day (from Table 2).

It is possible to make another estimate of the daily requirement. Fig. 8(g) and (h) gives the percentage in each copepodite stage during the period of the cruises. From this figure the approximate duration of stages can be estimated by Crisp's method (1954). Iles (in press) has adapted the method as follows: the number per m³ of each copepodite stage at a given date is expressed as a percentage of all stages at that date. The area under each stage curve is measured in cm², say x cm²; let 1 cm along the abscissa be 1 day and the approximate duration of the copepodite stage in days is given by x cm²/100 cm². A necessary part of the method is that only one generation is involved. That this is so appears partly from Fig. 8(a) and also from the general biology of *Calanus*. The values of stage duration, which includes mortality in this method are:

Stage	
I–II	15·8 days
II–III	14·5
III–IV	12·5
IV–V	22·8
V–VI	4·6
	70·2 days

From length measurements we have average weights at each stage and calculate as follows:

Stage	wt (mg)	Days	Δ wt	Δ wt/d	$\dfrac{(\Delta \text{ wt/d}) \, 100}{\text{wt}}$
I	0·0031	15·8	0·0161	0·00102	33%
II	0·0192	14·5	0·0792	0·00546	28%
III	0·0984	12·5	0·1676	0·01341	14%
IV	0·2660	22·8	0·4475	0·01963	7%

The specific growth rate is that needed to grow from stage to stage and so the 33 per cent/d between stages I and II is expressed as a ratio of the weight in stage I. It will be seen that the daily weight gain from stage IV–V is 7 per cent; therefore k_1 from Table 2 is 16 per cent and the daily ration/ body weight is 45 per cent. The information to calculate the figure from stage V–VI is lacking. It is likely that the stage duration is underestimated because the four last cruises were made in empty water when food was short and so the daily ration/body weight of 45 per cent is underestimated. It is suggested that superfluous feeding takes place when this value exceeds 70 per cent.

We return to Table 3, which derives the daily requirement of the *Calanus* V population, the daily ration/body weight which is high, the daily volume swept clear ($G \times$ per cent wt *Calanus* V/n litre of *Calanus* V), which is also high, the reproductive capacity of *Calanus* as number of eggs/*Calanus* ♀/day and the feeding opportunity of *Calanus* as *Calanus* lengths/cell (of 10,000 μ^3). We may summarize Table 3 as follows:

	Daily ration/body wt	Reproductive capacity	Feeding opportunity
Cruises 5–7	Superfluous feeding (370%)	Many eggs (18·5/♀/d)	No swimming for food (0·88 lengths/cell)
7–10	Adequate feeding (26%)	Some eggs (2·0/♀/d)	A little swimming for food (1·93 lengths/cell)
10–13	Low feeding (0·8%)	No eggs	Much swimming for food (4·5 lengths/cell)

Thus the nature of feeding, low, adequate or superfluous is linked with the degree of feeding opportunity, the distance the animal has to swim to find food. It will be seen that superfluous feeding exists only when the animal does not need to swim at all. It is suggested that the apparent excess feeding is really a destruction of algae. The reason for the excessive feeding capacity is probably to allow the animal to live in the barren water; it is possible that the algal quantities have been underestimated at this time, μ-flagellates not having been counted. *Phaeocystis* was present in the sea and *Calanus* guts were still green in the late cruises (10–13). However, there was not sufficient food in the sea for reproduction. The very fact that the animals had green guts suggests that the high volumes swept clear are real.

DISCUSSION

A comparison has been made between the grazing of herring (mainly on *Calanus*) and the grazing of *Calanus* on algae. There is a likeness between the two systems in that grazing is dependent on prey density, Ivlev's formulation for planktophagic fish resembling Cushing's (1959) for plankton animals. Growth of the herring appears to be greatest when the prey is of the size of *Calanus*, at a rather low grazing efficiency, as if the fish takes the largest prey for its density in unit volume searched—thus obtaining the greatest weight in the volume searched. There is a difference between the herring/*Calanus* relation and the *Calanus*/diatom relation in that the herbivorous copepod appears to graze excessively; expressed in terms of food eaten as proportion of body weight, the herring's food amounts to about 3·0 per cent of its body weight, but that of the *Calanus* can amount to many times its body weight at the height of the spring outburst. There is an apparent superfluous feeding by *Calanus* probably much in excess of the animal's need for maintenance and growth. It is possible that the reproductive load is higher than it appears superficially and that the animal's need for all vital processes should be doubled to include reproduction—which is limited to the period of superfluous feeding. Even then there would be an apparent excess of grazing by nearly three times. This suggests that algae are killed without being assimilated, as shown in the experiments of Monakov and Sorokin (1961). It appears that *Calanus* can feed to excess without swimming far, whereas the herring must swim considerably if it is going to aggregate on to food patches (Cushing, 1955) Therefore at the peak of the spring outburst the energy loss in the conversion of assimilated food by *Calanus* for its needs is minimal, although that caused in algal destruction is very high. Very roughly – using the daily ration and the daily requirement – it can be shown that two-thirds of the algal production is destroyed and not assimilated. The conversion of the other third is presumably carried out as efficiently as is possible by such small animals.

The high grazing rates used have frequently been attacked. The volumes swept clear make the physical imagination boggle. The algal productive rates are said to be much too high. It is said that a component of grazing has been omitted. Each argument has struck a vulnerable point. I. The animals cannot filter more than some mls/day, but by swimming, hopping and sinking with their antennules extended, they could search large volumes. II. The algal productive rates are not higher than those found in culture and were checked by observations at sea. It is true that no factor

GRAZING IN THE SEA

for nutrient lack has been included in the calculations, but phosphorus, silica and nitrate were all high during the period of the spring outburst; indeed phosphorus did not fall below 0·6 μg-atom P/litre during the whole period, but the nitrate values did fall towards the end. A productive rate of 30 per cent/day has been observed in the northern Pacific by McAllister, Parsons and Strickland (1960); with such a value, superfluous feeding can be shown to take place during the spring outburst — the daily ration reaching perhaps 200 per cent of the body weight. III. All possible herbivores were examined, from ciliates to euphausiids.

The most revealing evidence in support of the high grazing rates is that from the specific growth rate of *Calanus*. It means that the high grazing rates are not only possible, but necessary, in order to account for the stage durations found. The question arises: what happens in the water empty of food after the spring outburst? The quantity eaten, with a high reproductive rate used in the calculation, becomes reduced to 1 per cent of the body weight. The animals no longer produce eggs and they have perhaps enough to respire, but do they have enough to grow? Hence it is likely that the duration of stages might become extended, unless the fat reserves are used for growth. The data on which the duration of stages was estimated included four cruises in water empty of food. Hence it is likely that the stage duration in the spring outburst itself is overestimated and the quantity needed for food underestimated for that limited period.

In general, the high grazing rates are shown to be needed by the herbivores. In 1954 in the North Sea the herbivores were to all intents and purposes the *Calanus* population and the productive cycle has been described in terms of a high productive rate and a high grazing rate only. All stages of *Calanus* showed the same high percentage of food eaten to body weight, because the total quantity estimated to have been eaten was divided amongst the herbivore categories by weight. If the algal productive rate is low after the spring outburst, the herbivores will get a very small quantity to eat indeed, 0·1–1·0 per cent of body weight, rather than 1–5 per cent. It is the high grazing rate which allows them to do this. Therefore I believe that the high algal productive rates (which were checked independently at sea) are roughly of the right order.

The traditional view of the productive cycle is that at the peak of the spring outburst nutrients have declined sufficiently to reduce the algal productive rate and reduce production and hence stop the spring outburst. In terms of the algal productive rate this point has not been shown, nor is the correlation between the decline of nutrients and the timing of the decline of the algal standing stock very striking. In the spring of 1954 in the North

Sea, the control of the algal outburst is attributed solely to grazing, the effect of nutrients being irrelevant; the evidence for this is:

1. The high level of nutrients all through the spring outburst.

2. The algal productive rate observed at sea during the spring outburst.

3. The quantity of food needed by the herbivorous copepods in order to grow and, after the spring outburst, to live.

REFERENCES

BATTLE H.I. *et al.* (1936) Fatness, digestion and food of Passamaquoddy young herring. *J. biol. Bd. Can.*, **11**, 401–429

BEKLEMISHEV K.V. (1957) Superfluous feeding of the zooplankton and the problem of sources of food for bottom animals. *Trud. vsesoyuz. gidrobiol. Obshch.* **8**, 354–358

BEKLEMISHEV K.V. (1961) Superfluous feeding of marine herbivorous zooplankton. *Symposium on Zooplankton production*, Paper 6, ICES 1961

BLEGVAD H. (1917) On the food of fish in the Danish Waters within the Skaw. *Rep. Danish biol. Sta.* XXIV, 17–72, 1916

BURD A.C. & CUSHING D.H. (1962) I.—Growth and recruitment in the herring of the Southern North Sea. II.—Recruitment to the North Sea herring stocks. *Fish. Invest.*, *Ser. II* **23**, (5)

CRISP D.J. (1954) The breeding of *Balanus porcatus* (da Costa) in the Irish Sea. *J. Mar. Biol. Ass. U.K.* **33**, 473–494

CUSHING D.H. (1955) Production and a pelagic fishery. *Fish. Invest., Lond., Ser. II* **18** (7)

CUSHING D.H. (1959) On the nature of production in the sea. *Fish. Invest., Lond., Ser. II* **22** (6)

CUSHING D.H. & TUNGATE D.S. (1963) Studies on a *Calanus* patch I: The identification of a *Calanus* patch. *J. Mar. Biol. Ass. U.K., N.S. II*, **43**, 327–337

CUSHING D.H. (1963) Studies on a *Calanus* patch II: The estimations of algal productive rates. *J. Mar. Biol. Ass. U.K., N.S. II*, **43**, 339–347

CUSHING D.H. & NICHOLSON H.N. (1963) Studies on a *Calanus* patch IV: Nutrient salts off the north-east coast. *J. Mar. Biol. Ass. U.K., N.S. II*, **43**, 373–386

CUSHING D.H. & VUCETIC T. (1963) Studies on a *Calanus* patch III: The quantity of food eaten by *Calanus*. *J. Mar. Biol. Ass. U.K., N.S. II*, **43**, 349–371

HARVEY H.W., COOPER, L.H.N., LEBOUR M.V. & RUSSELL F.S. (1935) Plankton production and its control. *J. Mar. biol. Ass. U.K., N.S.* **20**, 407–441

HARVEY H.W. (1937) Note on selective feeding by Calanus. *J. Mar. biol. Ass. U.K., N.S.* **22**, 97–100

ILES T.D. (in press) The duration of maturity stages of spring, autumn and winter spawning herring

IVLEV V.S. (1960) On the utilization of food by planktophage fishes. *Bull. Math. Biophys.* **22**, 371–389

JOSEPH J. & SENDNER H. (1958) Uber die horizontale Diffusion im Meere. *Dtsch. Hydrog. Z.* **11**, 49–57

KAMSHILOV M.M. (1951) Determination of the weight of *Calanus finmarchicus* Gunner on the basis of body length measurements. *Dokl. Akad. Nauk SSSR* 74 (6), 945–948

LUCAS C.E. (1936) On certain inter-relations between phytoplankton and zooplankton under experimental conditions. *J. Cons. int. Explor. Mer* 11, 343–362

McALLISTER C.D., PARSONS T.R. & STRICKLAND J.D.H. (1960) Primary productivity and fertility at Station 'P' in the north-east Pacific Ocean. *J. Cons. Int. Explor. Mer.* 25 (3), 240–259

MONAKOV A.V. & SOROKIN I.I. (1959) Experimental studies of the carnivorous feeding of cyclops by means of an isotope method. *Dokl. Akad. Nauk SSSR* 125 (1–6), 319–321

MONAKOV A.V. & SOROKIN I.I. (1961) Experimental investigation of Daphnia nutrition using C^{14}. *Dokl. Akad. Nauk SSSR* 135 (6), 925–926

PETIPA T. (1959a) Feeding of copepod, *Acartia clausi* Giesbr. *Trud. biol. Sta. Sebastopol* 11

PETIPA T. (1959b) Feeding of *Acartia clausi* Giesbr. and *A. latisetosa* Kritcz in the Black sea. *Trud. biol. Sta. Sebastopol* 12

RILEY G.A. (1947) A theoretical analysis of the zooplankton population of Georges Bank. *J. Mar. Res.* 6, 104–113

SAVAGE R.E. (1931) The relation between the feeding of the herring off the East Coast of England and the plankton of the surrounding waters. *Fish. Invest., Lond., Ser. II* 12 (3)

SAVAGE R.E. (1937) The food of the North Sea Herring 1630–1934. *Fish. Invest., Lond., Ser. II* 15 (5)

WINBERG G.G. (1956) Rate of metabolism and food requirements of fishes. *Nauchnye Trudy Belorusskovo Gos. Univ. imeni, Minsk* 1956

ZEUTHEN E. (1947) Body size and metabolic rate in the animal kingdom with special regard to the marine microfauna. *CR Lab. Carlsberg* 26 (3)

16

GRAZING BY COPEPODS IN THE SEA

S. M. MARSHALL AND A. P. ORR

The Marine Station, Millport

ABSTRACT

The effect which the zooplankton grazing has on the phytoplankton depends on a number of factors. The food requirements of zooplankton copepods, the volume of water they can filter and the relation of these to the food available in the sea are discussed in the light of recent work.

INTRODUCTION

In the sea only a few of the economically important fishes eat plant food directly. The chief link in the food chain between the plants and the fishes is formed by the copepods, small crustaceans ranging in length from under 1 mm up to several mm. These are found in all the oceans of the world and many of them graze on the phytoplankton. It is only in coastal waters that other phytoplankton-grazing organisms besides the copepods are abundant. These include the planktonic stages of bottom living mollusca, echinoderms and worms.

The gut contents of the copepods usually reflect the composition of the microplankton in the sea at the time. However, only the indigestible remains of the food eaten can be seen, e.g. skeletons of diatoms, dinoflagellates and crustaceans. Naked forms, which may possibly be important, are not recognizable.

By the movement of their mouth-parts in swimming, copepods create currents which pass through the maxillae. These can be, and very often are, used for filter feeding. Not all copepods are filter feeders; some are purely carnivorous and perhaps the majority can act sometimes as predators, or can follow and select their food. *Calanus* and *Pseudocalanus* have been seen grasping large cells and sucking out the contents (Beklemishev, 1954; Cushing, 1955; Petipa, 1960). *Acartia* can be induced to pursue a *Coscinodiscus* cell held on the end of a needle (Petipa, 1959) and has also been observed eating an *Artemia* nauplius (Conover, 1960). Copepods living in deep water are probably chiefly predatory and Vinagradov (1962) and Wickstead (1962) have suggested that diurnal migration enables the deeper living copepods to prey on those in the upper layers. Since filter feeding is probably the chief method of feeding for many copepods and goes on automatically for a great part of the time, it is the capacity of the copepod for filter feeding which has been most closely studied.

There are several questions which require to be answered. How much food do copepods need to sustain themselves both during the winter when the temperature is low and when food is scarce, and during the spring when the temperature is higher, food is abundant and the copepods are reproducing actively? How much water can the different filter-feeding copepods filter daily? Finally, how do the food requirements and the feeding capacity compare with the food available in the sea?

FOOD AND FEEDING

The minimum food requirements of the copepods can be calculated by measuring the respiration. The value depends on the temperature and whether or not the copepods have been feeding; there are also seasonal changes with the different broods. The respiration is about doubled for a ten degree rise in temperature (Marshall and Orr, 1958). Conover (1960, 1962) has found that a fed copepod uses more oxygen than a starved one, and that carnivorous copepods have a relatively higher respiration than herbivorous. There is also a considerable seasonal variation in respiration but whether this is caused by the food present in the sea, or by the varying weight of the copepods, or some other factor or combination of factors, is not yet clear. Fig. 1 shows the seasonal variations in the respiration of *Calanus finmarchicus*. Values are low in winter when food is scarce and the sea temperatures are low, and high in spring when *Calanus* are heaviest and the food supply is maximal. In the lower part are shown the values for ripe females, unripe females and Stage V copepodites throughout the year in the Clyde sea-area, all measured at 10°C. The increase in spring is most marked in ripe females, least in Stage V. The upper part shows the same results corrected for sea temperatures. It should give a picture of the variations in the food requirements of the *Calanus* during the year. Small species of copepods have a higher oxygen consumption per unit weight than large (Table 1), and they too show a seasonal variation in respiration.

The respiration data in Table 1 give only the amount of food required for the maintenance of adult copepods and do not take into account what is required for reproduction. The fraction of the energy intake which goes to growth in the developmental stages of copepods has not been measured.

Richman (1958) has found that in the pre-adult stages of *Daphnia pulex* 55–58 per cent of the energy intake goes to growth.

The second question, how much food a copepod can take in and how much water it can clear of food daily, has been attacked in different ways. The simplest method is to observe the number of faecal pellets produced while the copepod is in a food culture. This, because faecal pellets vary in

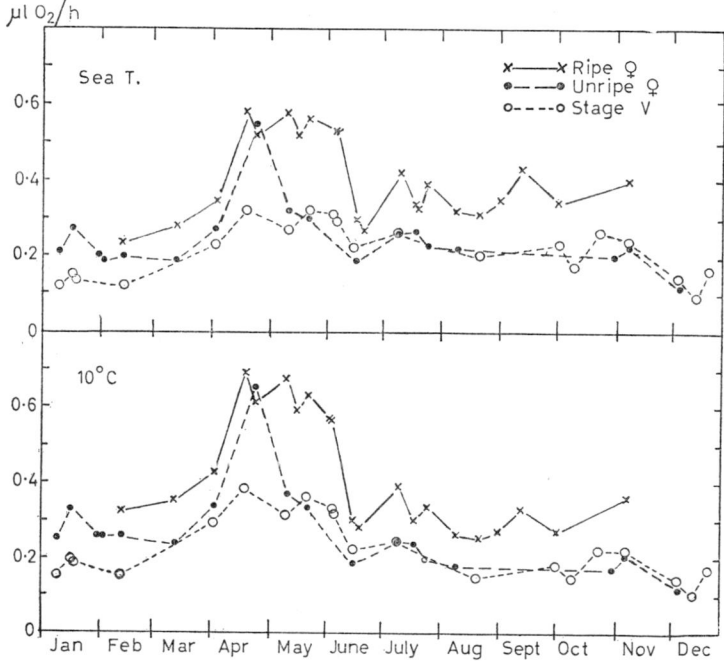

Fig. 1. Lower figure, respiration of ripe and unripe female and Stage V *Calanus* at 10°C in the laboratory. Upper figure, respiration corrected for sea temperatures in the Clyde sea-area.

size and content, is only a rough guide to what has been ingested. With a few species of food organism, it is possible to count the number of skeletons in the pellets but this method can be used only with a very limited number of organisms. Another way is to keep the copepod in a food culture of known concentration and to count the cells present after a known time. All these methods measure what has been ingested but do not tell us how much has been assimilated.

TABLE I

Respiration and food requirements of female copepods

Species	Size mm	T°C	μl O_2/cop./ day	μl O_2/ mg dry wt/ day	carbohydrate needed μg/day
Bathycalanus sp.	13	5·1	163·4	9·1	217
Calanus hyperboreus	(5·5–6)	<10	25·0	5·8	33
Pareuchaeta norvegica	5·1	<10–17	49·5–114·8	12·8	66–153
Rhincalanus nasutus	4·2–4·7	6·5	14·4	14·9	19
Euchirella rostrata	2·9–3·1	6·5	25·5	29·0	34
Pleuromamma robusta	(2·7)	8	17·3	60·4	23
Calanus finmarchicus	2·3–2·8	10	2·7–17·7	—	3·6–23·6
Calanus helgolandicus	2·6	10	4·6–11·5	—	6·1–15·3
Metridia lucens	1·8	10	4·7–7·1	—	6·3–9·5
Centropages hamatus	0·7–1·5	10–20	1·7–3·4	142–155	2·9–4·0
Centropages typicus	1·3	17	4·3–6·9	—	5·7–9·2
Temora longicornis	0·5–1·3	10–20	0·2–4·7	190–328	0·3–6·3
Pseudocalanus minutus	0·8–1·4	10–20	0·7–2·2	196–257	1·7–2·5
Acartia clausi	0·7–1·3	5–20	0·2–2·2	43–304	0·3–2·9
Acartia tonsa	0·9–1·1	20	1·1–2·6	181–318	1·5–3·5
Acartia bifilosa	0·8–0·9	20	1·5–2·8	319–394	2·0–3·7
Acartia discaudata	0·7–0·8	20	0·8–1·6	207–436	1·1–2·1
Eurytemora herdmani	0·9	15	2·1	—	2·8
Oithona similis	0·5–0·7	10	0·2–0·8	—	0·3–1·1

Figures in brackets denote sizes from Sars, 1903.

Yet another method is to label the food culture with a radioactive tracer, ^{32}P, and estimate the amount ingested and digested by measuring the radioactivity of the copepod and the faecal pellets. This is a simple and accurate measurement (Rigler, 1961), but it does not take account of excretion in solution, and since ^{32}P does not reach equilibrium within the body until the copepod has fed for some days, most of the phosphorus excreted during the first twenty-four hours is radioactive. This means that the figures for volume filtered are an underestimate and those for percent digested an overestimate.

Recently Corner (1961) has measured the organic matter present in sea-water before and after passing through a vessel with a number of Calanus in it. He found that by filtering 10–36 ml per day, a female Calanus could cover its food requirements as measured by respiration.

Each of these methods has its drawbacks and the results obtained show a wide range. The state of the Calanus and the state of the culture on which they are fed are probably both very important. In general it may be said that in the laboratory a *Calanus* does not often filter more than 100 ml a day. The smaller copepods filter less but still relatively more than the large.

The rapid reduction of the phytoplankton in the sea by the grazing of the zooplankton and the large number of copepod faecal pellets found in tow-nettings have led some workers (Harvey *et al.*, 1935; Beklemishev, 1962) to the belief that copepods often feed 'superfluously', i.e. that they filter off and ingest much more phytoplankton than they can use and pass it through their gut unchanged.

Experiments on feeding *Calanus* with radioactive phytoplankton show that, even when food is being passed rapidly through the gut, a large proportion of at least the phosphorus containing part is digested. The fact that faecal pellets contain little phosphorus (Harvey *et al.*, 1935) is another indication of efficient digestion. There is a physical limit to the rate at which ingested material can be turned into faecal pellets and ejected; for *Calanus* the maximum rate is about twelve faecal pellets per hour.

Food available in the sea

Both the quality and the quantity of the microplankton available for the copepods are important. In the sea the most important photosynthetic organisms available are the diatoms and the flagellates. Many species of these are readily taken by copepods and it has been shown experimentally that the digestibility of many species is high. Cells below $5-10\mu$ are less efficiently captured than larger ones unless they are in chains because they slip through the mesh of the maxillary filter. Some organisms are apparently indigestible, for example some species of *Chlorella*, and some may even be poisonous, for example *Prymnesium parvum* and *Gymnodinium veneficum*.

Very little is known about the nutritive value of different food organisms but Provasoli, Shiraishi and Lance (1959) have reared a shore-pool harpacticid copepod, *Tigriopus*, in axenic culture through many generations. They used as food a number of different bacteria-free cultures of flagellates. They found that few species, if any, are complete foods in themselves; after a few or many generations fertility is reduced and finally the copepod populations die out. A mixture of the two flagellates *Rhodomonas* and *Isochrysis*, neither a complete food in itself, will maintain fertility indefinitely, or pure cultures may be supplemented by bacteria or accessory food stuffs. It cannot therefore be assumed that when there is a rich monotypic phytoplankton in natural waters, conditions are necessarily ideal for copepod feeding and reproduction. Provasoli and Shiraishi

(1959) were even able to rear the phyllopod *Artemia* under sterile conditions on dissolved foods with particles of starch present to promote the swallowing reflex. It is not suggested however that in the sea dissolved foods are of any significance.

Some idea of the quantity of food available in natural waters is given in Table 2, modified from Jørgensen (1962). Values for the total particulate organic matter and for the phytoplankton organic matter are low in the open oceans and in deep water while in coastal waters, both offshore and inshore, they are high. We can calculate from these figures that in coastal waters there is enough food available to cover the requirements of the copepods but, if these results are representative, they must starve in oceanic waters.

Because of the seasonal character of phytoplankton production in most areas, the problems of zooplankton nutrition cannot be investigated satisfactorily unless we measure not only the numbers of zooplankton organ-

TABLE 2

Particulate organic matter and phytoplankton in sea-water

Locality	Depth in m	Total particulate organic matter μg/l	Phytoplankton organic matter μg/l
Oceanic:			
(1) Pacific	surface	320	14
(2) Atlantic (oligotrophic)	waters	100	2–33
Coastal offshore:			
(3) North Sea (Fladen Ground)		20–600	3–59
(4) English Channel		950–2500	150–430
(5) Southern North Sea		2000	
(6) Long Island Sound	,,	1200–3100	
(7) Florida current			6–900
(8) S.E. Australia			10–210
Coastal inshore:			
(9) Aberdeen Bay		200–1700	20–200
(10) Dutch Waddensea	,,	1000–4000	100–1000
(11) Departure Bay, Canada		950	400
(12) Loch Striven		20–3400	
Deep sea:			
(13) Pacific Ocean	300–600	300	
(14) Atlantic Ocean	200–1000	80	
(15) ,, ,,	500–5000	25	

isms but also the food available for them at different times of the year. This involves fairly complete sampling of an area at frequent intervals and has been achieved only in a few coastal areas such as off the N.E. coast of England (Cushing, 1955), in the English Channel (Harvey *et al.*, 1935) in Long Island Sound (Riley *et al.*, 1949) and in some sheltered areas (e.g. Marshall *et al.*, 1934).

There seems to be general agreement that an outburst of plant growth is followed by an increase in the number of zooplankton organisms and

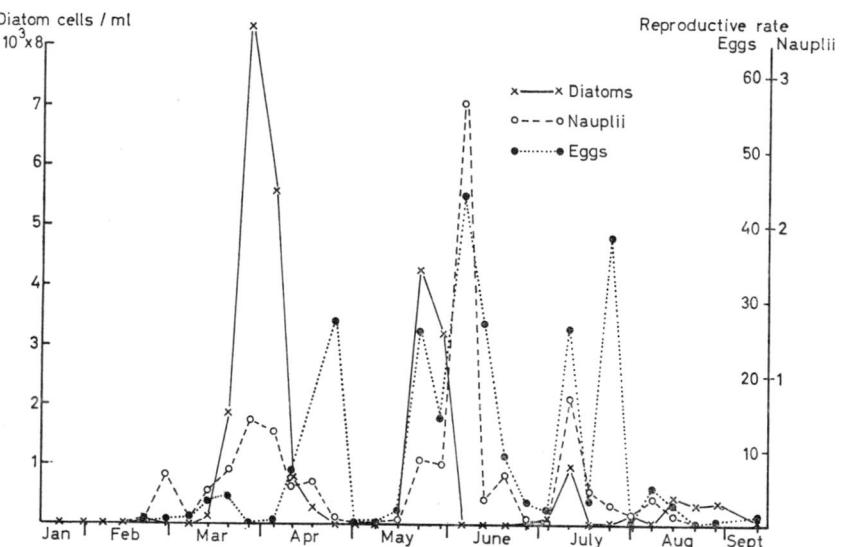

FIG. 2. Reproductive rate in *Calanus* in Loch Striven, 1933, in relation to diatom numbers.

indeed the connection between the increase in food supply and egg production is in some places close. We have shown this for *Calanus* in spring (Marshall and Orr, 1955, p. 76) and Edmondson (1962) has shown that with *Keratella cochlearis* there is a connection between the small phytoplankton and the rotifer's reproductive rate. This he defines as the number of eggs per female per day divided by the duration of development in days. We have applied this to the data for the copepod *Calanus* in Loch Striven in 1933 and the results are shown in Fig. 2. There is an agreement, though not very well marked, between reproductive rate and the diatom increases. Better agreement is shown when the nauplius stages of the copepod are used instead of the eggs; somewhat similar general agreement was found for other lochs investigated.

The relation between food and egg laying can be studied more closely in the laboratory. In experiments with *Calanus* it is found that, as expected, reproduction depends very closely on the food available. A ripe female

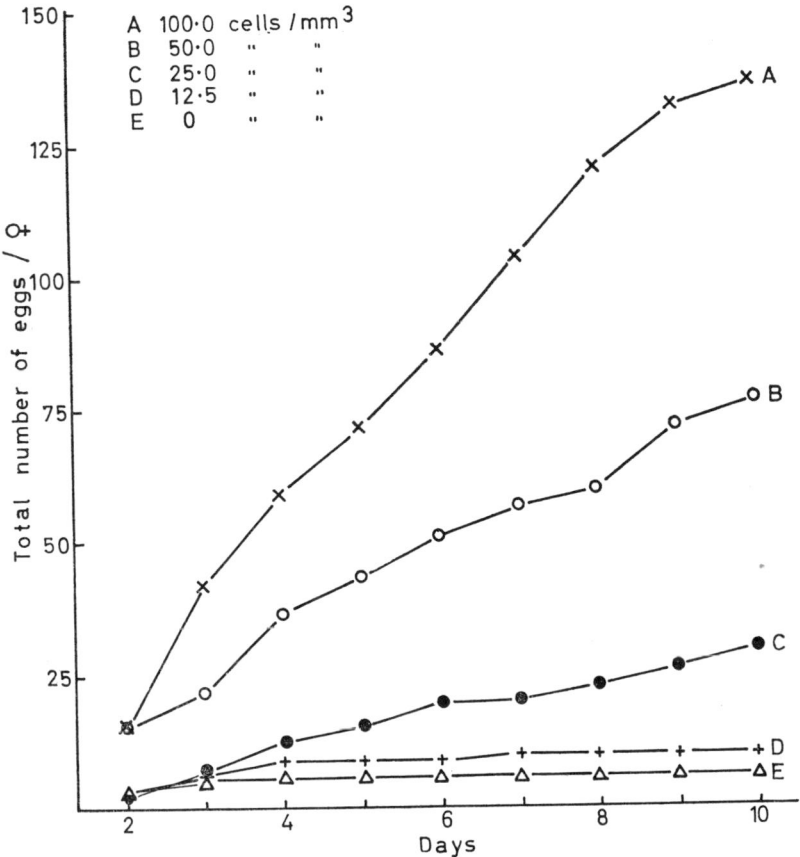

FIG. 3. Egg-laying by *Calanus* fed on different concentrations of *Skeletonema*.

when starved will stop laying eggs but she will start again if food is provided, and the number of eggs laid depends primarily on the quantity of food.

Fig. 3 shows the total number of eggs laid by ripe female *Calanus* fed at five different levels. A hungry *Calanus* will eat her own eggs and a possible explanation might be that all five sets had laid the same number but that the eggs in the less well-fed sets had been eaten. However, if egg eating is

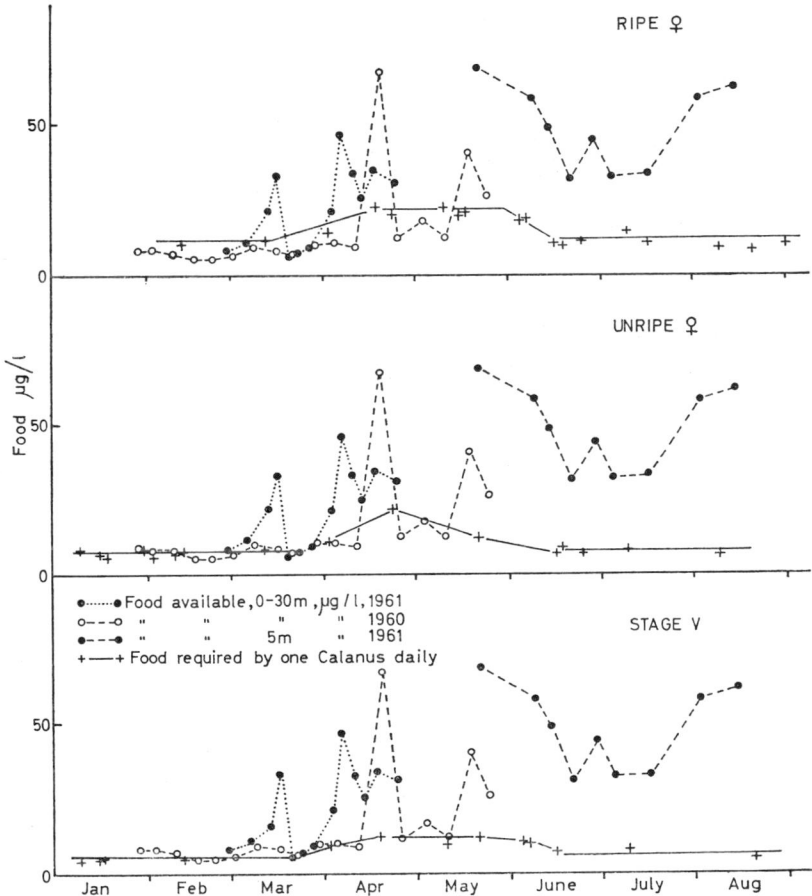

FIG. 4. Comparison of food available in the Clyde sea-area with the food requirements of a *Calanus*, assuming that it can filter 100 ml/day.

made impossible, the curves are not very different. In a laying *Calanus* a surprisingly large proportion of the food taken in goes to reproduction. This can be demonstrated by giving the female a meal of phytoplankton labelled with radioactive phosphorus (^{32}P) and measuring the ^{32}P which comes out again as eggs. In March, when egg production was high, an average of 47 per cent and a maximum of 72 per cent of a single meal was recovered in the eggs laid.

One of the difficulties of relating quantitatively the requirements of the zooplankton to the food available in natural waters has been the lack of a quick and reliable method for the measurement of the food value of the phytoplankton. Methods have varied from counting the phytoplankton organisms or measuring their volume to estimating their weight or one or more of their chemical constituents. Counting the numbers of organisms can be very deceptive because of differences in size even within the same species; weighing and subsequent analysis of filtered samples (Corner, 1961) is reliable but laborious. Of other methods available, the wet oxidation method for total carbon (Strickland and Parsons, 1960), the measurement of chlorophyll, and a colorimetric method for carbohydrate (Marshall and Orr, 1962a) all seem promising. Using the carbohydrate method we have followed the spring diatom increase simultaneously with counts of the diatoms in Loch Striven in 1960 and 1961. The diatom present was *Skeletonema costatum* and we have found from analyses of cultures that in it the carbohydrate represents between 20 and 30 per cent of the total organic matter. Parsons *et al.* (1961) found 32 per cent. We know too from feeding experiments on *Calanus* that 50–70 per cent of it is digested. Thus if we multiply the carbohydrate value by four to get the total organic matter and divide this by two for digestibility we can get approximate figures for the nutritive value of the phytoplankton during the spring increase. These are shown in Fig. 4. Miss Ågot Berner has kindly allowed us to quote her figures for carbohydrate at 5 m during the summer of 1961 in the Clyde sea-area.

The food requirements of *Calanus* are also shown based on its respiration and on the assumption that it can filter 100 ml of sea-water in a day. The curves show that for ripe and unripe female *Calanus* and for Stage V the food supply from the beginning of the spring diatom increase onwards was greatly in excess of their requirements.

During the winter the carbohydrate figure would appear still to cover or almost cover the requirements but this is more doubtful. Phytoplankton is absent during the winter and the carbohydrate is probably present then as detritus. In feeding experiments with detritus of different kinds *Calanus* females did not lay eggs nor even ingest much of it.

More observations on the quality of the food available for zooplankton in different areas of the oceans at different times are necessary before we can estimate accurately the effect of grazing on the phytoplankton.

REFERENCES

BEKLEMISHEV K.V. (1954) The feeding of some plankton copepods in Far Eastern Seas. Zool. J., 33, 1210–1229

BEKLEMISHEV K.V. (1962) Superfluous feeding of marine herbivorous zooplankton. Rapp. Cons. int. Explor. Mer. 153, 108–113

CONOVER R.J. (1960) The feeding behaviour and respiration of some marine planktonic Crustacea. Biol. Bull. Woods Hole, 119, 399–415

CONOVER R.J. (1962) Metabolism and growth in Calanus hyperboreus in relation to its life cycle. Rapp. Cons. int. Explor. Mer. 153, 190–197

CORNER E.D.S. (1961) On the nutrition and metabolism of zooplankton I. Preliminary observations on the feeding of the marine copepod Calanus helgolandicus (Claus.) J. mar. biol. Ass., U.K. 41, 5–16

CUSHING D.H. (1955) Production and a pelagic fishery. Fish. Invest., Ser. II 18, No. 7, 104 pp.

EDMONDSON W.T. (1962) Food supply and reproduction of zooplankton in relation to phytoplankton population. Rapp. Cons. int. Explor. Mer. 153, 137–141

HARVEY H.W., COOPER L.H.N., LEBOUR M.V. & RUSSELL F.S. (1935) Plankton production and its control. J. mar. biol. Ass., U.K. 20, 407–442

JØRGENSON C.B. (1962) The food of filter feeding organisms. Rapp. Cons. int. explor. Mer. 153, 99–107

MARSHALL S.M., NICHOLLS A.G. & ORR A.P. (1934) On the biology of Calanus finmarchicus. V. Seasonal distribution, size, weight and chemical composition in Loch Striven in 1933 and their relation to the phytoplankton. J. mar. biol. Ass., U.K. 19, 793–827

MARSHALL S.M. & ORR A.P. (1955) The biology of a marine copepod, Calanus finmarchicus Gunnerus. Edinburgh.

MARSHALL S.M. & ORR A.P. (1958) On the biology of Calanus finmarchicus. X. Seasonal changes in oxygen consumption. J. mar. biol. Ass., U.K. 37, 459–472

MARSHALL S.M. & ORR A.P. (1962) Food and feeding in copepods. Rapp. Cons. int. explor. Mer. 153, 92–98

MARSHALL S.M. & ORR A.P. (1962a) Carbohydrate as a measure of phytoplankton. J. mar. biol. Ass. U.K., 42, 511–519

PARSONS T.R., STEPHENS K. & STRICKLAND J.D.H. (1961) On the chemical composition of eleven species of marine phytoplankton. J. Fish. Res. Bd. Canada 18, 1001–1016

PETIPA T.S. (1959) Feeding of the copepod Acartia clausi. Giesbr. Tr. biol. Stat. Sebastopol, XI, 72–100

PETIPA T.S. (1960) Role of Noctiluca miliaris Sur. in feeding of Calanus helgolandicus Claus. C.R. (Doklady) U.S.S.R., Acad. Sci. 132, 961–963

PROVASOLI L. & SHIRAISHI K. (1959) Axenic cultivation of the brine shrimp, Artemia salina. Biol. Bull. Woods Hole 117, 347–355

PROVASOLI L., SHIRAISHI K. & LANCE J.R. (1959) Nutritional idiosyncrasies of Artemia and Tigriopus in monaxenic culture. Ann. New York Acad. Sci. 77, 250–261

RICHMAN S. (1958) The transformation of energy by Daphnia pulex. Ecol. Monog. 28, 273–291

RIGLER F.H. (1961) The relation between concentration of food and feeding rate of Daphnia magna Straus. Canad. J. Zool. 39, 857–868

RILEY G.A., STOMMEL H. & BUMPUS D.F. (1949) Quantitative ecology of the plankton of the western North Atlantic. *Bull. Bingham Oceanogr. Coll.* **12**, 3, 169 pp.

SARS G.O. (1903) *An account of the Crustacea of Norway. IV. Copepoda calanoida.* Bergen.

STRICKLAND J.D.H. & PARSONS T.R. (1960) A manual of sea water analysis. *Fish. Res. Bd, Canada., Bull.* **125**, 185 pp.

VINAGRADOV M.E. (1962) Feeding of the deep sea zooplankton. *Rapp. Cons. int. explor. Mer.,* **153**, 114–120

WICKSTEAD J.H. (1962) Food and feeding in pelagic copepods. *Proc. zool. Soc. Lond.,* **139**, 545–555

FEEDING IN PLANKTONIC COPEPODS

D. T. Gauld

Department of Zoology, University of Aberdeen

ABSTRACT

The common planktonic copepods feed in two different ways.
(1) By filtering water through stationary maxillae, as Cannon described in 1928.
(2) By a sweeping movement of the maxillae, first described for *Acartia* by Conover in 1956.
Acartia is small and uses its 'sweep-net' method of feeding to catch mainly diatoms and dinoflagellates, but the larger copepods, *Anomalocera* and *Labidocera*, use the same action with stronger maxillae to capture animal food. *Euchaeta norvegica* uses its maxillae as *Anomalocera* does, and in addition its large maxillipeds assist in the capture of active prey. None of these copepods filters as *Calanus* does.
It is shown that *Centropages*, *Temora*, *Pseudocalanus* and, to some extent perhaps, *Calanus* feed in two ways, by filtering small diatoms and flagellates, and by catching large diatoms or small animals with a sweeping movement of the maxillae. The volume of water from which they can collect food by these two mechanisms may be quite different and the extent to which they use the two mechanisms will vary with the nature of the food available. It is questionable whether measurements of an 'average filtering rate' can give a true estimate of the grazing rate of planktonic copepods under all conditions.

The grazing rate of herbivorous zooplankton is an essential factor in the assessment of the chain of production or energy transfer in the sea. It is usually measured in terms of a volume swept clear by the filtering activity of the animals, yet it is by no means certain that a single measurement of this kind can provide an adequate measure of grazing.

Two accounts of the feeding mechanism of calanoid copepods have been published and these show that copepods feed in two different ways:

(1) By filtering water through the stationary maxillae, as Cannon described in 1928.

(2) By a sweeping movement of the maxillae, first described for *Acartia* by Conover in 1956.

In Calanoid copepods the maxilla is a rather short, simple appendage lying more or less parallel to the ventral side of the head with a fringe of

239

from 14 to 28 long setae pointing forward. These setae are mostly provided on both sides with setules of varying size. When a copepod such as
Calanus is swimming slowly forward, it is propelled by the oscillations of
the anterior cephalic appendages, the antennae, mandibular rami and
maxillules. The maxillules have backwardly projecting epipodites with a
fan of long flexible setae, lying just outside the maxillae, and the movements of these epipodites draw a current of water forwards through the
setae of the maxillae. Small particles and microscopic algae suspended in
this water are strained out by the setae and their setules, which in *Calanus*
form a fairly close-meshed screen. The particles so filtered are combed off
the setae by the spines of the maxillary endite and passed to the mouth.

In *Acartia* the manner of swimming is somewhat different. Although
the maxillae are similar, there is no such current of water drawn through
them. Instead the maxillae are used actively with a sweeping or scooping
movement to sieve diatoms, etc. and other fine particles out of the water.
The setae of the maxillae are spread out downwards and sideways to form
a conical scoop net, and the gap between the bases of the maxillae, which
are set rather widely apart, is closed by the short maxillipeds. The bases
of the maxillipeds incidentally bear two long setae of identical form to
those of the maxillae, which are functionally part of the scoop net. One
important structural difference between these two types is that in *Calanus*
the maxillipeds, which lie immediately behind the maxillae, are long and
set widely apart, while in *Acartia* they are short and set close together,
effectively blocking from behind the space between the maxillae.

Acartia is a small copepod and uses its 'scoop net' to catch mainly diatoms
and dinoflagellates. The eleven principal setae of the maxilla (plus two on
the maxillipeds) are all exactly similar in form; but it is fairly clear that the
small number of setae on the maxillae and their uniformity is a consequence
of the general reduction in size that is suggested by the structure of *Acartia*,
like that of many other copepods. Another genus, nearly related to *Acartia*,
which does not show this evidence of reduction in size is *Anomalocera*:
here the maxillae differ from those of *Acartia* in the very distinct differentiation of the setae (other than a few small ones) into two main groups: a
basal group of seven, rather like those of *Acartia*, and a distal group of
eight longer and much stouter ones. *Anomalocera* is mainly carnivorous,
feeding on small planktonic animals including smaller copepods, and it
uses these stout distal setae with exactly the same scooping movement of
the maxillae as *Acartia* uses to catch and hold its prey. It apparently does
take some plant food. Lebour (1922) records 'green remains' in its gut, and
I have found similar traces too: these may be the remains of large diatoms

and dinoflagellates, but the basal setae are provided with quite fine setules and could retain moderately small plant cells. However in a suspension of small plant cells in which *Calanus* rapidly fills its gut, *Anomalocera* never contains more than a little food.

Acartia, Anomalocera and some other genera are set apart from the rest of the Calanoida mainly by structural features but also by their manner of swimming. However if one compares the maxilla of *Anomalocera* with

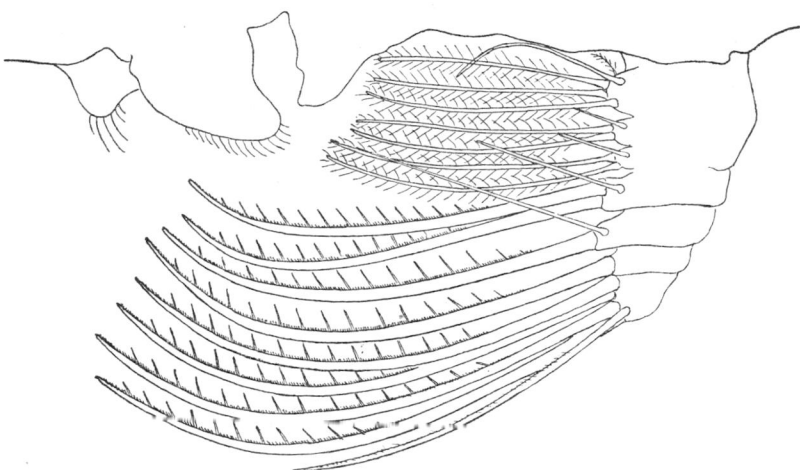

FIG. I. Maxilla of *Anomalocera*.

that of *Centropages*, a more typical calanoid, which indeed Gurney (1931) regards as the central type of the group, there is a remarkable similarity: there is the same basal group, this time of ten shorter, more slender setae and a distal group of six long, stout setae. There can be no doubt that *Centropages* uses these stout distal setae to capture and hold animal prey, just as both *Anomalocera* and another carnivorous copepod, *Euchaeta norvegica*, do: the size and form of the setae put this beyond question. Furthermore *Centropages* has long been known to feed, at least in part, on smaller copepods and nauplii.

Centropages also feeds on small plant cells, diatoms and flagellates, which it filters from the water in the way that *Calanus* filters its food. The filter is formed by the ten basal setae which are set with fine setules and form a filter screen just like that described by Cannon (1928). Thus *Centropages* can feed in two different ways — by the 'scoop net' system of *Acartia* and

17

Anomalocera, when it is catching smaller animals and perhaps large diatoms and dinoflagellates, and by the filter mechanism of *Calanus*, when it is catching smaller plants.

Although no observations have yet been made to confirm it, it is likely that other calanoids also use these two feeding mechanisms. Thus *Pseudocalanus* and *Temora* are known to filter and have basal setae which clearly form the necessary filter screen. They do not have a group of stout distal setae – the distal setae are shorter and if anything more slender than the basals – but near its tip each maxilla has a single, long, very stout seta, in the

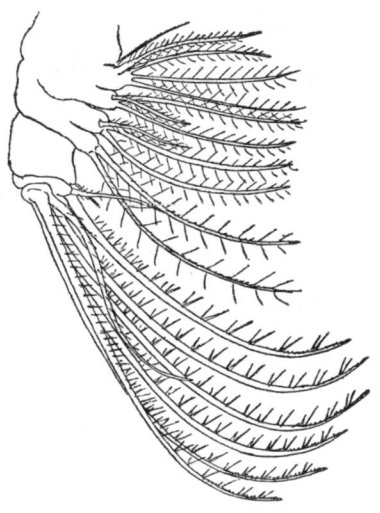

FIG. 2. Maxilla of *Centropages*.

form of a strong spine, which would be a very effective seizing and holding weapon.

In *Calanus* there is no obvious differentiation of the main setae into two groups. Marshall and Orr have shown however that in *C. helgolandicus* the setules are more widely spaced on the distal setae, but this is a very small difference and is not found in *C. finmarchicus*. But if the maxillae are examined in their natural position two facts emerge: (1) that while the first ten setae (on endites 1–4) lie quite well spaced out, so that their setules form an efficient filtering screen, the eight distal ones lie in a compact bunch, which certainly would not form an efficient filter; and (2) that in ventral view it is obvious that this distal bunch of setae lies at a different angle to the screen formed by the basal setae.

Now it is extremely difficult to see exactly how the setae are disposed when the animal is actually feeding and it may be that then these setae are spread out; but, since the entrance to the filter chamber is limited to the lower part of the maxillae, extending the filtering area does not seem to offer much advantage. Thus although there is no differentiation of form, it does appear possible to differentiate these two groups of setae in *Calanus* too.

Examination of the maxillae *in situ* brings out another significant point. In their detailed description of the maxilla Marshall and Orr (1956) des-

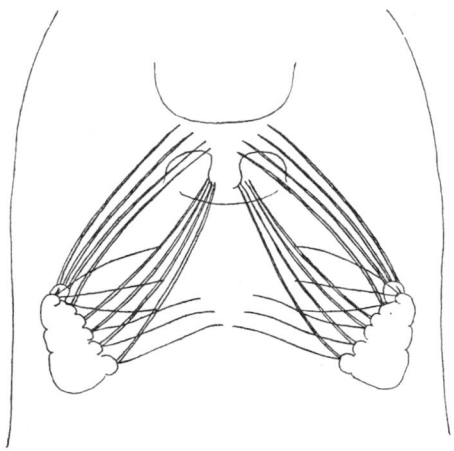

FIG. 3. Simplified diagram of the maxillae of *Calanus* from below. The maxillae have been separated distally to show the setae more clearly.

cribed four setae on the basal part of limb for which they could not suggest a function. It is clear from a ventral view that these four stretch across the back of the filter chamber, forming there a rather widely spaced screen. Here they will clearly help to retain in the filter chamber any particles which enter it; but they will also obstruct the entry of large particles. Since in *Calanus* these setae are approximately 40μ apart, the largest particles which will enter the filter chamber freely will be about 35μ in diameter. Yet *Calanus*, as is well known, feeds on diatoms much bigger than this.

Thus there is a bunch of distal setae, which apparently are not part of the filter mechanism, and a group of setae which apparently prevent some of the diatoms which *Calanus* is known to eat from entering the filter chamber. Both these groups of setae are comprehensible if we suppose that like *Centropages*, *Calanus* feeds in two ways: filtering as Cannon described, when it catches particles less than 40μ in diameter and 'scoop netting' with the distal setae spread out as *Acartia* does to catch mainly particles more than 40μ. This has not been confirmed by observation, but it seems a reasonable explanation of the anatomical data.

What are the implications of this suggestion?

First, it provides a possible mechanism for the 'selective feeding' to which reference is made from time to time. To give one example, Marshall and Orr (1955) describe how, in a mixed suspension of *Prorocentrum micans* and *Peridinium trochoideum*, *Calanus* which had been fed on *Peridinium* showed no evidence of eating *Prorocentrum* for the first hour and only slowly increased the proportion of it in their food, while *Calanus* fed on *Prorocentrum* immediately showed evidence of eating *Peridinium*. *Prorocentrum* is 43μ long and would be excluded from the filter chamber; to obtain any food at all in a culture of *Prorocentrum* a *Calanus* would have to use the maxillae as a scoop; if it went on doing this in a mixed culture, it would immediately obtain mixed food. *P. trochoideum* is only 25μ long and can be caught in the filter but a *Calanus* filtering in a mixed suspension would ingest only *Peridinium* because the *Prorocentrum* would be excluded from the filter. Future experiments on 'selective' feeding should be designed to investigate the possibilities of the two methods of feeding.

Secondly, all experimental measurements of grazing rates are measurements of a 'volume swept clear' in a given time. This is a valid way of measuring the grazing rate when the animal is filtering small food organisms which are evenly distributed in the water, and is equally valid for medium sized organisms which are being caught by active movements of the maxillae so long as the concentration is sufficiently high for the maxillae to be continuously or nearly continuously active. A volume swept clear in these circumstances is a real measure of the animal's grazing capacity, although the 'volume swept clear' by continuous 'scooping' may not be the same as that swept clear by filtering. But with less dense suspensions, and especially with larger diatoms, the maxillae may be inactive for much of the period of the experiment and the apparent 'volume swept clear' obviously refers only to the conditions of the experiment and cannot be applied outside them.

On the other hand, when much of the phytoplankton in the sea consists of medium or large diatoms which would be excluded from the filter apparatus the volume swept clear by the filter apparatus is quite irrelevant and what we need is some measure of the rate at which copepods catch diatoms at the concentration found at that time. In other words we need a new series of measurements of grazing rate, specifically related to a range of concentrations of large particles, possibly repeated for particles of different sizes. In such measurements the apparent 'volume swept clear' may prove to depend on the concentration of food particles.

Finally, if the rate at which copepods sweep up food particles of different sizes does prove to be different, it is obvious that knowledge only of the total amount of plant food available cannot give an accurate estimate of the food available to the animals: we need to know something about the sizes at least of the plants present and possibly something about their distribution within the water mass we are investigating.

REFERENCES

CANNON H. G. (1928) On the feeding mechanism of the copepods *Calanus finmarchicus* and *Diaptomus gracilis. Brit. J. exp. Biol.* **6,** 131–144

CONOVER R. J. (1956) Oceanography of Long Island Sound, 1952–1954. VI. Biology of *Acartia clausi* and *A. tonsa. Bull. Bingham oceanogr. Coll.* **15,** 156–233

GURNEY R. (1931) *British Fresh-Water Copepoda.* Vol. I. London, Ray Society

LEBOUR M. V. (1922) The food of plankton organisms. *J. mar. biol. Ass. U.K.* **12,** 644–677

MARSHALL S.M. & ORR A.P. (1955) On the biology of *Calanus finmarchicus.* VIII. Food uptake, assimilation and excretion in adult and stage V *Calanus. J. mar. biol. Ass. U.K.* **34,** 495–529

MARSHALL S.M. & ORR A.P. (1956) On the biology of *Calanus finmarchicus.* IX. Feeding and digestion in the young stages. *J. mar. biol. Ass. U.K.* **35,** 587–603

GRAZING BY MARINE BIVALVE LARVAE[1]

P. R. WALNE

Fisheries Laboratory, Conway, N. Wales

Bivalve larvae usually comprise a rather small part of the zooplankton but, because of the economic importance of the adults of some species (especially species of *Crassostrea*, *Ostrea* and *Venus*), methods of culturing the larvae have received a good deal of attention. Present methods are suitable for growing the larvae from the fertilized egg until it metamorphoses into the benthonic adult form. By comparing the growth rate and the proportion of embryos which reach metamorphosis, standards can be set for various culture conditions and for comparison with those obtained in the field.

The importance of the quality of the food supply has received particular attention and the results demonstrate quite clearly how much the various species of phytoplankton differ in their food value. Larvae are generally restricted, because of the size of the mouth, to food organisms measuring not more than 10 microns in one dimension. Species without a rigid cell wall are usually better as food than those with. For example, in the *Chlorophyceae* the genera *Chlorella* and *Chlamydomonas* give indifferent results compared with *Dunaliella* and *Pyramimonas*. The most satisfactory results are given by members of the *Chrysophyceae*, especially *Isochrysis* and *Monochrysis*.

The food must be present in suitable densities in the water. In the laboratory 50–100 cells of *Isochrysis* per μl are required for good growth. This is two or three times the densities recorded in the field but such populations only represent about 0·8–1·6 mg of dry organic matter per litre and this is well within the limits recorded in the field. It may be that some other energy source than small phytoplankton is also being utilized. A medium sized oyster larva requires about 0·14 μg dry organic matter per day of which about 75 per cent goes in growth and the remainder in respiration.

[1] Summary only.

GRAZING BY LITTORAL
AND BENTHIC ORGANISMS

AN ASSESSMENT OF PLANKTON GRAZING BY BARNACLES

D. J. Crisp

Marine Science Laboratories, University College of North Wales, Bangor

ABSTRACT

Barnacles feed on a wide range of suspended particles of all sizes from flagellates to small crustacea. Feeding is not indiscriminate, nutritious particles are taken more readily than non-nutritious ones and stimulate greater cirral activity; unwanted particles can be rejected.

The rate of capture by the cirri is generally proportional to the concentration of the food organisms. However, measurements of the rate of emission of faeces indicate that barnacles ingest only a limited amount of food, the excess material caught by the cirri being returned to the water, often in a damaged condition. Comparison of the rate of feeding in the laboratory with growth rates in the sea indicates a high efficiency of transformation of the ingested food. At the filtration rates observed in the laboratory, *Balanus balanoides* and *Elminius modestus* require for maximum growth a high concentration of suspended matter characteristic of rich inshore water.

The major factor determining both the size attained by individuals and the total amount of living tissue per unit area is the water movement carrying food within range of the animal. Intraspecific competition is important only in limiting individual size and fecundity; it has little effect on the total biomass produced in unit area. Different species have slightly different cirral behaviour and potential rates of growth. Such differences influence interspecific competition; *Elminius modestus* is less successful than *Balanus balanoides* in gathering food except in relatively still water.

Sessile animals may compete for food and for space. Since they depend almost entirely on water movement to bring them food they must, (a) utilize a catholic diet, (b) be capable of a wide range of growth rates according to food supply, and, (c) produce the maximum biomass and reproductive potential independent of wide variation in settlement density.

I. INTRODUCTION

The term grazing is usually applied to the removal of plants from a surface by an active herbivore. In the open sea the plants are widely dispersed throughout the depth of the photic zone and the grazing activities of the primary herbivores therefore extend throughout this layer. By analogy, the more rapidly moving predatory fish may be considered to graze on the primary herbivores, such as the copepods, and the baleen whales on the euphausids. The omnivorous feeding of barnacles may be regarded as an inverted system of grazing in which the animals are static and are spread out as a surface layer while the food material is carried past them by the movement of water. The energy relationships are essentially similar to those in classical systems of grazing but the inability of the animal to move in search of its food imposes certain constraints on the system that are without parallel in the normal grazing situation.

2. FEEDING IN BARNACLES

A co-ordinated set of movements of the body, the opercular valves and the appendages is responsible both for the capture of large and small food particles and for driving a current of sea-water through the mantle space and over the gills (Crisp and Southward, 1961). Although the movements involved in feeding and in respiration are closely integrated, food capture is not an entirely automatic process. Some degree of involuntary selection of the larger food particles must occur both within the cirral net, where the larger food organisms are caught, and in the filtering mechanism formed by the setae of the smaller cirri surrounding the mouth, where micro-feeding occurs (Southward, 1955). Some degree of selection and economy of effort is also achieved by a modification of the cirral beat occasioned by the presence or absence of food. When suitable food is present in the water a high proportion of the barnacles can generally be observed feeding with the cirral net fully extended. If barnacles are kept for some time in water in which the suspended matter is either absent or not nutritious, the proportion of the time they spend fishing by means of the cirri becomes progressively reduced and respiration is effected by a modified form of cirral activity, known as 'pumping', in which the cirri themselves are not extended into the water. Thus barnacles which have been starved for many weeks have a greatly reduced activity and display the normal cirral movements only for brief periods during each day.

The barnacle appears able to distinguish particles of food material from inert objects; the former are generally transferred to the smaller cirri and thence to the mouth, while the latter can be rejected in one of two ways. If the barnacle is feeding in a water current, particles can be removed directly from the cirral net simply by rotating it through 180° when the water current carries them away. Alternatively, unwanted particles may be rejected by the smaller cirri instead of being carried to the mouth.

The filtration rate for actively feeding barnacles was shown by Crisp and Southward (1961) to be more or less independent of the concentration of particles in the water above a certain size, suggesting that all the larger organisms that entered the cirral net were devoured. Very different results however were obtained when measurements were made of the amount of food actually ingested. *Balanus balanoides* and *Elminius modestus* adults were fed on nauplius larvae. The number of larvae ingested could be counted by examining the collected faecal strings in which each larval eye spot could still be seen, though partially digested. The volume of the faecal string could thus be related to the number of nauplii eaten. In actively feeding individuals of both species, the time required for food to pass through the

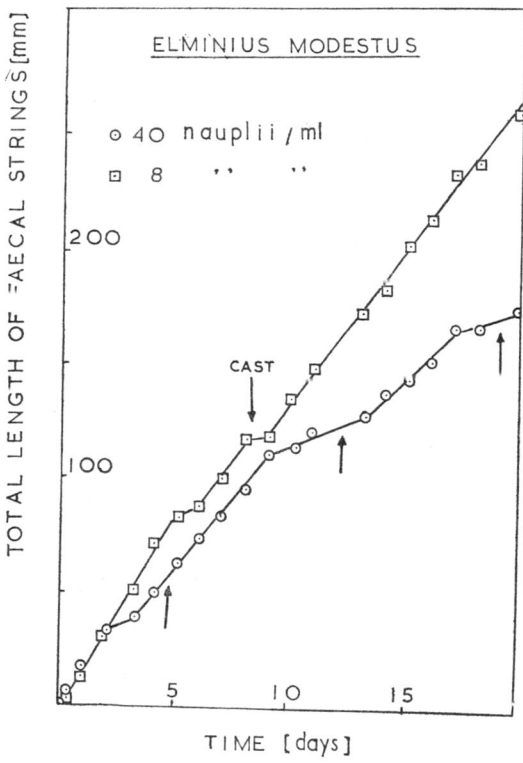

TIME [days]

FIG. 1. Rate of production of faecal strings by two specimens of *Elminius modestus*, weighing 88 (upper curve) and 84 (lower curve) mg wet weight respectively. The barnacles were fed on nauplii and the water gently stirred. The arrows indicate the occasions when the barnacle cast its cuticle. The individual shown in the upper curve was fed on a concentration of 8 nauplii ml.$^{-1}$ The individual represented by the lower curve was kept in a suspension five times as concentrated, but ingested food at a slightly lower rate.

whole length of the gut was from three to eight hours. Since for any such individual the faecal string was of roughly uniform diameter, the cumulative length of faecal string plotted against time gave a convenient measure of the rate of ingestion. Fig. 1 shows that the rate of ingestion did not depend upon the concentration of nauplii in the surrounding water, provided of course that it exceeded certain minimal requirements. Evidently, therefore, although the barnacles may capture and destroy most of the organisms that enter the cirral net, they ingest only the amount that they require. The nauplii that are captured but not ingested are usually damaged and fall to the bottom of the dish, thus contributing to the apparent rate of filtration when measured from the rate of disappearance of suspended food.

3. GROWTH RATE AND FOOD SUPPLY

No studies of energy flow appear to have been carried out on cirripedes although these animals would be extremely suitable. A comparison can, however, be made between the rate of tissue growth under natural conditions and the rate at which they could be expected to collect suspended matter from the sea. Table 1 gives the data for two specimens of *Balanus balanoides* and two of *Elminius modestus*. The second column gives the weight increment per day based on the linear part of the rate of growth curve for the species. Along this part of the growth curve the rate of increase in volume or weight is proportional to the product of the square of the linear dimension, l, and its rate of increase (Crisp, 1960a).

$$\frac{dV}{dt} = 3kl^2 \cdot \frac{dl}{dt} \tag{1}$$

The third column gives the weight increment per day in terms of dry tissue weight, excluding the weight of the shell. The dry tissue weight, which will be taken as the basis of comparison throughout, comprises • approximately one-tenth of the total wet weight of the barnacle.

The fourth column gives the rate of ingestion of food when plentifully supplied with nauplius larvae. Each nauplius larva was hatched from an egg of average volume 3.5×10^{-6} cc in which the embryonic nauplius was tightly packed. The volume occupied by one nauplius skeleton in the faecal string was approximately the same. Evidently the volume loss due to digestion of larval tissues compensated for the irregular packing of the larval skeleton in the faeces. Under these conditions of feeding, therefore, the volume of faeces produced per day approximately equalled the volume of living animal tissue ingested and the dry weight ingested shown in column V was approximately one-third of this.

TABLE I

Food requirements of specimens of *Balanus balanoides* and *Elminius modestus*

I	II	III	IV	V	VI
Species and dimensions	Total wet weight increment per day (from growth rate in the sea at 13–17°C)	Dry tissue weight increment excluding shell per day (1/10 of total)	Wet weight of tissue ingested per day (from faecal production at 15°C in laboratory)	Dry weight of food ingested per day (1/3 of wet weight ingested)	Calculated dry weight filtered per day (assuming 2 mg/L in sea, and filtration rates shown in brackets)
Balanus balanoides					
12 mm	5·7 mg	0·57 mg	4·8 mg	1·6 mg ⎫	0·72 mg
10 mm	4·0 mg	0·40 mg	3·25 mg	1·1 mg ⎭	(15 cc h⁻¹)
Elminius modestus					
10 mm	2·5 mg	0·25 mg	1·9 mg	0·6 mg ⎫	0·48 mg
8 mm	1·6 mg	0·16 mg	1·4 mg	0·5 mg ⎭	(10 cc h⁻¹)

The last column shows the quantity of dry organic matter which a barnacle of the size indicated could be expected to filter from the sea each day. The filtration rates are based on figures given in Crisp and Southward (1961) and an assumed value for the dry weight content of suspended organic matter in coastal water of two milligrams per litre (Corner, 1961; Armstrong and Atkins, 1950; Jones and Wills, 1956; see also Marshall and Orr, this volume, page 232). Rich estuarine water would be expected to contain somewhat greater concentrations, offshore water rather less.

Columns III, V and VI may now be compared. Column III represents the maximum growth rate of which the species is probably capable, when feeding in a strong current of water very rich in suspended matter. Column V probably represents the maximum rate of ingestion of suitable animal food. Since the daily ration is only two or three times the increment in tissue weight the conversion appears to be efficient, as in egg laying *Calanus* (Marshall and Orr, this volume, pages 231–6) and in other small crustacea such as the *Cladocera* (Richman, 1958). The amount of food available in average coastal water, as shown in column VI, is barely sufficient to maintain the maximum rate of growth for these two species. These results are therefore in agreement with the known effects of environment on growth rate. Growth rates increase in *Balanus balanoides* as the proportion of time available for feeding increases from high water to low water (Barnes and Powell, 1953). Growth rates of both species are greater in estuarine and inshore areas where the water has a high suspended matter content than in offshore areas where the water is clear (Crisp, unpublished observations). Growth rates are also greatly dependent on the free flow of water past the animal (Crisp and Davies, 1955; Crisp, 1960a). Moreover, since barnacles usually live in close proximity to one another they will tend to filter the same water thus reducing, in comparison with isolated specimens, the effective filtration and the rate of growth if food is limiting. A simple calculation serves to show how important is water movement in reducing the impact of this kind of intra- and inter-specific competition. If on a gently sloping shore there are five to ten barnacles per square centimetre projected on a vertical plane, and if these barnacles could each filter a separate volume of sea water equal to only twenty cubic centimetres per hour or one half litre per day, then they would require to strain completely a horizontal column of water, extending from 25 to 50 m offshore, daily. Strong turbulence would be essential to mobilize such a volume of water within range of the barnacles.

4. INTRA-SPECIFIC COMPETITION IN A BARNACLE POPULATION

Barnacles are very suitable for the study of intra-specific competition in two dimensional sessile communities which derive their food from the surrounding water. They can be made to settle according to a pre-arranged pattern by taking advantage of their predilection at settlement for small pits drilled in the surface. Details of the technique are given by Crisp (1960a), and Crisp and Patel (1961).

Using similar methods Dr Patel and I carried out a factorial experiment which will be reported in greater detail elsewhere in which cyprids of *Balanus balanoides* were allowed to settle on experimental panels at densities ranging from 0·25 to 15·0 individuals per square centimetre. Three series of panels were used, each in a different environmental situation. The first series was exposed from a raft moored in a rapidly flowing tideway where conditions for feeding would be ideal. The second series was fastened to an intertidal structure in the same area at about mean sea level where it would be exposed for half the tidal cycle to an unrestricted flow of water. The third series was placed in the same position, but enclosed in a large wooden box in which a few holes one centimetre in diameter had been drilled to allow a very limited flow of water through it. The cyprids settled on each series of panels at the same time, during early May, and the populations were artificially kept clear of any other settling organisms so that the barnacles could grow without restriction until the end of the experiment in December. By this time all the individuals that were capable of breeding would have contained fertilized egg masses. During growth, particularly of the denser populations, the area covered by the barnacles had greatly enlarged (Crisp, 1960b), while many had been eliminated by

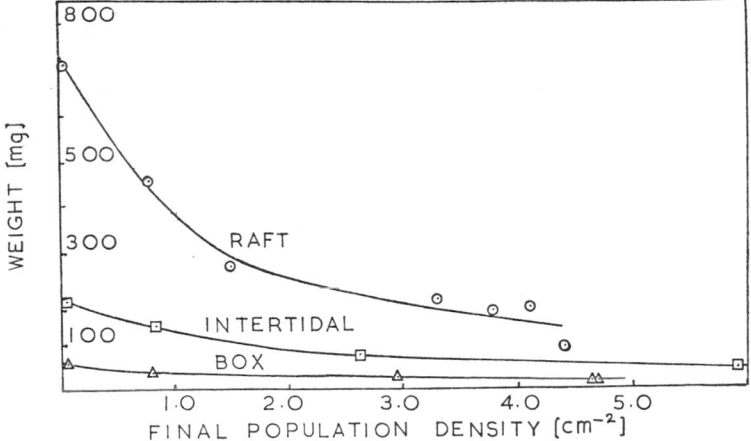

FIG. 2. Mean oven-dry weight of an individual barnacle (including shell) in mg plotted against the population density at the end of the experiment for each of the three environmental conditions.

competition (Connell, 1959). Consequently the final population density was usually considerably lower than the initial. A photograph was taken of each panel in order to measure the population density at the end of the experiment. Then each barnacle was carefully prized off, its egg masses removed, blotted dry of surplus water and weighed. The egg masses were then replaced and the whole barnacle oven dried at 110°C, then weighed.

Fig. 2 shows the mean individual dry weight in milligrammes attained by the end of the experiment, under each of the three sets of environmental conditions, plotted against the final population density. The success of the individual in gathering its food was determined mainly by the rate of renewal of food-bearing water around it, which was greatest in those continuously immersed from the raft and least in those enclosed in the box.

18

Competition from neighbours also influenced the rate of growth in each of the three environments. In Fig. 3, intra-specific competition has been demonstrated by plotting the data of Fig. 2 with the units on the ordinate modified to give the size attained as a percentage of the maximum size attainable in the absence of competition. The value taken for maximum growth was the intercept of the appropriate curve in Fig. 2 with the ordinate at zero population density. The points then fell on a similar curve,

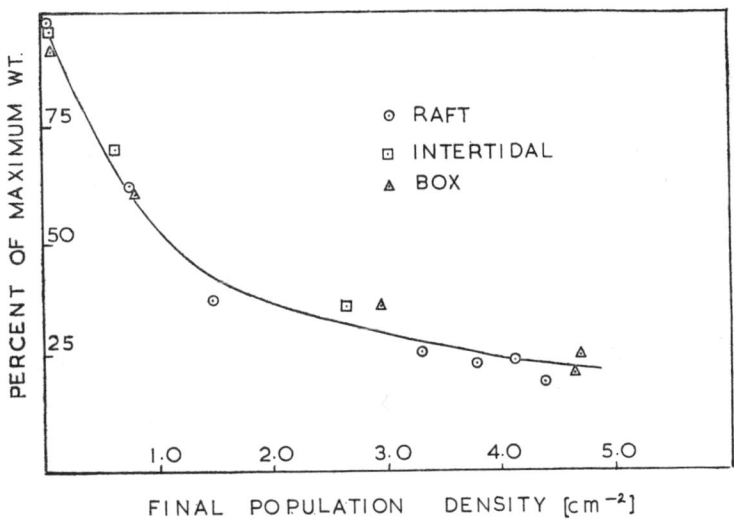

FIG. 3. Mean oven-dry weight of an individual barnacle, expressed as a percentage of the maximum weight attainable when growing in isolation in the same environment, plotted against the population density at the end of the experiment. The maximum weight attainable was taken from the intercept with the ordinate at zero population density of the appropriate curves in Fig. 2.

showing that competition from neighbouring individuals has much the same influence on food gathering and growth whether the food supply were rich or poor.

The success of a sessile animal such as a barnacle, which has a limited amount of surface available to it, depends not so much on the size attained by the individual as on the total biomass and the resulting production of eggs and nauplii that a unit area of this surface can sustain. Fig. 4 shows, for each of the three environmental conditions, the biomass per unit area that was attained in a single growing season in relation to the initial density of settlement of the cyprids. Provided the initial settlement exceeded five cyprids per square centimetre the biomass produced was constant and depended only on the nutritional conditions of the environment.

The explanation of this result was obvious on cursory examination of the panels. When the settlement density was low, the barnacles at no time covered the whole surface of the panel and their utilization of food particles carried to the surface was partial. When the initial settlement density exceeded the critical value, the barnacles became so closely packed to-

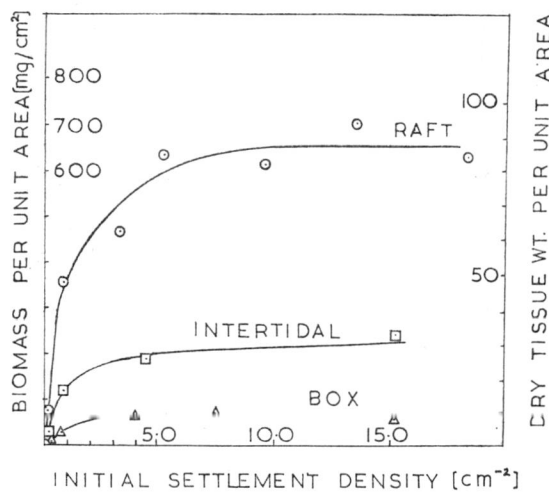

FIG. 4. The relationship between total barnacle biomass (dry weight) per unit area at the end of the first growing season and the initial settlement density of cyprids in each of the three environments.

gether that they formed a continuous layer on the surface. The constantly waving cirri of this sheet of barnacles would effectively remove any suspended particles that came into contact with it. Thus the rate of growth of the population would depend only on the rate at which the external water movements carried particular matter on to the surface.

Fig. 5 shows the relationship between egg production (wet weight) per unit area and the initial settlement density of the cyprids. As before, a minimum settlement density was required in order to achieve the maximum productivity; in this case the production of eggs by the population. However, it will be seen from a comparison of Figs. 4 and 5, that the differences in egg production between the three environments were much greater than the differences in total biomass. The rapidly growing indi-

viduals on the raft produced egg masses which were larger in proportion
to their size than were those produced by individuals growing in the intertidal zone, while the egg masses of individuals growing in the box were
relatively smaller still. Furthermore, a considerable proportion of the small
barnacles growing in the box were sterile, particularly those growing at
the higher population densities, so that the egg production actually de-

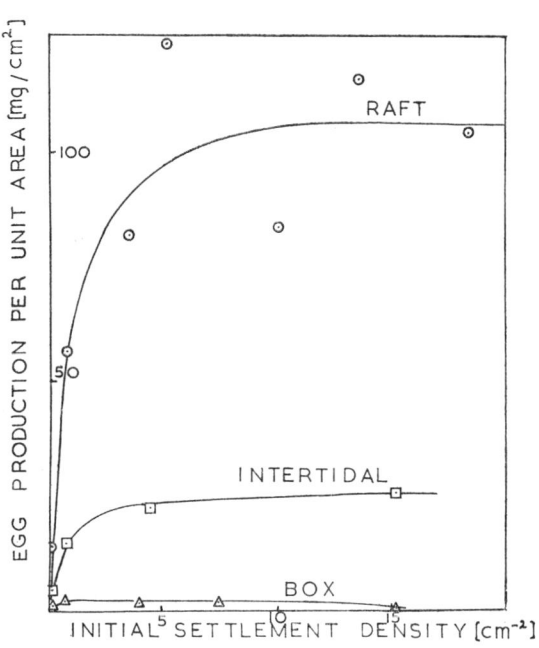

Fig. 5. Population fecundity per unit area, measured from the wet weight of
eggs produced per unit area of each of the three environments, plotted against
the density of cyprids at settlement.

creased with increasing population density. It is important to note that
only under these extremely rigorous and unnatural conditions was there
an inverse relationship between egg production and settlement density
such as would cause high settlement rates to be disadvantageous.

5. INTER-SPECIFIC COMPETITION

Growth rate is an important factor both in intra- and in inter-specific
competition, because it is usually the individual or species with the higher
growth rate that is able to grow outward at the expense of other indi-

viduals, causing them either to be displaced upward from the surface (Connell, 1961) or horizontally along the surface (Crisp, 1960b). In the experiment described above, a small number of specimens of *Elminius modestus* occasionally settled simultaneously with the rest of the population which consisted of *Balanus balanoides*. The former species normally has a lower growth rate than that of *Balanus balanoides* but it has a more rapid cirral beat (Crisp and Southward, 1961), and is therefore better adapted than *Balanus balanoides* for feeding in the absence of wave exposure or tidal current. Where the two species are found together *Elminius* dominates in sheltered situations and *Balanus balanoides* in exposed situations. The success of one species relative to the other may be measured in our experiments from the ratio of their mean dry weights at the end of the growing season. These are shown in Table 2. The most reliable sets of comparisons,

TABLE 2

Growth of *Elminius modestus* in competition with *Balanus balanoides*

| Condition | Settlement density | No. of comparisons | Mean dry weight | | Ratio Balanus/ Elminius |
			Balanus	Elminius	
Raft	0·68	46	506·7	124·9 mg	4·05*
Intertidal	0·15	4	191·0	107·9	1·77
	0·78	60	142·0	87·0	1·63*
	2·64	31	71·4	57·5	1·24
	5·47	2	38·0	56·4	0·67
Box	0·17	3	55·0	56·8	0·97
	0·80	94	36·1	27·8	1·30*
	2·95	6	21·9	23·8	0·92
	4·7	13	15·3	17·9	0·86

carried out at approximately the same population densities, are asterisked. The other results, though based on more limited data, are in reasonable agreement. They show that on the raft the balance of competition was very much in favour of *Balanus balanoides* with a weight ratio of four to one. In the inter-tidal zone the ratio was considerably less, while in the box the results as a whole show that *Elminius modestus* grew as fast as *Balanus balanoides*. Since *Elminius modestus* is a distinctly smaller species at maturity than *Balanus balanoides* it would almost certainly have the advantage under these conditions. The table shows also that, with increase in settlement density and, presumably, in the degree of competition between individuals, the advantage moved increasingly in favour of *Elminius*, the species with the greater potential for collecting sparsely distributed food particles.

6. GRAZING BY IMMOBILE TWO-DIMENSIONAL POPULATIONS

In this section I shall consider the limitations that the sessile habit imposes both on the individual and on the population. Only the genuinely sessile forms will be considered, excluding the semi-sessile forms, such as certain bivalves, which live in, and obtain their food from, bottom deposits. The truly sessile forms therefore whether they exist as close packed communities as do the shore barnacles, or whether they are distributed as isolated individuals and groups, depend very largely on the natural water movement to carry particles within the range of their food collecting organs. The advantage of this ecologically open system is that food can be derived from a very wide area with the minimum effort on the part of the animal. The disadvantage is that the animal must be content with whatever food arrives by chance and cannot afford the luxury of a specialized diet as can certain active predators. The majority of sessile forms, therefore, resemble the barnacles in accepting a wide range of food in their diet.

Since the flow of water determines the amount of food carried to communities of sessile animals, it is not surprising that these communities thrive best in narrow channels or estuaries where strong tidal currents pass up and down. In any given situation the efficiency of the food gathering activities, such as the captorial action of the cirri of barnacles or the feeding currents produced by the cilia of molluscs and polychaete worms, cannot increase the food supplies to the animal beyond a maximum which is determined by the transport of water and its content of suspended matter. Although the individual animal cannot control either of these factors there are two common adaptations which enable the species to increase its food supply. In the first, by growing outwards from the substratum, the animal gives itself access to water in greater volume and more rapid flow. It may raise the body on a simple stalk, as in the Lepadidae, or form branched colonies of feeding zooids, as in many hydroids and polyzoa, or develop prominent, usually branched, extensions of the body which serve both for feeding and for respiration, as in tubicolous polychaetes and holothurians. These adaptations usually depend for their success on a gentle flow of water past the animal and are therefore suited to animals which live in isolation or in small groups in relatively quiet water. In the second type of adaptation the animal encrusts the surface to the exclusion of other forms. Examples are afforded between the tide marks by mussels and barnacles and at lower levels by sponges, encrusting polyzoa and compound ascidians. By eliminating competition from other organisms, such colonies can, in theory, mobilize all the particulate matter that is brought within range of the surface. Some of these encrusting organisms form their colonies by vegetative growth over the surface. Such colonies are relatively small. Others form dense populations as a result of wide larval dispersal followed by subsequent settlement, usually gregarious. In order to be able to cover large areas of rocky surface so completely these animals must be highly successful and dominant forms.

Animals, such as barnacles, which form such two dimensional populations as a result of individual settlement, must experience three major limitations as a result of their lack of mobility.

The first is that they compete with their neighbours, not only for food but also for space. Barnacles have solved this problem by the extreme plasticity of form which they can adopt. In a closely packed population, columnar individuals may grow many times as high as broad without suffering any ill effect.

The second problem is the regulation of population density to achieve the maximum growth and fecundity. Territorial behaviour at settlement must help to prevent over-dense populations being formed and to spread out the settlement more evenly (Crisp, 1961). After settlement has taken place some limited mobility is still possible which would allow living individuals to extend into any spaces left by dead barnacles and enable crowded colonies to enlarge in area if space were available (Crisp, 1960b). The main safeguard, however, is the fact that the total growth of the colony and its reproductive potential are independent of settlement density over much of the range that is likely to occur in nature (see Figs. 4 and 5).

Thirdly, the barnacle, in common with all sessile forms, is entirely dependent for its food supply on conditions at the site of settlement. If food is lacking it cannot explore new grazing areas after settlement; consequently different individuals of the species may experience wide differences in nutrition throughout their life. Experiments show that the barnacle is well adapted to such a contingency. The ratio of sizes attained under different conditions was a hundredfold in some cases, while reproduction could still occur in individuals which were only one-twentieth of the maximum size. Furthermore, barnacles have been kept in the laboratory under conditions of virtual starvation for many months without dying. No doubt the reduction in cirral activity under such conditions helps the animal to conserve energy, just as the metabolic activity of other marine animals has been shown to be reduced when they are temporarily starved. However, the extreme variation in the range of normal growth and activity shown by barnacles may well be a feature characteristic of many other members of the sessile fauna.

ACKNOWLEDGEMENT

I am indebted to Mr Adrian Tibbetts who assisted me in the experiments on measuring ingestion rates of barnacles fed on nauplii by collecting and measuring the faecal strings daily.

REFERENCES

ARMSTRONG F.A.S. & ATKINS W.R.G. (1950) The suspended matter of sea water. *J. Mar. biol. Ass. U.K.* **29**, 139–143

BARNES H. & POWELL H.T. (1953) The growth of *Balanus balanoides* (L) and *B. crenatus* Brug. under varying conditions of submersion. *J. Mar. biol. Ass. U.K.* **32**, 107–128

CONNELL J.H. (1959) An experimental analysis of interspecific competition in natural populations of intertidal barnacles. *Proc. XV Int. Congr. Zool. Lond.* (1958) **3**, 290

CONNELL J.H. (1961) The influence of interspecific competition and other factors on the distribution of the barnacles *Chthamalus stellatus*. *Ecology* **42**, 710–723

CORNER E.D.S. (1961) On the nutrition and metabolism of zooplankton I. Preliminary observations on the feeding of the marine copepod *Calanus helgolandicus* (Claus). *J. Mar. biol. Ass. U.K.* **41**, 5–16

CRISP D.J. (1960a) Factors influencing the growth rate of *Balanus balanoides*. *J. Anim. Ecol.* **29**, 95–116

CRISP D.J. (1960b) Mobility of barnacles. *Nature Lond.* **188**, 1208–1209

CRISP D.J. (1961) Territorial behaviour in barnacle settlement. *J. exp. Biol.* **38**, 429–446

CRISP D.J. & DAVIES P.A. (1955) Observations *in vivo* on the breeding of *Elminius modestus* grown on glass slides. *J. Mar. biol. Ass. U.K.* **34**, 357–380

CRISP D.J. & PATEL B. (1961) The interaction between breeding and growth rate in the barnacle *Elminius modestus*. *Limn. & Ocean.* **6**, 105–115

CRISP D.J. & SOUTHWARD A.J. (1961) Different types of cirral activity in barnacles. *Phil. Trans. B.* **243**, 271–308

JONES D. & WILLS M.S. (1956) The attenuation of light in the sea and estuarine waters in relation to the concentration of suspended matter. *J. Mar. biol. Ass. U.K.* **35**, 431–441

RICHMAN S. (1958) The transformation of energy by *Daphnia pulex*. *Ecol. Monogr.* **28**, 273–291

SOUTHWARD A.J. (1955) Feeding of barnacles. *Nature Lond.* **175**, 1124

LIMPET GRAZING AND THE CONTROL OF VEGETATION ON ROCKY SHORES

A. J. SOUTHWARD

The Laboratory, Citadel Hill, Plymouth

ABSTRACT

The common limpet *Patella vulgata* uses a rasping radula to scrape algal food from the rocks of the seashore. Observations have been made on the rate of clearance of an algal film from the glass of an aquarium wall, and on the movements of the feeding limpet. On the shore, large and small algae are attacked. The effect of limpets on the vegetation of the shore has been studied by means of experiments involving removal of limpets and subsequent observations over a period of years. The results suggest that a cyclic relationship exists between limpets and algae. The point at which the cycle is temporarily stabilized is influenced by other factors, of which wave action is the most important. The sharp teeth of the limpet radula often remove some of the underlying rock with the algae when grazing, so that the contribution of limpets and other gastropods towards erosion of the rocks may be quite considerable.

1. INTRODUCTION

There are very few rocky shores in the world without an abundance of limpets and most people will have a memory of groups of these molluscs motionless on the rocks. The picture is obviously very different when the animals are covered by the tide; and they can also be found off their homes at low tide during the night or on damp days in the winter. Under such conditions, as many authors since Aristotle have testified, the limpets may be found feeding or moving to and from their feeding grounds and a careful listener will hear the noise made by their radulae scraping the rocks (for references, see Pieron, 1909).

2. FEEDING MECHANISM

The marks left by limpet radulae on the rocks, particularly on soft materials, or where there is a thick film of algae, have long attracted the attention of naturalists, and not a few of them have gone off from the beach with large masses of rock containing supposed fossil plants. The way in which the tracks are made by the grazing limpet has been described by several authors (e.g. Lukis, 1831; Hawkshaw, 1878; Hommeril and Rioult,

1962). The process is seen best in aquaria by introducing well-acclimatized but starved specimens of *Patella vulgata* into a tank in which the glass is thickly coated with a felted growth of algae. It is necessary to clear a patch for the limpet to allow it to grip the glass with its foot; feeding should then begin and last for some hours.

In feeding, the lips are closely pressed to the substratum and the buccal mass makes a succession of forward strokes, being withdrawn backwards under cover between the strokes. The toothed radula, borne on the buccal mass, acts as a rasp, with the teeth held at a narrow angle to the substratum. The strokes of the radula are made side by side so that the head slowly describes an arc in front of the foot. At the end of each series of strokes the position of the head or foot is changed slightly and another sweep begun in the reverse direction. The sweeps do not normally exceed an angle of 90° in front of the animal, but feeding can be carried out over half a circle occasionally. The sweeps are not absolutely regular and the forward movement of the animal is not uniform. Hence, sometimes a large area of substratum is covered, on bare or hard rock for example, and a series of widely spaced zig-zag marks is left; at other times the sweeps are close together and a slowly undulating track is produced, or else a small irregular patch is cleared of algae. The tracks are made more obvious by the small oblong patches of algae that are left between strokes and sweeps: that is, grazing is by no means total, though a large proportion of the swept area is cleared.

The typical grazing process described applies to the small encrusting unicellular or filamentous algae that are present on most shores, and are all that may be available as food for the limpets in wave-beaten localities. In the laboratory there does not seem to be any selection of food; green, blue-green and red algae are all grazed over, though the red colonies of *Ralfsia* seem very resistant, and survive for months in the aquarium tanks when all other algae have been removed. On the shore larger algae are also attacked. *Fucus* and *Ascophyllum* are trimmed along the edges of the thallus, hollows are excavated in the mid-rib, and eventually the holdfast is eaten through completely, liberating the damaged remains (Fischer-Piette, 1948; Jones, 1948; personal observations). In N.W. Europe the commoner species of limpets become very rare towards low water, and hence the large laminarian algae are preyed upon mainly by the smaller forms such as *Patina* and *Patelloidea*.

3. MEASUREMENT OF GRAZING RATES OF LIMPETS

The rate of feeding of *Patella* has not been studied to the same extent as its mode of feeding. From observations on a newly colonized sea-wall Moore

(1938) found a direct relationship between the volume of the animal, and the area it cleared and kept clear of Enteromorpha and filamentous green algae; this was approximately 75 sq. cm area to each cu. cm of limpet. No doubt these animals were growing rapidly under the uncrowded conditions and rich feeding of new habitat (cf. Orton, 1928a, b); on many shores there are in places 50 to 100 limpets per sq. m, which allows only 100 to 200 sq. cm for each, irrespective of size.

My own observations on the rate of clearance of an algal felt from an aquarium wall indicate a maximum initial rate approaching 1·5 sq. cm an hour for a limpet of 3·8 cu. cm volume. Later, an average rate of 2·8 sq. cm per day was found for the first week, declining to 0·85 sq. cm per day for the second week. That is, once the edge had been taken off the limpet's appetite, the area cleared became very much less and feeding became intermittent — occurring largely at night in specimens continuously immersed. However, it is probable that a good deal of time was wasted grazing over the area already cleared.

In this experiment the algal felt provided as food consisted largely of blue-green filaments, colonial greens and various diatoms: it contained 12·3 mg wet weight per sq. cm, and the rate of feeding is given below (Table 1).

TABLE I

Rate of feeding of *Patella vulgata*
(Specimen 3·8 cm³ calculated volume, 5 g estimated wet wt tissue)

	Area	Wet weight mg/day	Rate mg/day/g body wt
First few hours	1·5 cm²/hr	432	86
First week	2·8 cm²/day	33·6	6
Second week	0·85 cm²/day	10·4	1·8

4. CONTROL OF MARINE ALGAE BY LIMPETS AND BY OTHER HERBIVORES

Although the rate of feeding of a limpet is obviously low compared with copepods in the sea, the effect on the algal flora is just as drastic. Clearance experiments and observations made over a period of years have shown the importance of limpet grazing in controlling the plant populations of the shore, particularly in the north-temperate regions, where the mid-littoral may carry dense belts of fucoids. It is now well known that populations of these brown seaweeds are best developed on shores sheltered from wave action, and it used to be thought that their absence from wave-beaten shores was due entirely to the mechanical effects of the waves. However, the wave-beaten shores carry an abundance of limpets, which are much less frequent on sheltered shores. It can be suggested therefore, that wave-action operates indirectly, by encouraging larger numbers of limpets which then control the algae by grazing. The increased water movement of wave-beaten shores presumably favours the limpets by preventing the settlement of silt particles, which can clog the gills, and by increasing oxygenation, but may also increase the growth of the smaller algae on which the limpets maintain themselves when all the larger plants have been eaten. There is, of course, a further possibility that where wave-action is strong the limpets have to spend part of their time under water simply holding on, rather than feeding: though the rate of growth would be reduced, the area grazed over by each limpet would be smaller and a greater population density might develop. An explanation of this sort is believed to apply to the low growth-rate of small limpets living among dense barnacles, where movement is probably impeded by the rough surface of the barnacles (Fischer-Piette, 1948; Jones, 1948).

The dynamic balance between limpets and fucoids is well-shown by the series of experiments carried out on moderately wave-beaten rocks in the Isle of Man. In the first large-scale experiment begun in the winter of 1946–7, all large limpets and most small ones were removed from a ten-metre-wide strip of shore, running from high-water mark to low-water mark, over a series of gently sloping limestone terraces bearing only a sparse flora (Jones, 1948). An initial growth of diatoms, colonial and filamentous green algae, soon gave way to a dense cover of *Porphyra*, *Enteromorpha* and *Ulva* the following spring (Lodge, 1948). Pure stands of fucoids then developed in the second year, and by 1949–50 the strip was covered by thick growths of *Fucus spiralis*, *Fucus vesiculosus* and *Fucus serratus*, and hybrids between them (Burrows and Lodge, 1950).

A second experiment on a five-metre-wide strip a short distance away was begun in 1949, and a similar sequence of algal growth occurred; in this case the fucoids developed more quickly and a thick cover of the three species was found the second summer (Southward, 1953).

The result of both experiments was the establishment of thick fucoid cover within two or three years of the removal of limpets. By this time a limpet population had returned to the cleared areas. Close inspection beneath the *Fucus* canopy showed large numbers of small, thin-shelled, limpets — up to six times more abundant than the population existing before the clearance. The shape and shell form of these limpets indicated rapid growth in a favourable and damp habitat, that is, beneath the *Fucus*, and from size-group analysis it is likely that most of them had settled on the cleared area as spat, or moved on to it as very small juveniles during the first and second years following the clearance (Table 2).

TABLE 2

Algal cover and limpet population on 1 m² area at MTL
on experimentally cleared strip

	% cover of *Fucus vesiculosus*	No. of *Patella vulgata*, 5 mm groups								
		0–5	6–10	11–15	16–20	21–25	26–30	31–35	36–40	41–45	46–50
Sept. 1949 (before clearance)	nil	–	2	1	5	5	11	2	7	4	–
October 1950	100	–	10	52	30	25	12	2	1	–	–
October 1951	97	2	36	24	2	11	20	6	1	1	–
March 1954	22	–	2	6	6	10	20	32	24	8	4

In these large-scale experiments there was practically no migration of large adult limpets on to the strips from surrounding areas, although traces of their feeding activity could be seen at the margins.

With the reappearance of a large population of limpets the existing cover of fucoids gradually declined, most of them being eaten or removed by the limpets, and no further settlement of algae took place. After a further three to four years, that is five to seven years after clearance, the experimental areas were almost clear of algae, the numbers of limpets had fallen and most of them had the thick-shelled form typical of slower growth conditions on the open rock.

Similar experiments were tried on strips one to three metres wide on more wave-beaten vertical faces accessible only from a boat. The results were not conclusive, and as Aitken (1962) has recently reported, on the narrower strips the surrounding limpet populations moved in within a few days and no settlement of algae occurred. Aitken found that under such circumstances algal settlement could be obtained only by continued removal of limpets, or by reducing their numbers in the surrounding area. However, on a three-metre-wide strip a sequence of algal settlement was observed, with the same species as on gentler slopes, but their density, especially of fucoids, was very much less and consequently no heavy resettlement of limpets took place.

In the region where the large-scale experiments were performed limpets are sometimes cleared by natural forces, as for example by scouring due to a shifting pebble bank. In two cases of such scouring observed, the clearance was followed by growths of algae similar to those on the experimental areas. Later, limpet control was re-established, and the area reverted to the previous condition of practically bare rock and a few large

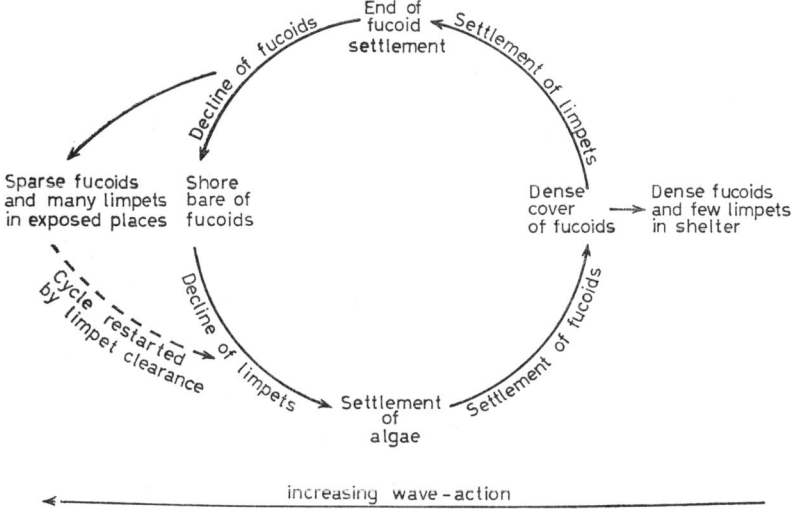

Fig. 1. Theoretical concept of the cyclic relationship between *Patella vulgata* and the fucoid algae.

limpets. Similar changes can be seen, sometimes more rapidly, on any new substrata exposed in the intertidal zone: on rock exposed by falls, or artificial structures such as concrete block breakwaters. The earlier growths of green algae are soon followed by a dense stand of fucoids, until the limpets once more gain control.

The experimental results and the observed natural changes suggest that a cyclic relationship exists and that the appearance of a shore, particularly the balance between the plants and the limpets, is due to temporary stabilization of the cycle at some point or other according to the influence of other factors, of which wave-action must be the most important. On the one hand we have wave-beaten shores where limpets are dominant, and where the cycle can be restarted by removing them, stability being re-gained only after periods of five years or more. At the other extreme we have the very sheltered shores where limpets are practically absent, due presumably to factors such as silt deposition and lack of water movement, and where interference can only lead to re-establishment of the fucoid cover. These relationships are shown diagrammatically on the chart opposite (Fig. 1).

It must be borne in mind that although limpets are the most obvious herbivores on the shore, and the most suitable for experiment because of their limited mobility, many other species of gastropods contribute to the control of vegetation. The top-shells and littorinids, although they often favour algal debris rather than attached plants, are all capable of grazing directly on the rocks, and their radulae leave substantially similar marks to those of *Patella* (Ankel, 1938). In warmer-water regions similar control is exercised in the sub-littoral by the large edible ormers and abalones, *Haliotis* and *Lottia*. Apart from gastropods, the sea-urchins *Echinus*, *Strongylocentrotus* and *Paracentrotus*, to name but a few, will also contribute to grazing effects, both sub-littorally and intertidally by migration during high water: these animals are, however, omnivores (Forster, 1959; Southward, 1958; Kitching and Ebling, 1961).

5. ROCK EROSION BY LIMPETS

Limpets also contribute to erosion of the rocks. During grazing the radula is applied to the surface with some force; the teeth are very hard chitin-protein complexes, reinforced at the tip with iron and silica (Runham, 1961). They are constantly renewed, and it is hardly surprising that some of the rock is removed with the algae during grazing. In addition, a good deal of unnecessary scraping goes on in the search for food, and there may well be active removal of calcareous rocks, when, as is often the case, algal growths are present within the porous structure. For *Littorina* species grazing at high-water mark on the Californian coast, North (1954) has calculated that pools and hollows in the sandstone are excavated at the rate of 1 cm per 16 years. On chalk rocks the gut of *Patella* is often filled with calcareous matter (Pieron, 1909; Hommeril and Rioult, 1962), and obser-vations made by Hawkshaw (1878) at Dover indicate the phenomenal rate of wear of 1·5 mm a year, said to be equivalent to all other erosive factors together. Even hard limestone does not escape: the Devonian limestone of south Devon is easily excavated by the limpets, to judge from their calcareous faecal pellets and their tooth-marks seen on the rock. On the hundred-year-old Plymouth breakwater, the occasional granite blocks stand proud of the more usual limestone ones by as much as 5 cm (Southward and Orton, 1954), and it is likely that a large proportion of the rate of wear of 0·5 mm a year is caused by limpets and other gastropods.

We may conclude that limpets and other grazing gastropods have great influence on the appearance of a shore, not only superficially by the control of the amount of algal cover, but more profoundly by a significant contribution to erosion of the rocks.

REFERENCES

AITKEN J.J. (1962) Experiments with populations of the limpet, *Patella vulgata* L. *Irish nat. J.* **14**, 12–15

ANKEL W. (1937) Wie frist *Littorina* I. Radula-Bewegung und Fresspur. *Senckenbergiana* **19**, 317–333

BURROWS E.M. & LODGE S.M. (1950) Note on the inter-relationships of *Patella, Balanus* and *Fucus* on a semi-exposed coast. *Rep. Mar. biol. Sta. Pt. Erin* **62** (1949), 30–34

FISCHER-PIETTE E. (1948) Sur les éléments de prospérité des Patelles et sur leur spécificité. *J. Conchyliol.* **88**, 45–96

FORSTER G.R. (1959) The ecology of *Echinus esculentus* L. Quantitative distribution and rate of feeding. *J. mar. biol. Assoc. U.K.* **38**, 361–367

HAWKSHAW C. (1878) On the action of limpets in sucking pits in and abrading the surface of chalk at Dover. *J. Linn. Soc. (Zool.)* **14**, 406–411

HOMMERIL P. & RIOULT M. (1962) Phénomènes d'erosion et de sedimentation marines entre Sainte-Honorine-des-Pertes et Port-en-Bassin (Calvados). Rôle de *Rhodothamniella floridula* dans la retenue des sediments fins. *Cahiers Océanographiques* **14**, 25–45

JONES N.S. (1948) Observations and experiments on the biology of *Patella vulgata* at Port St Mary, Isle of Man. *Proc. Lpool. biol. Soc.* **56**, 60–77

KITCHING J.A. & EBLING F.J. (1961) The ecology of Lough Ine XI. The control of algae by *Paracentrotus lividus* (Echinoidea). *J. anim. Ecol.* **30**, 373–383

LODGE S.M. (1948) Algal growth in the absence of *Patella* on an experimental strip of foreshore, Port St Mary, Isle of Man. *Proc. Lpool biol. Soc.* **56**, 78–83

LUKIS F.C. (1831) Remarks on the locomotion and habits of the Limpet. *Mag. Nat. Hist.* **4**, 346–351

MOORE H.B. (1938) Algal production and the food requirements of a limpet. *Proc. Malac. Soc.* **23**, 117–118

NORTH W.J. (1954) Size distribution, erosive activities and gross metabolic efficiency of the marine intertidal snails *Littorina planaxis* and *L. scutulata*. *Biol. Bull., Wood's Hole* **106**, 185–197

ORTON J.H. (1928a) Observations on *Patella vulgata* pt. I. Sex phenomena, breeding and shell-growth. *J. mar. biol. Ass., U.K.* **15**, 851–862

ORTON J.H. (1928b) Observations on *Patella vulgata* pt. II. Rate of growth of shell. *J. mar. biol. Ass. U.K.* **15**, 863–874

PIERON H. (1909) Contribution a la biologie de la patelle et de la calyptrée. L'ethologie-les phénomènes sensoriels. *Bull. sci. Fr. Belg.* 7e ser. **43**, 183–202

RUNHAM N.W. (1961) The histochemistry of the radula of *Patella vulgata. Quart. J. micr. Sci.* **102**, 371–380

SOUTHWARD A.J. (1953) The ecology of some rocky shores in the south of the Isle of Man. *Proc. Lpool biol. Soc.* **59**, 1–50

SOUTHWARD A.J. (1958) The zonation of plants and animals on rocky sea shores. *Biol. Rev.* **33**, 137–177

SOUTHWARD A.J. & ORTON J.H. (1954) The effects of wave-action on the distribution and numbers of the commoner plants and animals living on the Plymouth Break-water. *J. mar. biol. Ass. U.K.* **33**, 1–19

GRAZING AND THE LIFE CYCLES OF BRITISH NUDIBRANCHS

T. E. Thompson

Zoology Department, University College of South Wales
and Monmouthshire, Cardiff[1]

ABSTRACT

Information regarding diet is available for over sixty of the ninety or so British species of nudibranchs. Post-larval nudibranchs are carnivores feeding on Porifera, Cnidaria, Cirripedia, Polyzoa and Ascidiacea. Each family usually contains species which feed on similar types of prey. Some nudibranchs feed on a single species of prey; others attack a variety of organisms. In the latter it seems that each species may have a single preferred food-organism but in the absence of this will attack other prey. Preferences may alter with age and locality.

Nudibranchs preying on organisms which form stable, abundant populations in certain types of locality have annual life cycles and, usually, a single breeding period each year. Those which feed on more transitory prey usually pass through a number of generations each year and grow more quickly to sexual maturity.

It is probable that new populations of nudibranchs are commonly established in favourable regions through the exercise of the ability of the veliger larvae to recognize and settle upon some component of the diet of the benthic stages.

The order Nudibranchia comprises the modern representatives of, probably, a number of independent lines of evolution within the Gastropoda. Most nudibranchs are marine, and the great majority are carnivorous, in contrast to the related order Ascoglossa (or Sacoglossa) which are herbivorous marine and brackish slugs; many of these possess shells of some kind. Post-larval nudibranchs are invariably shell-less, but may exhibit a variety of compensatory defensive mechanisms (Thompson, 1960a). More than ninety species of nudibranchs are recorded from the shores and shallow waters of the British Isles (Winckworth, 1932, 1951). Information regarding diet is available for over sixty of these species and is summarized in the Appendix. It is with these alone that this paper deals.

1. PLANKTONIC LARVAL STAGES

So far as is known, the life cycles of all British nudibranchs include a planktonic larval phase. The duration of this phase may be short and feeding

[1] Present address: Department of Zoology, University of Bristol.

275

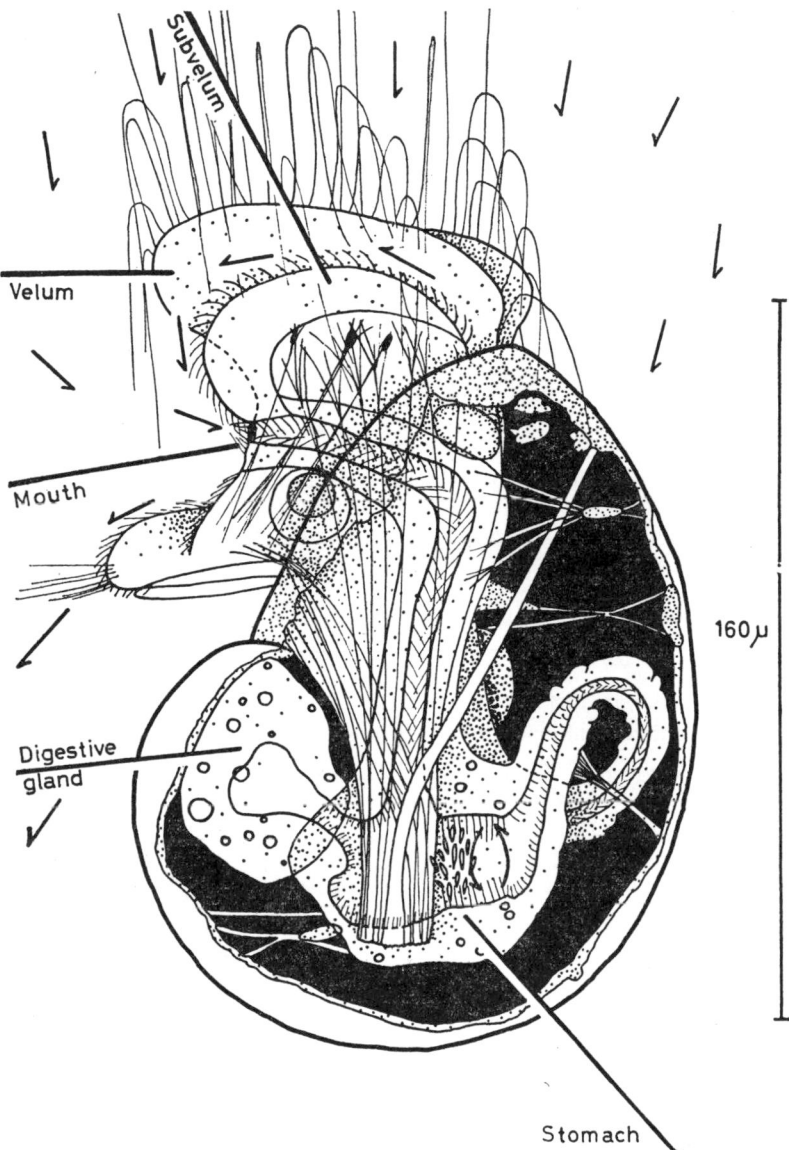

FIG. I. Newly hatched veliger larva of *Onichidoris muricata* (camera lucida drawing from life; optical section from the left lateral aspect. Ciliary currents are indicated by arrows. The perivisceral cavity is shown black.

unimportant in a few species (*Embletonia pallida*, Rasmussen 1944; *Adalaria proxima*, Thompson, 1958; and the lecithotrophic *Tritonia hombergi*, Thompson, 1962). Most nudibranch larvae must feed if development through metamorphosis is to occur normally. They possess a cephalopedal ciliary apparatus (Thompson, 1959), by means of which suspended fine matter is captured and passed towards the mouth (Fig. 1). Their natural diet is unknown but certain nannoplanktonic organisms have been used in the laboratory to feed a variety of these larvae. Allen and Nelson (1911) kept larvae of *Archidoris pseudoargus* alive for several weeks in a suspension of *Pleurococcus mucosus*. Food vacuoles have been observed in cells of the larval digestive gland of *Adalaria proxima* after feeding on *Chlorella stigmatophora* and *Isochrysis galbana* (Thompson, 1958) and in those of *Archidoris pseudoargus* after feeding on *Phaeodactylum tricornutum* (Thompson, 1959). Food-selectivity in these suspension-feeding larvae may involve the cessation of the feeding current on encountering unpalatable material, or the acceptance only of particles within a certain range of mass or volume. Larvae of *Coryphella lineata*, for instance, were seen in the laboratory to reject carmine particles 20–30 microns in diameter whereas those between 10 and 15 microns in diameter were ingested and passed to the stomach.

2. BENTHIC STAGES

(*a*) *Diet*

British post-larval nudibranchs are epifaunal carnivores, feeding almost exclusively on species of Porifera, Cnidaria, Cirripedia, Polyzoa and Ascidiacea. None is herbivorous. The Appendix shows that each family of British nudibranchs comprises species which feed on broadly similar types of prey. Thus the Coryphellidae, Dendronotidae, Dotöidae, Eubranchidae, Facelinidae, Heröidae, Lomanotidae and Tergipedidae contain species which feed on Hydrozoa. The British species of Aeolidiidae feed mainly on Actiniaria. The Glossodorididae includes species which feed on sponges. In the Okeniidae are a number of species which feed on ascidians, but a few of these may, from time to time, take also polyzoan food. The Proctonotidae and Onchidorididae contain species which attack polyzoans; *Onchidoris fusca* feeds, however, on sessile barnacles. Members of the Tritoniidae all feed on alcyonarian corals. Insufficient data are available regarding the diets of members of the Arminidae, Hancockiidae and Scyllaeidae. Two remarkable cases occur in, respectively, the Calmidae and Fionidae: *Calma glaucoides* feeds mainly on the eggs of shore fishes; *Fiona pinnata* attacks chondrophores (*Porpita*, *Velella*) and barnacles. Certain aeolidiid, facelinid and tritoniid nudibranchs may, in aquaria, feed on carrion or attack other nudibranchs (sometimes of their own species); such behaviour is associated with artificially crowded conditions, and is probable of little importance in Nature.

(b) Manipulation of the prey

There is a general, though not precise, correlation between the organization of the nudibranch and the form of the prey. Nudibranchs whose food is a flattish incrustation (for example, many sponges, *Alcyonium*, barnacle-aggregations, polyzoans and ascidian colonies) usually have a broad flattened foot and are more or less oval in outline. Their radula is usually broad and, with a few conspicuous exceptions among the Tritoniidae, they lack strong mandibles; in nature they are frequently well camouflaged through their shape, colouration and behaviour. Nudibranchs feeding on arborescent, more erect organisms (for example, hydroids, actiniarians and some Polyzoa) are usually of smaller size (with occasional conspicuous exceptions such as *Dendronotus frondosus*), and of more elongate shape, with a long, narrow foot adapted for clinging to this type of prey. Such nudibranchs are active, voracious forms, in which cannibalism may often be seen in laboratory conditions. They frequently possess brightly coloured dorsal papillae, and often do not appear to seek concealment: they are generally conspicuous to the human eye in their natural habitat.

The defences of the prey include frequently internal or external spicular concretions, or an exoskeletal refuge into which the soft parts may be rapidly retracted, the aperture often being furnished with an opercular system. The prey may further be rendered unpalatable by its possession of nematocysts (Cnidaria) or a strongly acidic internal fluid (Ascidiacea). In overcoming these defences, the secretion by the nudibranch of great quantities of mucus from oral, propodial and other glands is of essential importance (Graham, 1938; Forrest, 1953). Ingested food is liberally covered and mixed with mucus, as a protection against abrasion; despite this, it is recorded that sponge spicules often pierce the stomach wall of *Archidoris pseudoargus* (Forrest, 1950). To manipulate the food the nudibranch is provided with a muscular buccal mass containing the radula and, often, a pair of mandibles. The mode of functioning of the components of this buccal apparatus varies greatly in different species. In some species (for instance, *Archidoris pseudoargus*, Forrest, 1950, and *Jorunna tomentosa*, Millott, 1937) mandibles are absent and the prey is scooped up, fragmented and passed into the foregut solely by the action of the broad radula and its musculature. *Tritonia plebeia*, on the contrary, possesses a broad radula which is employed only to transport intact pieces of the prey into the fore-gut after they have been sliced away from an alcyonarian by the action of the powerful mandibles. By the action of the buccal mass the opercular plates of barnacles (in the case of *Onchidoris fusca*, Barnes and Powell, 1954) or of polyzoans (in the case of *Adalaria proxima*, Thompson, 1958) may be broken open and the soft parts sucked out by pulsating dilations of a muscular buccal diverticulum (Forrest, 1953); pieces of *Alcyonium* as broad as a shilling piece may be cut cleanly away and forced into the foregut (*Tritonia hombergi*, Thompson, 1962); calyptoblastic hydroids may be cropped and tubularians decapitated by facelinids, eubranchids and other nudibranchs.

Whereas some nudibranchs (for instance, *Archidoris pseudoargus*, *Tritonia hombergi*) kill and ingest their prey with little waste, others (for instance, *Facelina auriculata* and *Aeolidia papillosa*) often kill more of the prey than they ingest and wastage is considerable. It is of interest that *Archidoris* and *Tritonia* have a highly restricted diet while *Facelina* and *Aeolidia* are known to feed on a variety of cnidarians. In the former cases, dietary specialization has clearly been paralleled by higher manipulative efficiency.

(c) Specificity and selectivity

In some nudibranchs, for instance, *Archidoris pseudoargus* and *Tritonia hombergi* (which are, incidentally, two of the largest species), the prey may consist of a single species in each case. Observations throughout the year on a population of *A. pseudoargus* on a shore (Traie Meanagh) in Port Erin bay, Isle of Man, showed its complete dependence through all the benthic stages of the life cycle on *Halichondria panicea*. The dorids were nearly always found on an incrustation of this sponge, often partially imbedded in it. The faeces proved invariably to contain spicules of *H. panicea*, and the process of ingestion of the prey was observed both in the field and in the laboratory. Experiments showed the colouration of these dorids (which is usually procryptic in this habitat) to be independent of the colour-variety of the sponge consumed, contrary to the view of Cuénot (1903), but in agreement with that of Garstang (1890). It is of interest that specimens of the well known red variety, *A. pseudoargus flammea*, are said to feed exclusively on *Hymeniacidon perleve* and to refuse *Halichondria* in tests (McMillan, 1942).

Tritonia hombergi is almost invariably found in association with the soft coral *Alcyonium digitatum*. Observations on dredged samples from a rich *Alcyonium* area at 16–30 fm. off the south of the Isle of Man confirmed that the sole natural diet of this nudibranch is *A. digitatum*. The related *T.*

plebeia is, however, known to feed both on *Alcyonium* and *Eunicella verrucosa*. Another example of high specificity of diet is provided by *Trinchesia aurantia*, which feeds mainly on two species of *Tubularia*, *T. indivisa* and *T. larynx*, on which it is commonly found in the Menai Straits, particularly, in my experience, on the pier at Menai Bridge. According to Braams and Geelen (1953), adult *Trinchesia aurantia* can recognize these hydroids at a distance and are preferentially attracted to them in laboratory tests with a number of cnidarians.

In most other nudibranchs, diet-specificity is not so rigid as in the above instances, and many species are known to take a variety of prey. *Doto fragilis* and *Eubranchus exiguus*, for example, feed on several species of calyptoblastic hydroids; *Acanthodoris pilosa* has been seen to attack a number of encrusting intertidal polyzoans. Several species of nudibranchs have been recorded feeding on a large number of species of food-organisms. *Doto coronata* has been found to attack more than twenty species of hydroids (mainly thecate forms). *Calma glaucoides* has been recorded from the eggs of numerous species of shore fishes. In only a few cases have preferences been elucidated. One such case is the small dorid *Adalaria proxima*, which is common intertidally in the Menai Straits. If given a choice in the laboratory between the polyzoans *Alcyonidium polyoum*, *Electra pilosa*, *Flustrella hispida* and *Membranipora membranacea*, these dorids almost invariably attack a colony of *E. pilosa*. In the Menai Straits they are usually found on this polyzoan, although all these species are abundant on the shore. In aquaria, adult *Adalaria* feed on the other species only if denied access to *Electra*. Information regarding selectivity is available also for *Aeolidia papillosa*, a nudibranch which preys on actinarians. Miller (1961) states that it prefers *Actinia equina* to other anemones, and confirmation of this is furnished by Swennen (1961) who was able to rear young *Aeolidia* on a diet of *Actinia* or of *Metridium senile*, but not on diets of *Diadumene cincta*, *Sagartia troglodytes* or *Sagartiogeton undata*. *Aeolidia* is, in laboratory tests, attracted at a distance to *Actinia* and *Metridium*, but not to a number of other cnidarians (Stehouwer, 1952; Braams and Geelen, 1953). That preferences may differ in different parts of the geographical range of a species is indicated by Robson's observation (1961) that, in the Danish Sound, *Aeolidia papillosa* prefers *Stomphia coccinea* to *Metridium*, *Tealia* or *Sagartia*. The case of *Aeolidia* illustrates that all known components of a nudibranch's diet may not be of equal palatability and nutritive content. Swennen (1961) cites also the instance of *Trinchesia aurantia* which is known to occur and feed upon the two common species of *Tubularia* but 'often' grows larger if fed on *T. indivisa* than if fed solely on *T. larynx*. It is also suggested that *Facelina auriculata* may grow to a larger size if fed on *Tubularia* than if fed on calyptoblastic hydroids. Further instances of diet-selectivity in nudibranchs are given for *Trinchesia caerulea* which Miller (1961) states prefers *Sertularella polyzonias* to the other recorded constituents of its food, and *Polycera quadrilineata*, which is usually found feeding on *Membranipora membranacea* in the Menai Straits and which shows a similar preference in the Isle of Man (Miller, 1961).

In a few cases it has been suggested that food preferences may alter with age. Young *Dendronotus frondosus* are abundant on *Sertularia cupressina* in the Menai Straits during the winter months, while older specimens (up to 5 cm in length) may be found on the shores and sea-bottom in the neighbourhood of the Suspension Bridge feeding on *Tubularia indivisa* in spring and early summer. Clearly a change in diet occurs during benthic life, correlated with the change known to occur in the arrangement of the lobules of the digestive gland (Thompson, 1960b). Swennen makes a similar deduction (1961) for *Dendronotus frondosus*, as does Miller (1961) for this species and for *Lomanotus genei*. It seems likely that *Calma glaucoides* takes other food during seasons when no fish eggs (its customary diet) are available; a record of its occurrence on *Hydractinia* (Marine Biological Association, 1957) provides a clue to the possible nature of the diet of this nudibranch during these periods. A further instance of seasonal variation in diet is given by Swennen (1961) who suggests that, while adult *Goniodoris nodosa* attack encrusting colonial ascidians, the young stages feed on the polyzoan *Alcyonidium polyoum* and perhaps on other polyzoan species (Miller, 1961).

3. LIFE CYCLES OF NUDIBRANCHS

In those few British species which have received close study, the maximal life-span has proved to be one year or less. Some of these species have annual life cycles, with one breeding period per annum (but occasionally two), while others may pass through numerous generations in a year. To consider first the annual species: Fig. 2 shows the kind of picture of the life history which may be built up from observations on routine hand or dredge collections of samples at various seasons. Confirmatory data were obtained in some of these species by histological examination of the gonads of sub-samples (*Adalaria, Archidoris, Tritonia*), by maintaining small populations in laboratory culture through the whole cycle (*Adalaria*), and by occasional discoveries of senescent, post-sexual individuals in the field (*Archidoris*). These annual nudibranchs feed on organisms which have one

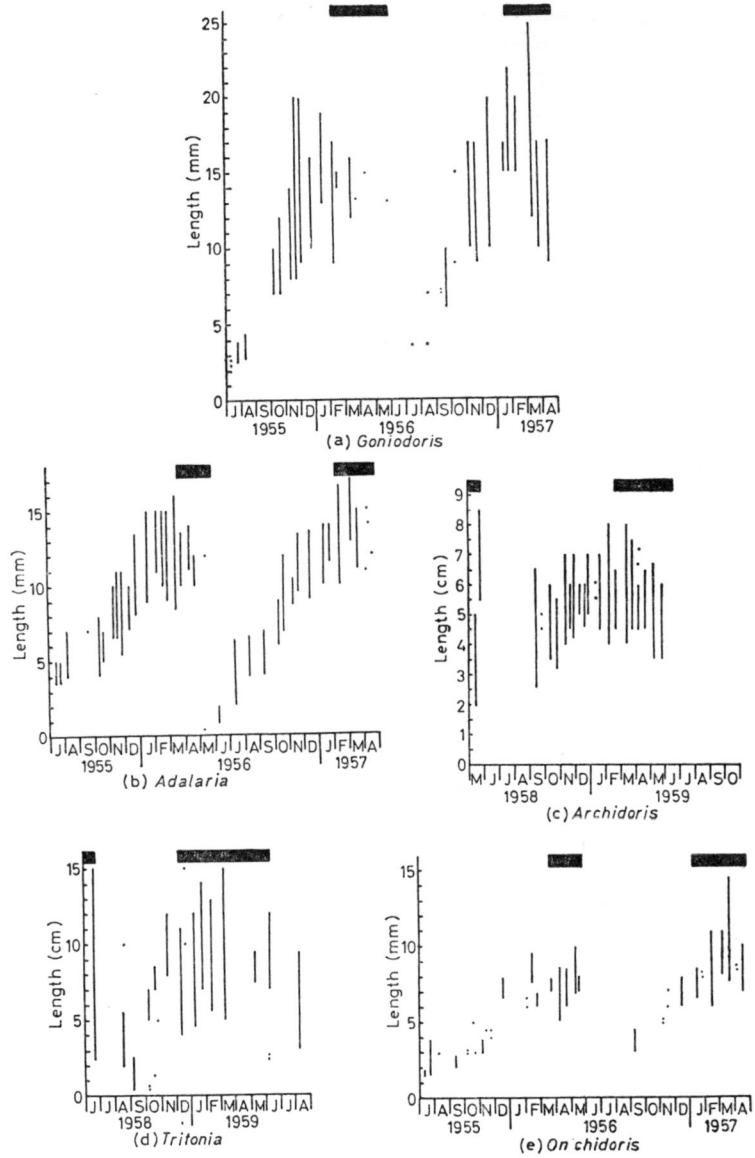

(a) *Goniodoris*

(b) *Adalaria*

(c) *Archidoris*

(d) *Tritonia*

(e) *Onchidoris*

conspicuous quality in common: their extreme abundance and stability in certain types of locality at all seasons of the year. The polyzoans and tunicates consumed by *Adalaria, Goniodoris* and *Onchidoris* are common intertidally on rocky British coasts. *Halichondria panicea*, the food of *Archidoris*, is often the most common littoral sponge. *Alcyonium*, the sole food of *Tritonia*, occurs in certain sub-littoral areas where it may form a thick carpet over a large area. The following questions arise: by what means are populations of these species of nudibranchs re-established at each generation in suitable areas, and how are they maintained? The first question may be answered by reference to the behaviour of the larvae of *Adalaria proxima* (Thompson, 1958) and *Tritonia hombergi* (Thompson, 1962). The minimal length of the planktonic phase of *Adalaria* was normally one or two days, but searching behaviour might continue for as long as a fortnight before the veligers died (at 9–10°C). The searching, eyed larvae settled and metamorphosed only if a live healthy colony of *Electra pilosa* was provided. Settlement would not occur on dead *Electra*, nor on live colonies of other polyzoan species unless live *Electra* was also present. As was mentioned earlier, *Electra pilosa* forms the preferred diet of post-larval stages of this species of nudibranch. Similarly, searching veligers of *Tritonia hombergi* are able to recognize, settle and metamorphose upon tissues of *Alcyonium* in the laboratory. It is clear that these behavioural mechanisms must bring about in nature the establishment of populations of these species in areas favourable for post-larval development. The maintenance of this position probably results from a combination of a number of factors: these nudibranchs are adapted for clinging to the prey, they are usually well camouflaged, and they probably possess chemical and other defensive mechanisms (Thompson, 1960a). Their behaviour is such that

---

FIG. 2. Annual life cycles of some British nudibranchs. The samples of *Tritonia* were obtained by dredging; the others were hand-collections. Black rectangles show the natural spawning seasons during the years under consideration. Vertical lines show the size range of animals collected, dots indicate the size of individual specimens.

(a) *Goniodoris nodosa* at Church Island, Menai Straits.
(b) *Adalaria proxima* at Church Island, Menai Straits (from Thompson, 1958).
(c) *Archidoris pseudoargus* at Traie Meanagh, Isle of Man.
(d) *Tritonia hombergi* off the south of the Isle of Man (from Thompson, 1961a).
(e) *Onchidoris muricata* at Church Island, Menai Straits (from Thompson, 1961b).

they move about little so long as there is sufficient food in their vicinity; this has been established in a number of species. Adult *Archidoris*, for instance, have been noted normally to move less than one metre in a month when living in an area rich in sponges; they may move, however, with surprising speed if starved in aquaria.

Those nudibranchs which are known to pass through a number of generations in a year are all species which feed on more or less transitory prey, such as hydroids, which spring up seasonally on sub-marine surfaces and may be cropped to extinction within a few days. Nudibranchs which attack such organisms possess certain attributes in common. They often grow to sexual maturity very rapidly, reducing the risk of dying without progeny. They are the most active and voracious of nudibranchs, and many of them are known to attack a wide variety of food-organisms. Juveniles and adults are often found together; spawn may be observed in Nature over a much longer period than has been noted for annual nudibranchs like *Adalaria* and *Tritonia*. A distinct lack of synchrony of the life cycles of the individuals composing the population is a frequent feature of the hydroid-eating nudibranchs. In no case has the life history of a nudibranch of this type been analysed in detail, but, thanks to the work of Rasmussen (1944), Swennen (1961) and others, a great deal of information is available which supports the validity of the above generalizations. The following extracts will suffice to illustrate the basic features of the life cycles of the hydroid-eating nudibranchs.

In Danish waters *Embletonia pallida* was commonly found feeding on the hydroid *Gonothyraea loveni* growing on *Zostera* (Rasmussen, 1944). Spawn was noted in nearly every month of the year and the life cycles of individuals showed great variability: large and small specimens were found at all seasons. Post-larvae grew to maturity and deposited their spawn three weeks after metamorphosis (at 15°C). Swennen (1961) records that *Tergipes despectus* reared from eggs in the laboratory spawned after only five weeks, *Facelina auriculata* after forty days. He found spawn of *F. auriculata* in the field in most months of the year, samples often containing large and small individuals. *Trinchesia aurantia*, according to Swennen, may begin to spawn when a body-length of eight millimetres has been attained; large and small slugs were found in all months of the year near Den Helder and spawn from May to December.

Just as has been shown for certain annual species, it is clearly probable that the veliger larvae of these nudibranchs have the ability to recognize and settle preferentially on the prey of the adult. Orton (1914) describes some particularly illuminating observations on the colonization of a raft moored in Cawsand Bay: after six weeks this was covered with scattered growths of *Obelia geniculata* on which were adult *Eubranchus exiguus* (with spawn), *E. pallidus* (with spawn), *E. tricolor, Tergipes despectus* and young *Doto coronata* and *Facelina auriculata*, all of which had almost certainly reached the raft initially as planktonic larvae. Experimental confirmation of this suggestion of high larval behavioural selectivity has come from Swennen (1961) who records that in the laboratory veligers of *Trinchesia aurantia* may be reared through metamorphosis only if allowed access to *Tubularia indivisa*. Finally, the case of *Tergipes despectus* (which feeds mainly on species of *Laomedea* and *Obelia*) must be mentioned again. Swennen's observations enabled him to state that 'The animals multiply so strongly that the *Laomedea* colonies are soon finished, after which the slugs disappear ... new colonies of polyps develop in other places and every time slugs turn up on them.'

There is now a considerable body of evidence supporting the view that new populations of nudibranchs are commonly established in favourable regions by the exercise of the ability of the searching veliger larvae to recognize and metamorphose upon some component of the diet of the benthic stages. That they possess this ability is proven in the case of some species, and indicated by circumstantial evidence in many others. What is not known is whether the larvae of those nudibranchs which as adults feed on a variety of organisms have less precisely specific settlement-preferences than those of species with a more rigid adult diet.

REFERENCES

ALDER J. & HANCOCK A. (1845–55) *A monograph of the British nudibranchiate Mollusca.* Ray Soc. Publ.
ALLEN E.J. & NELSON E.W. (1911) On the artificial culture of marine organisms. *J. Mar. Biol. Ass. U.K.* **8**, 421–474
BARNES H. & POWELL H.T. (1954) *Onchidoris fusca* (Müller); a predator of barnacles. *J. Anim. Ecol.* **23**, 361–363
BEAUMONT W.I. (1900) The fauna and flora of Valencia harbour on the west coast of Ireland. XII. The opisthobranchiate Mollusca. *Proc. Roy. Irish Acad.* (3rd ser.) **5**, 832–854
BEHRENTZ A. (1931) Trekk av *Lamellidoris muricatas* biologi og av dens generasjonsorganers bygning. *Nyt. Mag. Naturvidenskaberne* **70**, 1–26
BERGH R. (1880) On the nudibranchiate gasteropod Mollusca of the north Pacific Ocean, with special reference to those of Alaska. Part I. *Proc. Acad. Nat. Sci. Philad. for* 1879, 71–132, pls. I–VIII
BRAAMS W.G. & GEELEN F.M. (1953) The preference of some nudibranchs for certain coelenterates. *Arch. Néerl. Zool.* **10**, 241–264

COLGAN N. (1911) Marine Mollusca. Clare Island Survey, part 22. *Proc. Roy. Irish Acad.* **31**, section 2, 1–36

COLGAN N. (1913) Some additions to the nudibranch fauna of Co. Dublin. *Irish Nat.* **22**, 165–8

COLGAN N. (1914) The opisthobranch fauna of the shores and shallow waters of County Dublin. *Irish Nat.* **23**, 161–204

CORNET R. & MARCHE-MARCHAD I. (1951) Inventaire de la faune marine de Roscoff Mollusques. *Suppl.* 5 *Trav. Stat. Biol. Roscoff*, 80 pp.

CUÉNOT L. (1903) Contributions à la faune du bassin d'Arcachon III.—Doridiens. *Trav. Soc. Scient. Arcachon Stat. Biol. for* 1903, 1–22, pl. I

CUÉNOT L. (1927) Contributions à la faune du bassin d'Arcachon IX.—Revue générale de la faune et bibliographie. *Bull. Stat. Biol. Arcachon* **24**, 229–308

DALYELL J. G. (1853) *The Powers of the Creator displayed in the Creation*, vol. II. London

EDMUNDS M. (1961) *Polycera elegans* Bergh: a new species to Britain and discussion of its taxonomy. *Proc. Malac. Soc. Lond.* **34**, 316–322

ELIOT C. N. E. (1910) *A monograph of the British nudibranchiate Mollusca;* suppl. vol. Ray Soc. Publ. 1–198, pls. 1–8

ELMHIRST R. (1922) Notes on the breeding and growth of marine animals in the Clyde sea area. *Ann. Rep. Scottish Mar. Biol. Ass. for* 1922, pp. 19–43

EVANS T.J. (1922) *Calma glaucoides:* a study in adaptation. *Quart. J. Micr. Sci.* **66**, 439–455

FARRAN G. P. (1904) The nudibranchiate molluscs of Ballynakill and Boffin harbours, Co. Galway. *Rep. Sea & Inland Fisheries of Ireland for* 1901 part II, app. VIII, 1–10

FARRAN G. P. (1909) Nudibranchiate Mollusca of the trawling grounds off the east and south coasts of Ireland. *Sci. Invest. Fish. Board of Ireland for* 1907, 1–18

FISHER N. (1937) Notes on British opisthobranchs. I. The ecology of *Archidoris flammea* (A. & H.). *J. Conch.* **20**, 362–369

FORREST J. E. (1950) The structure and function of the alimentary canal in dorid nudibranchiate Mollusca. Unpublished Thesis, University of London

FORREST J. E. (1953) On the feeding habits and the morphology and mode of functioning of the alimentary canal in some littoral dorid nudibranchiate Mollusca. *Proc. Linn. Soc. Lond.* **164**, 225–235

GARSTANG W. (1889) Report on the nudibranchiate Mollusca of Plymouth Sound. *J. Mar. Biol. Ass. U.K.* **1**, 173–198

GARSTANG W. (1890) A complete list of the opisthobranchiate Mollusca found at Plymouth; with further observations on their morphology, colours, and natural history. *J. Mar. Biol. Ass. U.K.* **1**, 399–457

GARSTANG W. (1893) On the relations of Hesse's *Doto uncinata* to the genus *Hancockia*. *Conchologist* **2**, 110–112

GARSTANG W. (1894) Faunistic notes at Plymouth during 1893–4. *J. Mar. Biol. Ass. U.K.* **3**, 210–235

GRAHAM A. (1938) The structure and function of the alimentary canal of aeolid molluscs, with a discussion on their nematocysts. *Trans. Roy. Soc. Edinb.* **59**, 267–307

GRAHAM A. (1955) Molluscan diets. *Proc. Malac. Soc. Lond.* **31**, 144–159

HECHT E. (1895) Contribution a l'étude des nudibranches. *Mem. Soc. Zool. Fr.* **8**, 539–711, pls. I–V

HERDMAN W. A. (1890) On the structure and functions of the cerata or dorsal papillae in some nudibranchiate Mollusca. *Quart. J. Micr. Sci.* **31**, 41–63, pls. VI–X

HERDMAN W.A. & CLUBB J.A. (1892) Second report on the Nudibranchiata of the L.M.B.C. district. *Trans. Liverpool Biol. Soc.* **3**, 225–239, pl. XII

HUNT O.D. (1925) The food of the bottom fauna of the Plymouth fishing grounds. *J. Mar. Biol. Ass. U.K.* **13**, 560–599

LOYNING P. (1927) Nudibranchs from Bergen, collected in the neighbourhood of the biological station at Herdla. *Nyt. Mag. Naturvid.* **65**, 245–264

MACNAE W. (1957) The families Polyceridae and Goniodorididae (Mollusca, Nudibranchiata) in southern Africa. *Trans. Roy. Soc. S. Africa* **35**, 341–372, pls. XVII–XVIII

MARCUS E. (1957) On Opisthobranchia from Brazil. *Proc. Linn. Soc. Zool.* **43**, 390–486

MARCUS E. (1961) Opisthobranch mollusks from California. *The Veliger* **3** (suppl.), 1–85

Marine Biological Association (1957) *Plymouth Marine Fauna*, 3rd ed. M.B.A.: Plymouth

McMILLAN N.F. (1941) The marine Mollusca of Hilbre, Cheshire. *Proc. Liverpool Nat. Field Club for 1941*, 15–20

McMILLAN N.F. (1942) Food of nudibranchs. *J. Conch.* **21**, 327

McMILLAN N.F. (1944) The marine Mollusca of Greenisland, Co. Antrim. *Irish Nat. J.* **8**, 158–164

MILLER M.C. (1961) Distribution and food of the nudibranchiate Mollusca of the south of the Isle of Man. *J. Anim. Ecol.* **30**, 95–116

MILLOTT N. (1937) On the morphology of the alimentary canal, process of feeding, and physiology of digestion of the nudibranch mollusc, *Jorunna tomentosa* (Cuvier). *Phil. Trans. B* **228**, 173–217

M'INTOSH W.C. (1863) On the nudibranchiate Mollusca of St Andrews. *Proc. Roy. Soc. Edinb.* **5**, 387–393

MORTON J.E. (1958) *Molluscs.* Hutchinson: London

NEVILLE A. (1926) Notes sur les eolidiens. Un eolidien d'eau saumâtre. Origine des nématocystes. Zooxanthelles et homochromie. *Rev. Suisse Zool.* **33**, 251–289

ORTON J.H. (1914) Preliminary account of a contribution to an evaluation of the sea: the life-history of *Galvina picta*. *J. Mar. Biol. Ass. U.K.* **10**, 323–324

PELSENEER P. (1911) Recherches sur l'embryologie des gastropodes. *Mém. Acad. Roy, Belg. (ser. II)* **3**, livr. 6, 1–167

PRUVOT-FOL A. (1954) Mollusques Opisthobranches. *Faune Fr.*, no. 58, 460 pp.

PURCHON R.D. (1947) Studies on the biology of the Bristol Channel. XVII. The littoral and sub-littoral fauna of the northern shores, near Cardiff. *Proc. Bristol Nat. Soc.* **27**, pt. III, 285–310

RASMUSSEN E. (1944) Faunistic and biological notes on marine invertebrates I. The eggs and larvae of *Brachystomia rissoides* (Hanl.), *Eulimella nitidissima* (Mont.) *Retusa truncatula* (Brug.) and *Embletonia pallida* (Alder & Hancock), (Gastropoda marina). *Vidensk. Medd. Dansk Naturh. Foren. Kbh.* **107**, 207–333

REID J. (1846) On the development of the ova of the nudibranchiate Mollusca. *Ann. Mag. Nat. Hist.* **17**, 377–389

RENOUF L.P.W. (1935) Observations on periodic, sporadic, occasional and unusual appearances of certain organisms. *Acta Phaenologica* **3**, 110–154

ROBSON E.A. (1961) The swimming response and its pacemaker system in the anemone. *Stomphia coccinea. J. Exp. Biol.* **38**, 685–694

RUSSELL H.D. (1942) Observations on the feeding of *Aeolidia papillosa* L. with notes on the hatching of the veligers of *Cuthona amoena* A. & H. *Nautilus* **55**, 80–82

STEHOUWER E.C. (1952) The preference of the slug *Aeolidia papillosa* (L.) for the sea-anemone *Metridium senile* (L.). *Arch. Neerl. Zool.* 10, 161–170

SWENNEN C. (1959) The Netherlands coastal waters as an environment for Nudi-branchia. *Basteria* 23, 56–62

SWENNEN C. (1961) Data on distribution, reproduction and ecology of the nudi-branchiate molluscs occurring in the Netherlands. *Netherlands J. Sea Res.* 1, 191–240

THOMPSON T.E. (1958) The natural history, embryology, larval biology and post-larval development of *Adalaria proxima* (Alder and Hancock) (Gastropoda Opis-thobranchia). *Phil. Trans. B* 242, 1–58

THOMPSON T.E. (1959) Feeding in nudibranch larvae. *J. Mar. Biol. Ass. U.K.* 38, 239–248

THOMPSON T.E. (1960a) Defensive adaptations in opisthobranchs. *J. Mar. Biol. Ass. U.K.* 39, 123–134

THOMPSON T.E. (1960b) On a disputed feature of the anatomy of the nudibranch *Dendronotus frondosus* Ascanius. *Proc. Malac. Soc. Lond.* 34, 24–26

THOMPSON T.E. (1961a) The structure and mode of functioning of the reproductive organs of *Tritonia hombergi* (Gastropoda Opisthobranchia). *Quart. J. Micr. Sci.* 102, 1–14

THOMPSON T.E. (1961b) Observations on the life history of the nudibranch *Onchidoris muricata* (Müller). *Proc. Malac. Soc. Lond.* 34, 239–242

THOMPSON T.E. (1962) Studies on the ontogeny of *Tritonia hombergi* Cuvier. (Gastro-poda Opisthobranchia). *Phil. Trans. B* (to be published).

VEVERS H.G. (1955) *The Animal World of the Sea*. Rathbone: London

WALTON C.L. (1908) Nudibranchiata collected in the North Sea by the s.s. 'Huxley' during July and August, 1907. *J. Mar. Biol. Ass. U.K.* 8, 227–240

WALTON C.L. (1913) The shore fauna of Cardigan Bay. *J. Mar. Biol. Ass. U.K.* 10, 102–113

WINCKWORTH R. (1932) The British marine Mollusca. *J. Conch.* 19, 211–252

WINCKWORTH R. (1951) A list of the marine Mollusca of the British Isles: additions and corrections. *J. Conch.* 23, 131–134

APPENDIX

DIETS OF BRITISH NUDIBRANCHS

Swennen (1961) suggests that the following criteria must be satisfied before accepting that a particular substrate is of importance as food to a benthic carnivore. (A) The carnivore should customarily be found in the field on or near the suspected food-organism. (B) Ingestion of the prey should be confirmed by direct observations in the field or in the laboratory. (C) The carnivore should be able to survive for some time on a diet consisting solely of the prey in question. It is unfortunate that few authors, other than Swennen, describe their mode of approach in any detail. The following list includes what I judge to be firm records of predation; circumstantial records of associations between a nudibranch and a particular substrate are prefixed by the word *on*. Records of cannibalism are not included. Asterisks denote records which in my view are so remarkable that further confirmation seems desirable.

NOMENCLATURE

The scheme adopted for the nudibranchs is that of Winckworth (1932; 1951), except for the merging of *Tritonia alba* with *T. hombergi* (Thompson, 1962) and the inclusion in the list of *Polycera elegans* (Edmunds, 1961). Within each genus of nudibranchs, species are listed alphabetically. Other animals are named so far as possible in accordance with the Plymouth list (Marine Biological Association 1957). Inverted commas mark records of species of whose precise taxonomic position I am uncertain. Personal records are denoted by the letter P.

FAMILY	SPECIES	DIET
Glossodorididae	*Echinochila laevis*	Sponges (Forrest, 1950)
	Rostanga rufescens	*Microciona atrasanguinea* (Hecht, 1895, Cuénot, 1927); *on Ophlitaspongia seriata* (Colgan, 1911)
	Aldisa zetlandica	No data.
	Archidoris pseudoargus	*Grantia compressa* (Alder & Hancock, 1845–55); *Halichondria panicea* (Alder & Hancock, 1845–55, M'Intosh, 1863; Garstang, 1890; Herdman & Clubb, 1892; Forrest, 1953; Miller, 1961; Swennen, 1961; P); *Hymeniacidon perleve* (P); juveniles found at Arcachon *on Myxilla incrustans* and 'Esperella aegagropila' (Cuénot, 1903); *Tethya aurantia* (Miller, 1961).
	A. pseudoargus flammea	*Hymeniacidon perleve* (Fisher, 1937; McMillan, 1942 states refused *Halichondria panicea*).
	Archidoris stellifera	*Hemimycale columella* (Forrest, 1953); *on H. columella* (Marine B.A. 1957).
	Doridigitata derelicta	Sponges (Cuénot, 1903).
	Doridigitata sticta	No data.
	Geitodoris planata	No data.
	Jorunna tomentosa	*Halichondria panicea* (Millott, 1937; Miller, 1961, P); *on H. panicea* (P).
Limaciidae	*Aporodoris millegrana*	No data.
	Aegires punctilucens	?Encrusting polyzoans (Miller, 1961).
	Limacia clavigera	Polyzoans (Macnae, 1957); *Callopora dumerili, Cryptosula pallasiana, Electra pilosa, Membranipora membranacea, Porella concinna, Schizoporella unicornis, Umbonula littoralis* (Miller, 1961).
	Crimora papillata	No data.
	Thecacera capitata	No data.
	Thecacera pennigera	*Bugula* (Garstang, 1889; Marcus, 1957).
	Thecacera virescens	No data.

20

FAMILY	SPECIES	DIET
Limaciidae (contd.)	Polycera (Palio) dubia	Cryptosula pallasiana, Escharella immersa, Microporella ciliata, Schizoporella unicornis, Smittina reticulata (Miller, 1961).
	Polycera elegans	On simple ascidians (Edmunds, 1961).
	Polycera (Palio) nothus	Bowerbankia imbricata (McMillan, 1942); 'branching Bryozoa' (Graham, 1955).
	Polycera quadrilineata	Callopora dumerili, Schizoporella unicornis (Miller, 1961); Electra pilosa (Miller, 1961, P); * herbivorous (Alder & Hancock, 1845–55; Garstang, 1889); Membranipora membranacea (Elmhirst, 1922; Miller, 1961, P).
	Acanthodoris pilosa	Alcyonidium gelatinosum (Graham, 1955; Miller, 1961); Alcyonidium hirsutum, Callopora dumerili, (Miller, 1961); Alcyonidium polyoum (Miller, 1961 & P); Flustrella hispida (P); on Alcyonidium gelatinosum (Walton, 1908; Swennen, 1961); on Alcyonidium polyoum (Purchon, 1947; Swennen, 1961).
	Acanthodoris subquadrata	No data.
	Adalaria loveni	On polyzoans (Loyning, 1927).
	Adalaria proxima	Alcyonidium polyoum, Electra pilosa, Flustrella hispida, Membranipora membranacea (Thompson, 1958).
	Onchidoris depressa	'Encrusting Bryozoa' (Graham, 1955); ? Escharella immersa (Miller, 1961); on Lepralia (Alder & Hancock, 1845–55).
	Onchidoris fusca	Balanus balanoides (Barnes & Powell, 1954, Swennen, 1961 ; Miller, 1961); Balanus crenatus (Barnes & Powell, 1954; Swennen, 1961); Balanus porcatus (Miller, 1961); Elminius modestus (Swennen, 1961); 'encrusting Bryozoa and Balanus' (Graham, 1955); * dead fish (Bergh quoted by Marcus, 1961); on barnacles (Farran, 1909; Swennen, 1959).
	Onchidoris inconspicua	Cellaria sinuosa (Miller, 1961); on Cellepora pumicosa (Alder & Hancock, 1845–55).
	Onchidoris (Atalodoris) luteocincta	Smittina reticulata (Miller, 1961).
	Onchidoris muricata	Alcyonidium polyoum (Swennen, 1961); Celleporella hyalina, Cryptosula pallasiana, Electra pilosa, Escharella immersa, Microporella ciliata, Porella concinna, Schizomavella linearis, Schizoporella unicornis, Smittina reticu-

FAMILY	SPECIES	DIET
Limaciidae (contd.)	Onchidoris muricata (contd.)	lata, Umbonula littoralis (Miller, 1961); Membranipora membranacea (Behrentz, 1931; Miller, 1961, P).
	Onchidoris oblonga	Cellaria fistulosa, C. sinuosa (Miller, 1961); on Cellaria (Garstang, 1894).
	Onchidoris (Atalodoris) pusilla	Escharella immersa, Escharoides coccineus, Microporella ciliata, Porella concinna (Miller, 1961).
	Onchidoris sparsa	On Cellepora pumicosa (Alder & Hancock, 1845–55); on a polyzoan (Farran, 1904).
	Goniodoris castanea	Botrylloides leachii (Garstang, 1890; Miller, 1961); Botryllus (Walton, 1908, 1913); Botryllus schlosseri (Garstang, 1890; Forrest, 1953; Miller, 1961; Swennen, 1961).
	Goniodoris nodosa	Young ones feed on Alcyonidium polyoum, adults on Dendrodoa grossularia and Botryllus schlosseri (Swennen, 1961); Botryllus schlosseri (Forrest, 1953; Miller, 1961); Callopora dumerili, Flustrella hispida (Miller, 1961); Dendrodoa grossularia, Diplosoma listerianum (McMillan, 1942; Miller, 1961); on 'molgules' (Pelseneer, 1911).
	Okenia (Idaliella) aspersa	On Ascidiella (Marine B.A., 1957).
	Okenia elegans	Ciona, Molgula (Pruvot-Fol, 1954); 'Cynthia tuberosa' (Alder & Hancock, 1845–55).
	Okenia leachii	No data.
	Okenia (Idaliella) pulchella	No data.
	Ancula cristata	Botrylloides leachii, Botryllus schlosseri, Diplosoma listerianum (Miller, 1961).
Tritoniidae	Tritonia hombergi	Alcyonium digitatum (Alder & Hancock, 1845–55, Dalyell, 1853; M'Intosh, 1863; Hunt, 1925; Miller, 1961; Thompson, 1962); oysters (Alder & Hancock, 1845–55); on Alcyonium (Walton, 1908; Farran, 1909).
	Tritonia (Duvaucelia) lineata	Alcyonarians (Pruvot-Fol, 1954).
	Tritonia (Duvaucelia) plebeia	Alcyonium digitatum (Hecht, 1895; Miller, 1961; Swennen, 1961, P); Eunicella verrucosa (Graham, 1955); *hydroids (Graham, 1938); on Alcyonium (Alder & Hancock, 1845–55; Walton, 1908; Farran, 1909; Colgan, 1913; Swennen, 1959).

FAMILY	SPECIES	DIET
Lomanotidae	*Lomanotus flavidus*	On *Nemertesia* (Alder & Hancock, 1845–55).
	Lomanotus genei portlandicus	Hydroids (Graham, 1955); *Nemertesia antennina* (Miller, 1961).
	Lomanotus marmoratus	On *Nemertesia* (Farren, 1904).
Hancockiidae	*Hancockia uncinata*	On '*Antennaria indivisa* and *Tubularia tricoides*' (Garstang, 1893).
Scyllaeidae	*Scyllaea pelagica*	Cnidarians (Pruvot-Fol, 1954).

Dendronotidae   *Dendronotus frondosus*   *Dynamena pumila, Hydrallmania falcata, Sertularia argentea* (Miller, 1961); young ones feed on *Sertularia cupressina*, adults on *Tubularia indivisa* (Swennen, 1961, P); *Tubularia* (Elmhirst, 1922; Vevers, 1955); *Tubularia indivisa, T. larynx* (Miller, 1961, P); attracted by scent of *Tubularia larynx* (Braams & Geelen, 1953); on *Abietinaria abietina, Hydrallmania falcata* (Herdman, 1890); on '*Plumularia*' (Reid, 1846); on *Sertularia argentea* (Pelseneer, 1911, Cuénot, 1927); on *Sertularia cupressina* (Cuénot, 1927); young ones on *Dynamena pumila* (P).

Dotöidae   *Doto cinerea*   No data.

       Doto coronata   *Abietinaria abietina, Bougainvillia ramosa, Campanularia verticillata, Clava multicornis, Coryne muscoides, Diphasia tamavisca, Dynamena pumila, Halecium beani, H. halecinum, Hydrallmania falcata, Kirchenpaueria pinnata, Lafoea dumosa, Nemertesia antennina, Plumularia setacea, Sarsia eximia, Sertularia argentea, Tubularia larynx* (Miller, 1961); *Laomedea flexuosa* (McMillan, 1942; Miller, 1961); *Nemertesia*, '*Plumularia*', *Sertularia* (Graham, 1938); *Obelia dichotoma* (Swennen, 1961); *Obelia geniculata* (Miller, 1961; Swennen, 1961); on *Abietinaria abietina* (Alder & Hancock, 1845–55); on *Clava multicornis* (Herdman, 1890); on *Dynamena pumila* (Alder & Hancock, 1845–55; Cornet & Marche-Marchad, 1951, P); on *Hydrallmania falcata* (Alder & Hancock, 1845–55; Reid, 1846; Walton, 1908); on *Nemertesia, Plumularia*, calyptoblastic hydroids (Marine B.A., 1957); on *Obelia geniculata* (Garstang,

FAMILY	SPECIES	DIET
Dotöidae (contd.)	Doto coronata (contd.)	1890; Loyning, 1927; Orton, 1914); on Lafoea and Sertularia argentea (Farran, 1909); on Sertularia cupressina (P); on Sertularia operculata (Cornet & Marche-Marchad, 1951, P).
	Doto cuspidata	Nemertesia ramosa (Miller, 1961).
	Doto fragilis	Nemertesis antennina, N. ramosa (Miller, 1961); on Nemertesia antennina, near bases (Alder & Hancock, 1845–55); on Nemertesia ramosa, Halecium halecinum, at bases of clumps (Farran, 1909).
	Doto pinnatifida	Nemertesia antennina (Miller, 1961); on N. antennina (Alder & Hancock, 1845–55; Garstang, 1890).
Arminidac	Armina loveni	Probably alcyonarians (Pruvot-Fol, 1954); feeding is suctorial (Morton, 1958).
Proctonotidae	Proctonotus mucronifera	On Halichondria panicea (Alder & Hancock, 1845–55).
	Antiopella cristatus	Bugula (Hecht, 1895); Cellaria (Graham, 1955).
	Antiopella flagellatus	No data.
	Antiopella hyalinus	?Nemertesia antennina, ?Tubularia indivisa (Miller, 1961); on Bugula (Cornet & Marche-Marchad, 1951).
Heröidae	Hero formosa	Abietinaria abietina, Hydrallmania falcata (Miller, 1961); Tubularia indivisa, T. larynx (Miller, 1961, P).
Coryphellidae	Coryphella gracilis	On Nemertesia antennina, Sertularia argentea, Tubularia larynx (Walton, 1908).
	Coryphella lineata	Hydrallmania falcata, Sarsia eximia, Sertularia argentea (Miller, 1961); Tubularia (Graham, 1955); Tubularia indivisa (Miller, 1961, P); T. larynx (P); on Coryne (Swennen, 1961); on Tubulariae (Marine B.A., 1957).
	Coryphella pedata	Abietinaria abietina, Hydrallmania falcata, Tubularia indivisa, T. larynx (Miller, 1961); on Flustra foliacea (Herdman & Clubb, 1892); on Garveia nutans (P).
	Coryphella pellucida	Hydrallmania falcata, Sarsia sp. (Miller, 1961); Tubularia indivisa (Miller, 1961, P).

FAMILY	SPECIES	DIET
Coryphellidae (contd.)	Coryphella verrucosa rufibranchialis	Clytia johnstoni, Dynamena pumila, Hydrallmania falcata, Laomedea flexuosa, Sarsia eximia, Tubularia larynx (Miller, 1961); Eudendrium arbuscula (Swennen, 1961); on Garveia nutans (P); on Tubularia (Walton, 1908).
Eubranchidae	Eubranchus cingulatus	Kirchenpaueria pinnata (Miller, 1961); on Nemertesia (Walton, 1908; Marine B.A., 1957); on Plumularia Cornet & Marche-Marchad, 1951; Marine B.A., 1957).
	Eubranchus exiguus	Hydrallmania falcata, Laomedea flexuosa, Plumularia catharina (Miller, 1961); Obelia geniculata (Miller, 1961; Swennen, 1961); Obelia longissima (Swennen, 1961); on Laomedea flexuosa (McMillan, 1944); on Obelia dichotoma (Colgan, 1913; 1914); on Obelia geniculata (Alder & Hancock, 1845-55; Orton, 1914; Marine B.A., 1957).
	Eubranchus pallidus	Hydrallmania falcata, Obelia geniculata, O. longissima, Tubularia indivisa (Miller, 1961); on Hydractinia echinata (McMillan, 1942); on Obelia geniculata (Orton, 1914); on Sertularia cupressina (Walton, 1908); on Tubularia (Marine B.A., 1957); on Tubularia larynx (Swennen, 1961).
	Eubranchus tricolor	Abietinaria abietina, Hydrallmania falcata, Nemertesia antennina, N. ramosa, Tubularia indivisa (Miller, 1961); Obelia geniculata (Garstang, 1890; Miller, 1961); on Obelia, Clytia, Tubularia, Bougainvillia (Elmhirst, 1922); on Obelia geniculata (Orton, 1914).
	Eubranchus vittatus	On 'Antennularia' (Farran, 1904); on Obelia, Clytia, Tubularia, Bougainvillia (Elmhirst, 1922).
	Cumanotus beaumonti	?Tubularia (Cuénot, 1927).
Tergipedidae	Embletonia minuta	No data.
	Embletonia pallida	Cordylophora lacustris (Neville, 1926); Gonothyraea loveni (Rasmussen, 1944); Protohydra leuckarti, Psammohydra sp. (Marcus quoted by Swennen, 1961); on Laomedea and Cordylophora (Swennen, 1961); on Obelia dichotoma (Colgan, 1913).

FAMILY	SPECIES	DIET
Tergipedidae (*contd.*)	*Embletonia pulchra*	*Hydrallmania falcata* and its epizoitic hydroids, *Nemertesia antennina* (Miller, 1961); on *Nemertesia* (Marine B.A., 1957).
	Tergipes despectus	*Aglaophenia pluma*, *Clava multicornis*, *Sarsia eximia* (Miller, 1961); *algae on stem and branches of *Obelia geniculata* (Garstang, 1889); *Bougainvillia* (Marine B.A., 1957); *Gonothyraea loveni* (Swennen, 1961); *Laomedea flexuosa* (Miller, 1961, Swennen, 1961); *Laomedea gelatinosa* (Swennen, 1961); *Obelia* (Graham, 1938); *Obelia dichotoma* (Colgan, 1914; McMillan, 1942; Swennen, 1961); *Obelia geniculata* (Miller, 1961); *Obelia longissima* (Swennen, 1961); on *Laomedea gelatinosa*, *Obelia geniculata* (Alder & Hancock, 1845–55); on *Obelia* (Hecht, 1895; Cuénot, 1927); on *Obelia geniculata* (Orton, 1914); on *Obelia longissima* (Swennen, 1959).
	Cuthona amoena	*Halecium beani*, *H. halecinum* (Miller, 1961); on *Sertularia argentea* (Walton, 1908).
	Cuthona concinna	*Laomedea flexuosa*, *Sertularia cupressina* (Swennen, 1961); on *Sertularia argentea* (Alder & Hancock, 1845–55); on hydroids (Pelseneer, 1911).
	Cuthona couchii	No data.
	Cuthona nana	On *Hydractinia* (Walton, 1908).
	Cuthona pustulata	No data.
	Precuthona peachii	*Hydractinia echinata* (Swennen, 1961, P); *Tubularia indivisa* (Elmhirst, 1922); on *Hydractinia* (Beaumont, 1900; Farran, 1904; Marine B.A., 1957; Swennen, 1959); on *Tubularia* (Marine B.A., 1957).
	Diaphoreolis northumbrica	No data.
	Trinchesia aurantia	*Bougainvillia ramosa*, *Sarsia eximia* (Miller, 1961); *Tubularia indivisa*, *T. larynx* (Miller, 1961; Swennen, 1961, P); on *Garveia nutans* (Marine B.A., 1957); attracted by scent of *Tubulariae* and of *Obelia longissima* (Braams & Geelen, 1953).
	Trinchesia caerulea	*Halecium halecinum*, *Hydrallmania falcata*, *Sertularella polyzonias* (Miller, 1961).

FAMILY	SPECIES	DIET
Tergipedidae (*contd.*)	*Trinchesia foliata*	*Dynamena pumila* (Swennen, 1961); *Obelia geniculata, Sertularella polyzonias, Tubularia indivisa* (Miller, 1961); on *Tubulariae* (McMillan, 1941; Cornet & Marche-Marchad, 1951).
	Trinchesia glotensis	* *Crisia* (Graham, 1955).
	Trinchesia stipata	On *Sertularia* (Alder & Hancock, 1845–55).
	Trinchesia viridis	On '*Antennularia*' (Alder & Hancock, 1845–55); on hydroids (Farran, 1909; Marine B.A., 1957); on *Sertularia* (Cornet & Marche-Marchad, 1951).
Calmidae	*Calma glaucoides*	Eggs of *Cottus, Lepadogaster, Liparis, Gobius minutus* (Evans, 1922); eggs of *Lepadogaster lepadogaster* (Miller, 1961); on eggs of *Blennius ocellaris* (Renouf, 1935; Marine B.A., 1957); on eggs of *Gobius niger* (Farran, 1904); on eggs of *Lepadogaster* (Cornet & Marche-Marchad, 1951); on *Hydractinia* (Marine B.A., 1957).
Fionidae	*Fiona pinnata*	Barnacles (Eliot, 1910); *Porpita* (Marcus, 1961); stalked barnacles (Marcus, 1961); *Velella* (Bergh, 1880; Eliot, 1910; Cornet & Marche-Marchad, 1951; Marcus, 1961).
Facelinidae	*Favorinus branchialis*	Hydroids (Graham, 1938); *Obelia geniculata, Sertularia argentea* (Miller, 1961); spawn of other nudibranchs (Alder & Hancock, 1845–55); on spawn of *Archidoris pseudoargus* (Renouf, 1935).
	Favorinus carneus	No data.
	Facelina annulicornis	Other nudibranchs (Alder & Hancock, 1845–55).
	Facelina auriculata	'*Campanularia johnstoni*', '*Cordylophora carpia*', *Dynamena pumila, Obelia longissima* (Swennen, 1961); *Clava squamata* (McMillan, 1942); *Lucernaria* (Alder & Hancock, 1845–55); '*Lucernaria auriculata*' (Swennen, 1961); *Tubularia* (Graham, 1938); *T. indivisa* (Miller, 1961, P); *T. larynx* (Miller, 1961, Swennen, 1961, P); other nudibranchs, worms, carrion, etc. (Dalyell, 1853; Eliot, 1910; Swennen, 1961).
	Facelina elegans	No data.

FAMILY	SPECIES	DIET
Aeolidiidae	Aeolidia papillosa	Actinia, 'Anthea' (Eliot, 1910); Actinia equina (Miller, 1961; Swennen, 1961, P); Anemonia sulcata (Miller, 1961); Diadumene cincta (Swennen, 1961); 'Metridium marginatum' (Russell, 1942); Metridium senile (Swennen, 1961, P); Sagartia troglodytes (Miller, 1961; Swennen, 1961); Sagartiogeton undata (Swennen, 1961); Stomphia coccinea (Robson, 1961); Tealia crassicornis (McMillan, 1942); Tealia felina (Miller, 1961; Swennen, 1961, P); Tubularia indivisa (Miller, 1961); attracted by scent of Metridium senile and of Actinia equina (Braams & Geelen, 1953).
	Aeolidiella glauca	'Heliactis bellis' (Neville, 1926); Sagartia elegans (Miller, 1961).
	Aeolidiella inornata	No data.

NOTE ADDED IN PROOF

Since this paper was read in April 1962, two important works on nudibranch life-cycles have been published. Miller (1962) describes his observations on a number of species from the Isle of Man; many of his conclusions show an encouraging agreement with my own. Tardy (1962) describes how veliger larvae of Eubranchus exiguus settle and metamorphose in the laboratory on the adult's food, the hydroid Kirchenpaueria pinnata echinulata.

MILLER M. C. (1962) Annual cycles of some Manx nudibranchs, with a discussion of the problem of migration. J. Anim. Ecol. **31,** 545–569.

TARDY J. (1962) Observations et expériences sur la métamorphose et la croissance de Capellinia exigua (Ald. et H.) (Mollusque Nudibranche). C.R. Acad. Sci. **254,** 2242–2244

GRAZING IN THE INTERSTITIAL HABITAT: A REVIEW

P. J. S. Boaden

Department of Zoology, Queen's University, Belfast

ABSTRACT

Marine sand provides three different types of habitat, the epi-, endo-, and mesopsammon. Little is known of the feeding habits of the interstitial (mesopsammic) fauna, though generalizations can be made. The basic food sources are detritus, dead plankton, bacteria and autotrophs, such as diatoms. Various mesopsammic and endopsammic species graze from individual sand grains. The interstitial fauna forms part of the food source of larger indiscriminate sand grazers. Very few interstitial species have pelagic larval development but dispersion of the fauna may be aided by shore-grazing birds. Thus grazing phenomena may affect the interstitial fauna in three ways—nutrition, depletion and dispersal.

Marine sand and shell gravel provide three different types of habitat each with a distinctive fauna. The animals living on the sand surface can be termed an epifauna and their habitat the epipsammon. Within the substrate two habitats, the endo- and meso-psammons can be broadly defined. Endopsammic species actively displace sand grains by pushing them aside or by ingestion thereby forming a burrow or progressing through the sand. Mesopsammic species, however, are able to progress through the pore system formed by the spaces between individual sand grains and thus live without displacing the sand.

Most present day knowledge of the interstitial fauna has resulted from work in France and in Germany where study of the mesopsammon was initiated by Remane in the mid nineteen-twenties. Representatives of most of the invertebrate phyla have been found in this habitat. The Protozoa (especially ciliates), Platyhelminthes (Turbellaria), Nematoda, Gastrotricha, Annelida and Arthropoda (mainly Crustacea) are the commonest phyla. Representatives of the Cnidaria, Nemertini and Mollusca occur fairly often; members of other phyla such as the Polyzoa and Echinodermata occur occasionally.

Marked adaptation to the environment is shown by many interstitial species. Usually the body is either long and thin for gliding through the interstices or short and leaf-like for progression around individual sand grains. The longest interstitial animals belong to the former category, for instance various Protozoa Ciliata attain a length of 4 mm. On the other hand various metazoan groups are represented in the mesopsammon by very small species. Thus the opisthobranch genus *Microhedyle* Hertling is less than 1·5 mm in length and the archiannelid *Diurodrilus* Remane less than 450 μ. Adhesive glands and organs are widespread. Reproduction and development tends to take place within the sand. Such trends or conformation to a 'Lebensformtyp' have been illustrated well by Remane (1951) and Delamare Deboutteville (1960).

The population density can be very high. At Traeth Bychan on the east coast of Anglesey there are over 1,200 animals per litre of the upper sand layer at L.W.N. On the same beach just below H.W.N., where the archiannelid *Trilobodrilus heideri* Remane occurs in patches of superabundance due partially to periodic aggregation (Boaden, 1963), the interstitial fauna reaches a density of 8–10 animals per c.c of sand. It is obvious that rich food sources must be present to maintain such an abundant fauna.

Little is known of the feeding habits of the interstitial fauna but various broad types of feeding can be distinguished. Remane (1951) gives a diagram of the food cycle within the sand environments.

The basic food sources are dead organic matter, in the form of detritus and fallen plankton, and live matter in the form of a micro-flora encrusting the individual sand grains or free in the interstices. The film of organic matter around each grain consists of bacteria and detritus often with adhering autotrophs, especially diatoms. Peridinians, Chlorophycae and Cyanophycae are also found but, like the diatoms, are usually limited to the upper sand layer. Pearse, Humm and Wharton (1942) report bacterial concentrations in the range of 50,000–500,000 per c.c of beach sand. Pennak (1952) reports up to 20,000 diatoms per c.c.

The encrusted sand grains form a pasture on which many interstitial animals graze. Various marine Nematoda, Copepoda, Ostracoda and Rotifera scrape their food off individual sand grains. As far as is known most Archiannelida feed in this manner and the buccal pieces found in the marine genera *Nerillidium* Remane, *Thalassochaetus* Ax and the closely related subterranean species *Troglochaetus beranecki* Delachaux probably aid in abrasion of the food; some species, however, may feed by means of their large ciliated palps (Boaden, 1961).

In a fine paper Wieser (1953) has shown how mouth structure of free living Nematoda can be correlated with habitat. Four types of structure are distinguished:

1A. Without mouth cavity. Food obtained by pharyngeal suction.

1B. With unarmed mouth cavity. Food obtained by suction and movement of lips.

2A. Mouth cavity with light armature. Food scraped off surfaces or food object pierced and sucked.

2B. With powerful armature. Mostly predators.

In fine littoral sands that are rich in deposits groups 1B and 2A dominate and feed by pumping in detritus and diatoms or by grazing the grain epigrowth. Groups 2A and 2B dominate in sublittoral shell gravel and coarse sand where there is usually a good epigrowth and rich interstitial fauna. In beaches of clean sand there are remarkably fewer grazing nematodes and predatory forms dominate.

Endopsammic species such as various Amphipoda and Cumacea which graze food from individual sand grains have been termed 'sand-lickers' by Remane (1933, 1951). Feeding in the sand-living Cumacea has been studied by various authors. Recently Wieser (1956) has described a mode of feeding in *Cumella vulgaris* Hart in which sand grains are picked up by the maxillipeds and revolved whilst the food is scraped into the mouth. Similar feeding has been observed in other cumaceans by Foxon (1936) and Zimmer (1933). Thus some competition for food probably occurs between the interstitial grazers and the endopsammic sand-lickers. The latters' food will include some adhering eggs or small representatives of the interstitial fauna which are scraped off the sand grains with the epigrowth.

More serious depletion of the interstitial fauna is caused by the endopsammic sand-swallowers. These are forms such as various polychaetes and oligochaetes which graze through sand swallowing the grains more or less indiscriminately and thereby ingesting any adhering fauna and flora. As stated previously, many mesopsammic inhabitants are equipped with adhesive glands and the immediate reaction to disturbance is adhesion to one or more of the neighbouring sand grains. Most species lay sticky egg cocoons or eggs which attach to sand grains soon after liberation.

Very few interstitial species have a pelagic development but there is a tendency for a small but steady production of young in advanced stages within the substrate. This has been summarized by Swedmark (1958). In some genera, for instance the cnidarian *Otohydra* Swedmark and Teissier (1958) and in the gastrotrich *Urodasys* Remane (see Wilke, 1954) actual viviparity occurs. Dispersal of the fauna and colonization of new areas of sand must therefore be dependent on means other than pelagic larval stages.

The displacement by wave or current action of sand grains with adhering eggs and individuals, followed by deposition in a new locality probably forms the main mode of transportation. Another possible mode of dispersion is by adhesion of sand and/or animals to the feet of shore-grazing birds. This idea was mooted by Dr T. G. Karling of Stockholm at a small symposium on interstitial fauna organized by the Nordic Marine Biology Council in Sweden during August 1961. The idea received support from various authorities including Professor Lang of Stockholm who had once examined brushings from the feet of shore-birds for interstitial species but met with only limited success. Brushings from the mallard and other ducks yielded copepods, nematodes and larval hydracarids (personal communication).

In summary it must be said that little is known of the feeding habits of the interstitial fauna and further research needs to be done before any detailed account can be given. Sand grain epigrowth provides an important food source which is grazed either from individual grains by the action of the pharynx or mouthparts of many interstitial and some endopsammic species, or from collections of grains taken into the gut by various endopsammic deposit feeders. The latter must derive further nourishment from the simultaneously ingested interstitial animals and their eggs. It is possible that birds feeding on the shore may aid distribution of the interstitial fauna but this phenomenon also needs further investigation.

REFERENCES

BOADEN P.J.S. (1961) *Meganerilla swedmarki* nov. gen. nov. spec. an archianellid of the family Nerillidae. *Ark. Zool.* (2) **13,** 553–559

BOADEN P.J.S. (1963) Behaviour and distribution of the archiannelid *Trilobodrilus heideri* Remane. *J. mar. biol. Ass. U.K.* **43,** 239–250

DELAMARE DEBOUTTEVILLE C. (1960) *Biologie des eaux souterraines littorales et continentales.* 740 pp. Hermann: Paris

FOXON G.E.H. (1936) Notes on the natural history of certain sand-dwelling Cumacea. *Ann. Mag. Nat. Hist.* **10,** 377–393

PEARSE A.S., HUMM H.J. & WHARTON G.W. (1942) Ecology of sand beaches at Beaufort, North Carolina. *Ecol. Monogr.* **12,** 135–190

PENNAK R.W. (1951) Comparative ecology of the interstitial fauna of fresh-water and marine beaches. *Colloq. int. Cent. nat. Rech. sci.* **23,** 449–480

REMANE A. (1933) Verteilung und Organisation der benthonischen Mikrofauna der Kieler Bucht. *Wiss. Meeresunters. Kiel.* **21,** 161–221

REMANE A. (1951) Die Besiedlung des Sandbodens im Meere und die Bedeutung der Lebensformtypen fur die Okologie. *Zool. Anz. Suppl.* **16,** 327–359

SWEDMARK B. (1958) On the biology of sexual reproduction of the interstitial fauna of marine sand. *XVth Int. Congr. Zool.* 327–330

SWEDMARK B. & TEISSIER G. (1958) *Otohydra vagans* n.g., n.sp., hydrozoaire des sables, apparenté aux Halammohydridées. *C.R. Acad. Sci., Paris.* **247,** 238–240

WIESER W. (1953) Die Beziehung zwischen Mundhöhlengestalt, Ernahrungsweise und Vorkommen bei freilebenden marinen Nematoden. *Ark. Zool.* (2) **4,** 439–484

WIESER W. (1956) Factors influencing the choice of substratum in *Cumella vulgaris* Hart (Crustacea, Cumacea). *Limnology and Oceanography* **1,** 274–285

WILKE U. (1954) Mediterrane Gastrotrichen. *Zool. Jb. (Syst.),* **82,** 497–550

ZIMMER C. (1933) Beobachtungen an lebenden Mysidaceen und Cumaceen. *S.B. Ges. naturf. Fr. Berl.* 1932, 326–347

AUTHOR INDEX

21

21§

SUBJECT INDEX

311